The Mammoth Book of Everest

From the first attempts to today,
40 first-hand accounts

Edited by
Jon E. Lewis

ROBINSON

RUNNING PRESS
PHILADELPHIA · LONDON

ROBINSON

First published in Great Britain in 2003
as The Mammoth Book How it Happened Everest
by Robinson

This edition published in 2015 by Robinson

A CIP catalogue record for this book
is available from the British Library.

ISBN 978-1-47212-018-2 (paperback)
ISBN 978-1-47212-019-9 (ebook)

Typeset in Plantin by Hewer Text UK Ltd, Edinburgh
Printed and bound on Great Britain by CPI Group (UK) Ltd,
Croydon CR0 4YY

Robinson
is an imprint of
Constable & Robinson Ltd
100 Victoria Embankment
London EC4Y 0DY

An Hachette UK Company
www.hachette.co.uk

www.littlebrown.co.uk

"Because it is there."
George Leigh Mallory, 1923

Contents

Glossary

abseil	descent of rock face or ice wall by sliding down a secured rope
alpine-style	lightning small-scale assault on mountain
arete	sharp rock or ridge
belay	securing of climber to an anchor with rope
bergschrund	the gap between a glacier and the upper face
bivouac	temporary encampment under makeshift shelter or none
carabiner	oval metal snap-link (also "karabiner")
col	dip or pass in ridge
cornice	overhanging mass of hardened snow
couloir	gulley
crampons	steel spikes fitted to sole of boot for gripping on ice and snow
crevasse	crack or gap
cwm	valley or hollow formed by action of a glacier (q.v.)
glacier	river of ice
icefall	feature formed by flow of glacier over declivity
jumar	metal friction device to enable climbers to ascend fixed ropes
karabiner	see *carabiner*
la	Tibetan for "pass"
moraine	mass of loose stone pushed along by glacier
neve	bed of frozen snow
oedema	Accumulation of fluid on brain (cerebral) or lungs (pulmonary) caused by, among other conditions, high altitude

pemmican	dried meat
pitch	distance between two belays
piton	metal pin, hammered into cracks in ice or rock, for use as runner or anchor
rappel	descent using rope and friction device (see also *abseil*)
serac	pinnacle of ice, usually unstable
scree	slope of loose stone
Sherpa	Tibetan mountain race; also settled Indian regions of Darjeeling and Kathmandu
sirdar	head Sherpa
traverse	horizontal climb
verglass	thin layer of ice

Foreword

Of all the great mountain ranges of the world the Himalayas are the youngest as well as the highest, with Everest reaching over 29,000 feet above sea level – and they are still rising. The Himalayas are a result of "alpine" uplift – formed between two continents in collision.

This is explained via the theory of tectonic plates whereby there was a break up of a once-single continent, and the various parts or "plates" drift on the earth's core and overlying mantle. Eighty million years ago India had become an island with the Tethys Sea in between it and Asia towards which it was heading. Over the next thirty million years the gap gradually closed. The Tethys Sea was reduced as the underlying plate rocks were forced down into the mantle and the sediments of the seabed were forced up in a complex of folds and overfolds as if squeezed in the jaws of a great vice. Such was the force from the Indian land mass that Asia was pushed 900 miles north. The sedimentary rocks under such pressure and heat metamorphosed and granitic rocks intruded into them from below.

As this great fold mountain range rose so it was eroded. The ancient rivers continued to cut through the Himalayan chain, producing ever-deeper valleys. The Arun River cuts through the Himalayas at its highest point between Everest and Kangchenjunga. Here there is a tremendous height differential and consequent range of temperature and diversity of vegetation from subtropical to alpine-arctic.

Ice age glaciation, rain and wind have also eroded into these great fold mountains so that the story could be told from the revealed rocks and fossils. On the flanks of the four peaks of the Chomolangma massif, Changtse, Lhotse, Nuptse, and on Everest itself the geological history of the Himalayas, that replicates across the whole range, can be seen. At the base of these mountains elemental forces produced schists consisting mainly of gneisses and migmatites that had been pushed up from the earth's mantle. Above the schists are intrusions of granite rocks known as Makalu granite formations. The rocks are grey and fracture into blocks and slabs so characteristic of Makalu seven miles east of Everest and also visible on the great southern flanks of Nuptse and Lhotse. Above the granite rocks lie metamorphosed sedimentary rocks from the Tethys seabed including shales, limestones and sandstones.

A wide layer of schistose shale cuts right through Everest, dipping down northwards where it forms the awkward sloping slaty rocks below the rock steps on the North Face and Ridge. It was here that Mallory's broken body was found in 1999 by Conrad Anker.

On the South-West Face of Everest the scarp edge of this schistose shale is exposed as the 800-foot, almost vertical band of rock. Although the rock dips down into the mountain and should be more favourable to climbing, the rock is in fact shattered by temperature change, making climbing and inserting anchors for belays very difficult, as Nick Estcourt and Paul Braithwaite discovered on the first ascent of it in 1975. The sandstone rocks above the rock-band are less shattered and more conducive to climbing, albeit steep, as I found with Dougal Haston a few days later. On the north side they form the well-known first and second steps that dogged the early attempts by the British during the interwar years. The very summit pyramid of Everest consists of grey limestone rocks. It is incredible to contemplate that the highest rocks on the planet were once on the ancient Tethys seabed, and that their rise from the depths is ongoing, by a few centimetres each year. These great arches of rock are still under pressure, as evidenced by regular tremors and periodic earthquakes that cause massive landslides and the destruction of roads and villages. There is a sentence in the Bible from the 121st Psalm that reads "I will lift up mine eyes unto the hills from whence cometh my help". I was reminded of that recently flying over the north Indian plains towards Kathmandu, above the rivers meandering down from the forested foothills of the Himalayas and the "abode of snow" arrayed behind spanning a total distance of 1,800 miles.

Naturally mankind revered such snowy mountains, for they do after all provide water, the most important element to sustain life after the air we breathe. As the population increased on the fertile plains, so extended family groups were forced into the mountain valleys for sanctuary and succour. There were those who entered the highest valleys seeking sanctuary from the distractions of worldly affairs, to contemplate the human condition and purpose, first in natural shelters and later in remote monasteries. Distant Himalayan valleys are places conducive to this inner journey, as everyone who goes there must sense. Beyond the last village where vegetation gives way to rock and ice at about 3,500 metres is the place where you take in a big breath of fresh air and with a satisfied sigh know "I'm back", with the realisation that it is so easy to forget how good it is to be up in the mountains where there is a keen bite to the air, where the air is so clear and the mountains all around are vibrant against the blue sky, where your spirits rise and the stars at night are bright right down to the edge.

All over the world, and in the West until the Renaissance and the age of "scientific enlightenment", people who lived close to nature were aware that the landscape was inhabited by forces, or spirits, of many forms that could help or harm; they were given many names. In Tibet a vivid appreciation of these beings corresponds to the vastness of the plateau, the awesome height of the mountains and the fearsome forces they can unleash. The pre-Buddhist Bonpo visionary shamans interpreted these forces as alien and separate entities that had to be appeased with animal and even human sacrifice.

In the eighth century Guru Rinpoche, the greatest of Tantric yogis, travelled from India to Tibet through Nepal via the Kyirong valley at the invitation of the King, Trison Detsun. His first task, before any formal meeting with the King, was to subdue and tame the ruling elemental spirit forces. Such was the clarity of his perception and single-minded resolve that he bound the gods and goddesses of the sky, mountain and earth to take a positive and protective relationship towards the Buddha Dharma and the teachings that were to liberate Tibet and the Himalayas. From that time on these forces have been content with offerings accompanied by prayers of compassion, of incense from scented woods such as juniper and blessed cakes (torma) made of barley flour and yak butter. At the time of this transformation, these powerful mountain gods and goddesses entered the official iconography of Tibetan Tantric Buddhism. Each one is portrayed with their special quality and symbol of unique power. Many texts have been composed and continue to be composed by enlightened masters, prescribing the appropriate mantra and prayer to invoke the protection and interdependent well-being of the environment and the local inhabitants. Nature is not separate from the human mind – when people are unhappy, demoralized and suffering then the earth responds accordingly. Fertility is reduced, crops, herbs, trees and animals all suffer too – a fact that is now being addressed in many parts of the world where agriculture is concerned and also where there has been deforestation and pollution right up onto the slopes of Mount Everest. Most of the seven British expeditions to the north side of Everest between the wars were blessed by the highly respected head lama, Ngawang Tenzing Norbu, of Rongbuk Monastery at 5,030 metres and only two hours below base camp. It is probably the highest permanently inhabited monastery anywhere. It was founded in 1902 and once had over 500 monks and nuns in residence. The head lama, after firmly establishing Rongbuk, travelled over to the Khumbu and Solu Khumbu in Nepal to establish monasteries under Everest at Tengboche (Thyangboche) and also at Thame, Takshingdu and at Chilong in Solu near Paphlu.

In 1921 the Rongbuk lama had been in retreat, so it was members of the 1922 expedition under General Bruce who first commented on his holiness: "full of dignity, with a most intelligent and wise face and an extraordinarily attractive smile". Everyone coming to the valley and surrounding area was forbidden to kill animals. The British kept to this rule and were constantly surprised and delighted to find how tame were the birds and animals of the region: they would eat from their hands and calmly graze around their tents.

Members of the 1936 expedition were presented with copies of a booklet to aid pilgrims visiting the monastery. It is of considerable interest in that it sheds light on this, for most of us, unseen, parallel world of nature spirits, as well as giving important references to the local name for Everest – JomoLangma. In the booklet's introduction the authors indicate that the area around the monastery is of special religious significance. The following extracts are taken from a translation that was produced in a note by Kempson in the 1936 Expedition Book *Everest the Unfinished Adventure*:

The Earth, originally occupied by evil beings was after a long time rendered by the Vajradhara habitable by heaven-dwellers, chiefly sky-roaming demons. With the growth of Buddhism came many teachers, including Padmasamb-hava, and blessed many hills, lakes and mountains ... In Ron-phu-rdza (Rongbuk Valley) Padmasambhava spent seven months and realized the highest Siddhi (spiritual attainment): he ordained the region to be a place of salvation to all who beheld, heard or thought of or touched it. At that time, in a place where the auspicious long-lived Five Sisters (Tashi Tseringched Nga) walked the earth, in view namely of the high, self-created, ice mountain named Jomolangma, he exorcised Miyolansangma and the others by his word, and blessed the place to be a chief scene of Siddhi. Especially Mkhan-pa-lun of Sbas-yul, he named as taking the lead.

This evidently refers to the valley of Rongbuk monastery, which is in full view of Everest, standing magnificent and proud of any other mountains, at the head of the valley. There is no doubt that Jomo langma (pronounced Chomolungma by Tibetans and Sherpas) refers specifically to Everest the mountain and not the whole Everest massif.

There has been some debate as to the reason for using the name Chomolungma. There is little doubt that "Jomo" is a common title for a holy or noble lady. The titles "Jobo" (Lord) and "Jomo" (Lady) are quite often used for mountain gods. "Ma" at the end is a common feminine nominalizing particle of speech. The debate has centred around the part of the word "glang". The only readily acceptable meaning is bull, or ox, although researchers have suggested "wind" from "rlung" or "ling" meaning "place". If these are correct it could be either Goddess of the Place or Goddess of the Wind, which might refer to the wind-plume that often blows from the upper part of the mountain. Yet another name found in Tibetan dictionaries is Jomo-kang-chen-ma-ri, Queen of the Snow Mountains. Another explanation and one favoured by Edwin Bernbaum in his *Sacred Mountains of the World* associates the name with the actual goddess of the mountain. Of the Five Sisters of Long Life the chief sister, Tseringma, is associated with Gauri Shankar and is depicted in thankas riding a snow lion. Of the four other sisters the one called Miyo Langsangma shown riding a tiger is the goddess of Everest. It is more than possible, since the Tibetan language often condenses long words, that Langma is short for Miyo Lang zang ma; certainly she is much revered amongst the sherpas of Nepal. In the eleventh century, the Tseringma sisters were severely admonished by Jetsun Milarepa (1040–1123) who lived and died in this region. They had caused livestock to perish and the inhabitants to suffer severe and contagious diseases since shepherds had upset the goddesses with smoke from their fires. Milarepa went to the villagers and said "I have had indications from a dream that the pestilence now prevailing in this area was caused by the local goddesses because you offended and injured them by the fires you kindled. In revenge they have spread diseases. You should now perform suitable ritual and make various offerings." As a result of offerings of huge tormas, oblations and prayers to the Devas and spirits, the people rapidly regained their health. To this day the local people living around Chomolangma are careful with their fires and strongly discourage expeditions burning rubbish, and especially plastic, that produces thick black smoke.

In 1940 the head lama of Rongbuk died, ten years before the Chinese invaded Tibet, and long before his monastery was destroyed during the "cultural revolution" of the 1960s. (It has since been rebuilt and occupied by monks and nuns under Chinese supervision.)

As the north side closed down to climbing so it became possible to access Everest from the south through newly opened Nepal. All the early expeditions, and most contemporary ones, seek the blessing of the Abbot of Tengboche Monastery, Incarnate Lama Ngawang Tenzin Rinpoche. Rinpoche has in the past given out cards depicting, in a woodblock print, the goddess Miyo Lang Zang. She is also depicted on the murals inside Rongbuk and Tengboche monasteries and during the Mani Rimdu Festival, at Tengboche (November), the monks offer prayers to the goddess and dedicate a yak to her, which is released on to the open hillside to wander in protected freedom. All this is to bring blessing and prosperity to the people of the area. That those who venerate her will be nourished is indicated in the murals where she is seen as a golden goddess holding in her left hand a mongoose spitting jewels while in her right hand she holds a basket of magic fruit. Only the monks and nuns on the north side of Everest, along with local farmers, would have considered the mountain that significant until it was known to be the highest point and when outsiders came marching in to climb it. Only the tip of Everest can be seen from the southern valleys and in fact Khumbila, nearly 10,000 feet lower than Everest, but rising up in the centre of the Sherpa homeland above Namche Bazar, Khunde and Khumjung, is of far more religious significance to the Sherpa people. While Sherpas often climb Everest they could never desecrate Khumbila by climbing up it and upsetting the local deity, Khumbu'i Yul-lha.

The significant events leading to the identification of Everest as the world's highest mountain began in 1808 with the mapping of the whole Indian subcontinent by the India Survey. By the 1830s they had triangulated their way from the south of India to the foothills of the Himalayas. The surveyors could go no further as Nepal refused entry, fearing for its independence. They tried to work around the problem by taking readings on Himalayan peaks from a distance of up to 150 miles and often in extreme conditions of malarial, jungle-covered hills. Many of

the British surveyors died as a result. By 1849 there had been
enough observations of Peak "b" to calculate the height purely
on the readings as 30,200 feet. The Surveyor General at the
time, Andrew Waugh, then spent two years taking into account
refraction, which was a variable due to differences of prevailing
temperatures and barometric pressure. By then Mountain "b"
became XV and in March 1856 Waugh informed his deputy
that Pk IX (Kangchenjunga) was 28,156 feet and that XV was
29,002 and was "most probably the highest mountain in the
world". Kangchenjunga, for a time considered the highest,
was demoted to third highest two years later when K2 was
found to be the second highest. While K2 has continued to be
labelled with the old survey number (K for Karakoram), a
name simply had to be found for the highest mountain. As
with Kangchenjunga, the Survey had sought local names for
the peaks, but in the case of XV Waugh pushed for the label
Everest after George Everest who had taken charge of the
Great Trigonometral Survey, becoming the Surveyor General
in 1830 and going on to oversee the completion of the Great
Arc of the Meridian, by which the true shape of the earth
could be known.

Despite the fact that Chomolungma was known to be the
Tibetan name, and despite George Everest's personal dislike
of the idea, Everest prevailed as the designated name. In Paris
during 1733, D'Anvilles' map of China and Tibet was
published, in which the name Tschoumou-Lanckma appears
for what is now called Everest. Other names were mentioned
elsewhere, which strengthened Waugh's case basing his choice
on the fact that there was no single clear alternative, so the
highest mountain should be named after his industrious predecessor. In 1865, just one year before Everest died, the Royal
Geographical Society officially accepted "Mount Everest".
The debate, however, continues, with Chomolungma the main
contender – and with justification. To muddy the waters,
during the 1950s the Nepalese came up with an invention of
their own – Sagarmatha. It means approximately "Head in the
Sky" and was applied at a time of increased Nepalese national-
ism and foreign interest in "their" mountains. The significant
events leading up to a comprehension of the geography

surrounding Mount Everest commences with the French geographer D'Anville. He amassed his information via the Jesuits operating in Beijing who in turn trained native Tibetans, including lamas, to gather all relevant facts and figures in the same way British topographers later trained and sent Indian "pundits" onto the Tibetan plateau. The pundits performed an incredible service towards the mapping of southern Tibet; travelling in disguise, at considerable personal risk and suffering great hardship, they unravelled the source of the rivers and plotted mountains, towns and villages. The first two pundits to be selected began their course of training at Dehradun in 1863. The most famous was Nain Singh who, once trained in clandestine surveying techniques, travelled up through Nepal and entered Tibet via the frontier town of Kyirong. He eventually reached Lhasa where he plotted its exact location and established approximately its height above sea level. In all he covered 1,200 miles, walking back along the Upper Tsangpo to its source and then heading south back into British India. There were many other such visits that enabled the British to construct reasonable maps beyond the Himalayas. More detail was added as a result of the Younghusband "mission" to Lhasa in 1903. Captains Rawling and Ryder were allowed to lead a reconnaissance party into western Tibet. At one point they were only sixty miles from Everest. Rawling was quite enthusiastic about the possibility of climbing the North Ridge. In 1907 Natha Singh, an Indian Survey assistant, was officially allowed into Nepal to reconnoitre a route to Everest. He advanced up the Dudh Kosi, mapping all the peaks to a point beyond Lobuche as far as the snout of the Khumba Glacier. It was not until the Anglo-American visit in 1950 that the foot of the icefall was reached and only in 1951 that it was climbed, paving the way for the first ascent of Everest in 1953. Meanwhile during the 1920s and 30s, only Tibet would allow access and that was for British climbers. After the brilliant reconnaissance expedition of 1921 there followed a strong attempt on the peak in 1922, when seven Sherpas died in an avalanche below the North Col. Finch and Bruce reached 8,320 metres on the North Ridge using oxygen. In 1924 Norton reached 8,580 metres without oxygen, only some

800 feet below the summit. This was a very significant performance at the time and for many years to come Norton's
magnificent effort was an inspiration. It was truly a big step
into the unknown and yet none of the 8,000-metre summits
were ascended until 1950, although it has to be said that the
north side of Everest presents few technical problems until
high on the mountain. Also the 8,000-metre peaks in Nepal
were all out of bounds until 1950 when the French first
climbed Annapurna.

During the 1930s there were four more attempts that all
failed on account of bad weather, ill health or poor organization. The first serious attempt to climb Everest from the
south was made in the spring of 1952 by the Swiss and they
almost made it, with Lambert and Tenzing Norgay reaching
a high point of 8,595 metres, well up the South-East Ridge.
This was a tremendous effort by these newcomers to Everest
and on a completely untried route. However, they did have
Tenzing with them who had now been to Everest's north
side on four occasions. They made another attempt in the
autumn, but bad weather prevented progress beyond the
South Col. In 1953, Everest was climbed by Tenzing and
Hillary following the route pioneered by Tenzing and the
Swiss. This was a great team effort brilliantly led by Hunt.
They were able to take advantage of improved equipment
and clothing and also to rehydrate high on the mountains, as
by then there were improved pressure stoves. The physiology
of high altitude climbing was better understood and the need
to drink liquids was impressed on all the climbers by the
expedition physiologist, Griffith Pugh. Had it not been for a
failure of the oxygen apparatus at the south summit, Charles
Evans and Tom Bourdillon would have made it to the summit
on 26 May and become the household names that was the lot
of Sherpa Tenzing and Ed Hillary. There is so much luck as
to which expedition climbs a mountain first and who gets to
go to the summit.

Since then there have been many more ascents of the original route and altogether thirteen routes established on all
sides of the mountain, some very technical, such as the South-
West Face, and especially the South-West Pillar Route, but

none involved such commitment as that made by Willi Unsoeld and Tom Hormbein when way back in 1963 they took off from the west shoulder alpine-style to climb the unclimbed, unknown West Ridge to the summit and traverse over and down the South-East Ridge.

There have been other impressive performances on established routes, with Messner and Habeler first climbing Everest via the original route without resorting to "canned" oxygen. Two years later Messner climbed up the north side following Norton's route to completion, completely alone. His only support was his pregnant girlfriend down on the East Rongbuk Glacier. These two ascents made a big contribution to the progression of high-altitude lightweight and alpine-style climbing worldwide. In February that year, the Poles under the leadership of Zawarda made the first ascent of Everest in winter. Many other firsts were to follow, some of which were hardly that significant geographically although very courageous and no doubt gave the climber concerned enormous satisfaction. There has been the first married couple to reach the summit, the first father and son, the fastest ascent, the most ascents in one season and the most ascents overall. Records were set and periodically broken at both ends of the age spectrum – the youngest is currently thirteen and the oldest eighty. There are climbers with various disabilities who have battled their way up – one blind, another without a foot. Climbers have left the summit and descended by paraglider, on skis and now by snowboard, reaching the Rongbuk glacier in 2 ½ hours! One sobering statistic is that 1996 and 2014 proved to be the years with the heaviest death tolls on Everest, with fifteen and seventeen climbers dying respectively. Most of these climbers died on commercial expeditions, which by their nature leave inexperienced climbers exposed to the vagaries of the weather, the debilitating effect of altitude and the overwhelming ambition of clients, company and also personnel. One client, following a groove in the snow on a short leash of rope between guides, proudly boasted that Everest was the first mountain he had ever climbed. But did he "climb" Everest? A climber is someone who goes into the mountains to take responsibility for his or her own life and that of their companions, forever having to assess the situation and make judgements as to the prevailing snow and weather conditions, the pacing of the climb, when to turn back or to go for it. This implies serving an apprenticeship on other mountains so that climbing is second nature, knowing what to do instinctively and intuitively, at an altitude where there is only one-third of the oxygen in the atmosphere, when there can be a sudden storm with winds up to 120 mph and temperatures plummet to −50C and the snow in the air is indistinguishable from that on the ground. While the client is at risk so too is the climber, judging by the number of very experienced mountaineers and Sherpas who have perished on Everest.

For all those who go to Everest and reach the summit or at least the limit of endurance, the experience will lead to a degree of self-transformation and a better understanding of all and everything. The reader will discover in this anthology more about the aftermath of great climbs but also that such gains are made at enormous physical risk.

Doug Scott

Introduction

Around fifty million years ago movements in the Earth's crust caused India to collide with Asia. In the cataclysm of heat and pressure that followed, the leading edge of India was pushed upwards into a gargantuan fold of rocks 1,500 miles in length. Much the greatest brunt of the collision that bore the "Himalayas" came at the eastern end, where peaks were pushed to the highest heights in profusion. One of these erupted spires was the loftiest mountain in the world.

Not that this was known until AD 1856, when the Surveyor General of India emerged from complex theodolite measurements to announce that "Peak XV" was 29,002 feet. (The British India Survey's observations, obtained from distances of more than a hundred miles from Peak XV, were impressive: the most modern calculation as to the mountain's height, made in 1999 with Global Positioning System, is 29,035 feet/8,850 metres.) Feeling that such mountainous stature deserved a rather grander name than Peak XV, the Surveyor General proposed that the mountain be named after his predecessor, George Everest.

There were, in fact, existing local names for the mountain. The Tibetans called it Chomolungma, or "Mother Goddess of the World", while the Nepalese termed it Sagarmatha. In general the British India Survey preferred local nomenclature, in order to avoid accusations of imperialistic insensitivity, but in the case of Peak XV the name Everest was stuck on the map in 1865, and there for Westerners it has stayed.

Despite the official status granted Everest as the world's highest mountain, nothing more could be learned about it.

Squatted on the Nepalese–Tibetan border, it was inaccessible due to geography, and to politics, since both Nepal and Tibet had borders closed to foreigners. When the British traveller J.B.L. Noel infiltrated Tibet in disguise in 1913, he was the first Westerner to come within forty miles of Everest.

In 1921, however, the political problems were overcome, and the Tibetan government allowed a British reconnaissance expedition to Everest. After 400 miles over the Tibetan plateau Lt Col. Howard-Bury's expeditioners arrived at the mountain's north side. During the course of the reconnaissance, the East Rongbuk Glacier and the North Col were discovered, which seemed to offer a promising route to Everest's North-East Ridge and thence the summit itself. Much of this reconnaissance was undertaken by an English public school teacher whose name would become forever associated with the mountain: George Leigh Mallory.

All of the ensuing British expeditions pitted themselves against the North Ridge Route. In 1922 Geoffrey Bruce and George Finch climbed to more than 27,000 feet before exhaustion turned them back. Spring 1924 found the British again struggling up the North Col. On the expedition's first summit attempt, Somervell and Norton reached high on the North Face, Norton going on a little by himself to reach 28,126 feet/8,573 metres, just below the Great Couloir, which leads to the summit itself:

> I followed the actual top edge of the band, which led at a very slightly uphill angle into and across the big couloir; but to reach the latter I had to turn the ends of two pronounced buttresses which ran down the face of the mountain, one of which was a prolongation of a feature on the skyline ridge which we called the second step, and which looked so formidable an obstacle where it crossed the ridge that we had chosen the lower route rather than try and surmount it at its highest point. From about the place where I met with these buttresses the going became a great deal worse; the slope was very steep below me, the foothold ledges narrowed to a few inches in width, and as I approached the shelter of the big couloir there was a lot of

powdery snow which concealed the precarious footholds. The whole face of the mountain was composed of slabs like the tiles on a roof, and all sloped at much the same angle as tiles. I had twice to retrace my steps and follow a different band of strata; the couloir itself was filled with powdery snow into which I sank to the knee or even to the waist, and which was yet not of a consistency to support me in the event of a slip. Beyond the couloir the going got steadily worse; I found myself stepping from tile to tile, as it were, each tile sloping smoothly and steeply downwards; I began to feel that I was too much dependent on the mere friction of a boot nail on the slabs. It was not exactly difficult going, but it was a dangerous place for a single unroped climber, as one slip would have sent me in all probability to the bottom of the mountain. The strain of climbing so carefully was beginning to tell and I was getting exhausted. In addition my eye trouble was getting worse and was by now a severe handicap. I had perhaps 200 feet more of this nasty going to surmount before I emerged on to the north face of the final pyramid and, I believed, safety and an easy route to the summit. It was now 1 p.m., and a brief calculation showed that I had no chance of climbing the remaining 800 or 900 feet if I was to return in safety.

This was by far the highest that man had ever climbed. Mallory – on his third expedition to Everest – was determined to better it. He was accompanied by Andrew Irvine. They were last seen at midday on 8 June 1924 at the "second rock step" on the North-East Ridge. When they failed to return, their fellow climber Odell, in a staggering display of loyalty and endurance, searched the entire route from the North Col to 27,000 feet.

Mallory and Irvine became the great enigma of Everest. Did they reach the top? What fate befell them before they disappeared into thin air? Although Irvine's ice-axe was recovered in 1933 and Mallory's body in 1999, there are no answers, only more questions. Why did Mallory take the inexperienced Irvine? Was Mallory on a do-or-die mission? Mallory was certainly driven by ambition. As Sir Francis Younghusband wrote of Mallory:

He knew the dangers before him and was prepared to meet them. But he was a man of wisdom and imagination as well as daring. He could see all that success meant. Everest was the embodiment of the physical forces of the world. Against it he had to pit the spirit of man. He could see the joy in the faces of his comrades if he succeeded. He could imagine the thrill his success would cause among all fellow-mountaineers; the credit it would bring to England; the interest all over the world; the name it would bring him; the enduring satisfaction to himself that he had made his life worth while. All this must have been in his mind. He had known the sheer exhilaration of the struggle in his minor climbs among the Alps. And now on mighty Everest exhilaration would be turned into exaltation – not at the time, perhaps, but later on assuredly. Perhaps he never exactly formulated it, yet in his mind must have been present the idea of "all or nothing". Of the two alternatives, to turn back a third time, or to die, the latter was for Mallory probably the easier. The agony of the first would be more than he as a man, as a mountaineer, and as an artist, could endure.

After the disappearance of Mallory and Irvine, it was nine years before the British – who had an imperialistic monopoly on expeditions to Everest – were upon the mountain. Harris, Wager and Smythe all made Norton's 1924 record, but no higher. The 1936 expedition, one of the most powerful ever sent out to the Himalayas, was beaten back by storms and avalanches in a desperately early monsoon. Arguably its most propitious moment was when Frank Smythe allowed Sherpa Rinzing to take the climbing lead. Hitherto, Sherpas, a native people of Tibet, had only been used as porters, or mountain "coolies". Now they were climbers too.

Two years later, a small-scale British expedition set off in high hopes, but was defeated by the snows of another early monsoon. Everest seemed to be toying with the British who wished to climb it. "We are beginning to look ridiculous," moaned one old Everest hand, G.I. Finch.

With the arrival of World War II, the curtain came down on the first act of Everest expeditioning. Yet, for all the cumulative embarrassment and disappointment of the British on Everest, their achievements were remarkable. They had got very near the top on three occasions, and this with most rudimentary equipment. In photographs from the 1920s and 1930s, Everest climbers look dressed for a hill hike rather than an ascent of a mountain in temperatures zero and below. Here is Smythe describing his ascent kit from 1933:

> Our appearance muffled up in all the clothing we possessed resembled the Tweedledum and Tweedledee of *Through the Looking Glass*. I wore one Shetland vest, a thick flannel shirt, a thick camel-hair sweater, six light Shetland pullovers; two long pairs of Shetland pants, flannel trousers, and over all a silk-lined "Grenfell" windproof suit; my head was protected by a light Shetland balaclava helmet and an outer helmet of Grenfell cloth; and my feet were encased in four pairs of Shetland socks and stockings. The climbing boots were of necessity broad and lightly nailed, but they gripped admirably on the sloping slabs. The ideal gloves for Mount Everest have yet to be designed, but a pair of woollen fingerless gloves and over them a pair of South African lambskin gloves kept the hands reasonably warm.

Although all the British pre-war expeditions possessed oxygen (despite some members being against it on the ethical grounds that it was "cheating"), the equipment was heavy and often faulty. When its weight was taken into consideration, it probably gave no overall benefit. Many climbed without it.

The Second World War over, British climbers once again turned their thoughts to the pointed problem of Everest. With the new opening of the Nepalese border, Everest was approachable by a direct route from India and attention switched to Everest's south side. Reconnaissance in 1950 and 1951 determined that the only viable route on to the mountain was the Khumbu Glacier up to the Western Cwm, a glacier bowl held by Everest, Lhotse and Nuptse. To the disappointment of the British, the Nepalese granted the next permission for Everest – now on a first come first served basis – to the Swiss, who ascended the South Col in 1952 with Raymond Lambert and

Tenzing Norgay reaching 28,210 feet on the South-East Ridge. Near the top, but not the top.

And then in 1953 came John Hunt's British Everest Expedition, with all the weight of history – and experience – behind it. They followed the route they had reconnoitered and the Swiss had pioneered, and made their first bid on 26 May when Evans and Bourdillon reached the south summit, and could see the final ridge close up. But for the malfunctioning of Evans' closed-circuit oxygen equipment, they would have gone on to fame. The luck was with the second assault team, Edmund Hillary and Tenzing Norgay (using open-circuit oxygen), who reached the summit at 11.30 a.m. on 29 May 1953. Everest had at last been climbed. This is how Hillary described the moment when humankind reached the top of the world:

My first sensation was one of relief – relief that the long grind was over; that the summit had been reached before our oxygen supplies had dropped to a critical level; and relief that in the end the mountain had been kind to us in having a pleasantly rounded cone for its summit instead of a fearsome and unapproachable cornice. But mixed with relief was a vague sense of astonishment that I should have been the lucky one to attain the ambition of so many brave and determined climbers. It seemed difficult at first to grasp that we'd got there. I was too tired and too conscious of the long way down to safety really to feel any great elation. But as the fact of our success thrust itself more clearly into my mind, I felt a quiet glow of satisfaction spread through my body – a satisfaction less vociferous but more powerful than I had ever felt on a mountain top before. I turned and looked at Tenzing. Even beneath his oxygen mask and the icicles hanging from his hair, I could see his infectious grin of sheer delight. I held out my hand, and in silence we shook in good Anglo-Saxon fashion. But this was not enough for Tenzing, and impulsively he threw his arm around my shoulders and we thumped each other on the back in mutual congratulations.

In retrospect, the 1953 conquest was not the end of the Everest story, only its most important chapter. The mountain was still there, beckoning. The half-century since 1953 has seen over a thousand people struggle to the top of the world, most of them via the Hillary–Tenzing route. Of course, such is the climber's imagination that all manner of other routes have been devised to the top. In 1960 the Chinese ascended the mountain via the North-East Ridge – the route on which the British had repeatedly failed in the 1920s and 1930s – and in 1963 the Americans Tom Hornbein and Willi Unsoeld summited via the "unclimbable" West Ridge. The first Britons to the top – Hillary was a New Zealander in a British expedition – were Doug Scott and Dougal Haston, who scaled the virgin South-West Face in 1975. The East or Kangshung Face succumbed to the Americans Lou Reichardt, Kim Momb and Carlos Buhler in 1983. Even on these main faces and ridges there have been variations; in total, some fifteen routes have been found up Everest to date.

Of course, sometimes it's not just the way you go but the way that you do it. The Japanese climber Junko Tabei was the first woman to climb Everest, doing so in 1975. Reinhold Messner and Peter Habeler were the first to climb Everest – in 1978 – without oxygen, thus ending a decades-old argument as to whether it was possible to do so. "A single narrow gasping lung, floating over the mists and the summits," is how Messner described the experience.

It was Messner who then came back in 1980 to perform the feat of mountaineering on Everest *sans pareil*. He climbed it solo. Again, he climbed without supplementary oxygen.

By the 1990s, climbing Everest was the stuff of commerce. Adventure travel outfits took clients to the top. For the right money.

But anybody who thought that Everest was tamed was deluded. Everest magnanimously lets some crawl up it and down again. The mountain decided to show its unbroken power in 1996, with a sudden storm that left eight climbers dead in a day. They joined the other 150 men and women who have perished on Everest.

Such statistics fail to dissuade climbers from taking their

chances on Everest. There are more technically difficult mountains to climb, but only Everest is the highest place on the globe. Most of the Earth's atmosphere lies below its summit. Mallory once said he wanted to climb Everest "because it is there." He might have added that it is there to test human endurance and courage.

Everest is an irresistible adventure. Fixed ropes and better clothing may make it easier to ascend than in 1953, certainly more so than 1924, but not easy. And just to make sure that humans never take her for granted, the Mother Goddess of the World has a trick up her icy-cold sleeves.

Due to the continued clash of the Earth's tectonic plates and the accumulation of snow on her summit, she gets a little bit higher every year.

Everest 1913

In Disguise to Tibet

J.B.L. Noel

It was the eminent Victorian climber Clinton Dent, in his book
Above the Snowline *of 1885, who first mooted publicly the notion
of climbing Everest. Dent believed it was "humanly possible to do
so" and that the problems of "thin air" would be solved by acclimatization. In fact, the first ventures to Everest were not halted by
anything as etheric as oxygen but by prosaic Far Eastern politics.
The Tibetans were zealous in their exclusion of foreigners, as were
the Nepalese. Meanwhile, the British government, which might
have facilitated a British expedition through either Tibet or Nepal
(countries with which Britain had special friendship status), determined not to succour Everest-inclined mountaineers because of
"consideration of high Imperial policy". Effectively, the approaches
to Everest were shuttered down. Before the big expeditions of the
1920s, the closest a Westerner came to Everest was in 1913, when
the young British adventurer and photographer John Noel made
an illicit journey into Tibet. He at least caught a glimpse of Everest,
even if it was from forty miles away.*

Having already accomplished a good deal of mountain travel on
the borders of India and Tibet, I decided in 1913 to seek out the
passes that led to Everest and if possible to come to close quarters with the mountain. Everest! hitherto unapproached by men
of my race; guarded, so fantastic rumour said, by the holiest
lamas dwelling in mystic contemplation of the soul of the giant
peak, communing with its demons and guardian gods! It was an
alluring goal.

I thought that if I went with only a few hillmen from the
borders of Tibet and India, I should avoid the attention a

group of white men would attract. This proved to be the case. I was within forty miles of Everest before a force of soldiers turned me back.

To defeat observation I intended to avoid the villages and settled parts generally, to carry our food and to keep to those more desolate stretches where only an occasional shepherd was to be seen. My men were not startlingly different from the Tibetans, and if I darkened my skin and my hair I could pass, not as a native – the colour and shape of my eyes would prevent that – but as a Mohammedan from India. A Moslem would be a stranger and suspect in Tibet, but not as glaringly so as a white man.

I dared not hope to escape observation entirely, but thought I could minimize it and perhaps reach my goal before an intercepting party would catch me up. I planned the route from the writings of Sarat Chandra Das.

I intended to cross the mountains by a high pass that was not used by the Tibetans nor watched by them. It cut off the populated districts of southern Tibet round Khamba Dzong and Tinki, and it would open, I hoped, a high level road behind Kangchenjunga to the gorge of the Arun, and then to Everest's eastern glaciers.

All this was an ambition of years, and the result of careful study and preparation. It would have been impossible of accomplishment but for the help of the men who had travelled with me before. I could impart my plans to them. They were simple wild men of the mountains. I talked their tongue and they trusted me as I did them. If you travel with a man, you must either fall out with him or make him your good friend.

Adhu was a Bhutia with all the vigour of his race and the youth of the twenties. His broad Bhutia face smiled all day long whatever happened – that is chiefly why I took him.

Tebdoo was a Sherpa Nepalese, a rough but golden-hearted fellow who knew everything that there is to be known about mountains and wild sheep. After this journey he said he would come to work for me in India; and refused to believe that there were no wild sheep to hunt there. But at the end of the journey I had to part with him and send him back to wild Nepal. I honestly regretted doing so.

Badri, a little man from the mountains of Garhwal, had always been a favourite companion of mine on journeys in the Himalaya. I kept him beside me to carry the rifle and camera. He had a keen appreciation of mountain scenery; perhaps not for the beauty an artist would find in it but, born and bred among mountains, he felt their peculiar charm, that something which draws, gladdens and masters the soul of a hillsman. How impatient and miserable he was on the plains of India before we were able to start for the Himalaya! The keen, hardy, vigorous little figure felt lonely among the Hindoo people in that flat land. But as the days went on and the time for the start came nearer he responded to the delight of making "bandobast". Then all day he was light-hearted and happy.

I intended to be free to wander where I wished, unencumbered, so took no more baggage than would go into two small tin trunks from the native bazaar, a supply of blankets and two native tents. I concealed in the trunks two cameras and instruments for drawing and mapping; a boiling-point thermometer for altitudes; a good take-down model American rifle, that could be tucked away in any blanket, with plenty of ammunition; also my revolver, and automatic pistols for the men.

Enthusiasm filled me for this adventure. Darjeeling was to be made the base for meeting Adhu and Tebdoo and buying ponies. Then we would plunge into the heart of the great forests that clothe the foothills of the Himalaya. We would pass through the tangled thickets of the tropical forest, climb into the regions of pine, larch, juniper and rhododendron, then beyond the treeline through snowbound passes into unmapped Tibet.

"Why, look, Sahib! There are the mountains!"

I was awakened by little Badri, who had climbed into my carriage on the Bengal Express that runs from Calcutta overnight to Jalpaiguri and Siliguri. At Jalpaiguri at daybreak the traveller gets his first sight of the forests of the Terai with their stagnant morasses, clearings of ricefields and tea gardens. A dull green forest-clad wall of hills rises abruptly out of the hazy stretch of plain. Here and there on the distant slopes the white tin roofs of the tea planters' bungalows flash in the sunlight. Some of them occupy solitary clearings in the green mantle of forest that covers every inch of the hills.

If the morning is clear, far to the north, overtopping the tangle of green hazy foothills and rising to an incredible height, may be seen a serrated line of dazzling white peaks extending the whole length of the horizon from east to west, the great range of the Himalaya.

A little toy-like train starts from Siliguri. It is called the crookedest, and it is the tiniest mountain railway in all the world. Yet it does a giant's work. It climbs 8,000 feet in 40 miles to Darjeeling on the hilltop. It journeys from the plains through the heat of the tropical forests, through the Terai where tigers lurk and tea-planters cultivate clearings. Up and up it goes, turning and twisting and shunting backwards and forwards. A dozen times it makes figures of eight and zigzags and loops, where the engine passes the tail of the train, and the driver leans out and talks to the passengers in the end coach.

The track is laid along the cart road; and the engineer whistles to wake up the bullock carts and frighten away chickens and children in the village streets. At night time a man sits in front of the engine, holding a great tar torch to light the track and see that no stray tigers or elephants cause a bump!

At Ghoom comes the first view of the snows. That view rewards hours of waiting, when finally it reveals itself as the train, rocking from side to side, flies round a corner. So unexpected is the height of Kangchenjunga, the third highest mountain in the world, 28,000 feet, that people often mistake its silver spearhead for a cloud formation.

I remember the remarks of the people in the compartment, mostly residents, some invalids and businessmen who would not leave their newspapers to look at any mountains. They agreed that Kangchenjunga, a spire of ice that pierces the heavens, is a mighty sight, but their attention was given to collecting their parcels and guessing if "So-and-so" would perhaps be at the station to meet them. We were running into Darjeeling.

Darjeeling, like all Indian hill stations, is built on the very top of the hill. It has its fine clubhouses – its Gymkhana Club where a London quartette plays for dances, apparently all day and all night. There is a Scotch mission, a barracks, a hospital and an observation point to which tourists ride in a rickshaw, to lean over an iron railing and look down 6,000 feet into the steaming valleys below. From there the eye can sweep in a panorama embracing tropical forests and eternal snow.

At two o'clock in the morning, the hotel porter rings a twelve-inch brass bell outside your door, and comes again every ten minutes to make certain that you do not forget that ponies and rickshaws are waiting to take you to Tiger Hill where people go to see the sun rise on Kangchenjunga and Mount Everest. It is an unforgettable spectacle. Kangchenjunga commands the attention because it is so prominent, so near, and so huge. Far away to the west is a mass of huge peaks. Among them the guide points out a pyramid peeping behind the others and seeming to be smaller; that mountain is Everest.

Just as interesting as the first sight of the mountains is a first acquaintance with the hill people. In the marketplace on Sunday morning may be seen a throng entirely different from the people of the plains of India. They are jovial, happy folk, and you see no veiled women's faces. There are jolly Bhutia girls – very pretty some of them, but they win you most by their high spirits and their laughter. Everyone of them is naughty. They smoke cigarettes all day long. They do most of the hard work, while the Bhutia men collect in circles to gamble for hours with dice at the street corners, or else lounge against walls, grin broadly and doff their hats to anyone from whom they think they can get baksheesh. They are good-humoured; handsome; with gaily coloured clothes, raucous joking voices and tangled, loose, flowing hair. They earn enough to get drunk on by pulling rickshaws or by carrying luggage to the Everest Hotel. Both men and women are immensely powerful. There is a true story told of how a Bhutia woman porter once carried a grand piano unaided 500 feet from the station to this same hotel.

It is these people with whom one lives when wandering in

the forests and mountains beyond Darjeeling. They make jovial travelling companions; but the traveller must understand them and know how to manage them. They have a habit of calling at their pet drinking houses in outlying villages and getting hopelessly drunk, leaving him without bed and supplies the first night out.

I selected my ponies with great care. A man can entrust his life to a good pony and not even bother about holding the reins along the narrow paths through gorges and across precipices, they are so sure-footed.

Adhu and Tebdoo having been met according to plan, all was ready for the start. The cool of Darjeeling and the breeze that refreshed the hilltops changed rapidly as we dropped down and down into the Tista Valley nearly 7,000 feet below. We found ourselves entering the humid forest, whose vegetation grew thicker and thicker until the trees and the twisted creepers that climb over them, interlaced above, formed a tunnel of greenery hiding the sky.

We were dropping down mile after mile. The road was the hottest I had ever felt. The blazing sun boiled the thick, damp, rotting jungle into a thousand oppressive-smelling vapours. Swarms of insects filled the air with incessant hum and buzz. There came land leeches to attack our legs from the ground and fix themselves to our boots; others on the trees above, warned by some instinct – wonderful but horrible, since they are blind – swung their bodies in the air on our approach and dropped down on us as we passed below. There is no escape from the leech. You must make up your mind that you are going to lose a lot of blood. To compensate slightly there were remarkable butterflies on this road. They were gigantic, measuring up to four inches across the wings and unequalled for colour and diversity.

During the next few days' march, each bend of the road – and the track was twisting and turning continuously through the forests following the bank of the river – opened a new peep of the Tista, here a broad flood broken into foam by large boulders in midstream, and flanked by steep mountain walls, from which the superabundant vegetation hung down and trailed into the water. We crossed a chasm by a wire suspension bridge, a frail structure swinging and lurching under every step, where the torrent below had carved itself a gorge, only some 30 feet wide, but almost 300 feet deep.

As we continued day by day the path climbed higher and higher, and the scenery changed as if by magic. The tangled jungle dropped away and we entered a smiling valley. There were meadows dotted with pine, larch and rhododendron, with Alpine flowers and primulas beside clear streams that meandered through the pasturages.

Lachen occupies a shelf high above the torrent that tears and foams through a 500-foot cleft below. The village stands on a shelf thrown out from the flanks of snow-capped Lamadong, in a recess snug and protected from the cold. It was here I planned to leave the ponies and get six of the hardy hillmen of this village to come on with me to Tibet. They had been hunting with me on a former occasion.

Here, while making these arrangements, my men first seemed to realize the nature of our journey. They became filled with doubts and fears. "We have no man who knows those parts," they said. "How will we find the way to this mountain in Nepal that the sahib wishes to see?" They had little faith in my map; and, truth to tell, I had little too. They feared maltreatment should we enter Nepal; and they told stories of the fierceness and exclusiveness of the Nepalese.

We went on to a high grazing ground called Tangu, 13,000 feet, where I could acclimatize and prepare for the rough work. One day, in order to spy out the geography and to exercise my men, I decided to make the ascent of one of the surrounding peaks, which promised from its position to reveal the panorama ahead. We started before dawn to climb the snow-covered slopes. The ground was smooth and of even inclination, and there was no difficulty in making good pace all the way. Finally we gained the summit of the ridge, and found that we could not have taken a more lucky direction. We were looking at the giants of the Himalaya from their very midst.

It was shortly after dawn. The slanting rays of the sun caught the fantastic crest of the immense mountain Tsenguikang in a bright flaming glow. Mists scattered, and flying erratically in whirls and eddies, chased each other over the shining ridges, now hiding the peak entirely, now evaporating and revealing fresh vistas of ice and rock and precipice.

Looking west in the direction of Kangchenjunga we saw the first pass over the ridge towards the tangle of snow mountains into the heart of which we were to go. Deep below us was the cleft of the valley through which we had come from India. It continued to the north towards the Koru Pass that leads to Tibet, but is watched by Tibetans and guarded by the fortress of Khamba Dzong on the other side of the divide. There was no way for us into Tibet there. To the north we saw the landscape broadening, and in the far distance we got a glimpse of the plateau land of Tibet that stretches on for hundreds of miles, bleak deserted plains that roll away to Central Asia.

I could not have struck a better place for observation. The boiling-point thermometer measured the altitude as 16,700 feet. There was not a cloud to spoil the splendid view; and I lingered, contemplating the solitudes and admiring and storing in memory the beauties of the crystal air and turquoise sky. The men grew cold in the biting wind that blew in fitful gusts over the ridge. Although fine as a viewpoint, an exposed ridge at this height is no place for a doze.

From here I was to strike to the west and take a high level track that would take us out of the Indian Empire behind Kangchenjunga into southern Tibet.

We carried fourteen days' food with us. The first pass of 16,000 feet was no great obstacle. In two days we were across, spending one night at a Tibetan camping ground called Chabru, where there is a cave making a fine shelter. From there we looked down to the high verdant pasture lands of Lhonak where the Tibetan shepherds come in the height of summer by the Naku Pass from Khamba Dzong. The valley is a lofty secluded basin at an elevation of 16,000 feet, surrounded by walls of snow. In a hidden nook deep in the heart of undiscovered lands we stood alone among the solemn majesty of the sentinel mountains.

We sampled the variable Tibetan climate, where the sun shines in the rarefied air with dazzling brightness and burning heat. The rays parch the lips and tan the skin, even blistering it. Suddenly the sun may veil over and the wind spring up.

Then – pile on your thickest clothes if you would not feel perished with cold.

I challenged Tebdoo to a race down the hill. In the mountains it is often easier to run down slopes than to walk; and, indeed, when one is tired, it is often a relief to break into a run. But you must have strong knees and a good stick to lean back upon. Tebdoo, who was at heart only a boy, delighted in amusements of this kind, and won the race, at the cost of his skin boots. However, he could mend them quickly by sewing on a new piece of the untanned sheepskin that all hillmen carry in their bokkus.

We pressed forward through this country and got behind Kangchenjunga, where our course turned again to the north to cross the high Chorten Nyim Pass. The pass is a cleft in the mountains, blocked by snow and the debris of rock avalanches. I had learned that the Tibetans had abandoned the pass, and by crossing it I hoped to get into Tibet unobserved.

The day before crossing we made camp on a shelf looking right across to Kangchenjunga's precipices to the south. That evening I spent watching. It is in the evening that these mountains wear their most fairy-like aspect. Vapours and mists, evaporating, form themselves again, and coil worshipfully round the cliffs and ridges. Kangchenjunga's precipices rise 12,000 feet sheer from the glacier below. As I watched, the slanting shafts of light crept up the fluted precipices and caused their draperies of ice to scintillate as with fire. On the eastern side the shadows gathered. Twilight conquered, the depths became a dark chaos – in such shadows might have been enacted the primal mysteries before time began – but the summits of Kangchenjunga remained aflame, like beacons high above the night-enveloped world below, and seemed to shine with a luminosity all their own.

With the darkness came biting frost; and I turned quickly to creep into the tent and wrap a blanket round me.

I brought three of the men into my tent, as there was plenty of room, while their tent was overcrowded. They curled themselves up side by side, wrapped tightly in blankets, and so kept each other warm. I woke in the cold and darkness of the night to stir the smouldering juniper logs of the fire. Outside all was silent, and nothing could be seen except the still shining ghost-like mountain spires of Kangchenjunga.

Unable to sleep because of the cold, I remembered eerily how once, in a previous Himalayan adventure, I had seen at the monastery of Gantok, the capital of Sikkim, the annual festival of the worship of the god of Kangden-Dzod-Nga, Kangchenjunga – this mountain. The pageant took place in the presence of the Maharaja and Maharani before the Chief Magician's temple in the garden of their palace, with a retinue of brightly clad Lepcha guards.

The god is called Dzod-Nga, meaning "Five Treasures". He is the war god, and every year the ceremony must be held to placate him, and to foster the martial spirit of the nation, while the lamas invite Dzod-Nga to guard the faith of the state and to bring peace and security to the people.

Flashing sword dances are accompanied by the blare of lamas' trumpets, processions of temple gods and other religious ceremonies.

In the dance of the Dorge-Gro-Dosjidros – the mystic step – the triumph of truth over evil is believed to be accomplished. This dance is held with loud cries, led by the Maharaja at his throne and echoed in a chorus of thousands from his assembled subjects – "Ki-Kihubu! Ki-Kihubu!" It is the voice, as is also the thunder in the heavens, of the war god who consumes mountains of dead as his food and drinks oceans of blood as draughts and relishes the organs of the senses for dessert. "Ki-Kihubu – I am the blood-drinking and destroying god! Glory to Maha-Kala! Should any love his life, keep out of my way. Any wishing to die, come into my presence. I will cut the red stream of life – glory to Maha-Kala-Ki-Kihubu."

The dancers work themselves into a frenzy, wounding each other with their swinging swords, and imitate a fight between the followers of the war god and his enemy. Heralds of the Sword chant loudly:

"This blood-dripping sword is the despatcher of lives. It is made of the substance of the thunderbolt, welded by a thousand wizard smiths. In the summer it has been tempered in the white mountain tops, in the winter it has been tempered in the ocean beds. It has imbibed the heat of fire and the venom of the ocean. It has been dipped in poisons. Its edge has been ground on the man-slaughtering boulder. When waved over the head it emits sparks of fire. When lowered point downwards it drips blood and fat. It is my dearest and most cherished friend – My name is the Lightning-like Life Taker! Ki-Kihubu!"

All very ludicrous and, to the Western mind, when the first impressions begin to pall, even rather tiresome. But alone in these remote mountains, in the icy depths of their night, those raucous cries came echoing through my memory. This was the very home of that mountain god. Giant shapes flung themselves to the skies all round me. Who was I to violate with impudent temerity these forbidden solitudes? The wind howled, now miserably, now angrily round our tiny tent. I shivered, and although I told myself that it was the bitter cold, I began to wonder, if – after all . . . !

Next morning we shook ourselves up at an early hour, our blankets stiff with frozen dew. We had a hard march before us.

The pass looks like the work of a giant axe that has split a narrow cleft in the mountains, and left the bottom raw and splintered. Huge fingers of rock point vertically between cliffs on either side. When we reached the foot we found the debris of avalanches precipitated from above – the danger that had caused this pass to be abandoned by the Tibetans. Rocks fell as we climbed, and we met an exhausting obstacle in the loose shingle that slipped beneath our feet. Even the highest and loneliest Himalayan passes are crossed occasionally, as this one used to be, by shepherds, and in their migration in search of grass they perform amazing feats getting their yaks and sheep and goats, their families and foodstuffs across. The animals, each carrying a light load of tsampa and tea sewn into little wooden bags, balanced and strapped to each side, find their own way. The yaks are so surefooted, on ice and rock, that they can go almost anywhere a man or goat can go. The shepherds sing and whistle shrilly and hurl stones from their slings to urge and guide them.

But we were not yaks, and the men felt the burden of their loads, heavily laden as they were with our reserve food. One man complained of noises in the head; Adhu's nose started to bleed. The air was dead – mountain climbers know this condition as "stagnant air" – but the men called it "La-druk", the Poison of the Pass. They say it is the evil breath of the Zhidag – the Spirit of the Mountains.

But on the top we found good air and the men became happy and began to sing mountain songs. They built cairns, tied strips of coloured rags to them, lifted their caps and cried, "*Om mani padme hum*." These cairns were to counter the evil spirits.

But their flags did not drive away the low spirits that began to assail me. When I looked down to the desolation below, I felt discouraged. Ahead was the unknown – a foodless, inhospitable, forbidding waste. Moreover the obstacle of the pass we had just crossed would lie like a barrier across our homeward tracks. We did not dare to look back to the lovely grassy meadows of Lhonak, lest they should lure us from our goal. We had to nerve ourselves to go forward to the north – to Tibet. We would have to find some shelter by the glacier to spend the night. Next day, we would look for the pilgrim's shrine of Chorten-Nyim, reported by the early native explorers as lying where the mountains drop to the plains.

The men became anxious for our safe descent to Tibet, for the prospect was indeed threatening. A staircase of rocky ledges conducted to the terraces of ice that formed the head of the glacier below. Where glaciers at their source break away from the rock walls of the mountains, they leave gaping cracks, sometimes invisible under snow crusts, and a great danger when descending passes. We had to make our way, cautiously avoiding immense cracks down which we could look, sometimes fifty feet, into dark recesses.

That night we sheltered in a nook by a glacial lake. In the mountains I think one can scarcely find a prettier sight than these glacial lakes. They are like pale blue translucent cups filled with emerald water.

A night spent on a glacier holds many sensations. The stars at night in the rare air seem to be larger and brighter than you have ever known before. The slowly moving ice gives out weird noises as it rends itself, opening out new fissures with reports like pistol shots. Surface stones slip and gurgle down into the thinly frozen water of the lakes. Now and then louder noises, sometimes reaching a deafening crash, tell of rocks falling from above. The melted snow water, lodging in cracks during the day, freezes at night and expands and loosens the rock. You will hear also what the natives name "the music of the wind". Ice pinnacles whistle shrilly as their sharp edges cut the wind and the ice caverns moan deeply as it eddies in their hollows. Wrapped in your blanket, your breath freezing on its edge, uncomfortable on rough stones, your native companions – for you feel no colour bar when sleeping out in such conditions – huddle close. You are glad to have them near, as you wait for the dawn to come.

Morning showed no signs of life or vegetation. We found the way, avoiding boulders and crevasses, left the broken ice and walked to the side of the valley. After some miles we came unexpectedly to a little stone hut on a promontory where the valley closes to a neck. The hut was deserted. I expect it was the identical one mentioned by Sarat Chandra Das as the first Tibetan guard post; but it was no longer inhabited by any Tibetan guard.

Adhu discovered the shrine by following the line of chortens that are put up to guide pilgrims from the north and are built on the hillocks. The shrine, a place of special sanctity, lies hidden in a secluded nook. Numbers of tame birds and blue pigeons inhabit the cliffs and are fed by the nuns who live at the shrine. The spot has a special beauty in its solitude and in its gaunt surroundings. The valleys converge with white tongues of glaciers protruding from the cavernous mouths of the mountains that stand behind dark and solid.

The shrine is circled by a well-worn pilgrim's path, marked with mendongs and poles with flying prayer flags. As we approached we behaved as pilgrims, lifted our hats, cried, "*Om mani padme hum,*" and contributed stones to the foot of the chortens.

We entered and I took a dark corner to hide in while Adhu conversed with the nuns. We found that the chief nun and two others were quite blind, which relieved me of some anxiety. There were altogether seven nuns living at the shrine.

"Are you pilgrims?" they asked.

"No, we are travellers from India."

"Make offering to our shrine that no misfortune may overtake your journey. And take these potions to bring strength and love to your lives, for you Outer Men" (meaning men of earthly affairs) "prize these things for the body more than those things for the soul. Live more for the inner life," they said.

We made suitable offerings to the shrine, placed grains of rice in the bowls by the butter lamps beneath the god images; accepted the pills and love potions the nuns gave us. Then the nuns brought out goat-bladders of yaks' milk and *chung* from their bokkus and gave us to drink. Adhu talked with them and obtained information for our journey. The nuns said we were brave to come by the snowy road; they even said we might sleep here, but we feared other people might arrive. We thanked the nuns for the wise things they had told us, to which they answered, "We know your darkness" (ignorance) "and we will pray for you." Then we took our departure.

Here at Chorten Nyim we were at the exit from the high mountains. To the north we contemplated the plateau of Tibet, the highest desert of the world. It has much of the character and appearance of an Arabian or an Arizona desert, with the same breadth and space of sandy, rocky soil, intersected with ranges of undulating hills, bare of trees; but it has this difference, that the far horizons show snowy peaks.

In depressions between the hills, more like shallow basins than defined valleys, is seen the green of the marshlands along the banks of lakes and winding rivers. Beyond the grasslands sandy wastes continue ruffled and blown into dunes by the wind. As in all deserts, there is shimmering sunshine and clear sky, yet the sky of Tibet seems to have a special blue all its own. As in other deserts, the day is hot and the night is cold. Here is experienced a difference of 50° between day and night. All is peace and breadth and solitude; guarded by snowy mountain barriers that wall away the outer world and lend an impression of majestic loftiness to this peaceful plateau. We felt ourselves to be above the other world – veritably on the roof of the world.

We continued due west, following a high level line over the

spurs of the mountains, switchbacking over ridges and across deep glacier valleys. We could make little headway, and finally we were stopped altogether by deep canyons. We descended to the bottom of one by a funnel, but could not find any way out beyond. We were obliged to turn back and take a lower level route by the plain, hiding ourselves and passing villages at night, making detours to avoid the dogs that, hearing every movement of men and animals within the distance of a mile, barked and howled. These Tibetan mastiffs, found in all the Dok-pa shepherds' encampments, are magnificent yet savage animals. Attacking, they show fangs like wolves, and their ferocious appearance is heightened by the immense scarlet ruffs of yak hair, which the Tibetans place round their necks like Elizabethan collars. These dogs are prized for their ferocity, and the mark of their breeding is the depth of their bark. The Tibetans say their bark must ring like a well-made gong. Once I had to shoot one of these mastiffs that rushed out and bit one of my men badly.

We had now fairly well escaped the fortresses of Khamba Dzong and Tinki Dzong; and I wanted to bear into the valleys in the direction of Nepal, which promised more friendly concealment than the plains. But I was vague as to the way to the Langbu Pass, so we decided boldly to turn in to a certain village that we saw in the opening of a valley leading south-west.

Our approach caused the keenest excitement, the barking of dogs and the barring of doors. Along the skyline of the roofs were the flying prayer flags and bunches of dried grass, and we noted peeping heads observing us from the apparently deserted houses. Keeping on our way, and meeting people, we boldly insisted on being given a house to live in.

The people are forbidden by the lamas and Dzongpens to furnish information to strangers; but they do not do more than offer a passive resistance and answer "No" or "I do not know" to everything. They would, however, always give information in return for presents secretly conveyed, and at night time they would give us food in return for money. The Tibetan peasant himself is friendly, generous and hospitable, although with the same freedom that he gives his own things to you he will also make you a present of other people's things and take what he fancies of yours. In the spacious folds of his bokkus he stows away anything up to the size of a cooking pot.

A man and woman befriended us at this village, which we found was called Eunah, and gave us to eat and drink at their house. We climbed a wooden staircase to the living-room above the stable that always occupies the lower floor of a Tibetan house. There were no windows, but a circular hole in the ceiling let in light and let out the smoke of the yak-dung fire burning in the chula, or earthenware pot. There was also the dim light of the butter lamps burning before the family shrine. We sat round the fire on sheepskins and Tibetan woollen rugs and brought out our wooden tea bowls from our bokkus to drink buttered tea and eat tsampa.

I behaved just as one of my own men, except that I conversed in the Indian language, using a few Tibetan words that I knew.

Our visit, although no doubt causing our presence in the country to be reported to the governors of the fortresses, served its purpose, in that we found out from the people the way to the Langbu Pass. We got the information out of two boys who said, "Go to Changmu tomorrow – bridge to cross – go little along the river to two chortens. Then go up between high stones and you will find yak paths."

This we did, passing the curious rock-hewn settlement of Changmu, consisting of about a hundred caves like huge pigeonholes high up on the sheer face of a sandstone cliff. They were cave dwellings and we kept some distance away, not knowing what the hidden inhabitants would do. In Tibet there are many such caves, and they are said to be connected with passages leading out to the tops of the cliffs. They make splendid dwellings, protected from cold and heat and enemies alike.

We found the chortens the boys spoke of, and the yak paths that led into the mountains to the west. We breasted the bridge that separated us from the valley of the Langbu Pass. Below our feet was the winding valley of the Gye River. A track could be seen along the open red sandy hillsides. On we went, doing about eighteen miles that day by my paceometer, and camped by the stream, where we found fuel and could light a fire.

By climbing 1,500 feet up the hillsides I observed that evening the position of the Langbu Pass, also that of another pass to the south, leading back over the main chain to Nepal and giving access probably to the Kambachen Valley somewhere near the foot of the Kangchen Glacier. This would make a back door from Lhonak to southern Tibet through a corner of Nepal. There is still another pass that way, the Chabuk-la; but it is said to be very difficult.

Next day we struck out towards the Langbu Pass, crowned by the fine mountain called the Langbu Singha. The all-important question was: could Everest be seen from the top of the pass?

When I reached the top, I was staggered by a magnificent view of towering snow mountains. The centre peak of the range rose as a glittering spire of rock clothed with clinging ice and snow. Beyond rose a higher peak twisted like a hooked tooth, a precipice on the north side and a névé on the south. To the left of this again was a long, flat-ridged peak, fantastically corniced with overhanging ridges of ice.

What fine mountains! But they were none of them Everest: they were too near. Everest was still about sixty miles away. These mountains were about 23,000 feet in height. I named them – Taringban (meaning "Long knife" in the Lepcha language) and Guma Raichu (meaning "Guma's tooth" in Tibetan).

Presently, while watching the panorama, the shifting of the clouds revealed other high mountain masses in the distance; and directly over the crest of Taringban appeared a sharp spire peak. This, through its magnetic bearing by my compass, proved itself to be none other than Mount Everest. A thousand feet of the summit was visible.

Although this fine panorama and the discovery of mountains hitherto unknown was in itself a reward, still it was also a disappointment, because it indicated an utter barrier. The only existing map showed the Kama Valley joining the Arun at the same place as the Tashirak River. I had planned to follow down the Tashirak Valley to reach the Kama Valley and then to go up this valley to Mount Everest. The maps were entirely wrong. This mountain range stood between me and Mount Everest;

and the Tashirak River flowed south instead of west. I was opposed by an enormous mountain obstacle; and I felt it was impossible to overcome it. After remaining an hour on the top of the pass, during which time the men said copious prayers and built a chorten, to which they attached the usual strips of cloth, we went steeply down to the open meadows which surround the village of Guma; and there we found a shelter for the night among some dirty sheep pens and huts plastered with mud and dung. The people were not unfriendly.

We proceeded towards Tashirak in some trepidation as to whether we would be stopped by the Dalai Lama's Rice Officer, who holds the toll bridge with a guard of soldiers. There was nothing for it but to go straight on and talk to him. He requested us not to cross, so we went away and made a camp on our side of the river some distance off. We struck camp, however, at about two o'clock in the morning, forded the river in the dark under terrible difficulties and so lost two loads of our food. But I breathed again.

I hoped the valley would bend west towards the Arun. But it went on persistently south and we eventually found ourselves descending to forest lands with the valley becoming more and more narrow.

We met an encampment of Nepalese traders with their yaks carrying borax, salt, wool, skins and yak tails. They are enterprising, honest, engaging and handsome men and women, these Nepalese who spend their lives crossing the mountains, trading between Tibet and Nepal. They talked openly and pleasantly and told no lies in answer to my questions.

"This road does not go to Kharta," they said. "Down the river you will come to Hatia, which is in Nepal, and the Maharaja's guards live there to see that no strange people enter. Go up that valley," they said, pointing to a lateral valley to the west, "and you will find a Gompa (monastery) high up, from which you can see all mountains."

They spoke of a great mountain, Kangchen Lemboo Geudyong. Could this be Mount Everest? They knew Kangchenjunga, which they called Kangchenzeunga. They spoke of another great mountain that had a lake in its centre, which might well be a reference to Makalu, the "Armchair

Peak", which has been observed from India to have a curious cup-like formation near its summit. Geographers think this is filled with a glacier.

These Nepalese invited me and my men to stay in their camp, which we did for a little while, and they replenished our supplies of mutton, butter, ghee, salt and tea.

We regretfully parted from them; and struck off to the westerly valley to reach the monastery they had spoken of, and to look across, as I hoped, to Mount Everest.

We found a strongly fortified wall built across the valley – a wall that had been made during the wars between Nepal and Tibet. I little thought how useful that wall would soon be in other ways. Now we used it as a shelter against the wind where we made our camp; pretty soon it was to protect us against Tibetan bullets.

Next morning Adhu came to the tent to say that a Tibetan captain and guard sent to prevent us following the upper road to Pherugh were watching some little distance away. I went down with my men and, forcing the captain to dismount, asked him what he meant by posting soldiers on us as if we were common thieves. I found that he was the captain of the Tashirak guard, and in the background was no less a personage than the Tinki Dzongpen himself and his followers.

They rode shaggy Tibetan ponies bridled in brass and silver and saddled in coloured numdahs. Each pony carried bulky slung leather saddlebags and blankets; and from the general appearance of the party it was obvious they had travelled far. We learned later that the Dzongpen, hearing of our presence, had ridden 150 miles to meet us, covering the distance in three days.

An interview was arranged which lasted two hours, and was carried on for some time in rather a heated manner. The Dzongpen showed his surprise that we had been able to find our way into Tibet over the high pass, and was suspicious because we had chosen to come by such an unusual way.

"For what reason have you come to Tibet? At the time of the war" (the 1904 mission to Lhasa) "many white men and men of India came, but since that time no one has entered the country."

They repeated again and again the same sentences: "No foreigners may come to Tibet. We do not know what you want, or for what reason you come."

I complained that I had received only discourtesy and opposition in Tibet, whereas all Tibetans coming to India were free to travel where they wished, and were received as welcome visitors. This was, I protested, indeed a disgrace to Tibetan civilization and Tibetan culture.

The whole party became very excited at this juncture and all started to shout and talk together. The soldiers crowded round and unstrapped their matchlocks in a threatening manner. It was impossible to understand what they were shouting about or what plan they might be proposing. All I could make out was the Dzongpen saying: "Go back the way you came."

I argued, but he was insistent. Then I tried the Tibetan game. I temporized, told him I would think it over and give him a reply the following day. The discussion then took another turn. He dropped his blustering authoritative tone, and became delightfully courteous. He told me he would have to get permission from Lhasa for us to pass through his province, and he begged me by no means to travel on or it would cost him his head. So I consented to wait for instructions from his superior. But such a permission, in the unlikely event of his even seeking it, and in the unlikelier event of its being accorded, would take weeks to arrive. I knew they were only procrastinating. In a very few days the Dzongpen would inform me that Lhasa had refused, and that I was to quit Tibet immediately. I was tempted to steal away and push on with my hillmen. I was nettled, meeting this opposition when so near to my goal, and at the prospect of failure after so much effort.

I knew that his force of soldiers could not deter me. They were armed with an ancient variety of matchlocks, and at thirty yards range the charge of slugs they would fire would be harmless; but the Dzongpen had, in the latter part of the interview at least, been so polite that I naturally hated to do anything that would cause him to be beheaded!

Happily, this idea of fighting the Dzongpen forces was quickly dismissed. Certainly it would be impolite, and moreover there seemed to be no need of it. He returned to the charge and again urged me to quit Tibet immediately.

But it was my turn to procrastinate. Delay might produce an opportunity to steal away unobserved. When he saw that I would give him no decided answer, he said he would not remain in that inhospitable gorge until I had made up my mind, but would go home. He ordered me to remain where I was. He would return on the following day for my decision.

He galloped down the ravine, his party stringing along behind him. I watched them, none too pleased with the turn of events, and well "on the boil". Life at high altitudes does not conduce to placidity and evenness of temper, and the arrogance of the soldiers, and their unconcealed smug satisfaction at having discovered and made us halt, had distinctly got on my nerves. One of the men remained behind longer than the rest. Finally he too started, but in passing he jostled his horse against me rudely. I jumped ahead and seized his bridle. I meant to hold him and complain to the Dzongpen, but he struck me across the face with his whip and tore the bridle from my grasp. Highly enraged, I ran after him. He galloped for several hundred yards with me in pursuit. Then he dismounted and swung his clumsy matchlock into action.

I was fired on by that grotesque instrument! It made enough noise for a cannon. Where the slugs went I could never tell – all over the place, I think. I slipped behind the ruins of the Tibetan wall. I placed a shot from my American rifle over his head, and he went off so fast, and made me laugh so much, that I did not think it worthwhile to follow it with another one.

Things seemed to be none the worse for this incident, save that my face smarted a bit from the blow of the whip; but my men thought otherwise. They were tremendously excited and highly perturbed. With the exchange of fire they thought the whole of Tibet would descend on us. They absolutely refused to go on.

There was nothing to be done but to turn our backs on the approaches of Everest, the mysterious lamasery and the valley of the mountain.

Within forty miles, and nearer at that time than any white man had been! I leave you to imagine my chagrin and disappointment.

It took us six long weeks to get back to India.

Noel was not finished with Everest. He participated in both the 1922 and 1924 expeditions.

Everest 1921

Reconnaissance

C.K. Howard-Bury

And then in 1920, the Nepalese lifted their rock curtain and allowed a British expedition to Everest: the first ever from the West. The expedition, organized by the Royal Geographical Society and the Alpine Club, was placed under the leadership of a former Rifles officer, Lt Col. Charles Kenneth Howard-Bury.

At the beginning of the year, as soon as permission for the expedition had been granted, preparations were immediately begun to collect stores and to arrange for the alpine and scientific equipment that was to accompany the expedition. Most of the stores were bought in England, and all the alpine equipment, including skis and snowshoes, rope, crampons and alpine tents; the ordinary tents and a certain amount of food stores were bought in India. The scientific equipment included maximum and minimum thermometers, black- and bright-bulb solar radiation thermometers, hypsometers, George barometer, and aneroids in pairs to read from 15,000 to 22,000 and from 22,000 to 30,000 feet. The photographic equipment consisted of three stand cameras, one 7½ × 5 and two quarter-plate, all fitted with telephoto attachments. There was also a Panoram Kodak and several small Kodaks for use at great heights, where it would be impossible to carry up the larger cameras. The Imperial Plate Company kindly presented all the dry-plates for the expedition. The members of the expedition left England at different times, arranging to meet at Darjeeling by the middle of May, when it was hoped that the expedition would be able to start. Mr Raeburn was the first to arrive there, as he had gone ahead to collect coolies for the expedition. For high climbing a special type of coolie is needed, one who is strong and hardy and does not mind the cold and is also accustomed to live at great heights. The type of man who best fulfils these conditions is the Sherpa Bhotia, who comes from the north-east of Nepal from the districts that lie to the south of Mount Everest. He is a Buddhist by religion, and though at times quarrelsome and rather too fond of strong drink, yet he proves a very useful and capable type of man, who could be rapidly trained in snow and ice craft, and who was not afraid of the snow or the cold. We also picked up a few Tibetans from the Chumbi Valley on the way, and these proved to be as good as the best of the Sherpas; they were less trouble to manage, and could equally well carry loads at great heights. These coolies were all fitted with boots, and very difficult some of them were to fit with their broad feet – as broad as they were long. Blankets, cap comforters, fur gloves, socks and warm clothing were issued to all of them, and for those that had to sleep at the highest camps, eiderdown sleeping-bags were taken. The expedition also took two interpreters with them, Gyalzen Kazi, a Kazi of Sikkim, who came from near Gangtok, and Chheten Wangdi, a Tibetan who had at one time been a captain in the Tibetan Army, and then had been with the Indian Army in Egypt during the war. They proved quite invaluable to the expedition. They were both of them very hard-working, and saved the expedition many thousands of rupees in expense; their tact and knowledge of Tibetan ways and customs were of the greatest use in keeping up the friendly relations established between the expedition and the Tibetans.

Lord Ronaldshay, the Governor of Bengal, showed the expedition every kindness and hospitality, and went out of his way to help it in every way possible at Darjeeling. The stores from England, which had gone round by sea, were unfortunately late in arriving, owing to congestion in the harbour at Calcutta, and insufficient dock accommodation there. However, once they were landed, every one was most helpful, and the Darjeeling Himalayan Railway, which had given a free pass for them over their line, had everything brought up to Darjeeling by 16 May.

Arrangements had been made with *The Times* and with

certain Indian newspapers to publish periodical telegrams dealing with the progress of the expedition, and though this news was available to all other Indian papers, they took no advantage of it, and preferred to boycott the expedition.

Before going up to Darjeeling I had been to Simla, where I had had an interview with Lord Reading, the Viceroy, who had shown great interest in the expedition and had given a subscription of Rs.750 towards it. The Commander-in-Chief, Lord Rawlinson, I had also seen, and he had arranged to lend the expedition 100 government mules. These arrived at Darjeeling early in May and were to be our main transport. The mules were a fine lot, sleek and fat, and we had great hopes of them. On 18 and 19 May the expedition left Darjeeling in two parties, with fifty mules and twenty coolies in each party. Major Morshead had left on 13 May, travelling up the Teesta Valley, with his surveyors, and was to meet us at Kampa Dzong. We were unable to take all our stores at once, and left part of them behind, intending to make use of the government mules in bringing them on later. Throughout the journey across Sikkim the weather was very wet, with heavy rain each day; the mountain tops and ridges were all covered with clouds and prevented our obtaining any views. Owing to its heavy rainfall Sikkim is a country with a lavish growth and a marvellous vegetation; the path that leads across to the Tibetan frontier is a very trying one, as it is a series of steep climbs followed by equally steep descents into steaming tropical valleys. Wonderful butterflies of every shade and hue flitted across the path, scarlet clerodendrons made brilliant patches of colour in the dark green of the luxuriant forest among huge tree ferns. Creepers and ferns hung from every tree; white, orange, mauve or purple orchids grew among the mosses and ferns on the branches of the trees, and showed up in lovely clumps of colour. We passed big hedges of daturas on the way, fifteen to twenty feet in height and covered with hundreds of great white trumpet-shaped blooms, quite eight inches in diameter and fully a foot in length. At night they gave out a strangely sweet scent and seemed to gleam in the darkness with a curious kind of phosphorescence.

Ever since leaving Darjeeling our mules had been giving

trouble, and two or three from each party had to be left behind
after each march. After travelling for four days we stopped at
Rongli, hoping they might recover after a day's rest. Ten mules
had already been left behind and one had died. The next march
to Sedonchen was a short one of only nine miles, but the path
climbed from 2,700 feet to 7,000 feet, and this completely
finished the mules. For one party alone we had already hired
twenty-two ponies to take some of the loads, and after
Sedonchen we should have had to hire ponies to carry their
own line-gear as well as all our loads, so that there was now
nothing to be done except to send the mules back and rely on
what local transport we could get. The marches ahead of us
were longer and the climbing steeper than anything we had yet
done. We were, however, on the main trade route to Tibet, and
had passed hundreds of Tibetan mules coming down from
Tibet laden with bales of wool and others returning with rice,
grain and cloth bought in exchange. We were, therefore, able
to pick up sufficient mules to carry us to Yatung; if we had
taken the shorter route up the Teesta valley this would have
been impossible, as villages there are small and there is practically no transport passing along that route.

The path is really only a steep stone causeway up the mountain side, a regular *via dolorosa* and most unpleasant to walk
upon; but probably anything else would be washed away by
the torrential rain that falls here during most of the year.
Leeches abounded here, sitting up at the end of every leaf and
fern and waving at the passers-by. From Sedonchen to
Gnatong the path climbs 5,000 feet in the first five miles, and
as we rose higher we entered into the rhododendron forests
after passing through the zone of oaks and magnolias. The
rhododendrons at this time of the year were a glorious sight.
No photograph could do justice to the scene – it needed a
painter at least. The hillside was a blaze of colour – rhododendrons, orange, red, deep crimson, pink, white, cream-coloured,
formed a glorious mixture of colours. Every yard of the path
was a pure delight. Now appeared grassy fields carpeted with
primulas and many others of the purely alpine plants. Gnatong
was a very wet and cold spot with a rainfall of 180 inches, and
on the next day we crossed the Jelep La, 14,390 feet, in

pouring rain. This was the frontier between Sikkim and Tibet, and on going a few hundred feet down on the Tibetan side we emerged into fine weather with blue skies, having left the rain behind us on the Sikkim side. Everywhere were primulas and rhododendrons, the former appearing the moment the winter snow had melted from the ground. It was a steep and a stony descent of over 5,000 feet into the Chumbi Valley, but the rhododendrons in the great forest of fir trees showed up splendidly, the big pink blooms of *Aucklandi*, the orange bells of *cinnabarinum* and many a white and yellow one too, in striking contrast to the dark green of the firs. We now met birch, sycamore and willows, all pale green, with the tender green of early spring, white spiræas and clematis, yellow berberis, white and pink roses, purple iris and a mass of other wild flowers. The Chumbi Valley is one of the most fertile and prosperous valleys in all Tibet; the houses are large and well built, reminding one very much of Tirolese villages. The rainfall here is but a quarter of that which falls on the other side of the Jelap La; potatoes, barley, wheat, apples and pears all grow well here. The air everywhere at this time of the year was scented by the wild roses. From Yatung to Phari was twenty-eight miles, two days' easy march up the Chumbi Valley. We visited the Galinka and Donka monasteries on the way, both containing enormous prayer-wheels in which they said there were over one million prayers. Each time the wheel is turned a bell rings, and one million prayers have ascended to heaven. In other places we met prayer-wheels turned by water brought down in irrigation channels, and again in other parts the wind was used to do the same work, a kind of anemometer being fitted up to catch the wind. This latter was, perhaps, the most constant, as the wind blows both summer and winter in Tibet, whereas for six months in the year the water is frozen, and the waterwheel is silent and can offer up no prayers. In the Donka monastery was a famous oracle, a regular Delphic oracle who was consulted far and wide, and his oracles had a great reputation for truth. Here we were given the usual Tibetan tea, poured out into agate and silver teacups and made with salt, tea and butter, all churned up together. On a cold day this was a warming drink, but I never much took to it as a beverage, though I had to take many cups of it during the next few months and had to pretend to enjoy it.

Phari is a very dirty village, with a stone fort, and is situated at a height of 14,300 feet. It is always a cold windy spot, but it is an important trade mart, both to India and across the Tremo La to Bhutan. It lies at the foot of the sacred peak of Chomolhari – a very beautiful mountain, just under 24,000 feet, which stands at the entrance to the real Tibet, where the great plains and rolling downs begin with their far distant views. We left Phari on 31 May with a most marvellous collection of transport animals, comprising donkeys, bullocks, mules, ponies and yaks. There is a short way from Phari to Kampa Dzong, which takes only three days, but we were told that it was too early in the season to use that road, and that we would have to take the long way round. We afterwards found out that this was a lie, and that they had sent us the long way round in order to be able to charge us more. We had not yet got accustomed to Tibetan ways.

From Phari to Kampa Dzong by the long route took us six days. For the first two days we followed the ordinary trade route to Gyantse, over the Tang La, 15,200 feet, through Tuna to Dochen, keeping at a height of 14,800 all the way. Chomolhari was a magnificent sight the whole time, with its 7,000 feet of precipices descending right on to the Tuna plain. Near Dochen was the large shallow lake of Bam-tso, a lake with the most lovely colours, the shades varying from deep blue through purple to a light blue-green. In other parts of it the waters were quite red from a weed that grew in it, and in the still morning light the whole of the range of glacier-covered mountains that formed the background to the picture were reflected in its calm waters and formed a charming picture. Many bar-headed geese were seen swimming about, also some Brahmany duck and a few terns. On the plains roamed herds of kiang, the wild horse of Tibet, and many goa, the Tibetan gazelle, were feeding there, but the latter were very wary and would not allow us to get within 500 yards of them. It was at Dochen that our cook tried to boil a tin of fish without opening it first, and when he tried to open it afterwards when it was hot, to his surprise and fright, it exploded like a bomb in his face, and he and all his assistants in the kitchen were covered with small pieces of fish.

From Dochen we crossed the Dug Pass, 16,400 feet, to Khe, which was the site of the once-important town of Khe-tam. In those days the Kala-tso must have extended right up to it, but everywhere were traces of rapid desiccation. Ruins extended for more than a mile in every direction, and some of the buildings must have been of considerable size, but now there is no water in the valley, and all we could get that night came from a very dirty and muddy pond that was nearly dried up. From here we marched to Kheru, and camped at 15,700 feet with some nomads who were very friendly. The days were very warm, but at nights there were still sharp frosts. From Kheru there was a longer march of sixteen miles to Tat-sang, crossing two small passes of 16,450 and 17,100 feet. Tat-sang lies at a height of 16,000 feet on the edge of a broad plain, where there were some excellent springs full of fish, and below a small nunnery, which stands on a commanding rock. That night, again, there was a sharp frost. The next day's march to Kampa Dzong led for twelve miles along a barren and dry valley to a pass of 17,300 feet, and then gradually descended through a curious limestone gorge to Kampa Dzong, whose walls suddenly appeared towering above us on the cliffs. We passed many iris, light and dark blue, growing in the valley, and a curious pink trumpet-shaped flower that came straight out of the sand. Game was plentiful along the route, and I shot a gazelle and an *Ovis Ammon (Hodgsoni)* on the way. Here we met Morshead and his surveyors, who had come up the Teesta Valley and over the Serpo La.

Several of us, ever since leaving Phari, had not been feeling well, and had had stomach troubles owing to the change of climate and bad cooking on the part of our cooks. It took most of us some time to get acclimatized to the changed conditions. Dr Kellas, however, instead of getting better, gradually grew worse and weaker every day, until on the last march before reaching Kampa Dzong, while being carried in a litter over a 17,000-feet pass, his heart failed him, and he passed quietly away. The following day we buried him at Kampa Dzong, within sight of the three great mountains he had climbed in

Sikkim – Pawhunri, Kinchenjhow and Chomiomo – and in view of Mount Everest, which he had so longed to approach. Mr Raeburn, too, had been gradually getting worse, and there was no other alternative but to send him down with Mr Wollaston to Lachen and put him under the care of the missionaries there until he could recover. This was a very serious blow to the expedition, the loss of two of the members of the climbing party.

After Kampa Dzong our route lay across broad plains and along the flat and swampy valley of the Yaru with the snowy chain of the Himalayas to the south of us; from these heights, for we were about 15,000 feet, they did not appear nearly as imposing as they do from the south, and for the most part the northern slopes were not as steep as those on the south. Game was plentiful all the way to Tinki Dzong, and we passed many ponds covered with teal, duck and bar-headed geese. In these flat valleys the midges were very troublesome all day, surrounding us in clouds. Tinki Dzong was a picturesque old fort, situated on the banks of a large pond that swarmed with bar-headed geese, Brahmany duck and teal. They were wonderfully tame and came waddling round our tents, knowing no fear of man, for they had never been shot or killed here. For some years a lama, who had been sent from Lhasa, had lived here and made it his special object to tame all the wild animals around. The Jongpen rode out to meet us and escorted us to tents that had been pitched for us, where he had ceremonial tea, sweetmeats and chang – Tibetan beer – all ready for us. The Jongpen was very Mongolian in appearance, and was dressed in fine embroidered Chinese silks, and proved a most obliging and courteous host, presenting us with a couple of hundred eggs and four sheep. There were several large monasteries and prosperous-looking villages tucked away all around in the recesses of the hills. The barley here was just beginning to come up, for in Tibet it can be grown and ripened at heights of over 15,000 feet, and during the summer months I saw some of the finest crops that I have seen anywhere. It is nearly all irrigated, as they do not seem to put much faith in the rain.

On 11 June we left Tinki, and had the usual trouble in starting. Some forty-five families were supplying us with transport and, as each wanted the lightest loads for their animals, there was a babel of noise and nothing was done. The headman eventually settled the squabbling by taking a garter from each family and, after mixing them up, laid one on each load, and whoever was the owner of the garter had to take the load. Crossing the Tinki Pass we descended again into the Yaru Valley at Chusher Nango, passing on the way a curious dwarf gorse which carpeted the valley with yellow. Our yaks here proved very wild, and the plain was soon strewn with loads flung off by them as they careered away, tail in air, in every direction. We forded the Yaru here by a ford three feet deep and some eighty yards wide, and soon afterwards came to the fine country house of Gyanga Nangpa, which was the home of the Phari Jongpen. He rode out to meet us, and provided us with a very solid meal of soup and Tibetan dumplings with a chilli sauce. As we were given fifteen dumplings apiece we found some difficulty in making room for these. Europeans had never been seen before in any of these parts since leaving Kampa Dzong, so everywhere we were objects of the greatest interest to all the inhabitants who flocked out to see us.

Our next march proved a more exciting one, as after fording the Yaru again we had to cross a wide sandy plain full of shifting quicksands. When we arrived there a violent sandstorm was blowing, which our guides said would make the crossing easier. So off we started, dressed as though for a gas attack, with goggles over the eyes and with mouth and nose covered with handkerchiefs and mufflers. The sand was blowing in great clouds from off the sand-dunes, through which we wound our way, and under one we found some of our coolies halted and quite lost. After leaving the sand-dunes we had some wide stretches of wet sand to cross, over which the dry sand was blowing in smoke-like wisps, so that the whole ground appeared to be moving. In places where the wet sand shook and quivered we hurried on as fast as possible, and eventually we got everything over in safety. It was too late now to go on, so we camped in a howling gale among the sand-dunes, and it was many days afterwards before we got rid of the sand which had penetrated everywhere.

Close to this camp the Bong Chu and Yaru rivers meet and

flow south, cutting their way through the great Himalayan mountain range. Much to our surprise, there suddenly appeared just before sunset, and far away down the valley over the clouds, a lofty and very beautiful peak. This we eventually decided must be Mount Everest, and the next morning we were able to prove this was so by climbing one of the hills to the west of the camp, from which we could see the whole range of the Himalaya to the south of us. Our drivers called this peak Chomo-uri, the Goddess of the Turquoise Peak, but this can only be a very local name, as Everest is known and called by the Tibetans Chomo-lungma, Goddess Mother of the country. This is the official name in Lhasa, and this name was known throughout the country, so that this is apparently the correct Tibetan name for Mount Everest. From this point we now entered the valley of the Bhong Chu, and this we followed up to Tingri. Major Morshead and his surveyors were kept very busy all the time, mapping the country as they went along, for they were travelling now in unsurveyed country. From one peak to the north of the Bhong Chu we had a very extensive view, stretching from the snowy ranges beyond Chomolhari and 120 miles to the east of us to Kanchenjunga, and then on to Makalu and Everest, and from there passing on to the high snow peaks west of Everest and to Gosainthan, a range of some 250 miles of snow peaks; but above them all towered Mount Everest, several thousand feet above its neighbours.

Three days' march brought us to Shekar Dzong, where was the headquarters of the district with two Jongpens. There was also a large monastery here containing 400 monks. Shekar was a most remarkable place, on a rocky hill like a gigantic St Michael's Mount. The town is at the base of the hill, but the monastery, consisting of innumerable buildings with narrow streets, was literally perched on stone terraces built out from the rocky sides of the hill and connected by walls and towers with the fort, which was built still higher up, and this again was connected by turreted walls with a Gothic-like structure at the summit, where incense was freely burned every morning. Immense crowds came to see us and were most embarrassing in their attentions. While we were here we visited the monastery, which was a very rich one. In the largest temple, which, like all Buddhist structures, was very dark, were several life-sized gilded statues of Buddha, covered with precious stones and turquoises, and behind these was a colossal statue of Buddha fully fifty feet high. Round the temple were eight curious figures, about ten feet in height, and dressed in quaint flounce dresses, which were the guardians of the shrine. From the entrance to the temple we climbed up a steep staircase, almost in complete darkness, until we came out on a platform almost opposite the gilded face of the great Buddha. Here were offerings of grain and butter and some exquisitely carved bowls and teapots of silver. The abbot of this monastery was the reincarnation of a former abbot, and was looked upon as an extremely holy man. He had spent sixty-six years of his life in this monastery, and all the monks seemed to adore him for his gentle and charming personality. His attendants with much difficulty persuaded him to be photographed, as they wanted to have some picture of him, for they said that his time on earth could now only be short. They dressed him up in some beautiful gold brocades, and priceless silk hangings were put up for a background. This photograph proved afterwards most useful, and people hundreds of miles away used to beg for a print of it, as they put it in their shrines and worshipped it and burned incense before it, and I could not give any one a more welcome present than the picture of the old abbot of Shekar-chöde.

Two days' march from here brought us to Tingri, which was a large village and trading centre, situated on a small hill in the middle of the great Tingri plain. This was to be our first base while reconnoitring the north-western approaches to Mount Everest. We could get no information about the country to the south of us, so that it was necessary to send out parties in different directions. Information on any subject was always hard to get in Tibet. Most of the people knew nothing beyond their own village, and of those that had travelled further no two would tell you the same story. It was the same with distances; they would have no real measure of distance or time. It would be a long day's journey or a short one, and for short distances it was expressed by cups of tea, which means the time that it would take to drink one, two or three cups of tea. The representative of the Depon received us at Tingri, and put at our disposal the old Chinese Rest House, where we made ourselves quite comfortable. We had rooms in which to put away our stores, and another room we turned into a darkroom to develop all the photographs that we were taking. It had taken the expedition just one month to get to Tingri from Darjeeling.

No time was lost, as it was not known when the monsoon might break, and how strong it might be in Tibet, and on 23 June Mallory and Bullock started off to find the easiest method of approaching Mount Everest from the north-west. Mount Everest was clearly visible from Tingri, about forty miles away, and across a low range of hills and to the west of it were some fine snow peaks 25–27,000 feet in height, which dropped down to the Khombu Pass. It was just possible that a glacier might come from Mount Everest and join the Kyetrak River, so the following day Major Wheeler and Dr Heron started off to go towards the Khombu Pass. From now on Dr Heron was on the move all the summer, sometimes with one party, sometimes with another, and often by himself studying the geology of all the valleys and mountains. He travelled over more country than any other member of the expedition. Major Wheeler, too, began his photographic survey from the Khombu Pass, and most of the summer he spent by himself in lonely camps 18–20,000 feet high. The weather was very provoking, and often he would spend day after day, over 20,000 feet, on the top of a mountain in bitter cold and driving snow, waiting for the clouds to lift, to enable him to take his photographs. I think that he had the hardest and most trying time of all of us, and deserves the greatest credit for his work.

On 22 June Mr Wollaston rejoined the expedition, after having taken Mr Raeburn down to Lachen and handed him over to the care of the lady missionaries there. After his arrival I was now able to go away for a few days, and see personally where the various parties were and the general lie of the land, and I also wanted to find a place for our second base when we were reconnoitring the other side of Mount Everest. I first went and joined Major Wheeler and Dr Heron at Kyetrak, and, climbed up to the Khombu Pass – a fine glacier-covered pass of 19,000 feet – leading into Nepal and across which a certain amount of traffic comes. It is always a dangerous pass, but early in the season they appear to take yaks over it. To the east towered up the great cliffs of the 26,800-foot peak, and to the right were the icefalls of Chorabsang. From here, with Dr Heron, we crossed over the Pusi La or Marmot Pass (17,700 feet), a quite easy pass into the Rongshahr Valley and down to its interesting gneiss gorges. The Tibetan frontier in many places extends for several days' march south of the main watershed of the Himalayas, as it is easier to get from Tibet over the passes into the upper reaches of the valley than it is from Nepal. At a certain distance down the valleys they narrow into steep precipitous gorges up or down which the going is very difficult and often impassable in the rainy season, as the rivers are quite unfordable. This is the case with the Nyanam Valley, the Rongshahr Valley and the Arun Valley. On the south side of the passes there is a considerable rainfall and the vegetation becomes quite luxuriant. Near Tazang the white roses covered the hillsides, while spiræas, small yellow and white rhododendrons, yellow primulas, wild gooseberries and currants grew everywhere, and the shady sides of the hills were covered with forests of birch, while juniper covered the other slopes that faced south.

Owing to the amount of juniper that grows in it, and which is very aromatic and used as incense, the valley is looked upon as a sacred one, and there were several hermits that lived here in caves among the rocks. The nearest village supplied them with food, and morning and evening clouds of incense used to ascend from the mouths of their caves. After ten years of meditation the anchorite is supposed to acquire great holiness and to be able to support life on ten grains of barley a day. There was a female anchorite here, they told us, who had lived to 138 years and was greatly revered. She forbade any killing of animals, and hence we found the wild sheep everywhere very tame. After returning to Keprak we travelled east to Zambu, a prosperous-looking village, owning some 3,000 yaks, and with fine views looking up the Rongbuk Valley to Mount Everest, which was now only about twenty miles away. This valley led apparently right up to the foot of the giant precipices that come down from its north-western face. A large and unfordable glacier stream came down this valley, but at the monastery of Chöbu, three miles from Zambu, there was a footbridge across which the loads were carried by hand, while the yaks were swum across the river. Some of the yaks preferred to stop on an island in the middle of the stream. Throwing stones at them was no use as they refused to budge, but at length someone produced a sling, and the stones thrown by this method evidently stung the animals considerably more and produced the required effect. The Rongbuk Valley was wild and gloomy, with great cliffs coming down to the muddy glacier stream, but it was a strangely holy valley, too, for at a height of 16,500 feet there was a large monastery, and besides the inhabitants of the monastery they told us there were between three and four hundred hermits and nuns living in little solitary cells or caves. Here, far away from the outside world, under the shadow of the great precipices of Mount Everest, they could meditate in peace and in perfect seclusion. All the wild animals and birds in this valley were wonderfully tame. With my own eyes I watched the wild sheep coming down in the early morning to the hermits' cells and being fed not 100 yards from our camp, and I walked up openly to within twenty yards of a herd of burhel and they showed no signs of fear or paid the slightest attention to me. The rock pigeon would come and feed out of our hands, and so it was with all the other wild birds.

We found the alpine climbers in a camp further up the valley, on a sunny terrace about 18,000 feet, above the left bank of the Rongbuk Glacier, and commanding magnificent views of Mount Everest about seven miles away at the head of the valley. From here for a month they were able to train their coolies in snow and ice work, and to explore the side glaciers and the great spurs that come out to the west and north-west and which appeared so very impossible. At first, and up to 7 July, the weather remained pretty fine; but then the monsoon broke and rain and snow hindered the work of reconnaissance very much and made all high climbing impossible. From this point Dr Heron and I retraced our steps to Chöbu, and then in three marches, crossing the Doya La on the way, we reached Kharta and the main Arun Valley, or

Bhong Chu, as the Tibetans call it as long as it remains in Tibet. The people here were at first very frightened of us. Villages were quite deserted when we approached, but after a while they crept back one by one. The alpine flowers on the Doya La were exceptionally beautiful. The lovely blue poppy abounded and grew in clusters everywhere; pink, yellow and white saxifrages covered the rocks, and several varieties of gentian were just beginning to come out. The Doya La marks a distinct barrier, the country to the north being barren, while on the south the moister currents of air penetrate up the Arun Valley and its tributaries, giving it a distinctly damper climate. This was very noticeable in the vegetation as we descended – rhododendrons, willows, juniper, roses, clematis, currants, abounded, and the ground was in places carpeted with yellow and sweet-scented primulas.

After much trouble we at length found Kharta, for the old maps here were hopelessly wrong. It was really a large collection of villages, near where the Kharta River ran into the Arun. We rode up to see the Jongpen, who lives in the village of Kharta Shigar, some three miles up the Kharta Valley. He had a large Chinese tent pitched for us in his garden, which was well sheltered and shady with willow trees all round, and containing a large painted water prayer-wheel under a great poplar tree, turned by a gurgling little stream that ran through the garden. The Jongpen was quite a young man, though he had been there for some years, and was most friendly and hospitable. He insisted on giving us all our meals, but we were getting experienced now in the use of chopsticks, and the Tibetan cooking was often better than that done by our own servants. We were able to look round for a suitable place for our second base camp, as it would be necessary to explore the upper Kharta Valley and another valley that they told us about, that lay to the south of it. We eventually selected a house that stood all by itself on an old river terrace, and was surrounded by a shady garden of poplars and willows. The rent we had to pay for the house and garden amounted to 3½ *d.* a day; but living is cheap in Tibet, and you can get a house-servant there for 2*s.* 8*d.* a year!

The rains now broke in earnest, and we had a very wet

journey back to Tingri, going to Lumeh, with its huge poplar, forty feet in circumference, and crossing a dangerous ford over the Rongbuk river higher up at Tashi Dzong; but I got back in three days, riding thirty-six miles the last day in pouring rain. During my absence Major Morshead had been busy surveying the country to the north of Tingri, and on my return he and Mr Wollaston started off on a journey of exploration to the south-west, having had an invitation from the Jongpens at Nyanam to visit them, and they were able to see the great peak of Gosainthan and Gaurisankar, which was for a long time confused with Mount Everest, though over twenty miles away from it and 5,000 feet lower. It was a very striking and beautiful peak. They also visited Lapchi Kang, where the poet Mila Rapa had lived and which was a great place of pilgrimage. Its name was known far and wide, and some people even applied this name to Mount Everest. The weather, however, unfortunately spoilt their trip, as it rained nearly all the time. But Mr Wollaston managed to collect many natural history specimens and a great variety of new flowers. At Tingri, too, during this time, we had heavy storms of rain and thunder every night, fresh snow coming down as low as 15,000 feet; but most of it melted again during the day. The plains around Tingri were rapidly becoming marshes and the rivers soon became unfordable. The storms always formed to the north of us along the Sipri limestone ridge and the watershed between the Brahmaputra and Bhong Chu, and then gradually worked down towards the south. Fine weather came to us from the south, and when the south wind blew the rain stopped. It was seldom that the monsoon clouds brought rain directly to us. Every evening at Tingri we had brilliant lightning and loud thunder to the north, and our house proved to be very leaky. The rain poured in through the mud roofs.

On 24 July we started moving all our stores from Tingri to Kharta, and our first march was to Nezogu, where there was a bridge over the Kyetrak River. A couple of inches of snow fell during the night, and many of us who did not put on snow goggles soon enough suffered much the next two days from snow blindness. Wheeler, who had finished his survey of the Keprak and Khombu valleys, accompanied me as far as

Chöbu, where he started to go up the Rongbuk Valley. Here he remained for a month, having a very trying time with constant bad weather. Mallory and Bullock, finding the bad weather too much for them, joined us and came along to Kharta, and their coolies were also in want of a rest. From Chöbu to Rebu was a pleasant march through a fertile valley full of fields of barley, peas and yellow mustard, and the wild flowers were very beautiful along the irrigation channels – a black clematis, blue monkshood and delphinium predominating. The next day we crossed the Doya La, and on the 28th reached Kharta, where we established our camp in the garden belonging to the house that we had hired, the house itself being used for all our stores and for a darkroom. Here we were only at a height of 12,300 feet, and the valley was green with fields of peas and barley. Just below us flowed the Arun, now a majestic river over 100 yards wide, and a mile lower down it entered into its great gorges, where in the course of the next twenty miles it drops from 12,000 feet to 7,500 feet, a fall of over 200 feet in the mile. Every day the monsoon clouds came up through the gorge in thin wisps, but melted away always at the same spot, and though it poured with rain a mile below us, yet every day with us the sun shone brightly and it was very rare for any rain to reach us. Twenty miles away to the north again were heavy clouds, and storms and rain fell there daily, so that we seemed to be in a dry zone between the two storms. The forests of fir and birch came up to the limit of the rainfall, and then ceased suddenly when the rain stopped a mile below us.

On 2 August Mallory and Bullock left Kharta to explore the eastern approach to Mount Everest. Neither the Jongpen nor any of the inhabitants could tell us where the Kharta river had its source, and whether it was possible to get to Mount Everest that way. They said, however, that in the next valley to the south it was possible to do so. I followed the alpine climbers a couple of days later, as Mr Wollaston and Major Morshead had returned from their trip to Lapchi Kang. After going for seven miles up the Kharta Valley, which is very fertile, with every level space filled with barley-fields, and containing numerous villages and monasteries, we turned up a side valley and then crossed over a chain of mountains to the south by the Langma La, a pass 18,000 feet in height. This led us into the wonderful Kama Valley, a valley unexcelled in beauty anywhere in the Himalayas, with the most stupendous scenery – gigantic rocky cliffs towering up to heaven, and immense cliffs of ice torn and riven, breaking off and falling with a thunderous roar far down into the valley below; there were smiling pastures right up among the ice and snow, with fields carpeted with many varieties of gentian; rhododendrons, birch and fir trees surrounded some of the lower glaciers, and forests of some of the most magnificent fir trees grew in the lower parts of the valley, the whole forming a combination of beauty not often seen.

At the extreme end of the valley towered up Mount Everest with its great buttresses forming a huge semicircle, and like a great snake, the Kangshung glacier, with its bands of black moraine, crept up to the foot of the rock walls and cliffs that formed the eastern side of Mount Everest. It did not need a long survey of these faces to satisfy the alpine climbers that there was no practicable route up this side, but there was still an untried approach up the Kharta Valley, and to this valley they now turned their attention. But before we deal with the first reconnaissance of the Kharta Valley I should like to discuss the Kama Valley more fully; it was so very beautiful that I paid three visits to it at different times. From the upper Kharta Valley at the end of September, I paid my third visit with Major Wheeler and Mr Wollaston. We crossed over a high pass well over 20,000 feet, and descended into the head of the valley. The weather was fine, and we were able to get some good photographs of Everest and Makalu – the latter a mountain only a little over 1,000 feet below Mount Everest – yet a far finer mountain to look at and far more imposing. I was able to climb up on to a ridge between the two peaks, whence I got some superb views of the incredibly narrow peaks of Makalu, with its cliffs and formidable precipices often too steep even to be lightly powdered with snow. To the south we looked down over range upon range of snow mountains in Nepal. In the Kama Valley, Makalu is the most astonishing spectacle – its terrifically steep precipices descend sheer for 11,000 feet into the valley, and huge buttresses of perpendicular black rock support it with jagged black spires and towers. The Tibetans do not know the name of Makalu, but call the mountain Chomo Lönzo. From the northern peak the Kangdoshung glacier pours straight across the valley, forcing the stream that rises on Mount Everest itself to go under the glacier, entering it in an enormous black cavern. Rhododendrons, willows, mountain ash, blue poppies and iris now abound, and a few miles lower down begin the birch trees and the juniper, which grow with the greatest luxuriance, and in the autumn I never anywhere saw such beautiful colouring as the scarlet of the mountain ash and berberis, the yellow and gold of the birch and willows, and the deep red of the wild roses.

Towards the end of August, while waiting for the weather to improve, Mr Wollaston and I crossed over the Chog La and dropped down to Sakeding (the pleasant terrace), a small trade mart a little lower down in the Kama Valley, in order to pay a visit and investigate the lower parts of the valley. Here we entered at 12,000 feet into the zone of the real forests. Here were juniper trees of a size quite unknown, with stems twenty feet in circumference and rising for fifty and sixty feet without a branch. Then a little lower down we entered into the zone of the silver fir (*Abies webbiana*), where the trees grow 100 feet and more in height and with a girth of over twenty-five feet, and a little lower down at 9–10,000 feet the lovely feathery *brunoniana* grew over 150 feet in height, and with trunks over thirty feet in girth. In these zones grew also the great rhododendrons, *argenteum* and *falconeri*, for here was a climate of constant rain. These high mountains seemed to draw up the monsoon currents towards them, and every tree and bush was covered with long grey lichens that hung down and gently swayed in the wind; the hillsides were running with water and the path was a morass of black leafy mud, except where logs had been laid down on which to walk. Such conditions were favourable to leeches, and they abounded in this valley and to heights over 12,000 feet. They had evidently never tasted European blood, and were anxious to do so, thinking that we were a new kind of food and a great delicacy, for they climbed up the tent walls, on our clothes and legs and faces; they got on to our plates and cups and into our food, and we never knew

when we might not meet them. We travelled down to where the
Kama River joins the Arun River, at a height of 7,500 feet,
below the first great gorges of the Arun and some twenty miles
below Kharta. All this country is still in Tibet, as the Nepal
frontier runs along the Everest–Makalu Ridge, and then
continues eastwards, following the crest line of the ridge down
to the spot where it joins the Arun. The ridge is crossed by one
low pass of 14,000 feet, called the Popti La, and across this
pass a certain amount of trade is carried on with Tibet by
coolies during seven months of the year. For five months the
pass is closed by snow, but chillies, dyes and rice are sent over
from Nepal and are exchanged at Sakeding for salt. It is all
done by barter and no money changes hands.

Meanwhile Mr Mallory and Mr Bullock had been joined by
Major Morshead, and had gone up to the headwaters of the
Kharta Valley, and, after exploring it under bad conditions of
weather and with very soft snow, had decided that there was a
practicable means of getting on to Mount Everest by this
route. The rainy season, however, was still in full swing; far
more rain had fallen all through Tibet than we had ever
expected to meet; the rivers everywhere were unfordable now,
and all the bridges by which we had crossed in the spring had
been washed away, so that there was nothing to do but wait
until the weather improved. About the beginning of September
the weather showed signs of improvement, and Mallory,
Bullock and Morshead moved up to the advanced base camp
up the Kharta Valley, which was situated at a height of over
17,000 feet. Wollaston and I arrived there on 6 September.
Our tents were pitched in some little grassy hollows, which
formed a perfect alpine garden, as they were carpeted with
gentians and saxifrages, and all around grew a host of other
lovely little alpine plants. Unfortunately the weather broke
again, and until 19 September we had constant falls of snow
every day. The time was spent in carrying up fuel and stores to
the 20,000-feet camp, so that as soon as the weather improved
we might start off at once.

There was a temporary break on the 17th, and with Mallory
and Morshead we made one of the most delightful excursions
that I have ever taken part in. We started off at 2 a.m. with a

full moon shining with the most brilliant light, turning night into day, and we climbed up along the ridge south of the camp, which led to a peak 21,300 feet high that overhung the Kama Valley. When we started there were thirteen degrees of frost, and, except for the distant roar of the stream far away in the valley, there was no other sound, only an intense stillness. The valleys in Tibet, the great gorges of the Arun, the wooded valleys of Nepal, all lay buried under a white sea of clouds, out of which emerged the summits of the highest mountains, like islands out of a fairy sea. In the bright moonlight mountains like Kangchenjunga, 100 miles away, stood out sharp and distinct, and far away to the south, over the plains of India, was constant lightning. Here on this sharp ridge, at a height of 21,000 feet, with no obstruction to hide the view, sunrise came to us in all its grandeur and beauty. To the west, and close at hand, towered up Mount Everest, still over 8,000 feet above us, at first cold and grey, like the dead, and with a sky of the deepest purple behind. Then, all of a sudden, a flash of golden light touched the utmost summit of Mount Everest and spread with a glow of gold all over the highest snows and ridges of this wonderful mountain, while behind the deep purple of the sky changed to orange. Makalu caught next the first rays of the sun and glowed as though alive, and then the white sea of cloud was struck by the rays of the sun and gleamed with colour; then slowly rose and struck against the island peaks in great billows of fleecy white. Such a scene it has seldom been the privilege of man to see, and once seen leaves a memory that the passing of time can never efface.

By 20 September we had all moved up to the 20,000-feet camp, situated on a sunny terrace of stones between two glaciers. Even here a few flowers existed, and every night any food in my tent left unprotected was eaten by some mountain rats, though what they can find ordinarily to eat at these heights I cannot imagine. The nights here were cold, but the days delightfully warm, and the black-bulb thermometer registered sun temperatures of 195° and 197° Fahr. regularly. The sun at these great heights is one of the great foes that we have to contend with. It seemed to exhaust and draw off all one's vitality and leave us limp, and good for no exertion. The whole climate is trying, and the extremes are so great that your feet can be suffering from frostbite while you are getting sunstroke at the same time. It is only the young and thoroughly fit person that can withstand the extraordinary changes of climate and temperature that there are in Tibet, and can acclimatize himself properly to the changed conditions of existence and food.

We had been saddled with a very useless and incompetent sirdar, who was in charge of the coolies; he was a thoroughly untrustworthy man, and was always making mischief; we had sent him away to Kharta to get him out of the way, and once he was gone we never had any trouble with the coolies, who worked most willingly. On 22 September six of us moved up to the Lhakpa La, a col 22,320 feet in height, to which Mallory had been busy carrying up stores; from here the only possible way up to Mount Everest could be seen clearly. It necessitated first a descent of 1,200 feet on to a branch of the Rongbuk Valley, and then a steep climb up to the North Col, a col that joined Mount Everest with the North Peak, a peak some 24,600 feet in height. Mr Mallory with Mr Bullock and Major Wheeler went on the next day and reached the col at a height of about 23,000 feet; but the fates were altogether against them, and though the weather remained bright and clear, a north-westerly gale had already set in which made life even at the Lhakpa La camp very unpleasant, and conditions became absolutely impossible for any higher climbing. The whole slopes of Mount Everest seemed to be smoking with the snow being blown about in suffocating whirls and clouds, and with the iciest wind that made breathing almost an impossibility. After the monsoon there seems to set in a strong north-westerly current of air, with the force of a gale at heights over 23,000 feet, and nearly every day afterwards, throughout all our journey back, and right to the end of October, we could see the snow being blown off in great clouds from every peak over 23,000 feet, by a gale from the north-west, which would seem to preclude any higher climbs after the monsoon has ended in this easterly portion of the Himalayas. Tracks of hares, foxes and wolves were seen in the snow at great heights up to 21,000 feet, and the track of what was probably a large loping grey wolf, which had tracks very like that of a bare-footed man, gave rise to the legend of the snow man, which was well known to our coolies. As in many other countries, they have in Tibet a bogey man with which to frighten their children when naughty, and this takes the form of a hairy man that lives in the snow; and when they want to escape from him they must run downhill, as long hair from his head falls over his eyes when he runs downhill, and he is then unable to see, and so they can escape from him. Many such stories they have, and these wolf tracks in the snow, which looked at first sight like human prints, were at once accepted by them as being the tracks of wild men.

Defeated by the continuous gale, Mallory, Bullock and Morshead, with Raeburn, whom they had picked up at the 20,000-feet camp, returned straight to Kharta, while Wollaston, Wheeler and I crossed over a pass opposite the 20,000-feet camp and went round to Kharta after spending a few days in the Kama Valley, where we were lucky in getting some good photographs. It was not until 5 October that we were able finally to get away from Kharta. The autumn colours in the Kama Valley were magnificent, and near Kharta the willows and birches were all brown and gold. The crops of barley and peas had all been garnered, and the people of these villages were very satisfied, as they said that we had brought the rain with us, and that their crops were 50 per cent better than they were in most years.

We chose another route for the journey back, following up the valley of the Arun or Bhong Chu, as it is called in Tibet. This route was impassable during the summer months, when the rivers were in flood, but now with the snow and ice no longer melting its width was reduced by half, and it was fully ten feet lower, so that we could make use of the Heath Robinson bridge of twisted hide at Gadompa. Across these ropes each load and person were slowly pulled, and when the Tibetans wished to play a joke on anyone they let him slide rapidly down to the centre of the rope, where it sagged just clear of the water; but as a large wave formed in the rapids they had only to pause for a moment to allow the unfortunate passenger, who was helplessly trussed up, to get a ducking in this ice-cold water. At

Shilling, near the sand-dunes and the quicksands, we struck our old route and travelled back swiftly along it, as winter in these lofty regions was coming on apace, and between Kampa Dzong and Phari the thermometer fell to zero Fahrenheit, and we had a regular blizzard of snow. This time we came back by the shorter route, so that it only took the caravan three days to get from Kampa Dzong to Phari, but the marches were long, over twenty miles each day, and over 16,000 feet all the time. Darjeeling was reached on 25 October, and the expedition of 1921 was over. The expedition had accomplished what it had set out to do. All the approaches to Mount Everest from the north, north-west, north-east and east had been carefully reconnoitred, and a possible route to the top had been found up the North-East Ridge, and it was only climatic conditions that prevented a much greater height being attained this year.

The scientific results have not yet been fully worked out, but in general outline some 13,000 square miles of new country have been surveyed and mapped, part of this by the method of photographic survey and on a large scale; a large number of birds and mammals of all sizes have been collected; the geology of the whole region has been carefully worked out by the indefatigable Dr Heron, who is at present compiling a geological map of the district, and a series of photographs have been taken of a country quite unknown and containing some of the grandest scenery in the world.

Such, in brief, have been the results of the first year's expedition.

Everest 1922

Higher Than The Feet of Man Had Trod Before

T. Howard Somervell

Somervell was a member of both the 1922 and 1924 British Everest expeditions. "No mean mountaineer", in Francis Younghusband's words. Somervell was also gifted by the gods as a surgeon, photographer and painter; his landscape of Everest adorns a wall of the Royal Geographical Society's headquarters. He spent much of his life After Everest – *as Somervell titled his autobiography – as an Anglican missionary in India.*

Here Somervell recounts his summit bid of 22–3 May 1922. With him were Mallory, Norton and Morshead.

My first recollection of the actual ascent was the suddenness with which the west wind sprang up. We stepped onwards up the easy shoulder of the North-East Ridge, which was covered in places with good, firm snow. On the lower part of this ridge we kicked steps, but on the upper and steeper portion it became necessary to use the axe; progress was rapid, a single chip or two being all that was required.

As soon as we were conveniently able to get off to the left (east) side of the ridge we did so to avoid the wind. At a height of some 24,500 feet we traversed on rough rocks and over snow-filled gullies to attain a stony slope (25,000 feet) at an angle of about thirty degrees. This could not be called an ideal camping ground; but everything else was steeper and more rocky. So we built two little platforms and pitched our tiny camp, weighting the tent-ropes with large stones, as pegs would have been useless, and here, after pemmican soup and coffee, we proceeded to spend the most uncomfortable of nights, two of us in each tent. Wherever we lay, and in whatever position, there were always a few sharp stones sticking into the tenderest parts of our anatomy. We obtained sleep in snatches of the most fitful and unresting variety, so much so that on the following morning we were quite glad to get up and stand on our less tender feet.

When we crawled out of our shelters we had a bitter disappointment. The wind was not too bad, but fresh snow had fallen during the night, and our chances of getting to the top seemed very doubtful. Moreover, we had gone only a hundred yards or so when Morshead announced that he was not feeling at all well, and could not come with us. We knew that it was unwise for him to overtax his strength, and we knew Morshead well enough to realize that if he complained of his health he must feel pretty bad; so we went on without him, leaving him to go back to his tent and there to await our return.

For six hours or more we climbed steadily on, taking the lead by turns, as we did on all our climbs, thus sharing the responsibility and fatigue in truly democratic manner. We could progress only some 300 feet[1] in an hour, and every attempt to go faster than this for a few yards was perforce followed by a rest for a minute or so in order to regain breath enough to proceed. Our tempers were getting a bit edgy and, though no actual quarrels broke out, we were each feeling definitely quarrelsome. Our intelligence, too, was not at concert pitch. When, at a height of just under 27,000 feet, we discussed whether we should go farther or not, we chose the course of wisdom and retreat with the minimum of regret at not having reached the top of the mountain.

It was obvious that we must get back to Morshead in time to take him back to the North Col before nightfall if possible. The decision to go down at 2.30, wherever we might be at that time, had been made without disappointment and without disagreement. It was the right decision. Another night at 25,000 feet might have made it well-nigh impossible for Morshead to walk at all. That meant a risk of his losing his life,

---

1 Of vertical height.

for the active movement of body and limbs is the surest preventive of frostbite, and a certain prophylactic against being frozen to death. At 2.30 we had reached a sheltered ledge behind a large rock. Here we stopped for half an hour to eat, do a rapid sketch, and take some photographs.

Truly the view was magnificent, and the North Peak of Everest, itself 1,000 feet higher than the highest summit previously attained by man, was almost another 2,000 feet below us. Away to the north, beyond the cloudy and unsettled weather of southern Tibet, was a range of snow-covered peaks, some eighty miles distant. In the foreground Cho Uyo and Gyachung Kang, only ten miles from us and each over 26,000 feet high, were actually below the place where we stood. Of all the mountains we could see that day, only Everest, the one we were on, was higher than ourselves. However irritable and unintelligent we may have been rendered by the altitude, we were all enthralled by the magnificence of the view.

Yet we could not stay to enjoy it too long, and down we went, following our tracks, to the little camp 2,000 feet below. Morshead was not too bad – or so he told us with his wonted optimism; but he was by no means fit, and we started off right away in order to get back to No. 4 Camp at the North Col before nightfall. The fresh snow had obliterated our tracks of the previous day, and we made a mistake that almost cost us our lives in traversing back to the ridge at too low a level.

I was going last, and Mallory first, at a place where we had to cross the steep head of a long, wide couloir which swept down to the foot of the mountain, 3,000 feet below us. The man in front of me slipped at a time when I was just moving myself, and I, too, was jerked out of my steps. Both of us began sliding at increasing speed down the icy couloir. The second man checked our progress for a moment, but could not hold us. He, too, was dragged off his feet. But Mallory had had just enough time to prepare for a pull on the rope, digging his axe firmly into the hard snow. It held, and so did the rope, and the party was saved.

I remember having no thought of danger or impending disaster, but experimenting, as I slipped down, as to whether I could control my pace with the pick of my axe in the snow and ice of the couloir, and whether the rest of us could do so, too. I had just decided that my pace was constant, and was not accelerating, and was feeling rather pleased with myself when the rope pulled me up with a jerk. My experiment was stopped, for Mallory had saved my life and the lives of us all. It is strange how much of one's common sense and judgement is warped by the effects of high altitude; but, looking back on the incident, which we hardly noticed at the time, I am convinced that, by having the time and sense to do the right thing, Mallory prevented a serious disaster that day.

Chastened, and cursing at the effort required, those of us who had fallen kicked steps wearily in the snow and slowly ascended to join Mallory on his sound stance. From then onwards we were much more cautious. This was doubly necessary, for Morshead, though he stoutly endeavoured to appear normal, was obviously getting worse every minute, and we soon discovered that he had hardly the strength to walk. He kept suggesting a glissade or a slide, either of which might have spelt disaster to him, if not to us all. We had to use every possible persuasion to keep him moving and using his legs, and he was getting worse and worse. It was now dark and we were still some distance from the tents on the col. A jump of ten feet down an ice-cliff was successfully negotiated, Morshead being lowered on the rope. On we went through deeper snow, pushing and pulling our invalid, who persisted that he was all right, but was obviously not far from death.

We reached the tents at about ten o'clock – not a moment too soon. A great disappointment awaited us. We found all sorts of food, but no sign of stove or fuel. What had they done? Where had they put the stove before they left the camp in readiness for us to occupy? We were so indescribably thirsty that to eat a single morsel of food without a drink was unthinkable. And would Morshead last until the morning without sustenance?

A few spoonsful of strawberry jam, to stave off danger of actual collapse from hunger, were all that we could manage without liquid refreshment, and on the next morning we hurried down to No. 3 Camp. Again we were forced to use the utmost caution, for in many places an avalanche of the newly fallen snow seemed almost inevitable. Fortunately it never occurred, and before noon the four of us trudged into the camp on the glacier, all alive, but one of us only just snatched from death and already badly frostbitten in all his fingers and toes.

The lesson we learned from this episode is that a camp to which a party is returning, or is likely to return, should never be left unsupported. Did the Nanga Parbat Expedition of 1934 realize this? If they had acted upon it, the appalling disaster they underwent would most probably never have occurred.

What Morshead suffered during the next few weeks will never be known. Although outwardly and in company he was always cheerful, yet he used to get away by himself as often as he could, and cry like a child. After two months of torture his hands and feet cleared up, and though he lost portions of most of his fingers he was not seriously crippled. He was a stout fellow, an ideal member of a party of adventurers. Nevertheless, on the outing just recounted, he was at grips with death. Fortunately, we all realized it, or we might have been just a little careless or thoughtless, and given death the victory.

Anyway, we all arrived at No. 3 Camp alive – but with what a thirst! For thirty-six hours we had been struggling and panting in a dry, cold climate, losing pints of water from our lungs, and without any drink to repair the deficiency. I have never been so thirsty in my life; they tell me that I had seventeen large cups of tea without stirring from my seat. I expect we all did much the same.

It had been a fine and stimulating experience; we had been higher than the feet of man had ever trod before; but the mountain was not ours.

Somervell's record height lasted only until 26–27 May 1922, and the assault on the summit of Finch and Bruce (the latter on his first ever climb of a mountain), which achieved 27,300 feet before a broken tube on Bruce's oxygen set forced the retreat.

Avalanche

George Leigh Mallory

Mallory, born in England in 1886, was the pin-up boy of early twentieth-century mountaineering. He was charismatic, he was athletic, and women and homosexual men gushed over him ("George Mallory! ... My hand trembles, my heart palpitates, my whole being swoons at the words," wrote the smitten Victorian writer Lytton Strachey). As a climber Mallory had ability; more, he had ambition and nerve. He was also irritatingly forgetful and mechanically inept.

If Mallory was the passion of many, his grand passion, above even his wife and children, was Everest. And it was Everest that took his life in 1924 when he and the inexperienced Andrew Irvine departed Camp VI to climb the last 1,900 feet/600 metres to the summit. (See Odell's The Last Climb.*)*

Below, Mallory recounts an avalanche during the 1922 expedition.

The project of making a third attempt this season was mooted immediately on the return of Finch and Geoffrey Bruce to the Base Camp. There in hours of idleness we had discussed their prospects and wondered what they would be doing as we gazed at the mountain to make out the weather on the great ridge. We were not surprised to learn when they came down that the summit was still unconquered, and we were not yet prepared to accept defeat. The difficulty was to find a party. Of the six who had been already engaged only one was obviously fit for another great effort. Somervell had shown a recuperative capacity beyond the rest of us. After one day at the Base he had insisted on going up again to Camp III in case he might be of use to the others. The rest were more or less knocked out. Morshead's frostbitten fingers and toes, from which he was now suffering constant pain, caused grave anxiety of most serious consequences, and the only plan for him was to go down to a lower elevation as soon as possible. Norton's feet had also been affected; he complained at first only of bruises, but the cold had come through the soles of his boots; his trouble too was frostbite. In any case he could not have come up again, for the strain had told on his heart and he now found himself left without energy or strength.

Geoffrey Bruce's feet also were so badly frostbitten that he could not walk. Finch, however, was not yet to be counted out. He was evidently very much exhausted, but an examination of his heart revealed no disorder; it was hoped that in five or six days he would be able to start again. My own case was doubtful. Of my frostbitten fingertips only one was giving trouble; the extremity above the first joint was black, but the injury was not very deep. Longstaff, who took an interest which we all appreciated in preventing us from doing ourselves permanent injury, pointed out the probability that fingers already touched and highly susceptible to cold would be much more severely injured next time, and was inclined to turn me down, from his medical point of view, on account of my fingers alone. A much more serious matter was the condition of my heart. I felt weak and lazy when it was a question of the least physical exertion, and the heart was found to have a "thrill". Though I was prepared to take risks with my fingers I was prepared to take none with my heart, even had General Bruce allowed me. However, I did not abandon hope. My heart was examined again on 3 June, no thrill was heard, and though my pulse was rapid and accelerated quickly with exertion it was capable of satisfactory recovery. We at once arranged that Somervell, Finch and I, together with Wakefield and Crawford, should set forth the same day.

It was already evident that whatever we were to do would now have to wait for the weather. Though the lama at the Rongbuk Monastery had told us that the monsoon was usually to be expected about 10 June, and we knew that it was late last year, the signs of its approach were gathering every day. Mount

Everest could rarely be seen after 9 or 10 a.m. until the clouds cleared away in the evening; and a storm approaching from the West Rongbuk Glacier would generally sweep down the valley in the afternoon. Though we came to despise this blustering phenomenon – for nothing worse came of it than light hail or snow, either at our camp or higher – we should want much fairer days for climbing, and each storm threatened to be the beginning of something far more serious. However, we planned to be on the spot to take any chance that offered. The signs were even more ominous than usual as Finch and I walked up to Camp I on the afternoon of 3 June; we could hardly feel optimistic; and it was soon apparent that, far from having recovered his strength, my companion was quite unfit for another big expedition. We walked slowly and frequently halted; it was painful to see what efforts it cost him to make any progress. However, he persisted in coming on.

We had not long disposed ourselves comfortably within the four square walls of our "sangar", always a pleasant change from the sloping sides of a tent, when snow began to fall. Released at last by the west wind which had held it back, the monsoon was free to work its will, and we soon understood that the great change of weather had now come. Fine, glistening particles were driven by the wind through the chinks in our walls, to be drifted on the floor or on our coverings where we lay during the night; and as morning grew the snow still fell as thickly as ever. Finch wisely decided to go back, and we charged him with a message to General Bruce, saying that we saw no reason at present to alter our plans. With the whole day to spend confined and inactive we had plenty of time to consider what we ought to do under these conditions. We went over well-worn arguments once more. It would have been an obvious and easy course, for which no one could reproach us, to have said simply: The monsoon has come; this is the end of the climbing season; it is time to go home. But the case, we felt, was not yet hopeless. The monsoon is too variable and uncertain to be so easily admitted as the final arbiter. There might yet be good prospects ahead of us. It was not unreasonable to expect an interval of fine weather after the first heavy snow, and with eight or ten fair days a third attempt might still be made. In any case, to retire now if the smallest chance remained to us would be an unworthy end to the expedition. We need not run our heads into obvious danger; but rather than be stopped by a general estimate of conditions we would prefer to retire before some definite risk that we were not prepared to take or simply failed to overcome the difficulties.

After a second night of unremitting snowfall the weather on the morning of 5 June improved and we decided to go on. Low and heavy clouds were still flowing down the East Rongbuk Glacier, but precipitation ceased at an early hour and the sky brightened to the west. It was surprising, after all we had seen of the flakes passing our door, that no great amount of snow was lying on the stones about our camp. But the snow had come on a warm current and melted or evaporated, so that after all the depth was no more than six inches at this elevation (17,500 feet). Even on the glacier we went up a long way before noticing a perceptible increase of depth. We passed Camp II, not requiring to halt at this stage, and were well up towards Camp III before the fresh snow became a serious impediment. It was still snowing up here, though not very heavily; there was nothing to cheer the grey scene; the clinging snow about our feet was so wet that even the best of our boots were soaked through, and the last two hours up to Camp III were tiresome enough. Nor was it a cheering camp when we reached it. The tents had been struck for the safety of the poles, but not packed up. We found them now half-full of snow and ice. The stores were all buried; everything that we wanted had first to be dug out.

The snow up here was so much deeper that we anxiously discussed the possibility of going farther. With fifteen to eighteen inches of snow to contend with, not counting drifts, the labour would be excessive, and until the snow solidified there would be considerable danger at several points. But the next morning broke fine; we had soon a clear sky and glorious sunshine; it was the warmest day that any of us remembered at Camp III; and as we watched the amazing rapidity with which the snow solidified and the rocks began to appear about our camp, our spirits rose. The side of Everest facing us looked white and cold; but we observed a cloud of snow blown from the North Ridge; it would not be long at this rate before it was fit to climb. We had already resolved to use oxygen on the third attempt. It was improbable that we should beat our own record without it, for the strain of previous efforts would count against us, and we had not the time to improve on our organization by putting a second camp above the North Col. Somervell, after Finch's explanation of the mechanical details, felt perfectly confident that he could manage the oxygen apparatus, and all those who had used oxygen were convinced that they went up more easily with its help than they could expect to go without it. Somervell and I intended to profit by the experience. They had discovered that the increased combustion in the body required a larger supply of food; we must arrange for a bountiful provision. Their camp at 25,000 feet had been too low; we would try to establish one now, as we had intended before, at 26,000 feet. And we hoped for a further advantage in going higher than Finch and Bruce had done before using oxygen; whereas they had started using it at 21,000 feet, we intended to go up to our old camp at 25,000 feet without it, perhaps use a cylinder each up to 26,000 feet, and at all events start from that height for the summit with a full supply of four cylinders. If this was not the correct policy as laid down by Professor Dryer, it would at least be a valuable experiment.

Our chief anxiety under these new conditions was to provide for the safety of our porters. We hoped that after fixing our fifth camp at 26,000 feet, at the earliest three days hence, on the fourth day of fine weather the porters might be able to go down by themselves to the North Col in easy conditions; to guard against the danger of concealed crevasses there Crawford would meet them at the foot of the North Ridge to conduct them properly roped to Camp IV. As the supply officer at this camp he would also be able to superintend the descent over the first steep slope of certain porters who would go down from Camp IV without sleeping after carrying up their loads.

But the North Col had first to be reached. With so much new snow to contend with we should hardly get there in one day. If we were to make the most of our chance in the interval of fair weather, we should lose no time in carrying up the loads for some part of the distance. It was decided therefore to begin this work on the following day, 7 June.

In the ascent to the North Col after the recent snowfall we considered that an avalanche was to be feared only in one place, the steep final slope below the shelf. There we could afford to run no risk; we must test the snow and be certain that it was safe before we could cross this slope. Probably we should be obliged to leave our loads below it, having gained, as a result of our day's work, the great advantage of a track. An avalanche might also come down, we thought, on the first steep slope where the ascent began. Here it could do us no harm, and the behaviour of the snow on this slope would be a test of its condition.

The party, Somervell, Crawford and I, with fourteen porters (Wakefield was to be supply officer at Camp III), set out at 8 a.m. In spite of the hard frost of the previous night, the crust was far from bearing our weight; we sank up to our knees in almost every step, and two hours were taken in traversing the snowfield. At 10.15 a.m. Somervell, I, a porter and Crawford, roped up in that order, began to work up the steep ice-slope, now covered with snow. It was clear that the three of us without loads must take the lead in turns stamping out the tracks for our porters. These men, after their immense efforts on the first and second attempts, had all volunteered to "go high", as they said once more, and everything must be done to ease the terrible work of carrying the loads over the soft snow. No trace was found of our previous tracks, and we were soon arguing as to where exactly they might be as we slanted across the slope. It was remarkable that the snow adhered so well to the ice that we were able to get up without cutting steps. Everything was done by trenching the snow to induce it to come down if it would; every test gave a satisfactory result. Once this crucial place was passed, we plodded on without hesitation. If the snow would not come down where we had formerly encountered steep bare ice, *a fortiori*, above, on the gentler slopes, we had nothing to fear. The thought of an avalanche was dismissed from our minds.

It was necessarily slow work forging our way through the deep snow, but the party was going extraordinarily well, and the porters were evidently determined to get on. Somervell gave us a long lead, and Crawford next, in spite of the handicap of shorter legs, struggled upwards in some of the worst snow we met until I relieved him. I found the effort at each step so great that no method of breathing I had formerly employed was adequate; it was necessary to pause after each lifting movement for a whole series of breaths, rapid at first and gradually slower, before the weight was transferred again to the other foot. About 1.30 p.m. I halted, and the porters, following on three separate ropes, soon came up with the leading party. We should have been glad to stay where we were for a long rest. But the hour was already late, and as Somervell was ready to take the lead again, we decided to push on. We were now about 400 feet below a conspicuous block of ice and 600 feet below Camp IV, still on the gentle slopes of the corridor. Somervell had advanced only 100 feet, rather up the slope than across it, and the last party of porters had barely begun to move up in the steps. The scene was peculiarly bright and windless, and as we rarely spoke, nothing was to be heard but the laboured panting of our lungs. This stillness was suddenly disturbed. We were startled by an ominous sound, sharp, arresting, violent, and yet somehow soft like an explosion of untamped gunpowder. I had never before on a mountainside heard such a sound; but all of us, I imagine, knew instinctively what it meant, as though we had been accustomed to hear it every day of our lives. In a moment I observed the surface of the snow broken and puckered where it had been even for a few yards to the right of me. I took two steps convulsively in this direction with some quick thought of getting nearer to the edge of the danger that threatened us. And then I began to move slowly downwards, inevitably carried on the whole moving surface by a force I was utterly powerless to resist. Somehow I managed to turn out from the slope so as to avoid being pushed headlong and backwards down it. For a second or two I seemed hardly to be in danger as I went quietly sliding down with the snow. Then the rope at my waist tightened and held me back. A wave of snow came over me and I was buried. I supposed that the matter was settled. However, I called to mind experiences related by other parties; and it had been suggested that the best chance of escape in this situation lay in swimming. I thrust out my arms above my head and actually went through some sort of motions of swimming on my back. Beneath the surface of the snow, with nothing to inform the senses of the world outside it, I had no impression of speed after the first acceleration – I struggled in the tumbling snow, unconscious of everything else – until, perhaps only a few seconds later, I knew the pace was easing up. I felt an increasing pressure about my body. I wondered how tightly I should be squeezed, and then the avalanche came to rest.

My arms were free; my legs were near the surface. After a brief struggle, I was standing again, surprised and breathless, in the motionless snow. But the rope was tight at my waist; the porter tied on next to me, I supposed, must be deeply buried. To my further surprise, he quickly emerged, unharmed as myself. Somervell and Crawford too, though they had been above me by the rope's length, were now quite close, and soon extricated themselves. We subsequently made out that their experiences had been very similar to mine. But where were the rest? Looking down over the foam of snow, we saw one group of porters some little distance, perhaps 150 feet, below us. Presumably the others must be buried somewhere between us and them, and though no sign of these missing men appeared, we at once prepared to find and dig them out. The porters we saw still stood their ground instead of coming up to help. We soon made out that they were the party who had been immediately behind us, and they were pointing below them. They had travelled farther than us in the avalanche, presumably because they were nearer the centre, where it was moving more rapidly. The other two parties, one of four and one of five men roped together, must have been carried even farther. We could still hope that they were safe. But as we hurried down we soon saw that beneath the place where the four porters were standing was a formidable drop; it was only too plain that the missing men had been swept over it. We had no difficulty in finding a way round this obstacle; in a very short time we were standing under its shadow. The ice-cliff was from forty to sixty feet high in different places; the crevasse at its foot was more or less filled up with avalanche snow. Our fears were soon confirmed. One man was quickly uncovered and found to be still breathing; before long we were certain that he would live. Another whom we dug out near him had been killed by the fall. He and his party appeared to have struck the hard lower lip of the crevasse, and were lying under the snow on or near the edge of it. The four porters who had escaped soon pulled themselves together after the first shock of the accident, and now worked here with Crawford and did everything they could to extricate the other bodies, while Somervell and I went down into the crevasse. A loop of rope which we pulled up convinced us that the other party must be here. It was slow work loosening the snow with the pick or adze of an ice-axe and shovelling it with the hands. But we were able to follow the rope to the bodies. One was dug up lifeless; another was found upside down, and when we uncovered his face Somervell thought he was still breathing. We had the greatest difficulty in extricating this man, so tightly was the snow packed about his limbs; his load, four oxygen cylinders on a steel frame, had to be cut from his back, and eventually he was dragged out. Though buried for about forty minutes, he had survived the fall and the suffocation, and suffered no serious harm. Of the two others in this party of four, we found only one. We had at length to give up a hopeless search with the certain knowledge that the first of them to be swept over the cliff, and the most deeply buried, must long ago be dead. Of the other five, all the bodies were recovered, but only one was alive. The two who had so marvellously escaped were able to walk down to Camp III, and were almost perfectly well next day. The other seven were killed.

"We Shall Get To The Top"

George Finch

The first attempt on Everest had reached almost 27,000 feet, but was still more than 2,000 feet short of the summit. Another party, comprising just George Finch and Geoffrey Bruce, then made their bid – with the aid of oxygen.

On May 24, Captain Noel, Tejbir [a Gurkha NCO], Geoffrey Bruce and I, all using oxygen, went up to the North Col (23,000 feet). Bent on a determined attack, we camped there for the night. Morning broke fine and clear though somewhat windy, and at eight o'clock we sent off up the long snow-slopes leading towards the north-east shoulder of Mount Everest, twelve porters carrying oxygen cylinders, provisions for one day and camping gear. An hour and a half later, Bruce, Tejbir and I followed, and, in spite of the fact that each bore a load of over 30 lb, which was much more than the average weight carried by the porters, we overtook them at a height of about 24,500 feet. They greeted our arrival with their usual cheery, broad grins. But no longer did they regard oxygen as a foolish man's whim; one and all appreciated the advantages of what they naively chose to call "English air". Leaving them to follow, we went on, hoping to pitch our camp somewhere above 26,000 feet. But shortly after one o'clock the wind freshened up rather offensively, and it began to snow. Our altitude was 25,500 feet, some 500 feet below where we had hoped to camp, but we looked round immediately for a suitable camping site, as the porters had to return to the North Col that day, and persistence in proceeding further would have run them unjustifiably into danger. This I would under no circumstances do, for I felt responsible for these cheerful, smiling, willing men, who looked up to their leader and placed in him the complete trust of little children. As it was, the margin of safety secured by pitching camp where we did instead of at a higher elevation was none too wide; for before the last porter had departed downwards the weather had become very threatening. A cheerful spot in which to find space to pitch a tent it was not; but though I climbed a couple of hundred feet or so further up the ridge, nothing more suitable was to be found. Remembering that a wind is felt more severely on the windward side of a ridge than on the crest, a possible position to the west of the ridge was negatived in favour of one on the very backbone. The leeside was bare of any possible camping place within reasonable distance. Our porters arrived at 2 p.m., and at once all began to level off the little platform where the tent was soon pitched, on the very edge of the tremendous precipices falling away to the East Rongbuk and Main Rongbuk Glaciers, over 4,000 feet below. Within twenty minutes the porters were scurrying back down the broken, rocky ridge towards the snow-slopes leading to the North Col, singing, as they went, snatches of their native hillside ditties. What splendid men! Having seen the last man safely off, I looked to the security of the guy-ropes holding down the tent, and then joined Bruce and Tejbir inside. It was snowing hard. Tiny, minute spicules driven by the wind penetrated everywhere. It was bitterly cold, so we crawled into our sleeping-bags, and, gathering round us all available clothing, huddled up together as snugly as was possible.

With the help of solidified spirit we melted snow and cooked a warm meal, which imparted some small measure of comfort to our chilled bodies. A really hot drink was not procurable, for the simple reason that at such an altitude water boils at so low a temperature that one can immerse a hand in it without fear of being scalded. Over a post-prandial cigarette, Bruce and I discussed our prospects of success. Knowing that no man can put forward his best effort unless his confidence is an established fact, the trend of my contribution to the conversation was chiefly, "Of course, we shall get to the top." After sunset, the storm rose to a gale, a term I use deliberately. Terrific gusts tore at our tent with such ferocity that the ground-sheet with its human burden was frequently lifted up off the ground. On these occasions our combined efforts were needed to keep the tent down and prevent its being blown away. Although we had blocked up the few very small openings in the tent to the best of our powers, long before midnight we were all thickly covered in a fine frozen spindrift that somehow or other was blown in upon us, insinuating its way into sleeping-bags and clothing, there to cause acute discomfort. Sleep was out of the question. We dared not relax our vigilance, for ever and again all our strength was needed to hold the tent down and to keep the flaps of the door, stripped of their fastenings by a gust that had caught us unawares, from being torn open. We fought for our lives, realising that once the wind got our little shelter into its ruthless grip, it must inevitably be hurled, with us inside it, down on the East Rongbuk Glacier, thousands of feet below.

And what of my companions in the tent? To me, who had certainly passed his novitiate in the hardships of mountaineering, the situation was more than alarming. About Tejbir I had no concern; he placed complete confidence in his sahibs, and the ready grin never left his face. But it was Bruce's first experience of mountaineering, and how the ordeal would affect him I did not know. I might have spared myself all anxiety. Throughout the whole adventure he bore himself in a manner that would have done credit to the finest of veteran mountaineers, and returned my confidence with a cheerfulness that rang too true to be counterfeit. By one o'clock on the morning of the 26th the gale reached its maximum. The wild flapping of the canvas made a noise like that of machine-gun fire. So deafening was it that we could scarcely hear each other speak. Later, there came interludes of comparative lull, succeeded by bursts of storm more furious than ever. During such lulls we took it in turns to go outside to tighten up slackened guy-ropes, and also succeeded in tying down the tent more firmly with our alpine rope. It was impossible to work in the open for more than three or four minutes at a stretch, so profound was the exhaustion induced by this brief exposure to the fierce cold wind. But with the alpine rope taking some of the strain, we enjoyed a sense of security which, though probably only illusory, allowed us all a few sorely needed moments of rest.

Dawn broke bleak and chill; the snow had ceased to fall, but the wind continued with unabated violence. Once more we had to take it in turns to venture without and tighten up the guy-ropes, and to try to build on the windward side of the tent a small wall of stones as an additional protection. The extreme exhaustion and the chill produced in the body as a result of each of these little excursions were sufficient to indicate that, until the gale had spent itself, there could be no hope of either advance or retreat. As the weary morning hours dragged on, we believed we could detect a slackening off in the storm. And I was thankful, for I was beginning quietly to wonder how much longer human beings could stand the strain. We prepared another meal. The dancing flames of the spirit stove caused me anxiety bordering on anguish lest the tent, a frail shelter between life and death, should catch fire. At noon the storm once more regained its strength and rose to unsurpassed fury. A great hole was cut by a stone in one side of the tent, and our situation thus unexpectedly became more desperate than ever.

But we carried on, making the best of our predicament until, at one o'clock, the wind dropped suddenly from a blustering gale to nothing more than a stiff breeze. Now was the opportunity for a retreat to the safety of the North Col camp. But I wanted to hang on and try our climb on the following day. Very cautiously and tentatively I broached my wish to Bruce, fearful lest the trying experience of the last twenty-four hours had undermined his keenness for further adventure. Once again might I have spared myself all anxiety. He jumped at the idea, and when our new plans were communicated to Tejbir, the only effect upon him was to broaden his already expansive grin.

It was a merry little party that gathered round to a scanty evening meal cooked with the last of our fuel. The meal was meagre for the simple reason that we had catered for only one day's short rations, and we were now very much on starvation diet. We had hardly settled down for another night when, about 6 p.m., voices were heard outside. Our unexpected visitors were porters, who, anxious as to our safety, had left the North

Col that afternoon when the storm subsided. With them they brought Thermos flasks of hot beef-tea and tea provided by the thoughtful Noel. Having accepted these most gratefully, we sent the porters back without loss of time.

That night began critically. We were exhausted by our previous experiences and through lack of sufficient food. Tejbir's grin lost some of its expanse. On the face of Geoffrey Bruce, courageously cheerful as ever, was a strained, drawn expression that I did not like. Provoked, perhaps, by my labours outside the tent, a dead, numbing cold was creeping up my limbs, a thing I had only once before felt and to the seriousness of which I was fully alive. Something had to be done. Like an inspiration came the thought of trying the effect of oxygen. We hauled an apparatus and cylinders into the tent, and, giving it the air of a joke, we took doses all round. Tejbir took his medicine reluctantly, but with relief I saw his face brighten up. The effect on Bruce was visible in his rapid change of expression. A few minutes after the first deep breath, I felt the tingling sensation of returning life and warmth to my limbs. We connected up the apparatus in such a way that we could breathe a small quantity throughout the night. The result was marvellous. We slept well and warmly. Whenever the tube delivering the gas fell out of Bruce's mouth as he slept, I could see him stir uneasily in the uric, greenish light of the moon as it filtered through the canvas. Then half unconsciously replacing the tube, he would fall once more into a peaceful slumber. There is little doubt that it was the use of oxygen which saved our lives during this second night in our high camp.

Before daybreak we were up, and proceeded to make ready for our climb. Putting on our boots was a struggle. Mine I had taken to bed with me, and a quarter of an hour's striving and tugging sufficed to get them on. But Bruce's and Tejbir's were frozen solid, and it took them more than an hour to mould them into shape by holding them over lighted candles. Shortly after six we assembled outside. Some little delay was incurred in arranging the rope and our loads, but at length at 6.30 a.m., soon after the first rays of the sun struck the tent, we shouldered our bundles and set off. What with cameras, Thermos bottles and oxygen apparatus, Bruce and I each carried well

over 40 lb; Tejbir with two extra cylinders of oxygen shouldered a burden of about 50 lb.

Our scheme of attack was to take Tejbir with us as far as the
north-east shoulder, there to relieve him of his load and send
him back. The weather was clear. The only clouds seemed so
far off as to presage no evil, and the breeze, though intensely
cold, was bearable. But it soon freshened up, and before we
had gone more than a few hundred feet the cold began to have
its effect on Tejbir's sturdy constitution, and he showed signs
of wavering. Bruce's eloquent flow of Gurumuki, however,
managed to boost him up to an altitude of 26,000 feet. There
he collapsed entirely, sinking face downwards on to the rocks
and crushing beneath him the delicate instruments of his
oxygen apparatus. I stormed at him for thus maltreating it,
while Bruce exhorted him for the honour of his regiment to
struggle on; but it was all in vain. Tejbir had done his best; and
he has every right to be proud of the fact that he has climbed
to a far greater height than any other native. We pulled him off
his apparatus and, relieving him of some cylinders, cheered
him up sufficiently to start him with enough oxygen on his
way back to the high camp, there to await our return. We had
no compunction about letting him go alone, for the ground
was easy and he could not lose his way, the tent being in full
view below.

  After seeing him safely off, and making good progress, we
loaded up Tejbir's cylinders, and in view of the easy nature of
the climbing, mutually agreed to dispense with the rope and
thus enable ourselves to proceed more rapidly. Climbing not
very steep and quite easy rocks, and passing two almost level
places affording ample room for some future high camp, we
gained an altitude of 26,500 feet. By this time, however, the
wind, which had been steadily rising, had acquired such force
that I considered it necessary to leave the ridge and continue
our ascent by traversing out across the great northern face of
Mount Everest, hoping by so doing to find more shelter from
the icy blasts. It was not easy to come to this decision, because
I saw that between us and the shoulder the climbing was all
plain sailing and presented no outstanding difficulty. Leaving

the ridge, we began to work out into space. For the first few yards the going was sufficiently straightforward, but presently the general angle became much steeper, and our trials were accentuated by the fact that the stratification of the rocks was such that they shelved outward and downward, making the securing of adequate footholds difficult. We did not rope, however. I knew that the longer we remained unroped, the more time we should save, a consideration of vital importance. But as I led out over these steeply sloping, evilly smooth slabs, I carefully watched Bruce to see how he would tackle the formidable task with which he was confronted on this his first mountaineering expedition. He did his work splendidly and followed steadily and confidently as if he were quite an old hand at the game.

Sometimes the slabs gave place to snow, treacherous, powdery stuff, with a thin, hard, deceptive crust that gave the appearance of compactness. Little reliance could be placed upon it, and it had to be treated with great care. And sometimes we found ourselves crossing steep slopes of scree that yielded and shifted downwards with every tread. Very occasionally in the midst of our exacting work we were forced to indulge in a brief rest in order to replace an empty cylinder of oxygen by a full one. The empty ones were thrown away, and as each bumped its way over the precipice and the good steel clanged like a church bell at each impact, we laughed aloud at the thought that "There goes another 5 lb off our backs." Since leaving the ridge we had not made much height although we seemed to be getting so near our goal. Now and then we consulted the aneroid barometer, and its readings encouraged us on. 27,000 feet; then we gave up traversing and began to climb diagonally upwards toward a point on the lofty North-East Ridge, midway between the shoulder and the summit. Soon afterwards an accident put Bruce's oxygen apparatus out of action. He was some twenty feet below me, but strangled gallantly upwards as I went to meet him, and after connecting him on to my apparatus and so renewing his supply of oxygen, we soon traced the trouble and effected a satisfactory repair.

The barometer here recorded a height of 27,300 feet. The highest mountain visible was Cho Uyo, which is just short of

27,000 feet. We were well above it and could look across it into the dense clouds beyond. The great west peak of Everest, one of the most beautiful sights to be seen from down in the Rongbuk Valley, was hidden, but we knew that our standpoint was nearly 2,000 feet above it. Everest itself was the only mountain top we could see without turning our gaze downwards. We could look across into clouds which lay at some undefined distance behind the north-east shoulder, a clear indication that we were only a little, if any, below its level. Pumori, an imposing ice-bound pyramid, 23,000 feet high, I sought at first in vain. So far were we above it that it had sunk into an insignificant little ice-hump by the side of the Rongbuk Glacier. Most of the other landmarks were blotted out by masses of ominous, yellow-hued clouds swept from the west in the wake of an angry storm-wind. The point we reached is unmistakable even from afar. We were standing on a little rocky ledge, just inside an inverted V of snow, immediately below the great belt of reddish-yellow rock that cleaves its way almost horizontally through the otherwise greenish-black slabs of the mountain. Though 1,700 feet below, we were well within half a mile of the summit, so close, indeed, that we could distinguish individual stones on a little patch of scree lying just underneath the highest point. Ours were truly the tortures of Tantalus; for, weak from hunger and exhausted by that nightmare struggle for life in our high camp, we were in no fit condition to proceed. Indeed, I knew that if we were to persist in climbing on, even if only for another 500 feet, we should not both get back alive.

The decision to retreat once taken, no time was lost, and, fearing lest another accidental interruption in the oxygen supply might lead to a slip on the part of either of us, we roped together. It was midday. At first we returned in our tracks, but later found better going by aiming to strike the ridge between the north-east shoulder and the North Col at a point above where we had left it in the morning. Progress was more rapid, though great caution was still necessary. Shortly after 2 p.m., we struck the ridge and there reduced our burdens to a minimum by dumping four oxygen cylinders. The place will be easily recognised by future explorers; those four cylinders are perched against a rock at the head of the one and only large snow-filled couloir running right up from the head of the East Rongbuk Glacier to the ridge. The clear weather was gone. We plunged down the easy, broken rocks through thick mists driven past us from the west by a violent wind. For one small mercy we were thankful – no snow fell. We reached our high camp in barely half an hour, and such are the vagaries of Everest's moods that in this short time the wind had practically dropped. Tejbir lay snugly wrapped up in all three sleeping-bags, sleeping the deep sleep of exhaustion. Hearing the voices of the porters on their way up to bring down our kit, we woke him up, telling him to await their arrival and to go down with them. Bruce and I then proceeded on our way, met the ascending porters and passed on, greatly cheered by their bright welcomes and encouraging smiles. But the long descent, coming as it did on the top of a hard day's work, soon began to find out our weakness. We were deplorably tired, and could no longer move ahead with our accustomed vigour. Knees did not always bend and unbend as required. At times they gave way altogether and forced us, staggering, to sit down. But eventually we reached the broken snows of the North Col, and arrived in camp there at 4 p.m.

A craving for food, to the lack of which our weakness was mainly due, was all that animated us. Hot tea and a tin of spaghetti were soon forthcoming, and even this little nourishment refreshed us and renewed our strength to such an extent that three-quarters of an hour later we were ready to set off for Camp III. An invaluable addition to our little party was Captain Noel, the indefatigable photographer of the expedition, who had already spent four days and three nights on the North Col. He formed our rearguard and nursed us safely down the steep snow and ice slopes on to the almost level basin of the glacier below. Before 5.30 p.m., only forty minutes after leaving the col, we reached Camp III. Since midday, from our highest point we had descended over 6,000 feet; but we were quite finished.

Everest 1924

"It Has Been A Bad Time Altogether": Mallory's Diary

George Leigh Mallory

The disaster of the 1922 expedition notwithstanding, the British, a mere two years later, were back at Everest for another try. Inevitably, George Mallory was among them. Everest was Mallory's mountain, and he died on its heights in one of the most enigmatic chapters in the annals of mountaineering. But first came the hard grind of getting supplies up to the higher camps from the base camp near Rongbuk Monastery.

3 May

Irvine, Odell, Hazard and self to Camp I. Half the porters lagged badly. Having added a good deal of stuff on their own account to what we had given them to carry, they had big loads.

4 May

I decided to leave five loads not urgently required at Camp I and have five men to carry all the porters' blankets, etc. The result was good and the men must have gone well. Irvine and I had gone ahead and reached Camp II at about 12.30; we had hardly finished a leisurely tiffin when the first porters arrived. Camp II looked extraordinarily uninviting, although already inhabited by an N.C.O. and two others in charge of the stores (150 loads or so), which had already been carried up by Tibetans. A low irregular wall surrounded a rough compound, which I was informed was the place for the Sahibs' tents, and another already covered by the fly of a Whymper tent was the home of an N.C.O. The Sahibs' compound was soon put sufficiently in order; two Whymper tents were pitched there for the four of us, while a wonderful brown tent of Noel's was pitched for him. No tents were provided here for porters: the intention was to build comfortable huts or "sangars", as we call them, using the Whymper flys for roofs, but no sangars had yet been built, and accommodation for twenty-three men is not so easily provided in this way. However, I soon saw that the ground would allow us to economize walls, and Irvine and I with three or four men began building an oblong sangar, the breadth only about seven feet; other men joined in after resting. It is an extraordinary thing to watch the conversion of men from listlessness to some spirit of enterprise; a very little thing will turn the scale: on this occasion the moving of a huge stone to form one corner started the men's interest, and later we sang! And so these rather tired children were persuaded to do something for their comfort; without persuasion they would have done nothing to make life tolerable.

4–5 May

An appalling night, very cold, considerable snowfall and a violent wind.

5 May

Result: signs of life in camp very late. The first audible one in camps up to and including II is the blowing of yak-dung fire with Tibetan bellows.

The men were an extraordinarily long time getting their food this morning. The N.C.Os seemed unable to get a move on, and generally speaking an Oriental inertia was in the air. It was with difficulty in fact that the men could be got out of their tents, and then we had further difficulty about loads; one man, a regular old soldier, having possessed himself of a conveniently light load, refused to take a heavier one I wanted taken instead. I had to make a great show of threatening him with my fist in his face before he would comply, and so with much difficulty about it and about what should be left behind in the way of coolie rations and blankets and cooking-pots, and the degree of illness of those reported sick, we didn't get fairly away until 11 a.m.

Now, making a new track is always a long affair compared to following an old one, and on this occasion snow had fallen in the night. The glacier, which had looked innocent enough the evening before, was far from innocent now. The wind had blown the higher surfaces clear. The days, I suppose, had been too clear for melting and these surfaces were hard, smooth, rounded ice, almost as hard as glass and with never a trace of roughness, and between the projecting lumps lay the new powdery snow. The result of the conditions was much expend-iture of labour either in making steps in the snow or cutting them in ice, and we reached a place known as "The Trough", a broken trough in the ice, fifty feet deep and about one-third of the way up, knowing we should have all that we could do to reach Camp III. We followed along in the trough some way, a lovely warm place, and then came out of it into the open glacier where the wind was blowing up the snow maliciously. The wind luckily was at our backs until we rounded the corner of the North Peak, and then we caught it blowing straight at us from the North Col. As the porters were now nearly exhausted and feeling the altitude badly our progress was a bitter experi-ence. I was acting as lone horse, finding the best way, and consequently arrived first in camp. It was a queer sensation, reviving memories of that scene with the dud oxygen cylinders piled against the cairn that was built to commemorate the seven porters killed two years ago. The whole place had changed less than I could have believed possible, seeing that the glacier is everywhere beneath the stones. My boots were frozen hard on my feet, and I knew we could do nothing now to make a comfortable camp. I showed the porters where to pitch their tents at 6.30 p.m., got hold of a rucksack containing four Unna cookers, dished out three and meta [methylated fuel] for their cooking to the porters and one to our own cook; then we pitched our own two Meade tents with doors facing about a yard apart for sociability.

The porters seemed to me very much done up, and consid-ering how cold it was even at 6 p.m. I was a good deal depressed by the situation. Personally I got warm easily enough. Our wonderful Kami produced some sort of a hot meal, and I lay comfortably in my sleeping-bag. The one thing I could think of for our porters was the high-altitude sleeping-sacks (intended for Camp IV and upwards), now at Camp II, which I had not ordered to come on next day with the second party of porters (two parties A and B each of twenty had been formed for these purposes, and B were a day behind us). The only plan was to make an early start next morning and get to Camp II in time to forestall the departure of B party. I remember making this resolve in the middle of the night and getting up to pull my boots inside the tent from under the door. I put them inside the outer covering of my flea-bag and near the middle of my body but of course they remained frozen hard and I had a tussle to get them on in the morning. Luckily the sun strikes our tents early 6.30 a.m. or a little later at Camp III, and I was able to get off about 7. I left directions that half the men, or as many less as possible, should come one-quarter of the way down and meet the men coming up so as to get the most important load to Camp III.

I guessed that B party, after a cold night, would not start before 9 a.m., and as I was anxious if possible to find a better way over the glacier I wasted some time in investigations and made an unsatisfactory new route, so that it was after 8.30 when I emerged from the trough, and a little farther on I saw B party coming up. It was too late to turn them back. I found some of them had resolved they would not be able to get to Camp III and go back to Camp II the same day and consequently increased their loads with blankets, etc., determining to sleep at Camp III. This was the last thing I wanted. My chief idea at the moment was to get useful work out of B party without risking their morale or condition as I saw we were risking that of A. So after dispatching a note to Noel at II I conducted B party slowly up the glacier. After making a convenient dump and sending down B party I got back to Camp III early in the afternoon, somewhat done and going very slowly from want of food at the last. In camp nothing doing. All porters said to be sick and none fit to carry a load. Irvine and Odell volunteered to go down to the dump and get one or two things specially wanted, e.g. Primus stoves, which was done. The sun had left the camp some time before they returned. A little wall-building was done this day, notably round the N.C.O.'s tent, otherwise nothing to improve matters. The temperature at 5 p.m. (we hadn't thermometers the previous night) was observed to be 2 F. 30 of frost an hour before sunset; under these conditions it is only during the sunny, windless hours that anything to speak of can be done; this day there were such hours, but I gather that sahibs as well as porters were suffering from altitude lassitude.

7 May

The night had been very cold [minus] twenty-one degrees, i.e. Fifty-three of frost. Personally I slept beautifully warmly and yet was not well in the morning. Odell and Irvine also seemed distinctly unfit. I decided to send Hazard down with some of A party to meet at the dump and bring up some of B party (it had been arranged that some of this party should come up again). Investigation again showed that no porters were fit to carry loads; several were too unwell to be kept up at III. They had to be more or less pulled from their tents. An hour and a half must have been taken in getting their meals of tsampa, which they must clearly have before going down; and much time too in digging out the sicker men who tried to hide away in their tents; one of them, who was absolutely without a spark of life to help himself, had swollen feet and we had to pull on his boots without his socks; he was almost incapable of walking; I supported him with my arm for some distance and then told off a porter to do that; eventually roped in three parties in charge of the N.C.O. I sent them off by themselves from the dump, where shortly afterwards I met Hazard. Four men of B had gone on to Camp III, but not to sleep. Three others whom we now proceeded to rope up and help with their loads alone consented to stay there. A second day therefore passed with only seven more loads got to Camp III, and nothing done to establish the camp in a more comfortable manner, unless it counted that this third night each of the six men would have a high-altitude sleeping-sack; and meanwhile the morale of A party had gone to blazes. It was clear to me that the morale of porters must be established if possible at once by bringing B party up and giving them a day's rest to make camp.

8 May

I made another early start and reached Camp II at 9 a.m., and here met Norton and Somervell. By some mental aberration I had thought they would only reach Camp II on this day; they had proceeded according to programme and come to Camp II on the 7th. We discussed plans largely while I ate breakfast, in the mild, sheltered, sunny alfresco of Camp II (by comparison). Norton agreed with my ideas and dispatched all remaining B party to Camp III with Somervell, to pick up their loads at the dump and carry them on. A had been filled up the previous night with hot food and were now lying in the sun looking more like men; the only question was whether in future to establish the correct standard and make them carry all the way to Camp III and back as was always done in 1922. I was strongly opposed to this idea; the best way of re-establishing their morale, I thought, would be to give them a job well within their powers and, if they improved as I hoped, they might well carry loads the three-quarter journey to the dump on three successive days while B could ferry the last quarter once or twice on the two of the days when they would not be engaged in making camp. This was agreed to more particularly by Geoffrey Bruce, who really runs the porters altogether and who had now come up from Camp I.

A day of great relief this with the responsibility shared or handed over; and much lying in the sun and untroubled sleep at Camp II.

9 May

I intended going ahead of the party to see how things were moving at Camp III, for this day the camp was to be made wonderful. Seven men with special loads, fresh heroes from the base, were to go through to Camp III; the A men to return from the dump to Camp II. As it turned out I escorted the first batch who were going through to Camp III. The conditions when we emerged from the trough were anything but pleasant; under a grey sky a violent wind was blowing up the snow; at moments the black dots below me on the glacier, all except the nearest, were completely lost to view. The men were much inclined to put down their loads before reaching the dump and a good deal of driving had to be done. Eventually after waiting some time at the dump I joined Norton and Geoff, and we escorted the last three loads for Camp III the last bit of the way. On such a day I did not expect Camp III to be more congenial than it had been. However, it was something to be greeted by the cheery noise of the Roarer Cooker: the R.C. is one of the great inventions of the Expedition; we have two in point of fact, one with a vertical, and one with a horizontal flame, a sort of super-Primus stove. Irvine and Odell had evidently been doing some useful work. It has been a triumph getting the R.C. to Camp III, it is an extravagant load weighing over 40 lb. and it now proved to be even more extravagant of fuel than had been anticipated; moreover, its burning was somewhat intermittent, and as the cook, even after instruction, was still both frightened and incompetent when this formid-able stove was not functioning quite sweetly and well, a sahib had often to be called in to help. Nevertheless the R.C. succeeded in cooking food for the troops, and however costly in paraffin oil that meal may have been it made the one great difference between Camp III as A party experienced it and Camp III now. Otherwise on this day, set apart for the edifica-tion and beatification of this camp, the single thing that had been done was the erection of one Meade tent to accommo-date two more sahibs (only two more because Hazard came down this day). And no blame to anyone; B party was much as A party had been in a state of Oriental inertia; it is unfair, perhaps, to our porters to class them with Orientals in general, but they have this Oriental quality that after a certain stage of physical discomfort or mental depression has been reached they simply curl up. Our porters were just curled up inside their tents. And it must be admitted that the sahibs were most of the time in their tents, no other place being tolerable. Personally I felt that the task of going round tents and seeing how the men were getting on and giving orders about the arrangements of the camp now naturally fell to Geoffrey Bruce, whose "pigeon" it is to deal with the porters. And so presently in my old place, with Somervell now as a companion instead of Hazard, I made myself comfortable, i.e. I took off my boots and knickers, put on my footless stockings, knitted for me by my wife for the last expedition and covering the whole of my legs, a pair of grey flannel bags and two pairs of warm socks, besides my cloth-sided shoes, and certain garments too for warming the upper parts, a comparatively simple matter. The final resort in these conditions of course is to put one's legs into a sleeping-sack. Howard and I lay warmly enough and presently I proposed a game of picquet, and we played cards for some time until Norton and Geoff came to pay us a visit and discuss the situation. Someone a little later tied back the flaps of the two tents facing each other so that after Norton and Geoff had retired to their tent the other four of us were inhabiting, as it were, one room, and hopefully talked of the genius of Kami and the Roarer Cooker and supposed that a hot evening meal might sometime come our way. Meanwhile I produced *The Spirit of Man* and began reading one thing and another. Howard reminded me that I was reproducing on the same spot a scene which had occurred two years ago when he and I lay in a tent together. We all agreed that "Kubla Khan" was a good sort of poem. Irvine was rather poetry shy, but seemed to be favourably impressed by the Epitaph to Gray's *Elegy*. Odell was much inclined to be interested and liked the last lines of *Prometheus Unbound*. Somervell, who knows quite a lot of English literature, had never read a poem of Emily Brontë's, and was happily introduced. And suddenly hot soup arrived.

The following night was one of the most disagreeable I remember. The wind came in tremendous gusts and, in spite of precautions to keep it out, the fresh snow drifted in; if one's head were not under the bedclothes one's face was cooled by the fine cold powder, and in the morning I found two inches of snow all along my side of the tent. It was impossible to guess how much snow had fallen during the night when one first looked out. The only certain thing was the vile appearance of things at present. In a calm interval one could take stock of a camp now covered in snow and then would come the violent wind and all would be covered in the spindrift. Presently Norton and Geoff came into our tent for a powwow. Geoff, speaking from the porters' point of view, was in favour of beating a retreat. We were all agreed that we must not risk destroying the morale of the porters, and also that for two or three days no progress could be made towards the North Col. But it seemed to me that, in the normal course of events, the weather should now re-establish itself and might even be sufficiently calm to get something done that afternoon, and that for the porters the best thing of all would be to weather the storm up at Camp III. In any case it would be early enough to decide for a retreat next day. These arguments commended themselves to Norton and so it was agreed. Meanwhile one of the most serious features of the situation was the consumption of fuel. A box of meta, and none could say how much paraffin (not much, however), had been burned at Camp II; here at Camp III no water had yet appeared, and snow must be melted for everyone at every meal; a box of meta had to be consumed here too, and Primus stoves had been used before the Roarer made its appearance yesterday. Goodness knows how much oil it used. It was clear that the first economy must be in the number of sahibs (six) at Camp III. We planned that Somervell, Norton and Odell should have the first whack at the North Col, and Irvine and I finish the good work next day. Irvine and I therefore must go down first. On the way down Irvine suffered very much and I somewhat from the complaint known as glacier lassitude, a mysterious complaint, but I am pretty certain in his case that the sun and the dazzling light reflected from the new snow had something to do with the trouble. A peaceful time at Camp II with Beetham and Noel.

11 May

The weather hazy and unsettled looking. I dispatched fifteen loads up to the dump and arranged for the evacuation of two sick men, of whom one had badly frostbitten feet, apparently a Lepcha, unfit for this game, and the other was Sanglu, Kellas's old servant, who had been attached to Noel this expedition and last, a most valuable man, who seemed exceedingly ill with bronchitis. The parties had been gone half an hour before we were aroused by a shout and learned that a porter had broken his leg on the glacier. We quickly gathered ourselves into a competent help party, and had barely started out when a man turned up with a note from Norton to tell me, as I half expected, that he had decided to evacuate Camp III for the present and retire all ranks to the Base Camp. The wounded man turned out to be nearer at hand than, and not so badly wounded (a bone broken in the region of the knee), as I feared.

This same evening Beetham, Noel, Irvine and I were back at the Base Camp, the rest coming in next day.

Well, that is the bare story of the reverse so far as it goes. I'm convinced that Norton had been perfectly right. We pushed things far enough. Everything depends on the porters and we must contrive to bring them to the starting point, i.e. Camp III, at the top of their form. I expect we were working all the time in '22 with a smaller margin than we knew; it certainly amazed me that the whole bandobast, so far as porters were concerned, worked so smoothly. Anyway this time the conditions at Camp III were much more severe, and not only were temperatures lower but the wind was more continuous and more violent. I expect that these porters will do as well in the end as last time's. Personally I felt that I was going through a real hard time in a way I never did in '22. Meanwhile our retreat has meant a biff waste of time. We have waited down here for the weather; at last it looks more settled and we are on the point of starting up again. But the day for the summit is put off from the 17th to the 28th, and the great question is,

Will the monsoon give time?

12 May

It has been a bad time altogether. I look back on tremendous effort and exhaustion and dismal looking out of a tent door into a world of snow and vanishing hopes and yet, and yet, and yet there have been a good many things to set on the other side. The party has played up wonderfully. The first visit to the

North Col was a triumph for the old gang. Norton and I did the job, and the cutting of course was all my part; so far as one can enjoy climbing above Camp III I enjoyed the conquest of the ice wall and crack, the crux of the route and the making steps too in the steep final 200 feet. Odell did very useful work leading the way on from the camp to the col; I was practically bust to the world and couldn't have led that half-hour though I still had enough mind to direct him. We made a very bad business of the descent. It suddenly occurred to me that we ought to see what the old way down was like. Norton and I were ahead unroped and Odell behind in charge of a porter who had carried up a light load. We got only ground where a practised man can just get along without crampons (which we hadn't with us), chipping occasional steps in very hard snow or ice. I was all right ahead, but Norton had a nasty slip and then the porter, whose knot didn't hold, so that he went down some way and was badly shaken. Meanwhile I, below, finding the best way down, had walked into an obvious crevasse; by some miscalculation I had thought I had prodded the snow with which it was choked and where I hoped we could walk instead of cutting steps at the side of it, all the result of mere exhaustion, no doubt. But the snow gave way and in I went with the snow tumbling all round me, down, luckily, only about ten feet before I fetched up half blind and breathless to find myself most precariously supported only by my ice axe some-how caught across the crevasse and still held in my right hand and below was a very unpleasant black hole. I had some nasty moments before I got comfortably wedged and began to yell for help up through the round hole I had come through where the blue sky showed this because I was afraid my operations to extricate myself would bring down a lot more snow and perhaps precipitate me into the bargain. However, I soon grew tired of shouting; they hadn't seen me from above and bring-ing the snow down a little at a time I made a hole out towards the side (the crevasse ran down a slope) after some climbing, and extricated myself but was then on the wrong side of the crevasse, so that eventually I had to cut across a nasty slope of very hard ice and farther down some mixed unpleasant snow before I was out of the wood. The others were down by a better line ten minutes before me. That cutting against time at the end after such a day just about brought me to my limit . . .

My one personal trouble has been a cough. It started a day or two before leaving the Base Camp but I thought nothing of it. In the high camp it has been the devil. Even after the day's exercise I have described I couldn't sleep, but was distressed with bursts of coughing fit to tear one's guts and a headache and misery altogether, besides which of course it has a very bad effect on one's going on the mountain. Somervell also had a cough, which started a little later than mine, and he has not been at his physical best . . .

Norton has been quite right to bring us down for rest. It is no use sending men up the mountain unfit. The physique of the whole party has gone down sadly. The only chance now is to get fit and go for a simpler, quicker plan. The only plump fit man is Geoffrey Bruce. Norton has made me responsible for choosing the parties of attack, himself first choosing me into the first party if I like. But I'm quite doubtful if I shall be fit enough. But again I wonder if the monsoon will give us a chance. I don't want to get caught, but our three-day scheme from the Chang La will give the monsoon a good chance. We shall be going up again the day after tomorrow. Six days to the top from this camp.

Memories Of Mallory

Various

In the years after Mallory's death, many who knew him were asked to comment on his personality, and make their answer to the great conundrum: did Mallory and Irvine make it to the top?

John Noel

Mallory was no ordinary man. Raeburn, the veteran climber, before he was afflicted with the illness which unfortunately finished his climbing days, said that for sheer dash there was no one to touch this young climber. He applied himself to the task, which might have appalled most other men by its danger and magnitude, with indomitable energy and will. When he found his mistake over the missing of the East Rongbuk approach to Everest, he got his caravan of exhausted porters and his companions over the Lakpa-La in soft snow, nearly tearing their hearts out, and then encouraged them on still further even to surmount the greater obstacle of the terrible ice cliff.

With his physical strength he had a vivid imagination and a great heart. He seemed to live in a realm remote from everyday life. It could be seen that he had great imagination and ideals. He was stubborn to a degree; and his ideas were, perhaps, lacking in flexibility; but yet in another sense this same rigidity contributed to the strength of that determination which caused him to push through with dauntless energy any enterprise he might take up. In camp on the later expeditions, we often used to tease him in fun for his "advanced views". Some of these views on political and social questions were indeed advanced. (You see even in the camps on Everest, as in every remote corner of the world, men are wont to talk on politics forever.) He was lofty as the peaks he loved.

He was always young at heart and fond of a game. In America, after his sensational climbs in 1922, a photographer caught him climbing a fire escape at a New York skyscraper hotel, but not in the manner the builders intended. He was going up underneath the steps hand over hand, sometimes upside down!

But yet he always preserved a certain aloofness. If he had lived, after conquering the heights which were his ambitions no doubt he would with his intellect and energy have accomplished fine things. Above all, he was a mountaineer. By that I do not mean so much a climber of crags, but a man who lives among mountains and loves them. On Everest he seemed to have centred all his ambition and energy.

How this mountain obsessed him! He threw his whole body and soul into the fight against her. He seemed always as if he were measuring and calculating. Yet I always felt in my own acquaintance with him that some strange fatalism over-shadowed his ambition. I could notice that he was always trying to convince himself that he could beat the mountain but at the same time he seemed to show a consciousness somehow or other that the mountain held the mastery.

"The chances of a given party to reach the summit in a given time are fifty to one against." That was the expression, now become historic in the story of Everest, which he used on the occasion of the first public lecture he gave in London, after his return in 1921.

How the "personality", I might say, of this mountain had impressed itself upon Mallory can be traced in things he said from time to time. For instance, in 1924 when he started up the Rongbuk Glacier for the last time to make his biggest effort, the effort from which he never returned, he said, "We expect no mercy from Everest." But yet it will be well for her that she deign to take notice of the little group that approaches stealthily over her glaciers again, and that she shall observe among the scattered remnants she has thrice put to still a power to string her very nose tip.

T. Howard Somervell

I usually shared a tent with Mallory, in whom I felt that I had found a kindred spirit. Sometimes we played card games for two, such as picquet, but more often we read selections from *The Spirit of Man*, by Robert Bridges, or bits of modern poetry, each reading aloud to the other passages of which we were particularly fond. We discussed climbs in the Alps and planned expeditions for the future. We made, among other things, a detailed plan for the first complete ascent of the Peuterey ridge of Mont Blanc. Alas! the sad accident of 1924 put a stop to all the plans that Mallory and I had made of conquests of the Alps,

But during this and the subsequent Everest expeditions, George Mallory was the man whom I always felt that I knew the best, and I have seldom had a better or more intimate friend. When one shares a tent for days on end throughout the better part of six months with a man, one gets an insight into his character such as is vouchsafed to few other men. These many days of companionship with a man whose outlook on life was lofty and choice, human and loving, and in a measure divine, still remain for me a priceless memory. I forget the details of George Mallory's views on most of the many subjects we discussed, but in general he took always the big and liberal view. He was really concerned with social evils, and recognized that they could only be satisfactorily solved by the changing and ennobling of individual character. He hated anything that savoured of hypocrisy or humbug, but cherished all that is really good and sound. His was a great soul, and I pray that some of its greatness may live on in the souls of his friends.

Lt. Col. E.F. Norton

Mallory's was no common personality. Physically he always seemed to me the beau ideal of the mountaineer; he was very good-looking, and I have always thought that his boyish face – for he looked absurdly young for his thirty-seven years – was the outward and visible sign of a wonderful constitution. His graceful figure was the last word in wiry activity and he walked with a tireless swing which made him a man with whom few could live uphill; he was almost better downhill, for his years of mountain training had added balance and studied poise to his natural turn of speed.

But it was the spirit of the man that made him the great mountaineer he was: a fire burned in him and caused his willing spirit to rise superior to the weakness of the flesh; he lived on his nerves, and throughout two campaigns on Mount Everest (I never climbed with him elsewhere) it was almost impossible to make out whether he was a tired man or not, for he responded instantly to every call that was made on him, and while the call lasted his would remain the dominant spirit in any enterprise. The conquest of the mountain became an obsession with him, and for weeks and months he devoted his whole time and energy to it, incessantly working at plans and details of organization; and when it came to business he expended on it every ounce of his unrivalled physical energy.

Such was Mallory the mountaineer; but there was another and quite different Mallory, whom we knew in the mess tent and when there was no call for action. This aspect of him was curiously at variance with the other; it showed us a nature aesthetic and gentle combined with a keen and cultured intelligence; though here too a flash of the same impatience with which he urged on our flagging footsteps on the mountain would sometimes break out in our arguments and discussions; for his views were always clear-cut and decided and his nature masterful. We used to dub him a "high brow" and in fancy I can hear Longstaff chaffing him in 1922: "Mallory, you know the one good thing the Bolsheviks have done in Russia? They've obliterated the intelligentsia."

His death robs us of a right loyal friend, a knight "*sans peur et sans reproche*" among mountaineers and the greatest antagonist that Everest has had or is like to have.

R.L.G. Irving

Irving was Mallory's housemaster at Winchester, and introduced him to mountaineering.

Till he was eighteen George Mallory had been on nothing higher than the Malvern Hills. Then he was asked to join a small party in the Alps, and he came back with "the great door of the mountains" opened wide before him. You may see in that mere chance of the "Providence that shapes our ends"; in his case it is difficult to believe it was anything but the latter, for in climbing he found the perfect way of fulfilment for what his body and his soul desired.

The smooth oval face with its extraordinary likeness to a Botticelli Madonna was very different from the rough, rugged type we often associate with great mountaineers. It was not till you saw him at work on steep rocks or ice, the perfect balance and the completely natural grace of upward movement, that you knew M's body to be the perfect servant of his mind; and that mind was, above all else, a climbing mind. He was always striving after the higher, bigger things, the great truths to whose sources mountains pointed him. And so there was in him a continuous and rapid development of mind after the age at which education in the narrower sense is often regarded as complete. It is in mental grasp and breadth of outlook rather than in climbing technique that the Mallory of Everest differs from the youth who discovered the Slab Route on Lliwedd in recovering a pipe.

One feels, as one reads his letters from Tibet and his chapters on the Reconnaissance, that Everest is revealing itself to a man as fitted to understand its majesty as to accept its challenge. Everest in 1921 is a thing of mystery and romance. In 1922 and still more in 1924 it appears as the familiar, mind-obsessing goal at the end of the two miles of breathless, windswept, pitiless and almost hateful ridge that joins it to the North Col. I believe the abandonment of the enterprise after 1922 would have been no disappointment to Mallory. For him snow mountains were not simply opponents to be overcome; they were tilings that feed the springs of reverence and affection, making a man go with a lighter step and a more grateful heart along the road of life. But being asked to go, such a man could not refuse. And his fitness on the third expedition was amazing. His letters, always the most critical of his physical condition, are proof of it.

The story of his last climb is known to every reader of the Journal. Soon after midday on 8th June, just below the steep final step of the North Ridge, he was seen with Irvine "going strong for the top". That is the last glimpse we have of George Mallory. The progress of the great climb was being watched through the press by thousands who never before watched and will never again watch any other climb. And we who knew him saw the modest George obeying the call made upon his physical and spiritual vitality by the sight of any tip-ridge and wall of rock or snow, whether in Britain or the Alps or the Himalaya. Only, in the Everest expeditions, there was an element of duty, increasing in force with each succeeding attempt imparting for M a special nobility and sternness to the greatest mountaineering adventure of his life. Did he and Irvine reach the summit? It is probable that we will never know. And what wonderful justice there would be in the decree of fate that the honour of the first ascent should never be awarded to any but the man who explored the approaches to the mountain and found the only route, who saved his three companions on the return from the magnificent attempt in 1922, and who came back in 1924 to give his life to accomplish what he had set out to do. With better fortune in the matter of weather, with a less cumbrous means of carrying oxygen, Everest may be climbed, shall we say, a second time? How little it matters, after all, whether those last few hundred feet are still untrodden! It was George Mallory himself who wrote of the successful ending of a great climb: "Have we vanquished an enemy? None but ourselves. Have we gained success? That word means nothing here . . . To struggle and to understand, never this last without the other; such is the law." Let us leave him to his rest on Everest, this Galahad of mountaineering, pure of heart, high of purpose. To struggle and to understand . . . Has he won that goal seeing now face to face, knowing even as we are known? We may believe it if we cannot prove.

The Most Hateful Place
In The World

E.F. Norton

Edward Norton was a career army officer, born in 1884; he took over leadership of the 1924 expedition when General Bruce fell ill.

At 3 p.m. on June 1, Somervell and I with our six porters reached Camp IV, where Odell and Irvine took charge of us, allotted us tents and cooked and served us our meals, for they were now installed in their new role as "supporters". And a thankless job this was, for almost the whole day was taken up with performing alternately the menial duties of cook, waiter or scullion; going out to escort returning parties of porters or climbers across the crevasses and seracs leading to the North Col, or, not infrequently, descending to Camp III for more stores, while more fortunate climbers passed through and disappeared in succession up the mountain. Yet, thankless though the task may have been, Odell and Irvine gave such an exhibition of how it should be done that those of us who once passed through their hands are now spoilt for life; never again shall we enjoy such support as we were given by the "old firm". In a year when, to a conspicuous degree, all played for the side, none did so more conscientiously or with less thought of self than these two.

The morning of June 2 broke fine, and by 6.30 Somervell and I were off with our little party of six porters. The reader will understand that Mallory and Bruce were to have established Camp V overnight; this morning they should have been heading up the North Ridge for Camp VI, carrying with them the tent and sleeping-bags in which they had slept the night before. Our loads, therefore, must comprise one 10 lb tent, two sleeping-bags, food and "meta" (solid spirit) for ourselves for a possible three nights and for the porters for one; above the North Col porters' loads were always cut down to a maximum of 20 lb. a man, preferably a little under that weight. I cannot remember the exact details of the loads our men carried, but I know they were laden so near the limit that Somervell and I had to carry (as we had done the day before) a light rucksack apiece, with compass, electric torch, a few spare woollen garments, a change of socks, etc., for our own personal use.

Our route crossed the actual col just below the western lip and, as we emerged from the snow hummocks to traverse it, we suddenly found ourselves in shadow and exposed to the full force of the west wind from which we were completely sheltered both at Camp IV and in the intervening section; that was a bad moment, its memory is still fresh. The wind, even at this early hour, took our breath away like a plunge into the icy waters of a mountain lake, and in a minute or two our well-protected hands lost all sensation as they grasped the frozen rocks to steady us.

Some little way above the col we emerged into sunlight again, and though we got the full benefit of the wind all the way up the ridge, we never again experienced anything quite so blighting as those few minutes in the shady funnel of the col. Nevertheless the wind was all day a serious matter. Though it seemed to cut clean through our windproof clothes, it yet had so solid a push to it that the laden porters often staggered in their steps.

I should here explain that our kit was specially designed to exclude the wind. Personally I wore thick woollen vest and drawers, a thick flannel shirt and two sweaters under a lightish knickerbocker suit of windproof gabardine the knickers of which were lined with light flannel, a pair of soft elastic Kashmir putties and a pair of boots of felt bound and soled with leather and lightly nailed with the usual alpine nails. Over all I wore a very light pyjama suit of Messrs. Burberry's "Shackleton" windproof gabardine. On my hands I wore a pair of long fingerless woollen mitts inside a similar pair made of gabardine; though when step-cutting necessitated a sensitive hold on the axe-haft, I sometimes substituted a pair of silk mitts for the inner woollen pair. On my head I wore a fur-lined leather motorcycling helmet, and my eyes and nose were protected by a pair of goggles of Crookes's glass, which were sewn into a leather mask that came well over the nose and covered any part of my face which was not naturally protected by my beard. A huge woollen muffler completed my costume. Somervell was dressed in much the same style, and the porters were equally well equipped each in a light green canvas windproof suit over a variety of woollen and leather garments. We got used to one another's appearance in time, but every now and then I was struck afresh with the absurdly "gollywog" appearance of the party.

We followed our old route of 1922, the blunt ridge known as the North Arête. For the first 1,500 feet or more the edge of a big snow-bed forms the crest of the ridge, representing the very top of that great mass of hanging ice which clothes the whole of the eastern slopes and cliffs of the North Col. Ascending, we stuck to the rocks just clear of this snow-bed; descending, it is possible to glissade the whole length of it down to the col. The rocks are quite easy, but steep enough to be very hard work at those heights. About halfway up this day's climb was the spot where two years before I had, while taking a short rest, placed between my feet my rucksack, containing a few woollen comforts for the night, and something starting it off, it slipped from my grasp, and in a second was leaping and bounding like a great football with the evident intention of stopping nowhere short of the main Rongbuk Glacier below. This gives a fair picture of the general angle of the climb.

Somewhere about this same spot we heard something above and, looking up, were not a little disconcerted to see one Dor jay Pasang descending to meet us. He was Mallory's and Bruce's leading porter, their first pick and one of the men on whom our highest hopes centred. We had hardly heard his tale of woe and read a note he brought from Mallory when we saw above Mallory, Bruce and three more porters descending in his tracks.

The wind was too cold for a long conversation, and their story was distressingly simple. On the preceding day they had met a very bitter wind all the way up the arête on which we now stood, so bitter that it had quite taken the heart out of their porters. They had pitched two tents at Camp V at a little over 25,000 feet and spent the night, but next morning nothing, not even Bruce's command of the language and well-known influence over these men, would induce any of the porters to go higher, and the end of it was they had to return. Incidentally, Bruce had had to help the last two or three porters into camp the night before, carrying their loads for them for a short distance, and it was quite evident to us that these excessive exertions had affected him in some way, a surmise that was later confirmed by the discovery that he had strained his heart. So he himself was in no fit state to go on, though none who know him will doubt that he would have done so could the porters have been induced to accompany him. Now there is a moral attached to this story. My diary (written at Camp IV) for the day when this fatal wind was encountered mentions the fact that the weather was "quite perfect"; the porters who failed were the pick of the "Tigers", presumably among the best men we had. Yet these picked men, under the one sahib of all our party who knew best how to lead the Sherpa porter and on a day which at Camp IV appeared "quite perfect", were clean knocked out by wind and couldn't be induced to advance beyond 25,200 feet. How evident it becomes that it will never be possible to ensure success on any given day at these extreme altitudes!

As Camp V had been left all standing with tents and bedding destined to go higher that morning, Somervell and I were able to detach two of the porters who had accompanied us so far, to return with the descending party, and we now continued with four men, the three whose names I have already given and one Lobshang Tashi, a simple good-natured giant from the eastern borders of Tibet. We reached Camp V without incident about 1 p.m. We had no difficulty in finding the camp from Mallory's description and from certain strips of coloured cloth which each party carried to serve as signposts and which had been put up at the point where we were to leave the ridge.

The two tents were pitched one above the other on crumbling platforms built on the steep slope just over the edge, and on the east or sheltered side of the North Arête.

The afternoon was spent as every afternoon must always be spent under these conditions. On arrival one crawls into the tent, so completely exhausted that for perhaps three-quarters of an hour one just lies in a sleeping-bag and rests. Then duty begins to call, one member of the party with groans and pantings and frequent rests crawls out of his bag, out of the tent and a few yards – to a neighbouring patch of snow, where he fills two big aluminium pots with snow, what time his companion with more panting and groans sits up in bed, lights the meta burner and opens some tins and bags of food, say a stick of pemmican, some tea, sugar and condensed milk, a tin of sardines or bully beef and a box of biscuits.

Presently both are again ensconced in their sleeping-bags side by side, with the meta cooker doing its indifferent best to produce half a pot of warm water from each piled pot of powdery snow. It doesn't sound a very formidable proceeding, and it might appear that I have rather overdrawn the panting and groans; but I have carried out this routine on three or four occasions, and I can honestly say that I know nothing, not even the exertion of steep climbing at these heights, which is so utterly exhausting or which calls for more determination than this hateful duty of high-altitude cooking. The process has to be repeated two or three times as, in addition to the preparation of the evening meal, a Thermos flask or two must be filled with water for tomorrow's breakfast and the cooking pots must be washed up. Perhaps the most hateful part of the process is that some of the resultant mess must be eaten, and this itself is only achieved by will power: there is but little desire to eat, sometimes indeed a sense of nausea at the bare idea though of drink one cannot have enough.

When we had done our duty, I visited the tent where the four porters were packed like sardines, to persuade them to do theirs. For some time I could elicit nothing but grunts, but I succeeded at last in infusing some life into the comatose, unwilling figures, and it then appeared that some stones had fallen from our tent platform and, landing on the porters' tent, had cut Lobsang Tashi's head, a slight affair despite a good showing of blood, and Semchumbi's knee. The latter was a much more serious matter, a nasty gash right across the kneecap.

With one look at the panorama of glacier and mountain spread out below a world composed of three elements only, rock, snow and ice, the mountain-tops now gilded by the declining sun and Camp III just discernible in the cold shadow of the North Peak under our feet we turned in for the night, with gloomy forebodings for the morrow; for there was nothing whatever in the attitude of our porters tonight to encourage us to hope that we should next day succeed any better than Mallory and Bruce.

My diary records that we spent a "fair night"; only some 200 feet below we had seen the collapsed forms of two tents in which two years before Mallory, Somervell, Morshead and I had spent a truly miserable night, scarcely any of us getting any sleep. The difference was largely accounted for by improvements in our equipment and in the organization of our camp, and it is by this progressive raising of the standard of comfort high on the mountain that we shall some day reach the top.

On the morning of 3 June we were up at 5 a.m., and while Somervell busied himself with preparations for breakfast I climbed down to the porters' tent with some misgivings as to what their condition would prove to be. My fears were justified, and for some time groans were the only answer to my questions. But having at last, as I thought, inspired the men sufficiently to induce them to cook and eat a meal, I returned and had breakfast. I then again tackled them, for they seemed incapable of making any sort of a move without much stimulating, and it was at once evident that Lobsang Tashi was finished and useless for any higher climbing. His head wound was nothing, but he complained of sickness, and it was evident that his heart was not in the task of going any higher. Semchumbi was genuinely lame, his knee was much swollen and he looked an unlikely starter, despite the fact that he showed a good deal more spirit than the other wounded man.

Llakpa Chede I judged fit and willing to go higher provided that any of the others would, and so I concentrated most of my persuasive powers on Narbu Yishe. I talked for a long time to these men, pointing out the honour and glory that they would achieve if they would but carry their loads another 2,000 feet, thus passing by 1,500 feet the highest point to which loads had ever been carried.

I remember saying, "If you put us up a camp at 27,000 feet and we reach the top, your names shall appear in letters of gold in the book that will be written to describe the achievement." To make a very long story short I succeeded in inducing the three, Narbu Yishe, Llakpa Chede and Semchumbi, lame as he was, to come on, and we actually started from camp at 9 a.m., four hours after we had got up. Truly it is not easy to make an early start on Mount Everest! Lobsang Tashi was sent down alone to Camp IV; as soon as his face was turned in the right direction he showed considerable alacrity, and we had the satisfaction of seeing him reach that camp in safety an hour or two later.

Of our ascent of the ridge there is little to tell; it was a repetition of the climb of the day before and was over ground familiar to Somervell and myself, as we had traversed exactly the same route when making for our highest point two years before. Narbu Yishe and Llakpa Chede went splendidly when once they were started. Somervell was feeling his throat very badly and had constantly to stop and cough, so he took on himself the task of shepherding Semchumbi, who, to do him justice, performed a very fine feat indeed in climbing for four and a half hours with a 20 lb load, and, though inevitably slow and a drag on the whole party, he remained cheerful and willing and did his very best. The weather continued fine and the wind was markedly less severe than on the day before.

Some time after midday we recognized and passed the highest point that Mallory, Somervell and I had reached in 1922. As I have said before, one's sensations are dulled at these altitudes, but I remember a momentary uplift at the thought that we were actually going to camp higher than the highest point ever reached without oxygen. With a clear day ahead of us, and given favourable conditions, what might we not achieve!

About 1.30 it became evident that it would be impossible to urge the gallant Semchumbi much farther, so I selected a site for our tent, a narrow cleft in the rocks facing north and affording the suggestion, it was little more, of some shelter from the north-west wind. Here I set the two leading porters to scrape and pile the loose stones forming the floor of the cleft into the usual platform for a tent. I can safely say that in two excursions up and down the whole length of the North Arête of Mount Everest I have never seen a single spot affording the six-foot square level area on which a tent could be pitched without having to build a platform. As Somervell helped and encouraged Semchumbi up the last steep pitch, I went off for three-quarters of an hour to reconnoitre the beginning of the next day's climb.

About 2.30 we sent the three porters down. They had nearly 4,000 feet to descend, for we have since estimated the height of Camp VI at about 26,800 feet, and one of them was lame: so there was not too much time for them to reach Camp IV by daylight. I gave the men a note to be shown to the sahib in charge of each camp to say that they had done splendidly, and were to be fed on the fat of the land and passed comfortably to the Base Camp and a well-earned rest.

We afterwards learnt that on this day, Odell and Hazard, the latter of whom had reached Camp IV the day before, climbed to Camp V, returning to Camp IV the same night. Odell was after fossils, and actually found the first ever collected on Mount Everest, and Hazard accompanied him for air and exercise. This little stroll is a curious commentary on the fact that two years before the scientists were debating whether human beings could exist without oxygen at 25,000 feet.

Somervell and I spent the afternoon as on the day before, with the exception that we had now no porters to stimulate, and this was fortunate, for as you near 27,000 feet you have no great surplus of determination. My diary for the day finishes with the surprising entry: "Spent the best night since I left Camp I"; yet it was true in my case, and Somervell was at least fairly comfortable if he didn't sleep quite so well as I did. As one of our doubts had always been whether it would be possible to sleep, or even rest well, at 27,000 feet, this is an interesting point. Besides my boots I took to bed with me in my eiderdown sleeping-bag two Thermos flasks filled with warm tea; towards morning I found that one of these had got rid of its cork, and its contents no longer warm had emptied into my bed.

Once more our hopes of an early start were shattered; snow had to be fetched and melted to provide the essential drink for breakfast. If as I have before described vitality is low in the early hours at Camp III at 21,000 feet, it can be guessed how near the limit 6 a.m. found us at 27,000. Yet somehow the job was done and we were off at 6.40.

Perhaps an hour beyond camp we encountered the bottom edge of the great 1,000-foot-deep band of yellow sandstone that crosses the whole North Face of Everest from shoulder to shoulder, and is so conspicuous a feature of the mountain as seen from the north. This afforded easy going as we traversed it diagonally, for it was made up of a series of broad ledges running parallel to its general direction and sufficiently broken up to afford easy access, one to the next.

The day was fine and nearly windless, a perfect day for our task yet it was bitterly cold, and I remember shivering so violently as I sat in the sun during one of our numerous halts, dressed in all the clothes I have described, that I suspected the approach of malaria and took my pulse. I was surprised to find it only about sixty-four, which is some twenty above my normally very slow pulse. I was not wearing snow goggles except when actually on snow, a very small proportion of the day's climb, as I had found that the rims of my goggles somewhat interfered with a clear view of my steps. At a height of about 27,500 feet I began to experience some trouble with my eyes; I was seeing double, and in a difficult step was sometimes in doubt where to put my feet. I thought that this might be a premonitory symptom of snow-blindness, but Somervell assured me that this could not be the case, and he was undoubtedly right, for I have since been told that it was a symptom of lack of control and due to the insufficiency of oxygen in the air I was breathing.

Our pace was wretched. My ambition was to do twenty consecutive paces uphill without a pause to rest and pant elbow on bent knee; yet I never remember achieving it, thirteen was nearer the mark. The process of breathing in the intensely cold dry air, which caught the back of the larynx, had a disastrous effect on poor Somervell's already very bad sore throat and he had constantly to stop and cough. Every five or ten minutes we had to sit down for a minute or two, and we must have looked a sorry couple.

The view from this great height was disappointing. From 25,000 feet the wild tangle of snowy peaks and winding glaciers, each with its parallel lines of moraine like cart tracks on a snowy road, was imposing to a degree. But we were now high above the highest summit in sight, and everything below us was so flattened out that much of the beauty of outline was lost. To the north, over the great plateau of Tibet, the eye travelled over range upon range of minor hills until all sense of distance was lost, only to be sharply regained on picking up a row of snow-peaks just appearing over the horizon like tiny teeth. The day was a remarkably clear one in a country of the clearest atmosphere in the world, and the imagination was fired by the sight of these infinitely distant peaks tucked away over the curve of the horizon.

Towards noon we found ourselves just below the top edge of the band of sandstone and nearing the big couloir or gully which runs vertically down the mountain and cuts off the base of the final pyramid from the great northern shoulder. The line we had followed was one roughly parallel to and perhaps 500 to 600 feet below the crest of the North-East Arête; this was the line Somervell and I had always favoured in preference to the actual crest, which Mallory advocated.

At midday Somervell succumbed to his throat trouble. He declared that he was only delaying me, and urged me to go on alone and reach the top. I left him sitting under a rock just below the topmost edge of the sandstone band and went on. I followed the actual top edge of the band, which led at a very slightly uphill angle into and across the big couloir; but to reach the latter I had to turn the ends of two pronounced buttresses which ran down the face of the mountain, one of which was a prolongation of a feature on the skyline ridge which we called the second step, and which looked so formidable an obstacle where it crossed the ridge that we had chosen the lower route rather than try and surmount it at its highest point. From about the place where I met with these buttresses the going became a great deal worse; the slope was very steep below me, the foothold ledges narrowed to a few inches in width, and as I approached the shelter of the big couloir there was a lot of powdery snow, which concealed the precarious footholds. The whole face of the mountain was composed of slabs like the tiles on a roof, and all sloped at much the same angle as tiles. I had twice to retrace my steps and follow a different band of strata; the couloir itself was filled with powdery snow into which I sank to the knee or even to the waist, and which was yet not of a consistency to support me in the event of a slip. Beyond the couloir the going got steadily worse; I found myself stepping from tile to tile, as it were, each tile sloping smoothly and steeply downwards; I began to feel that I was too much dependent on the mere friction of a boot nail on the slabs. It was not exactly difficult going, but it was a dangerous place for a single unroped climber, as one slip would have sent me in all probability to the bottom of the mountain. The strain of climbing so carefully was beginning to tell and I was getting exhausted. In addition my eye trouble was getting worse and was by now a severe handicap. I had perhaps 200 feet more of this nasty going to surmount before I emerged on to the north face of the final pyramid and, I believed, safety and an easy route to the summit. It was now 1 p.m., and a brief calculation showed that I had no chance of climbing the remaining 800 or 900 feet if I was to return in safety.

At a point subsequently fixed by theodolite as 28,126 feet I turned back and retraced my steps to rejoin Somervell. In an hour I had gained but little, probably under 100 feet in height, and in distance perhaps 300 yards on the position where we had separated. Surveying is an exact science, and I must not quarrel with Hazard for fixing our highest point twenty-four feet below the height of Kinchinjunga, the third highest mountain in the world.

I feel that I ought to record the bitter feeling of disappointment that I should have experienced on having to acknowledge defeat with the summit so close; yet I cannot conscientiously say that I felt it much at the time. Twice now I have had thus to turn back on a favourable day when success had appeared possible, yet on neither occasion did I feel the sensations appropriate to the moment. This I think is a psychological effect of great altitudes; the better qualities of ambition and will to conquer seem dulled to nothing, and one turns downhill with but little feelings other than relief that the strain and effort of climbing are finished.

I was near the end of my powers, and had for some time been going too slowly to hope to reach the summit. Whether the height I had reached was nearing the limit of human endurance without the artificial aid of oxygen, or whether my earlier exertions and hardships in the month of May accounted for my exhaustion, I cannot, of course, say, but I incline to the latter opinion; and I still believe that there is nothing in the atmospheric conditions even between 28,000 and 29,000 feet to prevent a fresh and fit party from reaching the top of Mount Everest without oxygen.

One small incident will serve to show that I must have been very much below my proper form at this time, and that my nerve had been shaken by the last two hours of climbing alone on steep and slippery going. As I approached Somervell I had to cross a patch of snow lying thinly over some sloping rocks. It was neither steep nor difficult, and not to be compared to the ground I had just left, yet suddenly I felt that I could not face it without help, and I shouted to Somervell to come and throw me the end of the rope. Here again I remember the difficulty I had in making my voice carry perhaps 100 yards. Somervell gave me the required aid, and I could see the surprise he felt at my needing it in such a place.

Then came the descent. Soon after we started down, at about 2 p.m., Somervell's axe slipped from his numb fingers and went cartwheeling down the slopes below. This must have been somewhere about the point where an hour or two before he had taken his highest photograph; and it is a proof of the deceptive picture of the true angle of the mountain conveyed by these photographs that it does not give the impression that a dropped axe would go any distance without coming to rest, yet his never looked like stopping, and disappeared from our view still going strong.

We retraced our steps of the morning; we made very poor going, descending at a very much slower pace than we had made two years before when we turned back from our highest point some 1,000 feet lower.

We looked in at our tent at Camp VI, finding it without difficulty, collected one or two of our belongings and a section of tent pole as a substitute for Somervell's axe, collapsed and weighted the tent with stones and started down the interminable North Arête. Sunset found us level with Camp V, which we left below us on the right without departing from the blunt crest of the arête. We were unroped, for here the going was both safe and easy. Arrived on the big snow-bed I glissaded for some little distance before I realized that Somervell had stopped behind, and I had to wait quite half an hour for him to catch up. I concluded that he had stopped to sketch or photograph the effect of the sunset glow on the great panorama of peaks surrounding us, a proof that I had by no means realized his condition; actually he had been stopped by a more than usually severe fit of coughing which had ended by very nearly choking him, and he was probably only saved by coughing up the obstructing matter along with a lot of blood. When he rejoined me, coming very slowly down the rocks, as he could not trust himself to glissade on the snow, it was already dark and I lit up my electric torch.

As we neared the col I began to shout to Camp IV, for it was one of our rules that any party of porters or climbers descending from the mountain be met at the Col and escorted and roped over the intricate route into camp by one or more of the supporters, who knew the way by heart. At last I made myself heard, and an answering shout informed us that our escort was coming and was bringing an oxygen apparatus and cylinder. But there was something we wanted far more than oxygen, for we were parched and famished with thirst. I remember shouting again and again, "We don't want the damned oxygen; we want drink!" My own throat and voice were in none too good a case, and my feeble wail seemed to be swallowed up in the dim white expanse below glimmering in the starlight.

A hundred feet or more above the col, Mallory and Odell met us, and told us that Irvine was in camp hard at work preparing our dinner. Somervell had a go at the oxygen, but seemed to get no benefit from it, and I tried with the same result. But we were perfectly fit to get along without it, and perhaps another three-quarters of an hour saw us arrive in camp. Mallory and Odell were kindness itself, and they kept congratulating us on having reached what we estimated as a height of 28,000 feet, though we ourselves felt nothing but disappointment at our failure. We reached Camp IV at 9.30 p.m., and what a different welcome it gave us to that we had received at the same place two years before on our arrival at eleven at night in an empty and deserted camp! Young Irvine had both tea and soup ready for us, and we had something to eat; but our appetites were meagre, and herein lies one of the difficulties of high climbing: one eats from a sense of duty, and it is impossible to force oneself to take enough food even to begin to make good the day's wastage of tissue.

As Mallory and I lay in our tent, he explained that he had decided that if we two failed to reach the summit, he was determined to make one more attempt, this time with oxygen, and how he had been down to Camp III with Bruce and collected sufficient porters to enable the attempt to be staged. I entirely agreed with his decision, and was full of admiration for the indomitable spirit of the man, determined, in spite of his already excessive exertions, not to admit defeat while any chance remained, and I must admit that such was his will power and nervous energy he still seemed entirely adequate to the task. I differed with him in his decision to take Irvine as his companion for two reasons: firstly, that Irvine was now suffering from the prevalent throat trouble, though certainly not as badly as Somervell had been before the start of our climb; secondly, that he was not the experienced climber that Odell was, while Odell was obviously fit and strong, and, acclimatizing very slowly as he had done, was now beginning to show unmistakably that we had in him a climber of unequalled endurance and toughness. Mallory's reasons for his choice were that though Odell and Irvine were both thoroughly au fait with every detail of the oxygen apparatus, yet the latter had a peculiar genius for mechanical expedients, and had taken the lead in devising means to obviate its numerous shortcomings; and he insisted that those who were to use the apparatus must have faith in its efficacy. Odell, having used it with Bruce on the day of their abortive attempt to reach Camp IV without apparently benefiting from it, certainly had not this confidence.

But it was obviously no time for me to interfere with the composition of the party, and when I found that Mallory had completed his plans I made no attempt to do so.

Some time after eleven o'clock that night, as I was dozing off to sleep, I was suddenly wakened by sharp pain in my eyes, and found that I had been smitten with a severe attack of snow blindness. In the morning I found myself completely blind, and I remained in this condition for the next sixty hours, suffering a good deal of pain.

June 5 was spent in the usual preparations for Mallory and Irvine's climb, on which they were to start next day. I was only able to help by periodically coming to the door of my tent and talking to the porters, for, poor though was my knowledge of Nepalese, there was no one else at Camp IV who could do so even as effectively as I; Mallory had learnt a sufficient smattering of Hindustani to communicate with these men to an extent, but it was evident that his party might have trouble in getting their porters on from Camp V to Camp VI (though we hoped that their reluctance would be reduced to some extent by the fact that the carry had now been once successfully accomplished), and I had to do my best to stimulate the porters in advance for this crucial moment.

That afternoon Somervell descended to Camp III and thence next day went on down to the Base Camp, and Hazard arrived from Camp III to take Irvine's place, with Odell as supporter.

On June 6 at 7.30 a.m. we said goodbye to Mallory and Irvine, little guessing that we should see them no more. My last impression of my friends was a handshake and a word of blessing, for it was only in my imagination that I could see the little party winding its way amid the snow humps and ice crevasses leading to the col, the two climbers, never to return, accompanied by four or five porters.

About 10.30 a.m. Hingston arrived from Camp III with two

porters, to see what could be done for my eyes, of which Somervell had told him. Hingston is nothing if not efficient; he had already proved himself a remarkable goer on the glacier as far as Camp III, and we were scarcely surprised when he arrived in Camp IV with the matter-of-fact ease of an experienced mountaineer. Yet with a view to what followed it is worthy of note that he had never previously climbed a mountain in the alpine sense.

An examination of my eyes showed that nothing could be done to restore my sight at the moment, though there was little question that they would recover in a day or two; but I was anxious not to remain a useless encumbrance on the supporters at Camp IV and, Hingston volunteering to escort me with his two porters, I decided to go down, blind as I was, to Camp III. Hazard offered to accompany us as far as the top of the ice chimney to rope me from above down this steepest portion of the *rente*, including the chimney itself and the wall below it. Accordingly, about 11 a.m. we started the descent. The two porters, Xlma Tundrup and Churin, were both strong and steady climbers, and between them and Hingston, the last doing all the really responsible work, my every footstep was guided and my feet placed for me the whole way down, while Hazard held me with a rope down each steep section in succession. It was indeed a remarkable performance on the part of Hingston: he gave me the impression of having the steadiness and confidence of an alpine guide. I was shod with crampons, and thanks to them and to the help of my companions I never had an anxious moment, though it was necessarily a most laborious and tedious process. To make a long story short we reached the glacier without incident and hence sent one porter on to fetch six men, with the one-man carrier, from Camp III to meet me where our route took to the moraine; for on its rough boulders I could never have made any progress at all.

These six men took it in turns to carry me, and did so over the most appalling going, boulders, ice and frozen scree, without a single false step until, about 5 p.m., we reached Camp III; there I was welcomed by Bruce and Noel with that extraordinary solicitude and kindness which I have come to recognize as the one great reward that awaits the unsuccessful Everest climber.

Next morning I was beginning to see a little, and in two more days was completely recovered. Bruce, Noel, Hingston and I decided to remain at Camp III until the fate of Mallory and Irvine's attempt was decided. During the next four days we were to pass through every successive stage of suspense and anxiety from high hope to hopelessness, and the memory of them is such that Camp III must remain to all of us the most hateful place in the world.

The Last Climb

Noel Odell

Odell was the last person to see Mallory and Irvine alive, glimpsing them at the first step of the North-East Ridge through a break in the cloud on 8 June. What happened to them thereafter is a mystery. Almost a decade later an ice-axe belonging to Irvine was found at 27,500 feet/8,400 metres, suggesting an accident at that height. It is improbable that they reached the summit, still more than 1,300 feet/400 metres above them, Odell's hunch notwithstanding. In 1999 Mallory's body was discovered, almost perfectly preserved, by Conrad Anker (see pp 415–423).

At 8.40 on the morning of 6 June, in brilliant weather, Mallory and Irvine left the North Col Camp for Camp V. They took with them five porters carrying provisions and reserve oxygen cylinders. They used oxygen and, in the opinion of the porters, travelled well. On 7 June, when they were going from Camp V to VI, I went up in support to Camp V with the one porter that was available. Soon after my arrival Mallory's four porters arrived from VI, bringing me a message which said that they had used but little oxygen to 27,000 feet, that the weather promised to be perfect for the morrow's climb, and mentioning he was sorry the cooking-stove had rolled down the mountainside just as they were leaving Camp V – an occurrence which meant a cold supper and breakfast for me! As Nema, my porter, was suffering from mountain sickness, I sent him down with the four others to the North Col, and having the tent to myself, and a couple of sleeping-bags, I kept sufficiently warm to sleep well that night.

Next morning broke clear and not unduly cold. After a breakfast of "Force" and a little macaroni and tomatoes, I started my solitary climb to Camp VI, taking with me provisions for that

camp in case of need. My plan was to make a rather circuitous
route out on to the North Face in order to examine the structure of the mountain. Mist soon began to form, and although
the wind remained light I found myself immersed now and
then in squalls of sleet and light snow. By the glow of light
above me I could sometimes see that I was experiencing worse
conditions than quite probably Mallory and Irvine were at
their higher altitude.

At an altitude of about 25,500 feet I came upon a limestone
band which, to my joy, contained fossils – the first definite forms
found on Everest. I might very briefly refer here to the structure
of Everest and its bearing on the problem of climbing it. The
lower part of the mountain is formed of a variety of gneisses,
and on these rests a mass of rocks, mainly altered limestones,
which compose the greater part of its upper half. Here and there
have been intruded granitoid rocks, but these are relatively little
in amount. The general dip of the series is about 30° northward,
and since the slope of this face of the mountain above 25,000
feet is about 40° to 45°, the effect is to make a series of overlap-
ping slabs nearly parallel with the slope and presenting a number
of little cliff faces often up to fifty feet in height. Trying enough
for upward progress, these slabs are often sprinkled to a varying
depth with debris from above, and when to this is added freshly
fallen snow, the labour and toil of climbing at these altitudes
may perhaps be imagined. It is not the technical difficulty so
much as the awkwardness of a slope usually not quite steep
enough for the use of one's hands.

At about 26,000 feet I climbed a little crag, which could
possibly have been circumvented, but which I decided to tackle
direct, more perhaps as a test of my condition than for any
other reason. There was, perhaps, 100 feet of it, and as I
reached the top there was a sudden clearing above me and I
saw the whole summit ridge and final peak of Everest unveiled.
I noticed far away on a snow-slope leading up to the last step
but one from the base of the final pyramid a tiny object moving
and approaching the rock step. A second object followed, and
then the first climbed to the top of the step. As I stood intently
watching this dramatic appearance, the scene became
enveloped in cloud, and I could not actually be certain that I

saw the second figure join the first. I was surprised, above all, to see them so late as this, namely, 12.50, at a point that, according to Mallory's schedule, should have been reached by 10 a.m. at latest. I could see that they were moving expeditiously, as if endeavouring to make up for lost time. True, they were moving one at a time over what was apparently but moderately difficult ground, but one cannot definitely conclude from this that they were roped – an important consideration in any estimate of what befell them. I had seen that there was a considerable quantity of new snow covering some of the upper rocks near the summit ridge, and this may well have caused delay in the ascent. Burdened as they undoubtedly were with the oxygen apparatus, these snow-covered, debris-sprinkled slabs may have given much trouble. The oxygen apparatus itself may have needed repair or readjustment either before or after they left Camp VI, and so have delayed them. Or both these factors may have been operative.

I continued my way up to Camp VI, and on arrival there, about two o'clock, a rather severer blizzard set in and the wind increased. After a short rest I realized it was just possible that, balked by earlier bad weather higher up, Mallory and Irvine might be returning, and the concealed position of Camp VI would be almost impossible to discover in the blizzard. I remembered also that Mallory had told me in his note that he had left his compass at V, and asked me to retrieve it. So I went out in the direction of the summit, and having scrambled up about 200 feet and jodelled and whistled meanwhile, in case they happened to be within hearing, I then took shelter for a while behind a rock from the driving sleet. After about an hour's wait, realizing that the chances were altogether against their being within call, I found my way back to the tent. As I reached it the storm, which had lasted not more than two hours, blew over and the whole North Face of the mountain became bathed in sunshine. The upper crags were visible, but I could see no signs of the party. The little tent at Camp VI was only just large enough for two, and if I had remained and they had returned, one of us would have had to sleep outside in the open – an altogether hazardous expedient. But apart from this, Mallory had particularly requested me in his last note to return to the North Col, as he specially wished to reach there himself after their climb. Leaving Camp VI, therefore, about 4.30, and going down the North Ridge in quick time, I took to the hard snow near Camp V and glissaded down to the North Col, reaching the camp at 6.45. That night Hazard's brew of Maggi soup, made from a mixture of at least six varieties, went down really well! I was surprised, though, to find that I was not suffering from thirst – that bugbear of Everest – to anything like the extent I had expected.

We watched till late that night for some signs of Mallory and Irvine's return, or even an indication by flare of distress. Next morning we scrutinised through field-glasses the tiny tents of Camps V and VI, far up above us, in case they had returned late and had not yet started down. But no movement at all could be seen. At noon I decided to go up to Camp V and on to VI next day in search, and I arranged a code of signals with Hazard, who remained at the North Col. Two porters came with me and stayed the night at V, but in the morning I had to send them back to the North Col on account of indisposition. It was a bitterly cold night, and we slept little, if at all. Using oxygen, I started off from Camp V, and when within an hour or so of VI, I came to the conclusion that I was deriving but little benefit from the oxygen, which I had only been taking in moderate quantities from the single cylinder that I carried. I switched it off, and experienced none of the feelings of collapse and faintness that one had been led to believe ought to result. On reaching the tent at VI I found everything as I had left it: the tent had obviously not been touched since I was there two days previously. I dumped the oxygen apparatus and went in search up along the probable route that Mallory and Irvine had taken. There was a bitterly cold west wind, and now and then I had to take shelter behind rocks to restore warmth. After a couple of hours' search I realized that the chances of finding the missing ones were indeed small on such a vast expanse of crags and broken slabs, and that for any more extensive search towards the final pyramid a further party would have to be organized. I returned only too reluctantly to the tent, and then with considerable exertion dragged the two sleeping-bags up to a precipitous snow patch plastered on the little crag above the tent. With these sleeping-bags placed against the snow I had arranged with Hazard to signal down to the North Col Camp the results of my search. It needed all my efforts to cut steps out over the snow-slope and then fix the sleeping-bags in position, so boisterous was the wind. But fortunately the signal was seen 4,000 feet below, though the answering signal I could not make out. Closing up the tent and leaving its contents as my friends had left them, I glanced up at the mighty summit above me. It seemed to look down with cold indifference on me, mere puny man, and howl derision in wind-gusts at my petition to yield up its secret, this mystery of my friends. If it were indeed the sacred ground of Chomolungma, Goddess Mother of the Mountains, had we violated it? – was I now violating it? And yet, as I gazed again, there seemed to be something alluring in that towering presence. I was almost fascinated. I realized that no mere mountaineer alone could but be fascinated; that he who approaches close must ever be led on and, oblivious of all obstacles, seek to reach that most sacred and highest place of all. It seemed that my friends must have been thus enchanted also: for why else should they tarry? In an effort to suppress my feelings, I turned my gaze downwards to the North Col far below, and I remembered that other of my companions would be anxiously awaiting my return, eager to hear what tidings I carried. Alone and in meditation I slowly commenced my long descent. But it was no place for silent contemplation, for, buffeted by storm-blasts that seemed to pierce one through, it needed all one's attention and calculation to negotiate safely the exposed slabs of the ridge and prevent a slip on their debris-sprinkled surfaces. I quickened my pace lower down, but at times found it necessary to seek protection from the biting gale behind rocks and reassure myself that no symptoms of frostbite were imminent. Hazard had seen me coming and sent his one remaining Sherpa to meet and welcome me at the foot of the ridge. Arrived at the North Col Camp, I was pleased to find a note from Norton and to discover that I had anticipated his wishes that I should return to IV and not prolong my search on the mountain, seeing that the monsoon seemed likely to break at any moment. Next day Hazard, the porter and myself, leaving the tents standing, evacuated the North Col Camp and went down in good weather to Camp III, and later in the day with Hingston and Shebbeare to II, reaching the Base Camp on the 12th.

I have already mentioned the possible reasons why Mallory and Irvine were so late in reaching the point at which they were last seen – namely, an altitude which Hazard later determined by theodolite to be about 28,230 feet – and I must now very briefly speculate on the probable causes of their failure to return. They had about 800 feet of altitude to surmount to reach the top, and, provided no particularly difficult obstacle presented itself on the final pyramid, they should have got there about 3 to 3.30. This would be three or four hours late on Mallory's schedule, and hence they would find it almost impossible to reach Camp VI before nightfall, allowing five or six hours for the return. But at the same time it must be remembered there was a moon, though it rose rather late, and that evening it was fine and the mountain clear of mist, as far as could be seen. In spite of this they may have missed the way and failed to find Camp VI, and in their overwrought condition sought shelter till daylight – a danger that Mallory, experienced mountaineer that he was, would be only too well aware of, but find himself powerless to resist: sleep at that altitude and in that degree of cold would almost certainly prove fatal.

The other possibility is that they met their death by falling. This implies that they were roped together, which need not necessarily be inferred from their observed movements when last seen. It is difficult for one who knew the skill and experience of George Mallory on all kinds and conditions of mountain ground to believe that he fell. Of Sandy Irvine it can be said that, though altogether less experienced than Mallory, he had shown himself to be a natural adept and able to move safely and easily on rock and ice. Such had been my experience of him in Spitsbergen, in Norway, and on our home mountains. They were hampered, of course, by the oxygen apparatus – a very serious load for climbing with, as Mallory had mentioned in his last note to me. But could such a pair fall, and where, technically, the climbing appeared so easy? Experts nevertheless, I fear to remind you, have done so, under stress of circumstances or exhaustion.

It has been suggested that the oxygen apparatus failed and thereby rendered them powerless to return. I cannot accept the validity of this argument; for, from my own personal experience, being deprived of oxygen, at any rate when one has not been using it freely, does not prevent one from continuing, and least of all from getting down off the mountain. Mallory in his last note to me said they were using little oxygen, and they hoped to take only two cylinders each from Camp VI.

Hence I incline to the view first expressed, that they met their death by being benighted. I know that Mallory had stated he would take no risks in any attempt on the final peak; but in action the desire to overcome, the craving for victory, may have proved too strong for him. The knowledge of his own proved powers of endurance and those of his companion may have urged him to make a bold bid for the summit. Who of us that has wrestled with some alpine giant, in the teeth of a gale or in a race with the darkness, could hold back when such a victory, such a triumph of human endeavour, was within our grasp?

The question remains: "Has Mount Everest been climbed?" It must be left unanswered, for there is no direct evidence. But bearing in mind all the circumstances that I have set out above, and considering their position when last seen, I think there is a strong probability that Mallory and Irvine succeeded. At that I must leave it.

A word in regard to the oxygen and the benefit derivable from it. I think that its importance has been exaggerated, and provided one has acclimatized at a sufficiently high altitude, say 22,000 or 23,000 feet, one can do practically as well without it. I am prepared to go further and claim that oxygen used liberally may be regarded as a source of danger, preventing the user from proper acclimatization and greatly increasing the chances of his collapse if the apparatus break down. My own experience with the present apparatus is that its weight of about 30 lbs, combined with its bulk, quite obviates any advantage to be gained from it. It is interesting in this connection to compare Geoffrey Bruce's opinion in 1922 with his experience of it this year. I believe I am right in saying that he found he derived altogether less benefit from it this year than he expected he would. And this I feel sure was largely due to his higher degree of acclimatization. An interesting physiological point is that all members of the expedition who had been out previously acclimatized quicker than the newcomers. Finally, I consider that if oxygen be used by a high-climbing party in the future, if only in small quantities or as an emergency measure, it must be carried in an altogether lighter apparatus. Whether it be available in the gaseous state as at present, or can be carried in the much more convenient form of a liquid, is a matter for immediate research. But my firm belief is that Everest can be climbed without oxygen.

Everest 1933

First Over Everest

P.F.M. Fellowes, L.V. Stewart Blacker, P.T. Etherton and Lord Clydesdale

"The Houston Mount Everest Expedition" was an attempt on Everest with a difference. Equipped with two Westland biplanes, it sought to fly over the mountain and photograph it from above.

A sense of the great prize at hand dominated our efforts; we were all so ardent, our leader so confident, the need of securing good results so claimant, and a decisive victory over Everest seemingly so near, that only doubts as to the weather conditions clouded our thoughts. The work and preparation of more than a year, which had continued at their utmost tensity, seemed likely to be crowned with success.

But always the wind and the weather governed our deliberations, every sacrifice had been made; was the toil to be achieved?

Whenever the clearness of the sky allowed the theodolite observers to see the balloon up to 25,000 feet and above, the wind velocities became alarming, and seldom under seventy miles an hour.

Previous official estimates showed a thirty- or possibly forty-mile wind to be the highest in which it would be safe to make the attempt.

It will be understood that a strong wind from the west, its usual quarter, would tend to make the machines, travelling from south to north, drift sideways out of their course. Steering into the wind to counteract this would be equivalent to flying a longer course, and hence burning more fuel. Thus the stronger the wind "at height," the more fuel burned.

It was a question, therefore, if we made the attempt in a

stronger wind than that specified as permissible by the experts, whether there would be sufficient for the return journey.

As a precaution, we had prepared an advance landing-ground near Forbesganj, forty-six miles north of Purnea.

So we waited anxiously day by day for the wind at 30,000 feet to drop to a reasonable figure.

Sometimes, when the wind speed seemed promising the mountains would be covered in cloud, a matter fatal to photography. We could not even afford to have the valleys on the southern slopes of Everest cloud-filled, as this would cause a gap in the continuity of the all-important strip of air survey photographs.

In April the weather at Purnea seems to go in ten- or twelve-day cycles. It starts with a "disturbance," which might be a storm of rain. Then there are several clear days with little wind, but characterized by cloud-caps on the mountains. As these cloud-caps melt away and the peaks stand out clear, so the wind speed appears to rise. Every morning one of our scouting Moths went up to a few thousand feet, at which height the three great mountains were always clearly visible and it could be seen to what extent they were free from clouds. We waited anxiously for the evening telegram from Calcutta, with its weather forecast, and then for the early morning reports from the scout pilot, and the balloon observers. Should we ever get a moderate wind, without a mass of cloud? All seemed to depend on this. The weather factor had become a much greater one than we had anticipated.

Anxiously we all discussed the matter, always with the able advice of the meteorologists.

The Friday of that memorable week came, then the Saturday. The wind reports showed great, but diminishing velocities. On Sunday the speeds had lessened. We could scarcely sleep for anxiety. The evening telegram foretold a still further drop. Would it be borne out in the morning? Would the clouds have gathered, or the pendulum swing again back to greater winds? We decided that the risk must be taken of flying in a much higher wind and watching the fuel consumption carefully.

Then came Monday, an auspicious day, so said the astrologers. The scouting Moth reported the mountain crystal-clear, the meteorologists gave a wind of fifty-seven miles an hour at the altitude, not so great as to stand in the way of an attempt on Everest.

The die was cast; we drove breathlessly the ten miles to the landing-ground and fretted and fumed at the manifold last-minute preparations, which had to be made by our splendid skilled aircraftmen.

There were a hundred tasks to complete before the big machines were ready for the flight. Everything possible had been done the night before, but necessity compelled us to leave a number of details to the last minute.

Chief among the preparations was that of the cameras. The fine, impalpable, all-pervading dust was everywhere. For this reason the cameras could not be left on the aerodrome, still less in the machines themselves. In fact, it was found necessary thoroughly to clean every one of the numerous delicate items of camera equipment each night, and to wrap them up in a double layer of newspaper before putting them back each in its appropriate chest. Even these precautions were not excessive, but the result was that nearly an hour's hard work devolved on the aircraftmen every morning in installing all the many items; work that had to be done with great care and with the accuracy of the scientific instrument maker.

In addition to the fitting of the photographic equipment, there are many other minor tasks that could not be done over-night. Even the actual manhandling of the machines out of their tents took something like twenty minutes, so that it was not till after eight o'clock that the two aircraft were lined up in the aerodrome ready to take off.

We lowered ourselves clumsily into our machines, sweltering already in the heavy suits. The engines were ticking over and running as smoothly as could be; then a few final words with the leader and Etherton, who handed up the Everest mail containing letters to be carried over the mountain, the pilots opened the throttles, the huge engines roared and with a cheer and a wave they were off on the great adventure.

Let Blacker, chief observer in the Houston-Westland, tell the story in his own words:

"A few minutes after we left the ground I had to busy myself with my routine duties. At the start of all high-altitude flights, a number of vital checks must be made, and to avoid the chance of omitting any I had compiled a list. No less than forty-six separate jobs were included, and though each one was trifling in itself none could be omitted without risk to the eventual success of the work. It was the more necessary to prepare such a list since we were inhaling oxygen the whole time, and one of its effects on the human mind seems to be to create a tendency to concentrate on the idea or task that is uppermost to the exclusion of everything else. As most of the forty-six tasks were small details, it was all the more necessary to have them down in writing so that each observer could consult his list at any particular time during the flight, and thus ensure that every piece of work had been done by the appropriate time. The flight might be ruined, for instance, by omission to remove the caps from the lenses of all the cameras, and in this dusty climate they had to be left on till the last moment.

"The leading aircraftman photographer was responsible in the programme for removing all these caps, counting them and reporting to the observer the moment before the chocks were removed from the wheels.

"Everything passed off without incident as the two great machines soared up through the haze over the brown plains, except that just for a moment the dynamo refused, as electricians put it, to build up. This is a temperamentalism to which all dynamos are liable. So, almost in a panic, I had to take off the cover of the cut-out of the electrical system and undo the screws with my thumbnail, pressing the platinum contacts together by hand. All was well, the generator behaved perfectly throughout the flight and a supply of current kept us warm from first to last.

"By the time the initial batch of these tests was completed we had been flying for some ten minutes, and for the next half-hour I had nothing to do but to sit conning over and recapitulating in my mind my duties. This part of the journey was the more humdrum because the plains and foothills below were almost lost to view owing to the thick dust-haze which had, unfortunately, on that day, chosen to rise to a phenomenal height. Gradually the dull monochrome of the brown chequerboards of the ploughed fields of Bihar fused together into a uniform carpet, and every now and then the cluster of tiny rectangular roofs of a village stood out from the scene.

"This haze almost invariably ceases at about a 5,000- or 6,000-foot level; in the present case its continuance above that height was infuriating in the last degree.

"We did not rise clear of it until actually about 19,000 feet, and so the southern ground control, which was the river confluence near Komaltar, was practically invisible to the pilot. He could not find it with sufficient accuracy, a decided misfortune, since it was the point from which the photographic survey was started.

"Nevertheless, I was just able to see an infinite tangle of the brown mountains of Nepal, seamed with black forests, and caught occasional glimpses of the swift Arun river in its gradually steepening valley as now and then I opened the hatchway of the floor and looked down through thousands of feet of purple space. We crossed the frontier of this forbidden kingdom at 13,000 feet. Then, suddenly, a little after our craft sprang clear of the haze into the wonderful translucent air of the upper heights, and away to our right an amazing view of Kangchenjunga in all its gleaming whiteness opened out against the blue.

"For a few minutes nothing else could be seen against the sky but this.

"Fumbling with the catches in my thick gloves, I threw up the cockpit roof, put my head out into the icy slipstream and there over the pulsating rocker arms of the Pegasus, showing level with us, was the naked majesty of Everest itself. Just a tiny triangle of whiteness, so white as to appear incandescent, and on its right, a hand's breadth, another tiny peak which was Makalu. For some time nothing could be seen above this purple haze but these three incredible white peaks – Everest and Makalu just to the right of the engine, and Kangchenjunga behind the right wing. It was fortunate that the wind from the westward caused the machine to lie with a drift of eighteen degrees, obliquely to our track to the mountain, and thus we had a clear view of our goal straight beneath a point on the undersurface of the upper wing, eighteen degrees from the centre line.

"Gyachungkang was masked by the engine, but soon Gaurisankar showed over the port wing.

"I was not long able to remain watching these wonderful sights, for soon the machine soared upwards, unfolding innumerable peaks to right and left and in front, all in their amazing white mantles, but scored and seared with black precipices.

"The light on the snow was a wonderful thing in itself. A quality of whiteness, as much more brilliant than the snow to which ordinary human eyes are accustomed, as that snow is more vivid than the unclothed landscape.

"Somewhat to our dismay, there streamed from the crest of Everest away towards its sister peak, Makalu, eastwards, that immense ice-plume which is the manifestation of a mighty wind raging across the summit. Lifting from the prodigious cliff face, countless particles of ice are driven over the summit with blizzard force.

"Soon, very slowly it seemed, we approached closer and closer to the big white mountains, and all my time became occupied with work on the cameras.

"Now I crouched down over the drift-sight, peering through the great concave lens, and adjusted the wires across it. I rotated them carefully and this gave me the angle of drift of eighteen degrees. I passed this to the pilot, who needed it for navigation, and then I adjusted the big automatic survey camera, turning it through the same angle in its mounting.

"I had to look to the spirit-levels, longitudinal and transverse, and to adjust the tilt of the camera in both senses, until the bubbles rested in the middle of their travel. This required delicacy and judgement as the machine swayed every now and then. The adjustment had to be made in each case just at the moment when the machine happened to be level, neither one wing tip up nor down in either direction nor pitching. I glanced at the big aluminium actuating-knob, and saw that after twenty seconds or so it turned by itself as the pilot had switched on the current into its motor. The camera was warm, the current was running through it and all seemed well.

"Now, without getting up from a prone position, I could move myself back a little on my elbows, open the hatchway in the floor and look vertically down on the amazing mountainscape, bare of trees, seamed with great glaciers and interspersed with streaks of screen and shale. This was the beginning of the range, insignificant enough to our eyes at the height we were, which rises up to the culminating 24,000-foot peak of Chamlang. Then shutting the hatchway and laboriously taking great care to keep the oxygen pipe unentangled, and myself clear of all the various electrical wires, I could stand up and look again through the top of the cockpit. I caught a glimpse over the pilot's shoulder of the brilliant red light on his dashboard, which flashed for a moment as the camera shutter operated itself.

"Up went our machine into a sky of indescribable blue, until we came to a level with the great culminating peak itself.

"Then, to my astonished eyes, northwards over the shoulder of the mountain, across the vast bare plateau of Tibet, a group of snow-clad peaks uplifted itself. I hesitated to conjecture the distance at which they lay in the heart of that almost trackless country, for by some trick of vision the summits seemed even higher than that of Mount Everest. The astonishing picture of this great mountain itself, whose plume for a moment seemed to diminish in length and, with its tremendous sullen cliffs, set off the whiteness of Makalu, was a sight which must for ever remain in one's mind.

"I had been hard at work with the cameras first exposing plates, uncapping dark slides, winding and setting the shutters to seize a series of splendid views. The scene was superb and beyond description. The visibility was extraordinary and permitted the whole range to be seen on the western horizon. It seemed that the only limit to the view along the mountain was that due to the curvature of the earth's surface. The size of the mountains stunned the senses; the stupendous scale of the scenery and the clear air confounded all estimates of size and distance. So I went on, now exposing plates, now lifting the heavy cinema camera to run off fifty feet or so of film. I crouched down again, struggling to open the hatchway, to take a photograph through the floor. Everything by now, all the metal parts of the machine, was chilled with the cold, the cold of almost interstellar space. The fastenings were stiff and the metal slides had almost seized. I struggled with them, the effort making me pant for breath, and I squeezed my mask on to my face to get all the oxygen possible. I had to pause and, suddenly, with the door half-open I became aware, almost perceptibly, of a sensation of dropping through space. The floor of the machine was falling away below us. I grasped a fuselage strut and peered through my goggles at the altimeter needle. It crept, almost swung, visibly as I looked at it in astonishment, down through a couple of thousand feet. Now I had the hatchway open and the aeroplane swooped downwards over a mighty peak of jagged triangular buttresses, which was the South Peak.

"Below us loomed an almost incomprehensible medley of ridges, ranges and spurs of black rocks, with here and there the characteristic yellowy-red of Everest showing through. We had suddenly lost two thousand feet in this great down draught of the winds, and it seemed as though we should never clear the crags of the South Peak on the way to Everest now towering in front of us. However, the alarm was short-lived, for our splendid engine took us up through the great overfall. Again we climbed; slowly, yet too quickly for one who wants to make use of every moment, our aeroplane came to the curved chisel-like summit of Everest, crossing it, so it seemed to me, just a hair's breadth over its menacing summit. The crest came up to meet me as I crouched peering through the floor, and I almost wondered whether the tail skid would strike the summit. I laboured incessantly, panting again for breath to expose plates and films, each lift of the camera being a real exertion. Every now and then my eyes swam a little and I looked at the oxygen flow-meter to find it reading its maximum. So I bethought myself of the little cork plugs I had whittled down to fit the eye apertures of the mask. Tearing off the heavy gloves and fumbling with cold fingers, I managed to stuff them in.

"Now I had worked my way up again to a standing position, with the cockpit roof fully open and its flaps fastened back. I had my head and shoulders out into the slipstream, which had become strangely bereft of its accustomed force. I was astonished for a moment till I suddenly remembered that the wind here only weighed a quarter as much as at sea-level. Now I could take photographs over the top of the machine much aided by these fortunate cork plugs. Without them, if the aviator has his head sideways in the slipstream the oxygen tends to be blown from his mask and the flow stopped before it can reach his mouth, in much the same way that a trout may be drowned by pulling him upstream against the lie of his gills.

"Thus almost, and indeed before I expected it, we swooped over the summit and a savage period of toil began. The pilot swung the machine skilfully again towards the westward into the huge wind force sweeping downwards over the crest; so great was its strength that, as the machine battled with it and struggled to climb upwards against the downfall, we seemed scarcely to make headway in spite of our 120-mile-an-hour air speed. I crammed plate-holder after plate-holder into the camera, releasing the shutter as fast as I could, to line it on one wonderful scene after another. We were now for a few moments in the very plume itself, and as we swung round fragments of ice rattled violently into the cockpit.

"We made another circuit and then another as I exposed dozens of plates and ran off my spools of film. We could not wait long over the mountain-top for the oxygen pressure gauge needle in my cockpit was moving downwards, an ominous sign. We had no very exact idea of the length of time our return journey would take with that violent wind blowing, and fuel was needed for emergencies. After a quarter of an hour or so, which seemed perhaps on the one hand like a lifetime from its amazing experiences, and yet was all too short, we turned back. Soon we saw this wonderful view with serried peaks, row upon row, in fairy beauty, surmounted by Everest and Makalu almost grotesquely outlined by the aluminum-coloured fabric of our rudder. We came back towards the terrific Arun gorges over a bewildering medley of peaks, ranges and spurs, interspersed with broad grimy glaciers littered with moraine, screen and shale. These peaks must be a great height and yet they seemed insignificant enough to our eyes.

"160 miles home passed surprisingly quickly, the journey, marred by the discovery that the second film in the ciné-camera had become frozen despite its warm jacket, and was so brittle that I could not reload. My oxygen mask, too, plugged as it was with cork stoppers, had become a solid mass of ice. Steadily we came down, gradually losing height with the throttle of the engine fairly well open to guard against the carburettor freezing. It was in another struggle that I managed to change the magazine of the survey camera and adjust it to the drift now coming from the opposite side of the aeroplane.

"Soon the semicircle of gleaming peaks faded from our sight as the straight line of purple dust-haze rose to overwhelm it."

So much for the chief observer's record. Clydesdale and he had no communication during the flight, their positions were several feet apart, there was a bulkhead between them and their telephone had not been in an accommodating mood. The pilot was therefore in a position to form his own impressions independently and we cannot do better than quote the report made:

"This morning the Indian Meteorological Officer at Purnea, Mr S. N. Gupta, whose information and advice have been of great value to the expedition, reported from balloon observations that the wind, whose velocity previously had been unsuitable, had dropped to fifty-seven miles per hour at 33,000 feet, which altitude we had decided would be the most suitable working height for photographic survey.

"Our two machines took off from Lalbalu aerodrome, near Purnea, in still air, the Houston-Westland crewed by Col. L. V. S. Blacker and myself, and the Westland-Wallace piloted by Flight-Lieutenant D.F. McIntyre with Mr S. R. Bonnett, who is aerial photographer of the Gaumont-British Film Corporation, as observer. Our direct route to the summit meant flying on a track of 342 degrees. This necessitated changing the compass course at intervals more to the west, on account of the increase of wind velocity with height, according to our weather report.

"We had relied to some extent on overcoming the difficulty of accurate compass navigation caused by this frequent change of wind speed, by the good landmarks near and along the track.

"A heavy dust-haze, rising to a considerable height, almost completely obscured the ground from Forbesganj towards the higher mountain ranges. This (as it proved later) made aerial survey work impossible. We climbed slowly at low engine revolutions to a height of 10,000 feet. By this height, the crews of both machines had tested their respective electrical heating sets, and McIntyre and I signalled to each other that everything was satisfactory.

"After thirty minutes' flying we passed over Forbesganj, our forward emergency landing-ground, forty miles from Purnea and at a height of 19,000 feet. Everest first became visible above the haze. We flew lower than our intended working height in order to make every endeavour to pass over Komaltar, close to which is the ground control from which we were to begin our survey. It proved impossible to identify any landmarks at all until approximately within twenty miles of the summit.

"At nine o'clock we passed over Chamlang at an altitude of 31,000 feet. On approaching Lhotse, the South Peak of the Everest group, the ground rises at a steep gradient, and both machines experienced a steady down current due to deflection of the west wind over the mountain, causing a loss of altitude of 1,500 feet, despite all our efforts to climb. Both aeroplanes flew over the summit of Everest at 10.5, clearing it by 500 feet.

"The wind velocity was noticeably high near the summit, but no bumps were felt by either aircraft. Fifteen minutes were spent flying in the neighbourhood of the summit, and on account of the smooth flying conditions the taking of close-range photographs was rendered possible.

"The visibility of distant high peaks was very good. The great Himalaya range could be seen extending to great distances and provided a magnificent spectacle.

"The return journey was carried out at a slightly lower altitude, so as to secure better conditions for oblique photography. The machines landed at Lalbalu at 11.25. Both pilots pay the highest tribute to the splendid performance of the engines and aircraft."

So we landed, full of happiness, with the realisation that we had been where no man had been before.

But soon our jubilation was marred by the discovery that the survey photographs were not a success. That phenomenally amazing haze of dust had obscured the lower mountains to such a degree that the strips of photographs would neither overlap nor show the ground controls near the Komaltar Ridge.

The actual fliers were tired and entranced by their experiences and by what they had seen to the point of exaltation, so it took some time for the situation to be accurately appraised. In fact it was not until the next day that we were able to pin together the hundred prints from each film. Meanwhile the letters we had carried over the mountain were despatched to HM the King, the Prince of Wales and Lady Houston.

We were thrilled beyond description by what we had seen; but of all we had been through, our passage into the heart of that plume or jet of ice particles was the most intriguing.

Before the start of this flight, we had seen the mountain on several occasions from the Moths, from 5,000 feet up, which had taken us above the ground-haze, usually only 5,000 feet from the ground level, but enough to entirely obscure the mountains from the plains.

From the Moths we had seen what previous explorers had called "the plume" of Everest and had somewhat readily taken it for granted that it was merely a cloud, of which the component particles would naturally be frozen, and similar to that one usually sees in the vicinity of high mountains.

Kangchenjunga for instance, was seldom without such a cloud wreath throughout April.

When, however, the machines went actually into it, we realised that it was something quite different to what we had conceived. Here was no drifting cloud wisp, but a prodigious jet of rushing winds flinging a veritable barrage of ice fragments for several miles to leeward of the peak.

The force of the *rafale* was indeed so great as to crack the celastroid windows of the Houston-Westland's rear cockpit.

We soon realised too, that this "plume" could not be composed of frozen matter carried over by the blizzard from the windward face, for the reason that the windward faces, that is the western sides, were practically bare, as may be seen from the photographs.

Perhaps some day science will find a solution for this riddle, the enigma of the great mountain.

We ourselves are inclined to the opinion that this phenomenon is due to the immense overfall of the winds over the crest, giving rise to what aerodynamical experts call a "burble" on the leeward side, that is, a zone of reduced pressure, which tends to draw up the air from the Tibetan side and with it great masses of old snow and fragments of ice. Perhaps, too, drops of moisture are drawn up from lower levels, frozen in the process and projected back downwind when they come into the grip of this vast maelstrom.

This is merely a tentative theory, and we can but hope that scientists will take up the mystery of this singular "plume."

We realised that our passage through it, and through the complementary "downfall" on the windward side, hard by the South Peak ("Lhotse") had been the great adventure of our flight.

Still, it was not our business to have adventures, for adventures are eschewed by all well-organised expeditions.

The Long March

Hugh Ruttledge

Ruttledge led the 1933 Everest expedition, one of the strongest teams of climbers ever to head for the highest peak; it boasted Eric Shipton, Frank Smythe and Jack Longland, among others, as well as two former Everesters, E.O. Shebbeare and Colin Crawford.

The approach march was never the least aspect of the Everest endeavour. As Ruttledge found in 1933, the march in could have human as well as natural drama.

Darjeeling is separated from Kalimpong by the great valley of the Tista River. From a height of over 7,000 feet the road drops in endless zigzags to only 600 feet above sea-level, and then climbs nearly 4,000 feet to Kalimpong. That first march across the Tista Valley is a wonderful experience. One passes through so many zones from the pines of Darjeeling to the tropical forests beneath. At Pashok we descended through Mr Lister's tea estate, where it is the custom to record on his verandah wall the heights of expedition members. Greene's many inches now hold the record. Down, endlessly down the deep descent, to the detriment of one's toes, till at last the Tista bridge came in sight, and the motor-cars waiting to take us up to Kalimpong.

As it happened, the first and second parties left Kalimpong on successive Sundays, and each had the privilege of attending Divine Service at the Kalimpong Homes, where Dr Graham has laboured so long and so successfully. The first party left on 5 March and made a sensational exit; their ponies took charge and galloped for some distance in the wrong direction.

The second party, consisting of Shebbeare, Greene, Smythe, Birnie and myself, left on 12 March in more sedate fashion, after a pleasant gathering at Dr Graham's house. The children of the Kalimpong Homes lined the road and gave us a great send-off, and everybody pressed round to wish us success. We have very happy and grateful recollections of Kalimpong.

There is a singular sense of freedom during the march to Pedong. One is really off at last, motor-roads and towns are left behind. None but Mongolian faces are seen among the travellers coming and going. Life will be nomadic for the next five or six months. As if to mark the change, after seven miles of steady ascent past alders and bamboo clumps and white dhatura hedges, we found a market-day in full swing at Algarra. A country market, definitely. Open booths, not the stereotyped shops of a town civilization. Then we descended the five miles of execràble pavé mule track to Pedong dak-bungalow with its magnificent views over the Rangli-Chu. Here Wood-Johnson and Boustead joined us, the former from his tea garden, the latter post-haste from the distant Sudan. Wood-Johnson was like a schoolboy on holiday, and no wonder. For six long years he had prepared for this day.

Pedong is on the frontier between Sikkim and British India; soon after the start of the next day's march, our passes were closely scrutinised by a stern-looking little Gurkha policeman, and we were off down the steep 3,000-foot descent to the Rangpo River. The mountain ridges of this part of the country run roughly east and west; so the road to Gangtok is a series of enormous switchbacks, most trying for the untrained. Our thirsty troop was glad to find good oranges at the next halting-place, Pakhyong. From here, on the morning of the 14th, we had a wonderful view of Kangchenjunga, amazingly clear through miles of rain-washed air. One more valley had to be crossed, through a long avenue of rubber trees, and then we climbed up to Gangtok, the capital of Sikkim.

There was plenty to do here. Lobsang Tsering received full instructions for his postal service. His headquarters would be at Gangtok, but he had first to satisfy himself about the road through the Lachen Valley and over the Sebu La; he would then join the expedition at Kampa Dzong and accompany it to the Base Camp, thus familiarising himself with the whole route, and making arrangements with the Tibetan Dzongpens for the accommodation and support of his mail riders. From Gangtok our postal despatches and telegrams would be forwarded to Calcutta. In this the expedition received valuable help from the post and telegraph masters.

Williamson is the soul of hospitality, and we spent many happy hours with him at the Residency, admiring everything: his collection of Tibetan religious banners, arms and brasswork; his lovely garden; and the Sikkimese uniforms of his official and domestic staff. Our passport was ready with the official seal of the Tibetan government.

A translation of it may interest readers:

Be it known to the Dzongpens and headmen of Phari, Kampa, Teng-kye, Shekar and Kharta districts.

In accordance with the request contained in a recent written communication received from F. Williamson, Esq., I.C.S., the excellent Political Officer in Sikkim, we have, in view of the excellent friendly relations existing between the British and Tibetan governments, permitted

Mr H. Ruttledge,
Mr F. S. Smythe,
Major Hugh Boustead,
Captain E. St J. Birnie,
Mr C. G. Crawford,
Mr P. Wyn Harris,
Mr J. L. Longland,
Mr T. A. Brocklebank,
Mr E. O. Shebbeare,
Mr E. E. Shipton,
Dr C. R. Greene,
Dr W. McLean,
Mr G. Wood-Johnson, and
Mr L. R. Wager,

a total of fourteen British Officers, with about ninety servants, to ascend the snowy mountain of Chamalung, which is in Tibetan territory, in the first month of the Water-Bird year. The expedition requires about 300 baggage animals. Please supply these immediately on demand without any let or hindrance, taking hire without sustaining any loss. You should also render them such help as is possible in the country.

On their part, the sahibs and their servants must not roam about in regions not indicated in the passport at their will. They must not shoot birds or other wild animals at the various sacred places, an act which has the effect of offending Tibetan susceptibilities. They must not beat the people or subject them to any trouble. We have addressed a written communication to this effect to the Political Officer in Sikkim. You are required to give unfailing and unswerving effect to the foregoing. Therefore all of you should take responsibility and act unerringly in the matter.

Despatched on the 27th day of the 12th month of the Water-Monkey year (21 February, 1933).

Seal of the Ministers of Tibet.

We also had the pleasure of meeting His Highness the Maharaja of Sikkim, who has shown consistent friendliness to many expeditions, and of visiting his new gompa (temple) with its elaborate frescoes and paintings.

There was a good deal of lameness among our porters at this stage. They had been served out with their new English boots at Kalimpong, after a startling process which is Shebbeare's own patent. The boots were first thrown into a bath of water and then anointed with a terrible mixture of yellow soap and castor oil. This made them beautifully supple. The only difficulty was that they were of a generous size to permit of wearing several pairs of socks above the snowline. They were therefore too loose at present on the men's feet, and galled them.

With the prospect of long abstinence, or at least shortage, in view, the porters naturally caroused a little in the Gangtok bazaar; but there was no rioting, and they turned up for work on the 16th. Our principle was to give them only very light loads on the march to the Base Camp so as to have them fit and untired for the coming strain. They carried our cameras and light kit – enough to give them some sense of responsibility, and keep them out of mischief. It was important to get to know each man individually, and to study his character; by this means only should we be able to pick out the best for the higher camps. So we spent much time trying to distinguish one flat face from another flat face. It is humiliating to find oneself more than once addressing a man by his wrong name; and even when one got it right, there was the difficulty that Pasang, for instance, shared his name with at least five other Pasangs. But they were gently tolerant; besides, they were having far greater difficulty with our own names. They solved this characteristically by observing some individual trait of appearance or disposition and applying what they considered the appropriate label. All had been given numbered identity discs at Darjeeling. Crawford, in addition, suggested numbered linen squares such as adorn the backs of rugby football players. This worked well enough, besides amusing the porters, until dirt rendered the number and its background indistinguishable. By that time, however, we were more expert at identification, even of the non-committal Mongolian face.

From Gangtok, the pleasures of which were somewhat too much for our muleteers, we turned eastwards for the march to Karponang, ten miles away at a height of 9,500 feet. Not for many months should we live at so low a level. On this march, for the first time, we saw little patches of still unmelted snow. Primulas and magnolias were beginning to bloom, and a ringouzel was seen.

At Karponang we took the precaution to open all our kerosene and petrol tins. If this is not done at intervals, leakage occurs owing to variations in atmospheric pressure. In the evening, over a roaring wood fire, the climbing plans were brought out and further discussed. Shebbeare remembered that in 1924 the porters had been seriously affected by the long carry from Camp IV, at nearly 23,000 feet, to Camp V, at 25,200 feet. We thought that this might be remedied by an improved acclimatization, and that it was important to try to make a more comfortable Camp V. Above, owing to the need for a rapid advance while the weather was favourable the climbers would inevitably get ahead of their acclimatization. Norton's experience seemed to indicate that we must try to get to the top in three days from Camp IV.

The character of the country was now changing fast, forest giving way to slopes of grass and stone, of a generally Highland appearance. At Tsomgo, 12,500 feet, the lake was still frozen over, and there was snow around the bungalow. Great banks of dark cloud away to the west made it imperative to lose no time in crossing the Natu La, 14,300 feet, next day, lest the pass should become closed to traffic. We found a letter from Crawford, saying that the advance party had left only two days before. The sight of the magnificent rock peak of Chomunko, 17,500 feet, had been too much for the thrusters, and four of them successfully tackled it. This climb had a certain value, for it brought a renewed confidence to some, while to others it brought home the advantages of unhurried training.

Greene was rapidly becoming an expert dentist. He had already relieved an officer of the Telegraph Department of a molar at Pakhyong; he now did the same for Pasang Dorje, Shebbeare's servant. Dorje was sublimely indifferent to the absence of an anæsthetic. A sup of whisky, a quick wrench, and he went happily off with his piece of damaged ivory in his hand.

All were up early on the morning of the 18th for the crossing of the Natu La into Tibet. We hoped for a view of distant Chomo Lhari, 23,997 feet, before the clouds came up. As snow lay on the hills, goggles had been served out to the porters the previous evening. It was interesting to observe the first effects on the party of an altitude of over 14,000 feet. Those who had recently been in the Himalaya were practically unaffected, while others admitted to slight headaches.

We gathered round the fluttering prayer-flags on the top of the pass, the old hands almost envying the newcomers their first look over into Tibet; a vision of snow-streaked brown and purple hillsides, of sharp-cut outlines in the thin, clear air, of Chomo Lhari, fifty miles away, yet looking quite close. A new world of limitless horizons after the confined landscape of the foothills.

There was a good deal of ice on the northern slopes of the pass, making the descent by no means easy for the mules. But

Chumbitang bungalow, five miles on, was reached without accident. Though the sun was powerful enough overhead, a cold breeze blew up from the south, and a good fire was welcome that evening. Birnie, anxious for the welfare of our ponies, paid a surprise visit to their lines after dark, to find that their porter grooms had purloined the horse-rugs for their own use. After severely reprimanding them, he repeated the visit later on. The rugs again adorned the wrong bodies. This kind of thing had to be stopped, so next morning the culprits were brought to justice in the presence of the whole porter corps. The two principal grooms were summarily dismissed and sent back to Darjeeling, while sounds of strife outside indicated that Shebbeare was dealing faithfully with his own man – the rascally old Pasang Dorje, of the tooth episode. This early and drastic action had a good effect, for the men realised that we meant business.

It was a lovely march down to Yatung in the Chumbi Valley, through Scotch firs, rose trees, and scanty juniper. The Chumbi Valley must be one of the richest in Tibet, for through it passes the trade between Lhasa and India. The men conduct the carrying business, while their families cultivate the fertile, sun-bathed soil. We saw innumerable fields under rice.

Halfway down a great mountain spur, the road passes the red-hat Khajuk monastery, in a magnificent position. The head lama is himself a good artist, and has painted some remarkable frescoes depicting phases of human life. Among the many images was one of a white-faced, white-clad female figure, which we were assured represented Mount Everest. This was good enough for the porters, who smothered the image in votive scarves. The monks were very friendly and inquisitive. As usual, they wanted to know why we took all this trouble to visit Everest. Evidently no one, not even General Bruce, has yet been able to offer an explanation that conveys any meaning to the Tibetan mind.

At Pipitang, Shebbeare and I were stopped by a bland person – fortunately Karma Paul had joined us – who said that the Dipon (Tibetan Trade Agent) would be glad if we would call. The gateway of the house was adorned with various instruments of punishments, whips, thorny canes and cords, no doubt by way of discouraging potential malefactors. The Dipon, clad in the usual Chinese dress of silk, with a turquoise pendant from his left ear, greeted us smilingly. He had a somewhat nervous, anxious demeanour, but polished manners. We noticed that, although tea was served to us, in beautiful china cups but from a Japanese tin teapot, he took none himself. He was very concerned to know how many names were on our passport. It was necessary to admit that there were only fourteen, but a telegram to Williamson soon regularized the presence of Thompson and Smijth-Windham with the expedition. Reassured on this subject, the Dipon became more human and less official. He desired to know the exact relationship of myself to General Bruce and, of course, our purpose in going to Mount Everest. Mountaineering as a sport is incomprehensible to a Tibetan administrator. Possibly he thinks that we seek gold. Shebbeare, Karma Paul and I did our imaginative best, though our explanation was received with a courteous but obviously puzzled incredulity, and we retired from the presence thinking that we must improve upon our story.

On our way through the village we came upon a man lying on rugs in a courtyard. He asked for medical treatment, and the bystanders, who included many women, explained with amusement that he was a murderer who had just received 150 lashes by way of inducing him to confess. He made no attempt to deny this statement. The Tibetans are a tough people, in every sense of the word.

Beyond the village we met Captain A. A. Russell, the British Trade Agent, who was on his way to lunch with his "opposite number". He most kindly invited Shebbeare and me to stay at the Residency in Yatung, and showed the greatest hospitality to us all. Thompson and Smijth-Windham had meanwhile arrived from Kalimpong over the Jelap La.

At Yatung there is a garrison of Indian infantry to protect the trade route, since the Lhasa expedition of 1904, we have held as far as Gyantse; and the sepoys play football and hockey on a small, comparatively level space of ground. A few rocks break the surface here and there, adding a sporting element of chance to the games. On this ground the irrepressible Wood-Johnson proposed a game of polo, three-a-side, on the expedition's ponies. He could contribute two polo-sticks and a ball. For the rest, hockey-sticks borrowed from the Jemadar of the 103rd Mahratta Infantry would serve. It was a strange game, but an undoubted success from the point of view of the local inhabitants, who turned up in force. Some skill was required to keep our ponies from galloping away up or down the mountain-side, and to hit, occasionally, a rapidly disintegrating polo-ball (the rocks were very hard) with the short hockey-sticks. Luckily the second-hand reins and saddlery held together pretty well. The only accident was due to a horrible foul by Wood-Johnson, which involved Boustead in a toss, to the delight of the crowd. It is only right to add that Birnie, our one expert, appeared to have no difficulty in competing with the conditions.

Here we again opened our fuel tins, finding that there was already some slight leakage. The new porters' bell-tents were pitched and found to be of excellent quality though lacking ventilation. This was easily remedied by slitting holes in the tops. Meanwhile part of our equipment, on Pangda Tsang's fast mules, passed through Yatung without stopping. Birnie made a forced march that night in order to stop it at Gautsa, twelve miles on.

We followed along the stony track next morning, the 21st. Our way led through thick bush under a fierce sun, past the prosperous-looking village of Galinka to Lingmatang plain, where the ponies seemed to enjoy a gallop as much as we did. Then the hills closed in upon us again. A cold wind now sprang up, a few flakes of snow fell and, by the time we reached Gautsa, 12,500 feet, and the riotous welcome of the first party, it was evident that the milder conditions of our early marches had been left behind for good.

Gautsa lies in a deep defile among wonderful mountain scenery. Previous expeditions had noted its advantages as a place in which to acclimatise before entering upon the rigours of the Phari plain. But there was a look of snow in the sky, and it would not do to get caught here by a heavy fall. On the plateau beyond, the west wind prevents the formation of heavy drifts. We of the second party were for the most part tolerably well acclimatized; those of the first had spent several days here, and a few had pitched and occupied a camp up a side valley, considerably higher. Accordingly we decided to push on.

At Gautsa all the members of the expedition assembled for the first time. Most Englishmen are afflicted by shyness when meeting strangers, but this wore off as the march proceeded, and we were a happy company in which everyone had something fresh, of experience or outlook, to contribute. Crawford began the breaking of the ice with a most interesting disquisition upon Russia, which he had visited in the previous year. Wyn Harris and Shipton could discourse on Kenya and its many problems; Boustead on the Sudan: Shebbeare on the Indian forests; while in Greene we discovered a raconteur of unrivalled capacity. In a party drawn from so many professions everyone could offer something to the general stock, and we never had a dull evening. At Gautsa I appointed Shebbeare second-in-command.

The expedition split up once more into two parties for the march to Phari. Heavy snow fell during the night of 22 March, and early next morning it was so cold that some of us put on our windproof smocks. But the sun quickly put an end to that.

The Gautsa defile is thickly wooded; this was the last forest growth we were to see for many a day. Signs of change were all around us. Yaks with their slow, swinging stride and musical bells were coming down the road, shying at the Europeans. Trees soon gave place to grass-clad slopes, and steep-sided gorges to rounded hills and U-shaped valleys. Then after a long, slow climb we emerged with startling suddenness among the rolling downs of the real Tibet, and were struggling against the blast of the west wind. Quite close now, Chomo Lhari towered upwards. A short halt at a solitary tea-house, a mile or two round the flank of a hill, and Phari appeared in the distance. Mule-trains, with their wild-eyed drivers, passed on their way southwards bearing wool for the Indian markets. The flat plain was scarred by the burrows of the little mousehares, so that careful riding was advisable. Phari looked about two miles off; it was really five.

Here, for the first time, we pitched our Whymper tents, one for each member. From now on to the Base Camp, one's home was a canvas-covered space seven feet by seven. A very good home it was too. There was plenty of room for the "Trojan" camp-bed and for one's suitcases and kitbags. It was far more comfortable than the crowded rest-houses. Crawford, however, had some reason to disagree, for that night his servant Pemba Dorje, who had become a great deal too fond of chang, the barley beer of the country, disobeyed orders about his candle-lantern and contrived to burn a large hole in the end of his tent, besides ruining a suitcase. Fortunately the conflagration was discovered early and put out. Otherwise, with the wind that was blowing, the whole camp might have gone up in flames.

Russell was passing through on his way back to Gyantse. This was an opportunity to return in some small measure his hospitality. The mess tent was pitched in the courtyard of the rest-house, the three-ply tables rigged out and the bandalasta ware arranged in all its orange glory. Tenchaddar, our principal chef, was closeted in anxious conclave, hours in advance, with Shipton the mess secretary. Our small supply of Johnnie Walker was ruthlessly tapped. The resulting banquet, however primitive in reality, had some semblance of the genuine article, and the evening passed in merriment.

Phari (Hog Hill) has often been described, and it has not changed. Here the expeditions of 1922 and 1924 had many transport difficulties, for the place is on the main trade-route to Lhasa, pack animals are in constant demand and prices are mercurial. We blessed ourselves for having arranged with Pangda Tsang to see us right through to Kampa Dzong; for, as Tibetan Government Trader, he had first call on transport, and the responsibility was his. Yaks and mules appeared from a distant and apparently blank horizon. Both Dzongpens were away; their gyembos (assistants), men with a highly developed sense of business, seeing no way to profit by this arrangement, tried to give trouble. They failed, and the expedition moved out with no delay, on 25 March.

At this period of the year, perhaps at all periods, the traveller from Phari to Kampa Dzong must expect a rough passage, for he must cross the high ground formed by the northern spurs of that great mountain Pauhunri. We received news of heavy snow on the usual route, and our transport drivers insisted on a diversion towards the north, via the easy Tang La, 15,200 feet. After this we would turn sharply to the west. We camped beyond the pass that day, at the very foot of Chomo Lhari. The wind was blowing strongly at our camping-place, Shabra Shubra, but all thought of discomfort was banished by the view of that magnificent peak. Longing glances were cast on the tremendous arête of rock and ice which rises in one unbroken sickle-like sweep almost to the summit. As darkness came on, it seemed that the cold up there must be as that of interstellar space, and we thought of General Bruce's remark that Camp IV on Mount Everest is nearly as high.

That night was a presage of the future. The wind never stopped, and thirty-six degrees of frost Fahrenheit must have tried the baggage animals and riding ponies severely. Still, the morning was fine and there was a temporary lull, which enabled us to breakfast in the open while Phil and Flo, the mess tent mules, went off westwards across the snow-sprinkled plain. We started in our turn, leaving the long line of telegraph poles which runs remorselessly on northwards to Lhasa to link the modern world with the changeless solitudes which saw the cavalry of Genghis Khan.

The lull was short-lived. The wind came screaming across from the west, right in our faces; the snow, ripped in clouds from the flat plain, made direction-keeping difficult. Partly riding, partly walking to keep warm, we ascended very gradually towards a cleft in the distant hills among which, twelve miles away, was Lunge Bur. The wind in the cleft was tremendous, and we had difficulty on a snow-covered bank, where a cornice had formed and the ponies, led by their bridles, floundered helplessly down. The porters had a hard struggle to reach camp, and we pitched most of the tents ourselves. Shebbeare, usually indifferent to discomfort, considered this the hardest march he had ever done. Already we were at a height of about 16,000 feet and pulled a good deal when hauling on guy ropes, carrying heavy stones, or hammering in tent pegs. That evening the wind dropped, and we enjoyed a wonderful view of Pauhunri. Wager and I even summoned up energy for a scramble on the great gravel banks behind the camp.

After this rough introduction to plateau travel, the next day's march to Limbu was looked forward to with some trepidation, for it involved the crossing of the Dongka La and Chago La, both over 17,000 feet high. But the luck turned and we had a most enjoyable march, feeling the altitude but little. The great Sikkimese peaks, Pauhunri, Kangchenjau and Chomiomo, climbed years ago by Dr A. M. Kellas, gleamed blindingly against a sky of deepest blue.

The party had come along very well on this day, but acclimatization has its setbacks. Next morning several members complained of lack of sleep, and of feeling the cold (thirty-one degrees of frost). However, it was an easy ten miles to Tatsang, in perfect weather. There can hardly be anything more delightful than marching across the Tibetan levels in such circumstances, before the wind gets up. On the way we found some cliffs that positively invited a halt for a sunbath on the warm rock. Longland interpreted the invitation differently. To him anything steep is a direct challenge. Selecting a moment when I was at peace with the world, he departed stealthily round a corner, and was well on the way up a vertical pitch before I could develop my parrot-cry of "Safety first on the way to Mount Everest." However, Longland shares with lizards the faculty of adhering to perfectly smooth walls.

Tatsang boasts a nunnery maintained by the offerings of yak drivers. The ladies showed much interest in us, positively liked being photographed and encouraged a visit to their gompa. Theirs must be a hard life, for their supporters are few and poor themselves, and the surrounding soil does not look as if it made much of a return to labour. The wind here blew suffocating clouds of dust and sand through the camp. Already that distressing complaint of the Tibetan plateau, sore throat, was making its appearance. Many of us had, long ago, given up smoking; and we strove with nasal douches and throat gargles to keep the enemy at bay. Some escaped altogether, but the majority carried their sore throats with them to Mount Everest, and suffered a good deal.

Kampa Dzong was reached on the 29th, after a memorable march. The way led for nine miles up a gently ascending valley to a pass of about 17,000 feet. A herd of gazelle and a single kyang (wild ass) kept on our flank, like the scouts of an army. Longland, after some complicated manoeuvres, drove them across our front at very close range. They moved with that easy, effortless stride that conceals speed. Arrived on the pass, Shipton, Smythe, Wyn Harris and I thought we might test our acclimatization, and our theory of slow but continuous and rhythmical upward movement, by ascending a hill on our left about 1,000 feet higher. Brocklebank, Wood-Johnson, Longland and Wager followed. All found themselves going well, provided they did not hurry. Our reward was one of the grandest views imaginable, and our first sight of Mount Everest, nearly a hundred miles away. At our feet lay the plain of the Yaru river. Beyond it, the glittering northern wall of the Himalaya. The eye ranged over Pauhunri, Kangchenjunga and Chomiomo on the east; then Siniolchu, Kangchenjunga (with the Bavarians' ridge in full view), Jonsong Peak and innumerable unnamed summits; and, far away in the west, Makalu and a great snowy triangle which could only be Mount Everest. The snow had that yellow look that distance alone can give.

It was a glorious morning. The wind was still asleep, and we basked for an hour in the sun, one or other rising at intervals to use camera or telescope. There was little conversation, for a scene like this is best gazed upon in silence. Each, perhaps, was thinking of what his part might be in the battle for that distant summit. Reluctantly we turned to descend the easy scree slopes to the pass, on which poor Kellas died in 1921. Eight miles down, the steep-sided valley ended in a gorge that Gustave Doré would have loved to depict; and suddenly, round an abrupt corner, rose the soaring battlements of Kampa Dzong.

Most travellers to Mount Everest have happy memories of Kampa Dzong. Here they descend to 14,000 feet from the cold uplands of the Dongka La. The place is a perfect little suntrap and besides has architectural beauty of the highest order. Those old Tibetan builders had an eye for line and for proportion. The rounded towers, one above the other and connected by steeply mounting walls, lead up to the square-cut citadel with its sloping sides. The whole edifice, springing from precipitous rock, is a setting for a fairy story.

The Dzongpen of this place was away at Lhasa, being invested with the high title of Dzaza (General). His representative, the Nyapala, received us with great friendliness and procured our fresh transport without much delay. These Tibetan officials always turn out in beautiful costumes of Chinese silk, of purple, blue or claret, usually surmounted by a fur-edged hat with the official button on the top. The leader of a Mount Everest expedition has, of course, no official status. Not for him the cocked hat and gold-laced uniform of the political officer. Yet he must conduct negotiations clad in such a way as to "eat no shame", as they say in the East. The usual mufti of the West seems dull and unimpressive in contrast with the gorgeous silks of China. Accordingly we took thought, of which the outcome was, to say the least of it, singular. The expedition's ambassador received his visitor in the mess tent, arrayed in a Tibetan gown of watered silk lined with sheepskin with a red girdle, the whole surmounted by an opera-hat. The effect was all that could be desired. Here obviously was a man of standing in his own country. Deep called unto deep in the most friendly manner, with mutual respect; and our negotiations were completely successful. It should be added that the opera-hat had been brought along in no spirit of vanity. Its destination was intended to be the head of that porter who should do best on the mountain. The men gazed upon it with admiration, and were fascinated by its mechanism.

At Kampa Dzong we found our advance stores, all neatly stacked and guarded by the sirdar Nursang. To assist him, he had acquired a Tibetan mastiff, to whom he gave the astounding name of Police-ie. One-eyed and suspicious, Police-ie began by soundly biting Wood-Johnson, who approached the store-dump on his lawful occasions but without the formality of an introduction. The sacrifice was sufficient. Police-ie was reassured, and thereafter bit none but her own countrymen, of whom she spared neither sex nor age.

Though our friend the Nyapala was doing his best, the new transport did not turn up for four days; but there was plenty to do. Lobsang Tsering arrived direct from Gangtok with the post, reporting that the Sebu La was now open to traffic; despatches had to be written, stores overhauled. Longland, our quartermaster, worked overtime, assisted by relays of volunteers. The wireless officers assembled their equipment, hoping that we should be able to listen in on 1 April, and hear the result of the Boat Race. They were unsuccessful.

We explored the Dzong (fort) by invitation of the Nyapala. The way lies up a zigzag path under the southern precipice, past an enormous chorten (tomb), and one enters the fort up very steep steps through a wooden door with carved side-posts and lintel. On one side are prayer-wheels some three feet high, easily turned by a movement of the hand. The lower storey is occupied by a small carpet or rug manufactory, and access to the next is obtained by means of insecure-looking, slippery wooden ladders. It is just as well to let one's host go first, as the whole place is ill-lit and on each floor there is a savage mastiff, which is hastily grabbed by the attendants, often only just in time. After stumbling over many things and bumping one's head in odd corners, one emerges thankfully into brilliant sunshine on the roof, whence there is a magnificent view of the surrounding country. The sheer walls, mounting from the very edge of the precipice, give a tremendous impression of depth below. We are told that condemned criminals used to be hurled from this place.

Kellas's grave was next visited. The covering stone had been thrown down. We hauled a great slab into place, and carved on it a fresh inscription, with the assistance of some monks from the gompa on the hillside above, who, we hoped, might take some interest in its preservation. When all was done, Shebbeare, the oldest of us, read the 121st Psalm. Kellas's grave looks out over the plain to the great mountains that he climbed, and is in sight of Mount Everest.

The only drawback to Kampa Dzong was the dust, which added to the growing tale of sore throats. There was no escape once the wind had got up, at about eleven o'clock every morning. The dust penetrated everywhere, making our food and drink gritty and our throats dry. Several people had recourse to the Matthews respirator, and some heroic spirits even contrived to sleep with it on; but the effort of inspiration through the copper gauze, slight though it was, produced a feeling of claustrophobia that was too much for others.

On 2 April the new and very lively yak transport was loaded up, and we did the eighteen-mile march to Lingga, past Mende and its willow trees, and over the Yaru River. It was a day of terrible wind and dust. Lingga is surrounded by ponds and marshes, where the bar-headed goose and Brahminy duck hold high revel.

Thence to Tengkye Dzong, halfway from Darjeeling to Everest, where transport had again to be changed. This was a life of contrasts. Yesterday we had marched bent forward against the wind, muffled up to the ears and cursing the dust. Today the wind tarried and the sun shone brightly. Larks sprang into the sky before us in full song, or ran cheerfully about among the little dunes. Lizards basked in the warmth, and we followed their example whenever the sandy margin of a pool or some alluring outcrop of rocks suggested a halt. There was no need for hurry, as the distance was short and the mess tent awaited our convenience, a tiny green speck against the red hills in the distance.

Tengkye Dzong is a delightful spot at the mouth of a wide valley, with hamlets and gompas on the hillsides. The Dzong overlooks a little lake – a perfect setting. The resident Dzongpen is an amusing character: a native of Lhasa who would be perfectly at home in Paris, for he is a born boulevardier. Our arrival was a perfect godsend to this exile. He called at once, sampled some sloe gin with emphatic approval, asked innumerable questions and promised every assistance, including the use of his own mules. He administers, according to his own admission, an unruly and rapacious district; and he advised us to avoid the old route via Gyangkar Nangpa and go by a parallel route to the north, over the Bahman Dopté pass. Then he asked Shebbeare, Greene, Wood-Johnson and me to tea for next day, and tactfully left us to our work, waiving the formality of a return official visit.

In the evening several of us walked over to a charming willow grove about half a mile away, and found it full of birds – magpies, linnets, finches, a hoopoe and many others. It is a never-ending joy to find the birds of Tibet so tame; the place is a paradise for the ornithologist.

That acclimatization was improving was shown pretty

clearly here. Tengkye boasts level ground, and the porters started some energetic football, of which a few, including Lhakpa Chedi, knew the rudiments. This attracted every Tibetan man, woman and child from miles round, and our camp became an animated and most amusing scene. Rules, of course, were thrown overboard; numbers were immaterial. The great thing was to go for the ball, and propel it in any direction by feet, hand, or face. The Tibetans, to whom an altitude of 15,000 feet was as sea-level to us, were indefatigable. The seething mass, madly striving after an invisible ball, surged across the ground, and we watched, helpless with laughter, though tents might fall and guy ropes suffer.

Then Boustead gave a lesson in boxing, which was an instant draw. In no time our six sets of gloves adorned as many grimy pairs of hands, the owners of which busily endeavoured to exterminate anybody within reach, while the crowd roared in ecstasy. Two Tibetan children, perhaps six years old, fought a spirited and interminable round which fairly brought the house down, and were rewarded with many sweets.

A great afternoon's sport ended with an exhibition of pole-jumping by Longland, using a long bamboo. This took on at once, and as neither Sherpa nor Tibetan is content with the rôle of passive spectator, some very remarkable jumping, or rather falling, was observed. But these men are unkillable. Altogether a good day.

The tea-party in the Dzong was a great success, both socially and from the point of view of business. It was soon clear that the word tea was merely a "façon de parler," and that we were in for something much more strenuous. The friendly Dzongpen introduced us to his wife, a lady of much character, with a large black patch on her nose. The patch disappeared later, presumably because our hostess was reassured on the subject of the evil eye. A present of bandalasta ware and a needle-case, and Wood-Johnson's insinuating ways, secured her approval, and things went with a swing. Course succeeded course, rice, macaroni, mutton, wheaten biscuits. Tea was soon discarded in favour of chang. The moment you had taken a sip, your cup was filled again to the brim, and no excuses were accepted. Karma Paul was in his element, while Lewa and other sardars in their best bib and tucker sat in a solemn row, attended to by the domestic staff. Then two ladies were introduced, whose duty it is to dance and sing before distinguished strangers. Their voices were quite melodious, their dancing a rather stiff sort of shuffle and stamp. The dignity of the proceedings was only slightly disturbed by Shebbeare's judgement of Paris.

Our host was becoming mellow and benevolent. English travellers did not pass every day. He felt that he was appreciated. He remembered, as a boy, seeing Sir Francis Younghusband at Gyantse, where his father was Dzongpen. He would see that his guests were fairly treated. The headman of Gyangkar Nangpa was sent for and was obviously astonished to receive a stern and uncompromising order to supply transport, along a route at some distance from his village, at reasonable rates. When at last we were permitted to go, lighted through the darkness by torches, we felt that we had in the Dzongpen of Tengkye a sure ally. In the courtyard of his house he showed us his magnificent mules, with their earringed, long-haired, savage-looking drivers.

Perhaps we spoiled the Tengkye people with too much bread and games; for when work was needed, to get off on the morning of 5 April, a marked lassitude was apparent. But the Dzongpen came down himself and worked like a Trojan, allotting loads, even lifting them with his own hands, and cuffing recalcitrants. We said goodbye to him with sincere regret, as the long train of animals and men wound away up the valley for the eighteen-mile march to Khengu over the high Bahman Dopté pass. The dust at Khengu was appalling, and we were glad to move on to the meadows of Dochen, where the new Gyangkar Nangpa transport was to meet us. From here we could see the peak of Shankar-ri, 20,000 feet high, on which an attempt was made in 1922. It was taboo this time.

News came in, after our arrival, that Karma Paul's and Lobsang Tsering's ponies had both fallen. Karma Paul broke his little finger and Lobsang Tsering his collarbone. The one was soon dealt with, but the other nearly ended in tragedy. Greene and McLean went back and brought Lobsang Tsering in. It was decided to give him an anæsthetic and set the bone at once. Greene is an expert anæsthetist, and no difficulty was expected. But anæsthetics, it seems, can play queer tricks at over 14,000 feet. Lobsang went to sleep, and his collarbone was quickly set by McLean; but then he did not come to, and the doctors had to work hard with coramine and artificial respiration until the heart's beat was resumed, and a very green and shaky Lobsang returned to consciousness. Arrangements were made for him to stay several days with a local Tibetan family, after which he was to follow us to the Base Camp. He was very plucky over the whole business.

The Gyangkar Nangpa men, perhaps really impressed by the lecture given to their headman, brought the animals in good time – yaks and donkeys. But loading up the transport on the morning of the 7th was endlessly prolonged, and the donkeys seemed to be getting more than their fair share. It is amazing that these little creatures, with their pipe-stem legs, can carry 160 lb, the same as a yak. If given more than that they simply lie down, and the transport officer has to reallot loads, with the active non-cooperation of the drivers.

The ford at the crossing of the Chiblung-Chu caused both amusement and profanity; for the water was fairly high and everybody wanted to know if his own particular bedding was getting soaked, a question mainly of the size of his baggage animal. If there is a sandbank in the middle of a river, yaks love to assemble on it and defy the execrations of their drivers on the near bank. They will stay there in placid obstinacy until dislodged by some accurate stone-throwing.

We crossed the river again, to camp at Jikyop, by means of an extraordinary sort of stone pier, and spent some unpleasant hours among wind-driven sand. About this time various members again took to slow training walks up any convenient hill behind camp, going up perhaps two thousand feet or so, but always keeping a speed well within their powers. Having ridden a considerable portion of the day's march, they were fresh for a moderate climb in the afternoon. Memory lingers over these occasions when parties of two or three, informally arranged, would select each their own ridge and move off without haste, content to go so far as inclination or condition prompted and sure of some unforgettable picture of plain and hill and distant ice-clad peak. The level rays of the setting sun would pick out beauties unseen under the glare of midday, while harsh outline and lack of atmosphere were forgotten in contemplation of the ever newly revealed loveliness of colour. Then would come the effortless descent towards those little green tents far below that represented home; a few minutes perhaps with the porters collected round their cooking-pots and obviously enjoying themselves; and a return to the cheerful story and argument of the mess tent. Happy days, when everyone was strong and unstrained, and hope ran high.

The next two marches, to Trangso-Chumbab and Kyishong, were long and trying. The west wind seemed to be gathering strength, and to blow all day and most of the night, and the dust was everywhere. The transport officers had a particularly hard time getting into Kyishong through a full gale, which of course took a great deal out of the baggage animals. We searched in vain for a good camping site, for the village was aggressively pungent. But shelter from the wind could only be found behind a wall there. We just had to make the best of it and pray for the morn.

It was a relief when we started on the last stage to Shekar Dzong, which turned out to be actually shorter than the map indicated. Usually it had seemed to be the other way. The country about here was not inaptly compared by Shebbeare to the mountains of the moon. In every direction were isolated stony hills, of conical shape and very dry. Mounting a low pass, a mile or two beyond Kyishong, we looked across a wonderful landscape of plain and hill to the single pyramidal rock on which Shekar Dzong stands. Had the ancient Western geographers known of this place, it would certainly have been included among the wonders of the world. The name, which means "white glass", is sufficiently descriptive. The town of white houses is at the foot of the rock; halfway up, perched on steep ledges and built with cunning artistry, are the gleaming walls of two great monasteries; above them the Dzong, and on the highest pinnacle, about a thousand feet above the plain, a sort of lookout post. Even more than Kampa, it is a setting for a fairy story, a place of enchantment.

To Greene's just indignation, we camped close to the town,

on exposed ground swept by the evil dust-laden wind. A much better site should have been chosen, a mile away.

Our pleasure in seeing Shekar Dzong was spoilt by two things, the presence of a smallpox epidemic and the discovery that some of our equipment and stores had been looted on the way. The former was not really serious, since the porters as well as ourselves had been vaccinated before starting. The latter was a calamity. All hands had to be turned on to make a full inventory, the Dzongpen informed and a guard set – rather a case of locking the stable door after the horse had been stolen, though we had still five marches to go. The inventory disclosed the alarming fact that several pairs of porters' high-altitude boots, a Meade tent and sundry windproof smocks and pairs of warm socks were missing, and that many ration boxes had been opened and their contents rifled with a skill which indicated that the thief knew exactly what he wanted. The Dzongpen called soon after this work had begun. He was friendly and anxious to do his best to help us, and began by arresting a number of our transport drivers, who were under strong suspicion. According to Tibetan (and our own medieval) custom, he flogged them next day to make them confess, but without result. The stolen things were never traced, nor the culprits discovered. Shebbeare had proposed that he and Crawford should go on ahead to Rongbuk and begin making the route up the glacier. This programme fell through owing to the need for better supervision of the transport personnel and prevention of further losses.

Smallpox was at this time exacting a heavy toll from the neighbourhood. Apparently a knowledge of the benefits to be derived from vaccination had penetrated to this part of Tibet, and the Dzongpen wanted lymph. There was none in our medical stores, so I gave him a message for the British Trade Agent at Gyantse, asking for a supply.

The Shekar district is large and important, and includes the Rongbuk Valley and Mount Everest. It was particularly advisable to secure the goodwill of this Dzongpen, in order to recruit Tibetan porters for work at the glacier camps and organize supplies of fuel. Negotiations were opened at the first interview, with most satisfactory results. The Dzongpen placed at our disposal his Chonzay (steward), who had worked for other expeditions, and gave us excellent transport at fair rates. He was a nervous-looking, bent-backed little man, by no means impressive at first sight. But he was an honourable gentleman, and a good friend to us.

A pleasant interlude between the hours of stocktaking and inquisition was the pitching of the new arctic tents. They were pronounced to be a success, a sound provision against the blizzards of the East Rongbuk Glacier. Then it occurred to someone that a general hair-cutting might improve our appearance. Wyn Harris proved our most efficient barber, but very ill-advisedly submitted himself to Crawford's hands when his turn came. The resultant coiffure nearly caused a riot.

We visited the great monasteries, where the art of selling curios has, for some reason unknown, reached a high state of development. There are no trippers in Tibet. The lamas had set out a regular little shop in a room, and pushed their wares – banners, cups, spoons, carvings, charm-boxes – with the skill of professional pedlars. They were very good-tempered, and thoroughly enjoyed argument with both climbers and porters. The architecture of their monasteries is a delight to the eye; austere and perfect in line. At every point one saw unexpected beauties – possibly to some extent fortuitous and due to the accident of rock-formation, but with evidence of a definite artistic perception. We were admitted to one of the services, and then taken to see, in a very dim religious light, a gigantic image of the Buddha and some highly realistic busts of departed abbots, including the last incumbent, who so impressed the 1921 expedition. Judged from the photograph taken at that time, the likeness was excellent.

Emerging through the highest roofs, several of us climbed steeply up through the ruined Dzong to the lookout post, which seemed as if it might come crashing down at any moment. We brought a telescope, for it was known that Mount Everest, some fifty miles away, could be seen from here. Unfortunately there was now bad weather to the south, but we caught an occasional glimpse of the north-east arête and the North Ridge; a good deal more impressive than some had expected to find them.

The porters of course knew that Shekar was the last place of even moderate size that they would see before entering the wilderness of rock and ice. They broke out a little; especially the bootmaker, who got extremely drunk and was well hammered in the town. That did not matter, but our sleep also was interfered with in camp, and Birnie had to relieve me in successive suppressions of the now loquacious Lhakpa Chedi.

Our departure, on 13 April, was a dreadfully protracted affair. There seemed to be plenty of yaks and donkeys about, and the little Dzongpen, with all his staff, looked very busy; but his head clerk, and the lamas, still as anxious for barter as ever, delayed matters, and the last load did not leave for Pangle till noon. We paid a last ceremonial visit to the Dzongpen, photographed him at his own request in his full regalia and parted from him on the best of terms. He wrote to us from time to time while we were on the mountain, cordially inviting a return visit.

The last load had left Shekar, it is true; but our difficulties were not yet at an end. The first part of this march lay through a very narrow defile, where box after box was scraped off the donkeys' backs, till we seemed to be on the track of a defeated and retreating army. We had to work pretty hard, some retrieving the donkeys, which had taken advantage of the position, others helping the profane drivers to tie the loads on again.

Crossing the Phung Chu by an unusually good bridge, we were just in time to receive the full benefit of a furious gale of sleet, which lashed us unmercifully all the way to the snow-covered camping-ground of Pangle. It mattered little; the porters were in splendid form, now that the temptations of the cities were behind them.

We were now marching due south straight for Mount Everest. In front rose the Pang La, about 17,000 feet high, from which we hoped on the morrow to have a good view. To that end the big telescope was unpacked and assembled as quickly as frozen fingers would permit. An early start would have to be made, for there was a good deal of new snow about.

We were toiling up the slopes to the pass by 6 a.m. next day, but never got the view, clouds hiding everything to the south; so we descended without delay to that charming spot,

Tashidzom. The valley here may be said to be an eastern continuation of the Rongbuk gorge. Most of the water in the river flowing past had issued from the Rongbuk Glacier. Tashidzom boasts a delightful grove of willow trees, carefully maintained and well watered, standing among green meadows where we camped. The "Squire" of the place has obligations towards the Rongbuk monastery, which he supplies with wood and stores. He undertook to look after our ponies, which would be sent down the moment we reached Rongbuk; here, even at this early date, a certain amount of grazing could be had, and the large Tibetan pulse. Birnie, Shebbeare and I had a look at the old gentleman's own stables, and came to the conclusion that the ponies would do very well there, better than at Chö-Dzong, which is farther up the valley.

There remained only three more marches to the Base Camp. Mount Everest could not be seen, but we felt that it was very close, and that we were entering the battle-zone. During this long period of marching a close eye had been kept upon condition and form. So far we had been lucky, for there had not as yet been a single case of serious illness – just minor ailments such as sore throat and slight stomach troubles. None of the dreaded dysentery which saps a man's strength and is so hard to throw off.

Form was a different matter. No amount of organization or thought will make a party acclimatize at a uniform rate. Our experience conformed in many respects to that of 1924. Those who had been recently in the Himalaya – Smythe, Greene, Birnie, Shipton, Wood-Johnson and I – were sufficiently acclimatized to feel no distress on the passes. Boustead, of lean and active build, and Wyn Harris, who had been to over 17,000 feet in Kenya, were shaping well. Wager, toughened by two seasons in Greenland, showed no particular signs of wear and tear. Crawford, though he had kept himself in training, both in the Alps and in the Canadian Rockies, had not been in the Himalaya since 1922, and was not, at this stage, at his best. Longland and Brocklebank also gave cause for anxiety; they were clearly feeling the altitude. McLean was difficult to gauge, as he was riding most of his marches, but he seemed fit. On the other hand, Shebbeare, though tough as always, was walking too much, we thought, and carrying too heavy a rucksack, and he looked a little fine-drawn.

As for the porters, one had only to go round the camp of an evening to see that there was not much the matter with them. Away from the worries of civilization, their pay and maintenance secure for months ahead, they were a happy, carefree crowd. Tomorrow could look after itself. For all that, they were proud to be members of the expedition, and anxious to prove themselves mountaineers. The Sherpa does not come to Everest merely for what he can get out of it. He could earn as much money elsewhere. If you asked him why he came, he might prevaricate, or pass it off with an embarrassed laugh. Pride of achievement, or carrying through a dangerous job, or sheer love of the great mountains – and he now knows all about Everest's pride of place – or escape from the monotony of civilization? He may not be able to explain, or may not wish to, but he is of nomad stock. He knows, too, that the Englishmen who have come from so far have exactly the same feeling as himself. That is why he gets on so well with them from the very start, even with those who can hardly speak one word of his language. He understands them without the need of speech. How else can you explain his readiness to risk his life in company with men whom he has never seen before, and may never see again?

The composition of parties for work on the mountain was, of design, kept open till a late hour. This involved a certain amount of strain on individuals, but it would have been, for instance, unwise to tell A and B, at Kalimpong, "You two will climb together"; or to tell C and D, "You two will establish Camp IV." But here, at Tashidzom, some estimate of individual progress was possible, and a provisional allocation of duties could be made. Smythe and Shipton were evidently in splendid form. They had climbed together on Kamet, and knew each other's capacity, speed and rhythm. They became our "best bet" for the summit. Again, Wager and Longland had climbed much together. Wager's special qualities were steadiness, sound mountaineering methods and judgement; Longland's, a strong instinct for attack and a splendid rock-climbing technique. If Longland could acclimatize well during the next three weeks, this should make a very strong climbing party. Wyn Harris and Greene should also do well in double harness. Both were experienced mountaineers, and possessed the right temperament for the game. Others expected to go high were Wood-Johnson, Birnie and Boustead. They had Himalayan experience, but had never climbed together. Whether they took part in the final assaults or not, there was plenty of work for them: the establishment of the higher camps, for instance. At least one climber would be needed to escort the porters down if Camp VI were carried nearer to the summit than before, for on this part of the mountain it is unsafe to let them go alone. Meanwhile, Wood-Johnson could carry on as second transport officer; and Birnie made the welfare of the porters and their selection for the hardest work his special care.

A decision about Crawford and Brocklebank could wait on events. Both were thought to be slow acclimatizers. Crawford was the most experienced mountaineer of us all, spoke Nepali well, was liked by the porters and was the only man in the party with knowledge of the North Col. Brocklebank, the youngest, should be brought along slowly, and not allowed to get ahead of his acclimatization. His medical report had been a particularly good one, and he had given many proofs of staying power. A strong reserve was needed, in case of a breakdown or casualties among the first parties. His one idea was to be of service, and he never departed from it, now or later.

McLean's duties were expected to be primarily medical. He would be responsible for the health of the Base Camp and the glacier camps while Greene was on the mountain; but he might be called upon as a climber, should need arise.

Content with our tactical plan of assault, and with the provisional arrangement of parties, we marched up the wide valley to Chö-Dzong on 15 April. Norton had warned me to look out on the way for a sight of the mountain up a valley to the south, but there were heavy clouds in that direction during the march, so we crossed the boulder-strewn bed of the river to our very exposed campsite without delay. That evening, several of us climbed up the hill to the north, carrying the naval telescope, and were rewarded by a magnificent view of

Mount Everest now hardly more than twenty miles away as the crow flies. In spite of the recent cloudy weather, the North Face carried little snow, and with the telescope we could see, in some detail, the ledges along which Norton and Somervell had traversed and the North-East Arête which still held Mallory's and Irvine's secret. One thing was obvious: the second step was a formidable obstacle. Every mountaineer knows that you cannot judge rock accurately until you actually, as the late Captain Farrar used to say, "rub your nose on it." Nevertheless, the angle of the second step was certainly very severe; the step rose more than a hundred feet above the North-East Arête, overhanging slightly towards the top. Careful examination revealed signs of a fault in the rock about half-way up, which might permit of a turning movement on the right, and a steep snow slope seemed to lead up to an equivalent height on the other side. If this snow were in good condition, it might provide a means of avoiding the rock altogether and of reaching the arête again beyond, and to the west of, the second step; after this the route to the summit would lie well above the worst part of the North Face.

Norton's route, under the first and second steps and across the Great Couloir east of the final pyramid, looked remarkably difficult; but we were looking at it frontally and thus could not estimate the true angle. The final pyramid, though by no means easy, seemed practicable. The problem was to reach it across the frightful slabs of the couloir walls.

Darkness began to fall as long clouds drifted across the summit. We descended to camp in a mood of qualified optimism. At least we had been able, for the first time, to see for ourselves, to form a judgement of our own, and from a distance which allowed of a fairly true perspective. Henceforward we should be too much under the mountain to estimate our difficulties with any accuracy.

Excitement promoted early rising on the 16th. Only fourteen miles to Rongbuk monastery. Soon we were passing along the shelves of what looked like gigantic moraines but which Wager defined as river terraces. The valley narrowed as the hills closed in; and a powerful south wind drove into our faces. Grass disappeared. Boulder and scree, snow, blue ice and precipice would be our scenery for the next three months. As we turned into the Rongbuk valley proper, with its appearance of complete desolation, Tibetan men and women met us in considerable numbers. They were descending from worship or from the performance of more mundane duties at the Rongbuk monastery. The approach was dramatic. At one moment we were walking up the rough, snow-covered track, in a valley which seemed to lead to nowhere in particular. At the next, a last corner was turned and there was the monastery, with its great chorten; beyond, the wind-torn but still impenetrable mists behind which, we knew, was Mount Everest.

Rongbuk must be one of the highest permanently inhabited places in the world. It stands at well over 16,000 feet and is occupied, summer and winter, by more than 300 monks, whose maintenance must seriously tax the resources of the surrounding country. Still farther up the valley, along the steep-sided moraine shelves from which the place obtains its name, are a nunnery and some primitive cells where hermits pass a life of meditation in circumstances of hardship which baffle the imagination. It is sacred ground, and tradition has it that animals and birds have found sanctuary here for centuries past.

The head lama of the Rongbuk monastery is a man of great influence and reputation; and his blessing is eagerly sought, not only by the Tibetans of this region, but also by the Sherpas of Sola Khombu, four marches away over the Nangpa La, in Nepal. It was important to secure this for our men. Karma Paul, radiating Buddhistic fervour, hastened off to crave audience, while we pitched camp in a howling wind which blew straight off the snows. The expedition arrived in good health, but that wind found us out. In the afternoon the mists were driven off, and Mount Everest, sixteen miles away, stood forth in compelling majesty. Climbers and porters crowded round the big telescope, heedless of the gale. The result was a number of chills, some of which were to have more serious results, but for the moment all was animation and delight. Karma Paul returned full of cheer. He had arranged everything, and the great lama would bless the expedition in the morning. We settled down with the feeling that all was well and the omens propitious. The ponies were taken away down to Tashidzom for their well-earned rest. The transport animals would see us right through to the Base Camp.

Our moment of arrival was fortunate. Till recently the old lama had been in retreat, engaged in meditation and therefore unapproachable. He was now free again and, though sorrowing for the death of a beloved sister, was prepared to bless the men whom a strange madness had brought for the fourth time to Mount Everest. The porters were paraded in their best, and each man was given a rupee for an offering. Armed with a despatch-case, bandalasta ware, kincob brocade and scarves, we set off in close order for the monastery. The lama awaited us upstairs, in a curious little shed with real glass windows. Glass is very rarely seen in Tibetan houses. He has a most attractive smile, and an air of great authority. One had only to observe the demeanour of his monks to realize that here was a man completely master in his own house. He asked if there were any members of previous expeditions, so Crawford and Shebbeare were introduced. Then he wanted to know – they always do – if I were related to General Bruce; also my age and status. He told me to be very careful and to allow no killing of animals or birds in the Rongbuk Valley, and to treat his people well. Then he promised to pray for us.

After this, presents were exchanged, his consisting of various foods, and the blessing ceremony began. Each of us advanced in turn, put his head in at a glass window and was touched with the dorje and blessed. The old gentleman asked us Europeans to recite the mystic words "*Om mani padme hum*" (Oh, the jewel in the lotus), and chuckled with delight when Smythe's pronunciation failed him. We fell completely under his charm. Then followed Karma Paul, the Gurkha NCOs, the sardars and porters. It was an impressive little ceremony, perhaps less formal than the blessing at Darjeeling, but sincere and evidently regarded as a great privilege by men already in the shadow of danger and privation. Afterwards the lama consented pleasantly to come out into the open and be photographed. For all his dignity, he is very human and a good friend.

The expedition now set out in high spirits for the last four miles to the Base Camp. The weather was perfect. Clambering over the debris of the old moraines, past the nunnery and the hermits' cells, we crossed the ice of a frozen lake and camped at the foot of a terminal moraine, the same place as had been selected by our predecessors. Perhaps a mile to the south was the snout of the main Rongbuk glacier; above, on the left, the shelf along which we must proceed to Camp I, in the side valley to the east. The mountain, though still twelve miles away, looked enormous, completely dwarfing the North Peak, which is 24,730 feet high.

By this time the men were well drilled in their duties. After a quick survey of the ground, they had the tents up like magic, the mess tent and Whympers for the climbers, bell-tents and Meades for the rest. Ten-cheddar spread a great black yurt for his kitchen and stacked the firewood and yak-dung within easy reach, while the Tibetans built sangars (stone shelters). The boxes were quickly arranged in ordered rows. Then the baggage animals and drivers, with the unsolicited assistance of Police-ie, were off down the valley, leaving us to ourselves. It was Easter Monday, 17 April. The long march was over.

High Life

Eric Shipton

Shipton's name is almost as strongly associated with Everest as that of Mallory. Born in 1907, Shipton participated in no fewer than five Everest expeditions: those of 1933, 1935, 1936, 1938 and 1951. In this extract from his memoir Upon That Mountain, *Shipton recounts life at high altitude on the 1933 expedition.*

The work of carrying loads up from the Base Camp began on 19 April and on 2 May we established and occupied Camp III in the upper basin of the East Rongbuk Glacier at a height of 21,000 feet. We were now in full view of the North Col. At last we were confronted with a real mountaineering proposition, which would require some concentration of energy and skill. The prospect was a good one. Pleasant and intensely interesting though the journey had been, most of us I imagine had been keyed up by the anticipation of the toughest climbing of our lives. So far it had all been make-believe, and it was difficult to avoid the question, "When are we going to be called upon to do a job of work; when will we have something really to bite on?"

The eastern slopes of the North Col are composed of steep broken glacier and rise about 1,500 feet from the level ice below to the crest of the col. As the glacier is moving slowly downwards the slopes present a different appearance from year to year. Our task then was to find a way up them, to make a ladder of large safe steps and to fix ropes to serve as hand-rails over all the difficult sections, so that it would be possible for laden porters to pass up and down with ease and safety.

We started the work almost at once. It was about an hour's

walk from Camp II to the foot of the steep slopes below the
col. The ice of the upper basin had been swept clear of snow
by the wind. It was rather like walking on an ice-skating rink
and required some little practice to avoid sitting down heavily.
But fortunately the slopes above were composed of hard snow,
for it would have been a tremendously laborious task to cut
steps all the way up in hard ice, and also very difficult to fix the
ropes. As it was it was very hard work. Even at that height any
physical exertion left one gasping for breath. We took turns of
about twenty minutes each at cutting the steps. Even that
seemed an eternity and it was a great relief to be told that the
time was up. We climbed about a third of the way up to the col
on the first day.

There followed days of storm and wind, which rendered
work impossible. Below, we had experienced fairly severe
conditions, but Camp II was much more exposed to the
weather, which deteriorated a good deal during the fortnight
after our arrival there. I gathered from the Sherpas who had
been with the 1924 expedition that the conditions were very
similar to those experienced in that year. But we had an
additional item of equipment, which added enormously to our
comfort and rendered us impervious to the buffeting of the
wind. This was a large, double-skinned, dome-shaped tent of a
type that had been used by Watkins in the Arctic. It had a
circular floor about fifteen feet in diameter, and was built
round a bamboo frame, the outer skin fitting over the frame
while the inner skin hung from it, so that there was an air space
about a foot wide between the two. It was difficult to erect, but
once up it was as snug as a well built log hut.

As soon as there was a lull in the wind, we resumed work on
the slopes below the col. We found that the steps we had
already cut had been swept away, and that not a trace of them
remained. So as to take advantage of brief periods of fine
weather, we put a camp (III A) at the foot of the slopes. This
was a bleak and comfortless spot, and even more exposed to
the wind than Camp III, which was situated on rocks close
under the cliffs of the North Peak. The new camp was pitched
on hard, smooth ice on which it was difficult to anchor the
tents. One night, during a particularly violent storm, one of

them broke loose from its moorings, causing a certain amount of excitement. But the new position was a great help, and from it we were able to make progress. But our advance was very slow, and as we set out day after day I began to wonder if we should ever reach the col. The most difficult part was about halfway up. This consisted of an ice wall about twenty feet high, topped by a very steep ice slope. We had a lot of fun getting up it, and succeeded largely owing to a fine lead by Smythe. We hung a rope ladder down it for subsequent use.

At last, by 15 May, the road of steps and fixed ropes was complete, and we established Camp IV on an ice ledge, some twenty feet wide, about 200 feet below the crest of the Col. The ledge was formed by the lower lip of a great crevasse, the upper lip of which, forty feet above, almost overhung the ledge. The camp was well sheltered and quite comfortable, the only disadvantage being the danger of small snow avalanches falling from above.

For the next four days the storm was continuous, and we could do nothing but lie in our sleeping-bags. Nor was any communication possible with the camps below. But on the evening of the 19th, the wind dropped and Smythe and I climbed up the last 200 feet. Apart from the ice wall this was by far the steepest part of the North Col slopes. When we reached the narrow crest of the col we were met by a most glorious view to the west, over range after range of giant peaks, draped by dark cloud banners, wild and shattered by the gale. The mighty scene was partly lit by an angry red glow, and rose from a misty shadow-lake of deep indigo that often appears among high mountains in the evening after a storm.

The next day Wyn Harris, Birnie and Boustead started up with ten porters, intending to reach 25,500 feet to choose a site for Camp V. But they were forced to retreat from 24,500 owing to the wind. Actually there was some difference of opinion about the wisdom of this decision, and a hot-tempered argument raged most of the succeeding night, by the end of which the subject under debate had become rather confused. Nerves were already frayed, and we were all liable to lose our tempers at the slightest provocation, and to take our silly grievances sorely to heart. This seems to be a common manifestation

of the effects of life at high altitudes. In our case it was undoubtedly aggravated by the rough handling we had received from
the weather, and by having been forced to spend so much of
our time during the past month cooped up in a tent with too
little to do and too much to anticipate. Being unable to speak
above a whisper, I found it difficult to quarrel successfully with
anyone, and it would have been too exhausting to attempt to
pull my opponent's beard. Had I been psychoanalysed at the
time, I would no doubt have been found to be suffering from
some fierce repressions.

We were very comfortable at Camp IV. Cooking and breathing soon produced a pleasant fug in the tents: we had large
double eiderdown sleeping-bags, and our snow beds were
soon made to conform with the shapes of our bodies. The
crevasse provided a convenient latrine, though it required a
strong effort of will to emerge from the tent. It was only at the
upper camps that the cold compelled us to use a bedpan in the
form of a biscuit box. So long as we did not have to do anything,
the time passed pleasantly enough. Lethargy of mind and
body was the chief trial. Once one got going it was not so bad,
but the prospect of toil was hateful. At the higher camps, of
course, this lethargy increased tenfold.

Eating, however, was the serious problem, and one which,
to my mind, did not receive nearly enough attention. This was
entirely the fault of the individual, for we had more than
enough food, and its quality and variety could not have been
better. The trouble is that at such an altitude the appetite is
jaded, and unless a man forces himself to eat regular and
sufficient meals he does not consume anything like enough to
maintain his strength. Melting a saucepan full of snow for
water and bringing it to the boil took so long that people
tended to delude themselves that they had eaten a hearty
meal. Over and over again I saw men starting for a long and
exhausting day's work on the mountain with only a cup of
cocoa and a biscuit or two inside them; the cold and the wind
discouraged eating during the climb, and they were generally
too tired to eat anything much when they returned. This state
of affairs contributed largely towards the rapid physical
deterioration of the party. There was endless talk about

rations, and certainly these were carefully and efficiently planned beforehand; but in actual practice we ate whatever we wanted and whenever we felt inclined. Sweets were the easiest kind of food to swallow, but it is doubtful if haphazard sweet-eating is as beneficial as the taking of regular substantial meals, which it certainly discourages. In most cold climates people develop a craving for fat, which has a higher calorific value than any other food. Unfortunately at high altitudes fat of any kind is particularly repugnant.

On 21 May, Smythe and I climbed some 1,500 feet above the North Col for exercise. We both felt extremely fit, and without undue effort we maintained an average speed of 1,000 feet an hour, which would not have been a bad performance had we been at sea-level. Individuals differ very widely in their physical reactions to the effects of high altitudes; some vomit a great deal, some suffer from blinding headaches, some cannot sleep, while others can hardly keep awake, some gasp and pant even when at rest. I used not to suffer much from any of these maladies; my particular trouble was physical lethargy which grew progressively more intense the longer I remained at a high altitude. For example, in 1933 I made three climbs up the north-east spur above the North Col. On the first occasion, after six nights at Camp IV (about 23,000 feet), I felt very strong, and as though I could go on indefinitely; the second time, after eight nights at Camp IV, I was weaker, though I still went fairly well; on the third occasion, after two nights spent at Camp V (25,700 feet) and twelve at Camp IV, I only reached Camp V, for my second sojourn there, after a very hard struggle. Smythe and I reacted to the effects of altitude in very much the same manner, though in 1933 he deteriorated considerably less quickly than I did. For men with no previous Himalayan experience, and considering that they had spent a whole fortnight laid up at the Base Camp while the rest of us were working slowly up the glacier, Wager and Wyn Harris acclimatised remarkably quickly. Longland was slow in adjusting himself, which made his subsequent performance all the more remarkable. Crawford and Brocklebank were at their best when it was too late for further attempts on the mountain, and thus were robbed of the chance of going high, though they spent weeks of monotonous but vital work keeping the North Col route open.

Weather conditions now appeared to have reached that state of comparative quiet that we had expected just before the arrival of the monsoon. Wireless messages received at the Base Camp spoke of an exceptionally early monsoon in Ceylon and its rapid spread over India. This news was confirmed by the appearance of great banks of cloud from the south which, however, were still far below us. Obviously the critical moment had arrived. On 22 May Birnie, Boustead, Greene and Wyn Harris, with twenty porters carrying 12 lbs each, established Camp V at 25,700 feet. The plan was for these four climbers and eight of the porters to stop the night at Camp V and to carry Camp VI as high as possible on the following day; Birnie and Boustead would then return to Camp V with the porters, while Wyn Harris and Greene would stop at Camp VI and attempt to climb the mountain by the "ridge route". Meanwhile Smythe and I would follow up to Camp V on the 23rd, take the place of the first party at Camp VI on the 24th, and make our attempt on the summit on the 25th, choosing our route in the light of the experiences of the first pair. Greene unfortunately strained his heart during the climb to Camp V, and his place was taken by Wager who had accompanied the party for exercise.

It was hard to believe that the time for the supreme test had arrived. Waiting at the North Col on 22 May, I felt as I imagine an athlete must feel just before the boat-race, marathon or boxing contest for which he has been training for months. It was difficult to keep one's mind from the nagging questions, "Will the weather hold long enough to give us a decent chance?" "How will I react to the extreme exhaustion that must inevitably accompany the final effort?" "What is the climbing really like on that upper part?" "For all our previous optimism, is it, in fact, possible to climb to or even to live at 29,000 feet?" Three more days, seventy-two hours!

It was a great relief when, the next morning, the moment to start arrived. We had the whole day before us, and there was no need to hurry. The basis of all mountaineering is the conservation of energy by the three fundamental principles

– rhythmic movement, balance and precise placing of the feet. As far as possible, steps should be short so that upward motion appears as a gentle sway from the hips rather than a strong thrust by thigh muscles. It is better to use a small nail-hold at a convenient distance than a large foothold involving a long stride. If a long stride is necessary, the balance must be adjusted by lateral pressure by the hand or ice-axe. A practised mountaineer is, of course, in the habit of observing these principles even on the simplest ground; his ability to maintain them on difficult and complicated terrain determines in large measure his quality as a climber. Nowhere is perfection of technique so important as at high altitudes where the slightest effort takes heavy toll of the climber's reserves of strength; nowhere is it more difficult to achieve.

Above the North Col we were met by a strong wind, which increased in violence as we climbed. I have no idea what the temperature was. On the glacier below a minimum of twenty degrees Fahrenheit was observed. I doubt if we experienced less than that on the upper part of the mountain. Judged by winter temperatures in the Arctic or Antarctic, such cold is not considered severe. But at great altitudes it is a very different matter. Due to lack of oxygen, the various functions of heart, lungs and circulation are most inefficient, lost heat is difficult to restore and there is danger of frostbite even at freezing point, particularly when there is a wind blowing: one has constantly to watch for its symptoms. If a foot loses feeling it is wise to stop to remove one's boot and bang and rub it to life again. This is one of the greatest difficulties we have had in dealing with the Sherpas at high altitudes; it was most difficult to induce them to take these precautions.

We were not altogether surprised, when at about four o'clock we reached Camp V, to find that the whole party was still there. Though by now the wind had dropped, it had been even more fierce at Camp V than it had been below, and it had been impossible to move on up the ridge. There was no room for two more at Camp V, and, though we offered to go down again, it was decided that Smythe and I should change places with Wyn Harris and Wager, in the hope of being able to push on up the mountain the next day.

The site of Camp V was composed of two platforms, one about four feet above the other. Each was sufficiently large to accommodate two "Meade" tents pitched end on. The tents themselves were about six feet six inches long by four feet wide by four feet high, made of light canvas and weighed about 16 lbs each. The "Meade" tent is really a smaller edition of the "Whymper", and is named after the well-known mountainer C. F. Meade – I have asked him why, but he could not enlighten me.

I doubt if anyone would claim to enjoy life at high altitudes – enjoy, that is, in the ordinary sense of the word. There is a certain grim satisfaction to be derived from struggling on upwards, however slowly; but the bulk of one's time is necessarily spent in the extreme squalor of a high camp, when even this solace is lacking. Smoking is impossible; eating tends to make one vomit; the necessity of reducing weight to a bare minimum forbids the importation of literature beyond that supplied by the labels on tins of food; sardine oil, condensed milk and treacle spill themselves all over the place; except for the briefest moments, during which one is not usually in a mood for aesthetic enjoyment, there is nothing to look at but the bleak confusion inside the tent and the scaly, bearded countenance of one's companion – fortunately the noise of the wind usually drowns the sound of his stuffy breathing; worst of all is the feeling of complete helplessness and inability to deal with any emergency that might arise. I used to try to console myself with the thought that a year ago I would have been thrilled by the very idea of taking part in our present adventure, a prospect that had then seemed like an impossible dream; but altitude has the same effect upon the mind as upon the body, one's intellect becomes dull and unresponsive, and my only desire was to finish the wretched job and to get down to a more reasonable clime – with strong emphasis on the latter part of the programme. I found that I could sleep pretty well, providing I was reasonably comfortable, but the slightest irritation, such as a jagged rock sticking into my back, was enormously exaggerated, as it is when one is suffering from a high fever.

Tight Corner

Jack Longland

Jack Longland was a leading English rock climber of the interwar years. Selected for the 1933 British Everest expedition, he established with Wager and Harris Camp VI at 27,500 feet/8,382 metres, a then record height for a camp. On the descent from Camp VI Longland was caught in a blizzard, but achieved the notable feat of bringing his eight Sherpas down to safety. This experience he later regaled BBC radio listeners with in the programme A Tight Corner. *Sir Jack Longland died in 1993, aged 88.*

It was 29 May 1933, and during one of the attempts to climb Mount Everest – which means that struggling about in blizzards was not exactly a new experience. But I want to try and set those two hours on 29 May against their background, so as to show why they seemed worse and generally more desperate than anything else we ran into on Everest.

You get used to winds and storms when you're trying to climb the highest mountain in the world, but we had more than our share of them in 1933. A month's winter marching across the bitter uplands of Tibet landed us at Base Camp in mid-April with a crop of sore throats and skinned faces. Then a fortnight of slow struggle up to the foot of the mountain itself at Camp III. Getting acclimatized to 21,000 feet is bad enough in itself; you pant and puff and want to give up the ghost even when you are only walking gently uphill, but wind and cold make it all seem much worse. There were fifty degrees of frost on my first night at Camp III, and a blizzard that blew powdery snow right through the fabric of my little tent, and when I woke everything inside the tent was covered with a two-inch layer. But it isn't so bad while you are lying inside a double sleeping sack, even if it does sound as if the tent might carry away any minute – the nasty part is going out and facing the snow and wind next morning.

And that is what throughout the month of May we had to do. Day after day was spent struggling up the steep snow slopes towards the North Col, cutting hundreds of steps and fixing rope handrails to make the way safe for the loaded porters who were to follow, and day after day ended the same, with storms and driven snow forcing us back to uncomfortable tents. Next morning a blanket of new snow covered the steps and ropes and ladders, and the whole weary job had to be done over again. You come to feel that wind is a personal enemy on Everest, always cunningly hitting you when you are weakest from the struggle against cold and the effort of hauling yourself uphill with less than half the amount of oxygen to breathe that you get at sea-level. It was 15 May before we got Camp IV, at the top of the great snow slopes, occupied and provisioned, and another week of dodging and fighting storms before four tiny tents were perched to make Camp V on the windswept North Ridge of the mountain, at nearly 26,000 feet.

There were four climbers and eight porters crowded into those little tents on the night of the 22nd. They hoped to go on next morning and pitch Camp VI as near to the top as they could reach. What they got instead was a three-day blizzard which kept them cooped up in their tents, hardly daring to poke their noses outside. Two of them, Wyn Harris and Wager, ventured out for not more than ten minutes to fix a signal for the rest of us below at Camp IV. It took several hours to revive the warmth in their fingers and toes and save them from serious frostbite. What is more, we never saw the signal down below! Three nights of this were as much as anyone could stand, and when I struggled up the ridge on the 25th from Camp IV with fresh provisions I was thankful to meet the party from V on the way down. They had given up the idea of going further. We were not surprised – the eight native porters with them, the "tigers" who'd been specially picked for the job of pitching our high camps, were in no fit condition to go on. They all had frostbite, some of them losing fingers afterwards, and the only thing to do was to send them down to the relative comforts of Base Camp.

So there we were – Camp V abandoned 3,000 feet above us and the top of Everest looking as hopelessly far off as if we had never started. As a further blow, our wireless brought the news that the monsoon was on its way, nearly a month too early, and when the monsoon comes, covering all the mountain with feet of soft new snow, and sending avalanches pouring down all the steeper slopes, it's good-bye to all chances of climbing Everest for *that* year. We had a strange council of war, eight of us all sitting round in one of the big arctic tents at Camp IV, after the last of the battered porters had been helped down the ice slopes below. In the end Ruttledge, the leader, decided that Wyn Harris, Wager, Birnie and I should go up again to make a second shot at pitching Camp VI. If we could get that job done, there might still be time for one or possibly two parties to strike at the summit from there, before the monsoon arrived and put the stopper on everything.

So we picked another eight porters. It would not have surprised us much if they had refused, after seeing what a mess the first "tigers" were in after weathering the storms at Camp V. But they did not – the Sherpa porters are wonderfully loyal and plucky: one of them, Angtarke, had actually been one of the first party, and he afterwards became the only porter to go twice up to Camp V – and beyond. You could have no better man with you on a mountain: a little fellow with a long pigtail and an everlastingly cheerful grin.

We gave the party a day's rest, and then at 5 a.m. on 28 May we all set off again up the weary ridge to Camp V. It is a slow grind up easy rocks and scree – easy, that is, if there's not a wind to throw you off your balance. Scree is always exhausting, for your feet slip back at every step. It's specially beastly above 24,000 feet, when each step needs three or four breaths, and you have to stop and pant every few minutes. We must have looked a strange bunch of asthmatic crocks, but after five hours we had worked our way to the little sloping shelf, and found the tents at Camp V still intact.

You don't stay long to admire the view at that height; so after seeing the porters safely packed away, we crawled into our sleeping sacks and started the laborious game of cooking. Cooking is a courtesy title – what we really did was to fill our cooking-pots with snow, and wait for a cold hour or more till the water grew faintly warm, and we could produce something that was a mockery of soup or tea. At that height even boiling water is not hot enough to scald your hand. Then an uncomfortable night, trying to keep warm inside double sleeping sacks with all our clothes on. It must have been cold, because at 5 a.m. when I tried to pour the water out of the vacuum flask that had been filled with lukewarm water the night before, several small pieces of ice came out with it. We found a bitter wind blowing outside, and though it meant wasting valuable time, we finally decided to send the porters back to their tents, and we all cooked more warm drinks to fortify ourselves for the job ahead. At last, when the wind dropped a trifle and the sun was out, we set off at half past eight.

We aimed to hit the long East Ridge of Everest near a tower at about 28,000 feet, which we called the "First Step". The route took us over great slabs of outward-shelving rock, reminiscent of the tiles of a roof greatly magnified, and mostly coated with new snow and varied by belts of steep scree. We found no flat ledges to rest on at all, and there were long periods of difficult balancing where we had to depend on the friction of our bootnails against the smoothly sloping rock.

Birnie had to stay behind at Camp V – he'd crocked a leg, and was in no state for the difficult journey towards Camp VI. So I had to give up the idea of joining Wyn Harris and Wager in their attempt on the summit next day, and concentrate on the job of seeing the porters safely down again from Camp VI. On the way up Wyn Harris and Wager prospected the route, while I brought up the lamer dogs in the rear: but all the porters really climbed magnificently, like seasoned mountaineers, on ground where a slip would often have been fatal. The going was treacherous, particularly where the rocks were covered with loose pebbles, and a slither would have been hard to check – and if it *wasn't* checked it would only have ended when you reached the glacier, 8,000 feet below.

At the end of every fifty minutes we called a ten-minute halt, and I could encourage the most exhausted of the porters when

I had breath to spare to try out my few Nepalese phrases. Personally, I was about as glad of the halts as they were, though the porters were carrying ten pounds or more on their backs and we were unloaded. At last, just about midday, we struggled up over a steeper band of yellowish rocks, and found a little sloping snow-clogged ledge at about 27,500 feet. This was to be Camp VI – but there wasn't even room to pitch our tiny six-by-four tent until the porters had cleared away the snow and built up a sort of platform of small stones at the lower edge. Even then the tent sloped drunkenly downwards, and those who slept in it always found the man who had the upper berth slipping down on his companion during the night and disturbing his fitful sleep. Still, there it was – the final jumping-off place for the top, now not much more than 1,500 feet above. Our eight porters, "tigers" if any have deserved the name, had done a magnificent piece of work. They had carried up the highest camp that has ever been pitched, 700 feet higher and nearly a quarter of a mile nearer the summit than a tent has ever been before – or since.

There wasn't much time for resting – the porters had to be got down to safety at Camp IV before night came. But I remember catching a glimpse of the Rongbuk monastery below Base Camp, 10,000 feet below, and thinking how odd it was to see it lying there across those great depths after nearly six weeks' absence. Then we set off just before one o'clock, after the briefest of goodbyes to Wyn Harris and Wager in their little tent, and one final glance towards the summit, which looked invitingly close.

I had decided not to try and take the porters directly down the steep and slippery slabs by which we had climbed up from Camp V. Looking back, I have never blessed any decision more – if I had decided otherwise I doubt if I should be alive now. Instead we worked along horizontally, following a break in the steep Yellow Band and aiming to hit the top of the main North Ridge, which I thought would be safer for the tired porters to descend. As I was helping them down a steep little section just before the ridge was reached, I had a moment or two to look at the view. You are more than ordinarily stupid at that height – the brain is starved of oxygen, and so neither eyes nor ears nor any of the senses do their job properly. But I told myself that this was the best view I was ever likely to see, and did just manage to take in the fact that I was seeing distant peaks that must have been more than two hundred and fifty miles away: and all the high summits that had looked so proud from Camp IV were now insignificant humps below.

These glimpses of the view had a sudden and nasty interruption. Without any warning that I remember a great storm blew up out of the west. There weren't any more distant horizons – the most I could see was a snow-swept circle of twenty or thirty yards. A mountain storm is always rather unnerving, but its effect at 27,000 feet on cold and exhausted men is devastating. Worst of all I was responsible for the safety of eight men who had trustingly followed us to this height, and who had somehow to be got safely down to Camp IV. Worse even than that, we were now at the top of the North Ridge, and the whole length of it down to Camp V was entirely unknown to me, as our diagonal route of the morning had missed it out. That wouldn't have mattered so much on some ridges, even in an Everest hurricane, for a sharp ridge is easy to follow, even if you can't see more than a few paces. But the North Ridge of Everest is broad and badly defined – you can miss the best way even in calm weather – and here I was trying to collect my wits and mountaineering experience to follow it correctly when it was all I could do to stagger downhill at all, and when all the rest of my mind was occupied with the necessity of keeping the porters together, urging on the stragglers and seeing they kept away from the steep rocks, where a fatal slip might have occurred.

The snow began to cover the holds on the rocks, and give a slippery coating to the patches of scree, and the wind came in rather terrifying gusts, forcing us to cling or cower against the rocks to avoid being blown bodily away. My snow-goggles soon became quite useless, choked with snow. I took them off, only to find that eyelids and eyelashes coated up as well, forming an opaque film which had to be rubbed away every few minutes before I could peer out again and get a glimpse of the next few yards.

Every ten minutes I called a halt to count up my little band

and collect them together, and then with a few shouted words of encouragement in what I hoped was Nepalese, off we pushed again, fighting our way down against the bitterly driving snow.

We had a moment's respite in the lee of a small cliff, where we happened on the tattered remains of a green tent. It must have been the old Camp VI from which Mallory and Irvine left in 1924 for their attempt on the summit, and were never seen again. For a minute or two the least tired porters rummaged among the wreckage. One brought out a candle lantern and another an electric torch – the kind worked with a press-button. Even after nine years of storm and cold the torch still worked, so we pushed on rather heartened by these signs of human occupation, many years old as they were.

But the finding of the 1924 tent gave me my nastiest moment. I had a photograph in my pocket on which the position of Mallory's camp was marked. I was going to use it to mark accurately for Smythe and Shipton, who were to follow up Harris and Wager if the first attempt failed, the position of our own new Camp VI. I pulled the photograph out of my pocket now, and discovered to my horror that Mallory's camp was marked as being not on the main North Ridge at all, but on a subsidiary spur further east. This must mean that, in spite of all my care, we were not on the main ridge, and more than that, this second spur ran out on appall-ingly steep ice slopes overhanging the East Rongbuk glacier thousands of feet below. If once I led the party on to these slopes there was no escape – it would at best have meant a night in the open and to spend a night out at this height, even without a storm, would have been fatal.

I had to think desperately quickly – and it was a problem I couldn't possibly share with the porters, though if I went wrong they were equally involved in an unpleasant death. Looking at the photograph again I saw that if we *were* on the wrong ridge, I ought soon to see signs of a steep ice couloir on the left. Equally, if I *wasn't* wrong, that couloir ought not to appear. So the next half-hour or more was full of desperate anxiety, as I peered through the snow expecting and yet hoping not to see that steep funnel of ice on my left. When minute after minute of painful stumbling and struggling with the wind went by and no couloir appeared, I began to have a glimmer of hope that the marking of the photograph was wrong and that my mountain experience had led me right. But it was a pretty desperate chance – nine times out of ten map or photograph is bound to be right, and the bewildered climber lost in a storm is as certainly wrong.

Meanwhile the storm was telling: the more exhausted porters were beginning to sit down, even between our frequent halts. It took a lot of urging to get them to their feet again – it was so much easier to lie down and die! And all the time perhaps they were right – if I really was leading them down the wrong ridge, why not die quietly now rather than later after more hours of struggle and cold? That was the problem that made these two hours the worst I have ever spent – worse even than the storm and the effort of fighting on down against it.

All this time I was hoping for some short pause in the storm – just a minute of clearer view which would give me a glimpse of the North Peak and a chance of fixing our position. I believe I carried my compass in my gloved hand during most of the descent, but without a single landmark to be seen beyond the driving snow it was about as much use as a sick headache. The weaker porters were beginning to sit down more often now – more than once I had to lift a man up and set him going again; anything was better than continuing in the face of that diabolical and unrelenting storm. And still I hoped it was the right ridge – surely, if I was wrong, we ought to have come to the top of those great ice slopes by now. I don't remember much about the last bit of that descent – it was all slipping and staggering down icy screes and round little snowed-up cliffs. And then suddenly, down through the snow-scud appeared a little patch of green. I rubbed the ice off my eyelashes and looked again: and it *was* a tent, three, four tents – the little cluster that meant Camp V and safety, and an end to the tearing anxiety of two hours. Only two hours of storm – less than three since I'd left Wager and Harris at Camp VI; but I seemed to have crowded a lifetime of fear and struggle and responsibility into that short time. And it wasn't till a day or two later that I learnt that it was careless marking of the photograph that had made me think that Mallory's camp was not on the main North Ridge.

An awkward descent with the last porter down a final steep bit of rock, and then we were crawling into the warmth of the tents. Mugs of hot drink were pushed into our hands, and then Smythe and Shipton and Birnie were clamouring for the story. Smythe tells how he only recognized me by my voice – though that was croaking enough after months of high-altitude throat. This is how he described me: "Longland was unrecognizable; his face was clotted with ice; icicles hung from his nose; a chandelier of them was suspended from his beard; he brought great news!"

The news, of course, was of the porters and their successful establishing of Camp VI. Having given exact directions as to how to find the little tent there, I pushed off again after twenty minutes, to get my porters safely down to the lower levels and greater comfort of Camp IV. Two stayed behind at Camp V – they were too exhausted to go farther that evening. The rest of the way down was pretty tiring, for our legs grew wearier as we went. But the worst of the storm was over – and descending by a way we knew was like five-finger exercises after what had gone before. The stronger porters soon got ahead, but I had to stay with the man who was worst. Helping him with encouragement and an arm at the steeper places kept me fairly absorbed, and it was just getting dark when we got to the level ridge before the little rise into Camp IV. It was only then, when safety was close and certain, that I realized how desperately exhausted I was myself. Dragging myself up that little snow rise, only twenty or thirty feet at most, was the hardest struggle of the day – and I knew then how near the limit we had been. But in the big arctic tent there was comfort, and a wonderful welcome from Crawford and Maclean. Hot drinks and warm food, and then I was put to bed like a small child and did not wake until I went out at six o'clock next morning to watch through a telescope Harris and Wager's slow and steady progress towards the summit from the camp we had successfully established the day before. They didn't quite reach the summit, but that is another story!

Alone

Frank Smythe

On 1 June 1933 Frank Smythe and Eric Shipton left Camp VI for their attempt on the summit via the north side. Shipton, however, felt ill and quit near the First Step, leaving Smythe to go on alone.

There was never any doubt as to the best route. The crest of the North-East Ridge, leading to the foot of the second step, was sharp, jagged and obviously difficult. As for the second step, now almost directly above me, it *looked* utterly impregnable, and I can only compare it to the sharp bow of a battle cruiser. Norton's route alone seemed to offer any chance of success, and it follows the Yellow Band beneath a sheer wall to the head of the great couloir.

At first there was no difficulty and a series of sloping ledges at the top of the Yellow Band took me round a corner and out of sight of Eric. Then came a patch of snow perhaps thirty yards wide. There was no avoiding it except by a descent of nearly 100 feet, but fortunately the snow was not the evil floury stuff I had expected, but had been well compacted by the wind; indeed, such hard snow that step-cutting was necessary.

Step-cutting at nearly 28,000 feet is a fatiguing operation, and the axe seemed unconscionably heavy and unready to do its work. In the Alps one powerful stroke with the adze would have fashioned a step, but sudden spurts of exertion are to be avoided at 28,000 feet, and I preferred the alternative of several light, short strokes. I must have looked like an old hen grubbing for worms, but even so I had to cease work and puff hard after making each step.

High altitudes promote indecision. Projecting through the

snow was a rock and at first sight it seemed a good foothold. Then I thought it was too sloping and that I had better cut to one side of it. But I had no sooner changed my mind when I decided that perhaps after all it could be used as a foothold and would save me a step or two. I must have spent a minute or two turning this ridiculous little point over in my mind before doing what was the obvious thing – avoiding it. It is curious how small problems encountered during a great undertaking can assume an importance out of all proportion to their true worth.

When I had crossed the snow I again glanced back, but there was no sign of Eric following me, and I continued on my solitary way.

Contrary to accepted mountaineering practice, I found that the easiest as well as the safest method of traversing the slabs was to keep the ice axe in the outside hand as there were always little cracks and crannies to put it in. It was a third leg to me and an invaluable companion throughout the whole of the day.

Beyond the snow patch the slabs were covered here and there with loose, powdery snow. This had to be kicked or scraped away before I dared stand on the outward-sloping ledges. Progress was slow, though steady, and as I advanced and saw the final pyramid appear above the band of rocks beneath which I was traversing, there came to me for the first time that day a thrill of excitement and hope. I was going well now, better than when I had parted from Eric, and for a moment there seemed a chance of success.

The bed of the great couloir was hidden, but a subsidiary couloir and a buttress separating it from the great couloir were in full view. Both were sheltered from the wind and as a result were still heavily plastered with the snow of yesterday's blizzard. My hopes were dashed as I gazed at the buttress. It was considerably steeper than the rocks I was traversing, and snow filled every crack and was piled deeply on every sloping ledge. Was it climbable in such a condition? In the Alps perhaps, but not at 28,000 feet by a man nearing the limit of his strength. And the subsidiary couloir? Even supposing the traverse of the buttress proved practicable, what kind of snow should I find in this narrow cleft? Most likely unstable powder affording no certain footing and impeding every movement. True, it might be possible to avoid it by climbing the rocks at one side, but these, in their turn, were mostly snow-covered.

Instinctively I looked for an alternative. Could I climb directly upwards to a point above the second step and attack the final pyramid without having to continue this long, wearisome and unprofitable traverse? The wall rose above me like a sea cliff, in places it overhung, and every hold, every wrinkle and crack held its quota of snow. There was no visible break in it until the buttress where there was a gap, possibly the point reached by Norton in 1924, which might prove a feasible alternative to the subsidiary couloir. At all events direct ascent was impossible. One thing alone gave me hope: once the subsidiary couloir had been climbed and the rock band passed there seemed every reason to suppose that the principal difficulties were behind. I could see the face of the final pyramid and it did not look difficult. This was a scree slope at the base of it and higher a slope of light-coloured boulders. Energy alone would be required to surmount it. Of course it may hold its surprises, for Everest will remain a stubborn opponent to the last; but I feel confident that once the rock band is below, the change from difficult and dangerous climbing to safe and easy climbing will inspire the climber to outlast fatigue and altitude over the remaining 600 feet to the summit.

The angle of the Yellow Band steepened gradually as I approached the great couloir. In general direction the ledges were parallel with the band, but they were not always continuous, and once or twice I had to retrace my steps for a yard or two and seek an alternative route. But the climbing was never difficult – it required only unfailing attention to the planting of each foot on the sloping ledges, especially when these were masked by loose snow.

Presently the bed of the great couloir became visible. It was shallow enough not to necessitate any steep descent into it, and was filled with snow, perhaps thirty to forty feet wide, which ended beneath the rock band. Several hundred feet lower was a pitch of unknown height, beneath which the couloir widened out into a small hanging glacier, then fell steeply towards the Rongbuk glacier, a total height from my position of about 8,000 feet.

It was a savage place. Beyond was the steep and snowy buttress separating me from the subsidiary couloir, and hemming me in above was the unrelenting band of rock, and higher still the final pyramid, a weary distance away, cutting aloofly into the blue.

I approached the couloir along a ledge which bent round a steep little corner. This ledge was comfortably wide until it came to the corner, then it narrowed until it was only a few inches broad. As far as the corner it was easy going, but to turn the corner I had to edge along, my face to the mountain, in a crab-like fashion. The rocks above projected awkwardly, but it was not a place that would have caused a second's hesitation on an Alpine climb. One step only was needed to take me round the corner. This step I funked. The balance was too critical. With arms spreadeagled above me I sought for steadying handholds. They were not essential; balance alone should have sufficed, but I felt I could not manage without them. I could find none; every wrinkle in the rocks sloped outwards. For a few moments I stood thus like a man crucified, while my heart bumped quickly and my lungs laboured for oxygen, and there flashed through my mind the possibility of a backward topple into the couloir – an interminable slide into belated oblivion.

I retired a few yards, and apostrophized myself as a fool. I knew that the traverse was possible, and if Eric had been there I should not have hesitated. Being alone made all the difference.

I tried again, and once more found myself in the spreadeagled position but without the courage to take the one step that would have placed me in safety round the corner.

The only alternative was a ledge about twenty feet below. I was loath to lose even twenty feet of height, but there was nothing for it but to descend.

The slabs separating me from the ledge were reasonably rough, and though there were no very definite holds there were wrinkles and folds. For the rest friction should serve. Facing outwards and sitting down, I lowered myself gingerly off the ledge on the palms of my hands. The friction was even better than I had hoped for, and the seat of my trousers almost sufficed by itself to maintain me in position without the additional support of the palms of my hands. There was no awkward corner in the lower ledge; it was wide and honest, and though it sloped outwards and supported a bank of snow three or four feet deep, it brought me without difficulty to the snowy bed of the couloir.

Wyn and Waggers had found the same loose, disagreeable snow in the couloir as had Norton in 1924, but I suspect that they traversed the upper ledge and so crossed higher than I. The snow at my level, as a tentative forward dig with the ice axe revealed, had been hardened by the wind and step-cutting was again necessary.

One step, then a pause to gasp, while the snow at my feet and the rocks beyond swam uncertainly before me. Then another step and another bout of gasping. The snow was very hard and the angle of the great couloir at this point fully 50°. About a dozen steps – I was across at last.

Next, how to traverse the buttress? I must climb almost straight up it for about fifty feet before continuing more or less horizontally towards the subsidiary couloir.

The rocks were steep and snow had accumulated on them untouched as yet by the wind. How had the wind swept the snow in the couloir hard and left the slabs at this side unaffected?

When these slabs are snow-free they are probably not much more difficult than the slabs to the east of the great couloir. There are numerous ledges, and though the general angle is appreciably steeper, there is no necessity for anything but balance climbing, and I confidently believe no insuperable obstacle will prevent the climber from reaching the subsidiary couloir. But now snow had accumulated deeply on the shelving ledges and it was the worst kind of snow, soft like flour, loose like granulated sugar and incapable of holding the feet in position. As I probed it with my axe, I knew at once that the game was up. So far the climbing had been more dangerous than difficult; now it was both difficult and dangerous, a fatal combination on Everest. The only thing I could do was to go as far as possible, always keeping one eye on the weather and the other on the strength I should need to retreat safely.

The weather at all events was fair. In the shelter of the buttress and the wall beyond the subsidiary couloir there was not a breath of wind and the sun shone powerfully – too powerfully, for it seemed to sap my strength and my resolution. I was a prisoner, struggling vainly to escape from a vast hollow enclosed by dungeon-like walls. Wherever I looked hostile rocks frowned down on my impotent strugglings, and the wall above seemed almost to overhang me with its dark strata set one upon the other, an embodiment of static, but pitiless, force. The final pyramid was hidden; if only I were on it, away from this dismal place with its unrelenting slabs. The climber who wins across the slabs to the final pyramid must conquer a sickness of spirit as well as a weariness of body.

With both arms at breast-high level I began shovelling the snow away before me; it streamed down the couloir behind me with a soft swishing noise. Several minutes elapsed before a sloping ledge was disclosed, then I heaved myself up, until first one knee, and then the other, were on it. In this position, like a supplicant before a priest, I had to remain while my lungs, intolerably accelerated by the effort, heaved for oxygen. Then with another effort I stood cautiously upright.

More snow had to be cleared before I could tread a smaller ledge on the slab above; then, to my relief, came a step unattended by this prodigious effort of clearing away snow. But relief is short-lived on Everest and the ledge that followed was covered several feet deep in snow bevelled into a steep bank, yet without the slightest cohesion.

Presently I had to stop, as apart from the need to rest overstressed heart and lungs, immersing my arms in the snow brought such numbness to my hands, gloved though they were, that I feared I might let slip my ice-axe.

So slow and exhausting was the work of clearing the snow that I began to rely on feel alone. That is to say, when I could I trusted my foot to find holds beneath the snow rather than clear the snow away from the slabs until I could see the holds. I realised full well the danger of this, and whenever possible used my ice-axe pick as an extra support by jamming it into cracks. This last precaution undoubtedly saved me from catastrophe. There was one steeply shelving slab deeply covered with soft snow into which I sank to the knees, but my first exploring foot discovered a knob beneath it. This seemed quite firm and, reaching up with my axe, I wedged the pick of it half an inch or so into a thin crack. Then, cautiously, I raised my other foot on to the knob, at the same time transferring my entire weight to my front foot. My rear foot was joining my front foot when the knob, without any warning, suddenly broke away. For an instant, both feet slid outwards, and my weight came on the ice axe; next moment I had recovered my footing and discovered another hold. It happened so quickly that my sluggish brain had no time to register a thrill of fear; I had acted purely instinctively and the incident was over almost before I knew it had occurred. I did not even feel scared afterwards as I was climbing now in a curiously detached, impersonal frame of mind. It was almost as though one part of me stood aside and watched the other struggle on. Lack of oxygen and fatigue are responsible for this dulling of the mental faculties, but principally lack of oxygen. It is a dangerous state of mind and comparable to the mental reactions of a drunken man in charge of a car. He may believe that his judgement is unimpaired, even that he can drive more skilfully than usual; in point of fact, as statistics and the police court news reveal, he is much more prone to an accident in this condition.

Just before crossing the great couloir I had looked at my watch; it was 10 a.m. Now I looked again. An hour had passed, and I had made about fifty feet of height, not more. At least 300 feet of difficult rocks, all deeply snow-covered, remained to be climbed, before easier ground on the final pyramid was reached. Perhaps I could do another hour or two's work, but what was the use of it? I should only exhaust myself completely and not have the strength left to return.

I shovelled away the floury snow until I had made a space on which I could stand, though I did not dare to sit.

I was high up on the buttress separating the great couloir from the subsidiary couloir. Above me was the band of rock beneath which I had been, and was still, traversing. It looked impregnable except where it was breached by the subsidiary couloir, and the place already mentioned a few yards to the east of this couloir. For the rest, it is Everest's greatest defence, and stretches unbroken across the North Face of the mountain. The striated limestone rocks composing it actually overhang in places, and the section above the great couloir reminded me of the well-known pitch in the Central Gully, on Lliwedd, in North Wales.

It is possible, indeed probable, that weariness and altitude distorted my judgement, but there are two things I believe to be true. Firstly, that Norton's route is practicable, and that when the "tiles", as he calls the slabs, are free of snow, they can be traversed without excessive difficulty to the subsidiary couloir, and this can be climbed on to the face of the final pyramid. Secondly, that it is not a practicable route when snow covers the slabs. But there is no doubt that even in the best conditions this part of the climb will tax a climber's powers to the uttermost. The unrelenting exposure of the slabs, dependence on the friction of boot nails for hours on end, added to the physical and mental weariness and lethargy due to altitude, will require something more than strength and skill if they are to be countered successfully. The summit was just in view over the rock band. It was only 1,000 feet above me, but an æon of weariness separated me from it. Bastion on bastion and slab on slab, the rocks were piled in tremendous confusion, their light-yellow edges ghostlike against the deep-blue sky. From the crest a white plume of mist flowed silently away, like unending volcanic steam, but where I stood there was not a breath of wind and the sun blazed into the hollow with an intense fierceness, yet without warming the cold air. Clouds were gathering, but they were thousands of feet below me. Between them, I could see the Rongbuk glacier, a pure white in its uppermost portion, then rugged and uneven where it was resolved into a multitude of séracs and, lower still, a gigantic muddle of moraines as though all the navvies in the world had been furiously excavating to no logical purpose. Beyond it, the Rongbuk valley stretched northwards towards the golden hills of Tibet, and I could make out the Rongbuk monastery, a minute cluster of minute buildings, yet distinct in every detail through the brilliantly clear atmosphere. With this one exception, I remember no details. My position was too high, my view too vast, my brain too fatigued to register detail. There was nothing visible to challenge my elevation. The earth was so far beneath, it seemed impossible I could ever regain it. The human brain must needs be divinely inspired to comprehend such a vista, and mine was tied to a body fatigued by exertion and slowed down in all its vital processes by lack of oxygen. Somervell's description of the scene is simplest and best: "A god's view."

More by instinct than anything else, I pulled my camera out of my pocket. The photograph I took is pitifully inadequate.

I cannot enlarge on the bitterness of defeat. Those who have failed on Everest are unanimous in one thing: the relief of not having to go on outweighs all other considerations. The last 1,000 feet of Everest are not for mere flesh and blood. Whoever reaches the summit, if he does it without artificial aid, will have to rise godlike above his own frailties and his tremendous environment. Only through a power within him and without him will he overcome a deadly fatigue and win through to success.

Descending even difficult ground at high altitudes is almost as easy as descending at an Alpine level, and within a few minutes I regained the great couloir. Recrossing it, I halted on the broad, comfortable ledge to take a photograph. It is curious that I did not remember taking this photograph or the one from my highest point until the film was developed, so I think my action at the time was more automatic than reasoned, as before starting on the expedition I told myself many times that I must take photographs whenever possible. This lends colour to a theory I have long held, that in climbing at great altitudes, when mind and body are in the grip of an insidious lethargy, it is on the subconscious, rather than the conscious, that the climber must rely to push him forwards. Therefore, it is essential that the will to reach the summit of Everest be strengthened by a prior determination to get there. Perhaps it is not too much to say that Everest will be climbed in England.

After taking this photograph it occurred to me that I ought to eat something. I was not in the least hungry, indeed the thought of food was utterly repugnant, especially as my mouth was almost dry, and my tongue leather-like, but in duty bound I pulled a slab of mint cake from my pocket.

And now I must relate the curious incident described in "Everest 1933".

After leaving Eric a strange feeling possessed me that I was accompanied by another. I have already mentioned a feeling of detachment in which it seemed as though I stood aside and watched myself. Once before, during a fall in the Dolomites, I had the same feeling, and it is not an uncommon experience with mountaineers who have a long fall. It may be that the feeling that I was accompanied was due to this, which, in its turn, was due to lack of oxygen and the mental and physical stress of climbing alone at a great altitude. I do not offer this as an explanation, but merely as a suggestion.

This "presence" was strong and friendly. In its company I could not feel lonely, neither could I come to any harm. It was always there to sustain me on my solitary climb up the snow-covered slabs. Now, as I halted and extracted some mint cake from my pocket, it was so near and so strong that instinctively I divided the mint into two halves and turned round with one half in my hand to offer it to my "companion".

It was apparent when I recrossed the couloir that I would do better to return across the Yellow Band by a lower route. The angle of the band west of the first step is very slightly concave, and on such slabs a degree or two in angle makes all the difference. The western end of the band terminates below in a great cut-off, a sheer precipice which carries the eye in a single bound to the Rongbuk glacier. My return route lay a few yards above and parallel to the edge of this precipice. There was no difficulty whatsoever.

Great Effort

Hugh Ruttledge

This account of Wyn Harris and Wager's "great effort" on the summit was written from notes Ruttledge "recorded immediately upon their arrival down at Camp III, knowing that even the most accurate observer's memory for detail fades rapidly after a climb to high altitudes, and from narratives subsequently written by both men".

They had a somewhat disturbed night at Camp VI, after a light meal of Brand's essence of chicken, tinned loganberries, biscuit and condensed milk. Both men's appetites were poor, they were thirsty, and slept badly. Wager had the lower berth, so to speak, for the floor of the tent sloped downwards, and his companion kept slipping down upon him. Wyn Harris managed to sleep for about four hours. He was up at 4.30 on the 30th. A ten-mile-an-hour wind was blowing, and the cold was not excessive, considering the altitude. But the Thermos flask, prepared the night before, had not been able to keep its contents warm, and they were obliged to spend an hour heating water (obtained, of course, from snow), over a "Tommy cooker". After a very poor meal, during which they thawed out their frozen boots over another "Tommy cooker", they put on their windproofs, and emerged slowly and stiffly from their tent at 5.40 a.m. All movement is terribly slowed down when your oxygen supply from the air has been reduced to one third of normal.

The sun had not yet reached them, and they suffered much from cold during the first hour while traversing diagonally upwards towards the North-East Ridge. Wager noticed that excessive panting resulted in rapid loss of body heat. Both felt the beginnings of frostbite; and the moment the sun appeared, nearly an hour after they had left Camp VI, Wager sat down to remove his boots and rub his feet. Soon after this, about sixty feet below the crest of the ridge and 250 yards east of the first step, Wyn Harris, who was leading, found the ice-axe about which there has been so much controversy. It was lying free on smooth, brown "boilerplate" slabs, inclined at an easy angle but steepening considerably just below. It was in perfect condition, looking quite new. On the polished steel head was stamped the name of the maker Willisch of Täsch, in the Zermatt valley. I will state in a later part of the chapter the conclusions at which we have arrived from careful consideration of this discovery.

The climbers left the axe lying where they found it, and proceeded upwards to the foot of the first step, which is actually composed of two large towers on the ridge. It will be remembered that their first object was to reconnoitre the second step, now about two hundred yards away; to climb it if they could; and to ascend thence along the ridge itself and up the final pyramid to the summit. If the step could not be climbed, they would go by Norton's 1924 route, keeping more or less along the top of the Yellow Band, two or three hundred feet below the crest of the ridge, cross the Great Couloir and attack the slabs on its western wall, thus effecting a lodgement on the north face of the pyramid.

It was now 7 a.m. Their first thought was to turn the first step and climb straight up on to the ridge. But they soon saw that the ridge was difficult, and that it would be easier to traverse along the top of the Yellow Band. They could not, from their viewpoint, see that the cliffs directly below the second step were impregnable to direct assault; the step itself was obviously so. They therefore moved off horizontally westwards, over snow-covered slabs, keeping roughly to the line where the Yellow Band adjoins the bottom of the dark-grey limestone precipice forming the continuation of the first step. The going was not very difficult here, and they were still unroped. Arrived under the second step, they at once saw that, not only was the second step itself impossible from this side, but they could not even reach the foot of it. Above them rose the dark-grey precipice, smooth and holdless. From a distance the second step had seemed to be split by an oblique gully cutting down through it in a north-easterly direction. At close quarters even this could not be traced. But about 200 yards farther along appeared a gully of fair promise. It seemed to cut through both the dark bands that form the first and second steps. If it could be climbed, the second step would be turned and the ridge reached at a point beyond which there seemed to be a straightforward way to the summit. The traverse was accordingly continued along ground that now became more difficult, and the bottom of the gully was reached at about 10 a.m.

More than four hours had thus been spent in a detailed survey of this portion of the North Face. Knowing the men as I do, I feel very certain that their adverse opinion of the second step and its approaches carries great weight. They would not turn aside from a climb within the limits of the possible.

The gully was a delusion, a mere shallow scoop in the smooth walls. Moreover it did not even continue to the ridge. The party roped up here. In general, the rock was of a uniform, treacherous smoothness; in detail, a few knobby excrescences could be found, which, with less snow about, would afford a tolerably good foothold. For the hands there was nothing. Wyn Harris made an attempt to lead up the shallow scoop, but was brought to a standstill almost at once.

Two ways had now been prospected of which high hopes had been entertained through distant reconnaissance. It seemed that Norton was right, and that the ridge route was impracticable. About 150 yards farther along, round a corner, was the great snow couloir descending from the eastern foot of the final pyramid. The roped party climbed cautiously along immediately under the precipice, and were delayed by some very difficult going over snow-covered, sloping slabs near the corner. A single slip here would have been absolutely fatal. Actually they would have done better to traverse along a better ledge, some fifty to a hundred feet below, where the angle eased off. It was decided that they should give each other mutual support over any difficulties in the neighbourhood of the couloir, and that, if easier ground was discovered beyond, Wyn Harris, who was feeling the stronger of the two, should go on alone.

In the couloir a very awkward fifty feet of powder snow had to be crossed. The snow gave no support to the feet, cascading down at a touch, and the greatest care was necessary to prevent a slip. On the left, a few feet away, the rocks overhung. The couloir itself ran precipitously downwards to the main Rongbuk glacier, 10,000 feet below. It was a sensational crossing.

The rocks forming the western wall were even steeper than those just left behind, and they had more snow on them, being more protected on this side from the wind. It seemed just possible to find a way round the base of a flat buttress and then up between minor buttresses. The party crept slowly and carefully along for about 150 feet beyond the couloir, traversing slightly upward till they reached a point some fifty feet above the top of the Yellow Band, on the edge of a small gully where the snow was particularly deep and soft. Wyn Harris attempted to cross it, though knowing full well that Wager, precariously balanced on a slab affording no belays, could not possibly hold him should the snow slip away. It showed every sign of doing so. Suddenly came the realisation that the limit of reasonable climbing had been reached, if not passed. Wyn Harris retreated to the lesser evil of the slab, and the position was reviewed.

It was now 12.30 p.m. The height already reached was presumably over 28,100 feet, for, from Norton's description, he had reached approximately the same place. There remained, therefore, about 1,000 feet to the summit. The going above did not look absolutely impossible, but in the present conditions of snow on the slabs it would be difficult and very dangerous. Even worse was the prospect of a continued traverse across the little gully and the slabs to a biggish subsidiary couloir, which runs down to meet the main couloir about 200 feet below. In good conditions, with the rocks dry and free from snow, this might well be the best way to reach the easier slabs of the final pyramid above the black bands of the first and second steps. To go on in the existing conditions was to court disaster. The most optimistic estimate could not allot much less than four hours for completion of the climb. This would overstep the time-limit of safety, for the returning climbers must reach Camp V, at least, before dark. Camp VI, where Smythe and Shipton should by now have arrived, only held two men. Wager thought he might be able to continue upwards for another hour. Except in the last necessity, a man should not be left alone, either to wait or to climb, on ground like this. Lastly, both climbers had an uncomfortable feeling that they had not been able to explore fully the possibilities of the second step. If they could only prove, beyond cavil, that that route was wholly out of the question, Smythe and Shipton could go for Norton's traverse with undivided minds, and could probably reach the couloir in three hours from Camp VI. This would give them a far better chance for the summit.

The word was given for retreat. Neither man liked the thought of repeating the terrific traverse they had made on the ascent. They found a way downwards to a series of ledges between fifty and a hundred feet lower, and had less difficulty in crossing the great couloir and the slabs on both sides of it. This involved a slight diagonal ascent towards the foot of the first step, whence they intended to climb on to the ridge and have a final look at the second step. But they were very near exhaustion point, and the climb to the ridge between the steps proved to be beyond them. They continued slowly towards Camp VI; and while Wyn Harris retrieved the axe left there in the morning (abandoning his own in its place), Wager by a last effort dragged himself up to the ridge east of the first step. He is the only climber who has looked down the stupendous, ice-clad South-East Face of the mountain.

Harris and Wager reached Camp VI at about 4 p.m. and there found Smythe and Shipton who were on their way up the mountain.

I must now revert to the question of the axe that Wyn Harris found on the slabs, one hour's climbing above Camp VI. I have already stated that the maker of it was Willisch of Täsch. Our first thought was that the owner must undoubtedly have been Mallory, for the reason that Willisch is a master craftsman to whom first-rate amateurs like Mallory, who do their climbing without guides and therefore do their own step-cutting, would be likely to go for a really good axe. I have subsequently been informed, however, that a number of Willisch axes were supplied to the expedition of 1924, so it is possible that this one was carried by Irvine. To one of these two it must have belonged, for no other climbers have gone by that route previous to this year. Norton and Somervell traversed by a lower line, on their way diagonally upwards from their Camp VI to the couloir. Some have suggested that this was the axe dropped by Somervell soon after he and Norton turned to descend. But they were much farther to the west when this happened, and Somervell's axe fell straight down the mountain-side and disappeared from view "still going strong". Others proffer the theories that either Mallory or Irvine put down the axe in order to climb unencumbered, or even that it was planted on the summit and blown by wind in the course of time to the place where it was found.

As to the first of these theories, no mountaineer climbing the North Face of Mount Everest regards his axe as an encumbrance. It is his best friend and greatest safeguard. He uses it to help his balance on the outward-dipping slabs, to anchor himself when the treacherous gusts are tearing at his legs, to clear a foothold on the snow-covered rocks and, on occasion, to cut steps across hard patches of snow. The second theory is even less tenable. Supposing the axe to have been planted on the summit, for the reasons just given it would not be abandoned there. Even if it were, and supposing that the wind blew it away, it could only fall on one side or the other of the summit ridge; to north or south, to the main Rongbuk glacier, 11,000 feet below, or down the enormous southern face. By no conceivable combination of circumstances could it be carried down the eastern edge of the final pyramid, and almost horizontally eastwards for a distance of about two thirds of a mile.

We have naturally paid close attention to the problem. Firstly, it seems probable that the axe marked the scene of a fatal accident. For the reasons already given, neither climber would be likely to abandon it deliberately on the slabs, and its presence there would seem to indicate either that it was accidentally dropped when a slip occurred or that its owner put it down possibly in order to have both hands free to hold the rope. The slabs at this point are not particularly steep, but they are smooth and in places have a covering of loose pebbles, which are an added danger. A slip might easily occur, and would be difficult to stop. We have no means of knowing if Mallory and Irvine climbed roped together; it is not unlikely that they did. But the rope is a poor safeguard, for the climber has no secure foothold on which to brace himself against a shock. Below, the slabs steepen considerably. A fall once begun is likely to continue. Norton has pointed out that anything dropped almost anywhere on the North Face is lost for good, owing to the outward and downward dip of the strata. A flat and comparatively light object like an axe might, in this particular place, have failed to gather momentum and therefore have stayed where it was dropped or laid down; and the axe in question resisted the pull of gravity and of the wind for nine years. But the rule rather than the exception would govern the effect of any miscalculation or loss of balance by a climber.

Secondly, the evidence is insufficient to prove whether the accident occurred during the ascent or the descent. Prima facie, a slip would be more likely to occur during the descent. It is known that Mallory preferred to try the crest of the North-East Arête, and he may well have taken this line to reach it, even from the old Camp VI on the North Ridge. Would he have returned the same way, whether he succeeded in climbing the second step or was forced on to Norton's traverse? If he was forced on to Norton's traverse, the more direct route back would be that adopted by Norton and Somervell, lower down; but Mallory might have preferred to regain the line that he had taken on the ascent and therefore knew to be practicable. If he climbed the second step he would almost certainly return the same way. Odell believes that he saw Mallory and Irvine near the second step while he was ascending from Camp V in support. If he did see them, and if our theory as to the scene of the accident is correct, Mallory and Irvine fell on the descent.

Everest 1938

The Mountain Turned White

H.W. Tilman

The Everest expedition of 1938 was a radical departure from its predecessors. While they had been gigantic affairs, with platoons of porters, designed to besiege the mountain, the 1938 venture was small-scale: just seven climbers and fifty-seven porters. This economy was partly forced on the Mount Everest Committee by the economics of the Depression, partly because of the success of the recent micro-expeditions of Frank Smythe to Kamet, of Tilman to Nanda Devi and of Spencer Chapman to Chomolhari. These stood in stark contrast to the failures of the Committee's big battalions on Everest. To its credit, the Mount Everest Committee, once converted, decided to appoint as leader of the 1938 expedition the principal proponent of the "small is successful" climbing school: Bill Tilman.

It was bad luck on Tilman that the 1938 expedition, as he records below, encountered such disastrous weather on Everest.

That this year's expedition to Mount Everest was organized on a smaller scale than before is well known. For some time past a few have inveighed against the large expedition on more grounds than one – mobility, efficiency, expediency and economy – but it was probably the financial aspect that finally tipped the scale, especially after the experience of 1936 when, through no fault of those concerned, the party was unable to accomplish anything. It was felt that the time had come to give other methods a trial, if only for the reason that they were less expensive.

Permission to go this time was obtained through the persuasive powers of Mr B. J. Gould, whose Mission visited Lhasa in the winter of 1936. The Committee, having appointed a leader, gave him a free hand, and, since the money was raised privately through the generosity of friends and members of the party, they were also spared financial responsibility. A satisfactory arrangement was made with *The Times*, but it is a matter for regret on our part that through an unfortunate incident the terms of the contract were not fulfilled by us. We budgeted for a cost of something less than a quarter of previous expeditions.

The party which assembled in India at the end of February consisted of seven, all of whom were climbers: H. W. Tilman, E. E. Shipton, F. S. Smythe, N. E. Odell, Dr C. B. M. Warren, P. Lloyd, Captain P. R. Oliver. A dozen Sherpa porters were collected in Darjeeling, and the party left Gangtok on 4 March with sixty mules carrying the baggage. A week was spent at Tangu, where snow still lay deep, through which a track for the mules was cleared with the whole-hearted assistance of the Sikkim Road Engineer. The Sebu La was crossed on 18 March on a cold blustery day, but thereafter throughout the march across Tibet we enjoyed bright sunny days marred only by the wind which blew usually in the afternoons.

We reached Rongbuk on 6 April, ten days earlier than the earliest of previous expeditions, having taken the precaution of being there in time to avoid a repetition of the 1936 experience. As will be related the weather did break early, even earlier than in 1936, but until it broke the wind and cold made climbing impossible. The day after our arrival we were joined by forty-five Sherpas, who came over from Sola Khombu in accordance with arrangements, bringing with them 1300 lbs of food. They came by a 19,000-foot pass called the Nangpa La and the journey takes about a week. As women and children cross the pass later in the season, it must be easy; but we were told that no animal transport ever uses it because the guardian spirit of the pass takes the form of a horse, and any four-footed animal that presumes to cross is at once struck dead.

In spite of the mild conditions of the march, wind and dust had taken their usual toll: Oliver and Lloyd had colds, Odell a bad cough, Warren went to bed with what was called influenza and Shipton with colic. After the usual ceremonies at the monastery, when the old abbot blessed the whole party, Europeans and Sherpas, individually, we moved up to the original Base Camp. This was used only as a halting place; we took with us up the glacier everything we required and had no lines of communication to bother about. After making one carry to Camp I we reduced our porter strength from sixty-one to thirty-one, because we were in no great hurry to reach the mountain owing to the prevailing cold and wind. With this reduced porter strength four relays to each camp up the glacier were necessary, and it was not until 18 April that we occupied Camp II. There I went down with influenza and after four days in bed went down to Rongbuk on the 22nd. Before I went we discussed plans, and decided that after the North Col slopes had been examined Shipton and Smythe should go over to the Kharta valley for a rest, leaving the others to carry on and make an attempt if conditions allowed. The reason for this was that Shipton and Smythe, who had had most experience and were our most likely pair, were of the opinion that the end of May was the most probable time for an attempt and were averse to making an earlier one.

On the 26th I returned to Camp III where the others now were. They reported much ice on the North Col slopes and were not in favour of doing anything more yet on account of the extremely cold conditions. Temperatures of 46 and 47 degrees of frost at night were being recorded; moreover none of the party was fit: coughs, colds and sore throats were the tale of our infirmities, and on Mount Everest the only cure for these complaints is a lower altitude. On the 27th therefore Shipton, Smythe, Oliver and nine men crossed the Lhakpa La (22,000 feet) *en route* for the Kharta valley. The rest of us waited a couple of days and then followed them, the wind and cold showing no signs of abating. The alternatives to this move were to stay and carry on, or to go down to Rongbuk, which was nearer to the mountain but less beneficial to health. Before leaving England I had been strongly warned by Norton, who in 1924 had suffered in the same way, against committing the party too early with the probable result of putting some of us out of action with frostbite; and such were the conditions at this time that this was less of a probability than a certainty for any party above the North Col. Nor, as things turned out, would mere proximity to the mountain by our being at Rongbuk have helped us. Bitter weather continued until 5 May, when snow fell heavily and fell daily for the next week. The mountain turned white and was never again in climbable condition.

Our camp among grass and trees at the head of the Arun gorge was a change from the harsh conditions of the glacier camps. All enjoyed their stay there except myself, who went to bed on arrival with a recurrence of influenza and only left it to begin the march back on 10 May. Shipton and Smythe stayed behind, intending to return by the Lhakpa La in time to meet us at Camp III on 20 May. We returned by the Doya La and reached Rongbuk again on the 14th, whence our first view of the mountain was not reassuring. It was covered with snow and the plume was now blowing off the summit from the reverse of the familiar north-west direction. On reaching Camp III on 18 May we found drastic evidence of changed conditions: a foot of snow now covered the bare ice of the glacier, and water lay about in pools whereas before water was only obtainable by melting ice.

Early on 19 May clouds poured up over the Rapiu La in ominous fashion, bringing in their train intermittent falls of snow; but Odell and Oliver having examined the North Col slopes reported the snow in good condition. Lloyd was sickening for his turn of our common complaint, but on the 20th four of us and four Sherpas began making a route up to the col. The line we took almost directly up the middle was undoubtedly well adapted to act as an avalanche shoot, but the snow was good and the climbing easy until within about 300 feet of the top, when the angle steepened considerably, forcing us out to the left on a long traverse before we were again able to climb straight up. Oliver, who had done most of the work in front with his two Sherpas, was suspicious of the snow on the traverse and waited until the rest of us had come up before embarking on it with his two men, carrying a light line for fixing. A short way out they got bunched and the snow avalanched. The leading man, a Sherpa, was clear of the cleavage, and the line we were paying out got mixed up in their climbing rope so that we easily held them. Part of the route having thus been made safe, Odell and I took over the job of cutting and stamping out a track in the steep, soft snow. It was so hot that a little of this work was enough to send us back to camp at 4 p.m., where we found Shipton and Smythe, who had recrossed the Lhakpa La early that morning. They had watched our performance with interest and anxiety and were glad to see us coming down. That evening it snowed steadily for several hours and the roar of the resulting avalanches continued far into the night.

This heavy fall of snow gave rise to discussion. The slopes would be unsafe for three or four days, while if the wind for which we prayed came the probable formation of windslab might make them dangerous for an indefinite period. Having in mind the queer behaviour of the snow here in previous years our thoughts began to turn to the route up the west side, which had been warmly recommended by the 1936 party who had looked at it but not gone up it. We decided that Shipton and Smythe, taking half the porters, should go round, and if they succeeded in reaching the col should attempt the mountain. The contemplated division left both parties weak in porters, but it promised that one or other would reach the col.

A cold windy night followed by a promise of colder weather made us drop the plan for the moment, and next day, having examined the slopes, their condition seemed good enough to warrant a start. On 24 May, all the Europeans, less Lloyd who went down to recuperate, and twenty-five porters went up to the col. The route to the top was soon finished, ropes fixed, and by midday all were up. Loads were dumped on the 1936 site where the apex of one of their Pyramid tents showed through the snow. Next day Smythe and I took fifteen more porters up; we left early, were on the top by 10 a.m., and back in camp by midday. The outlook from the col was as depressing as from below. Clouds could be seen billowing up from both sides, the air was still, the mountain white, and the snow at our feet, deep and soft. More discussion followed, when it was decided that Shipton and Smythe should retire to Rongbuk, returning when the mountain was less white, and that we others should occupy the col in order to examine the snow higher up. Uncertain whether the west side would be practicable, we were reluctant to commit ourselves to that yet; meanwhile it was no good keeping more men than needful at Camp III. Nevertheless, when more snow fell the following day we reverted to the earlier plan, and on the 27th Shipton, Smythe and half the porters went down, with the intention of returning by the west side when conditions improved.

On the 28th Odell, Oliver, Warren, myself and thirteen porters went up to Camp IV on the col. It was very hot, mist hung over the slopes and the snow in places was rotting; we crossed the traverse one by one. Eight porters went down with orders to return next day with more loads if no snow fell, but a foot of snow fell that night, so nothing was done. There was more snow on the 29th, but on the 30th Oliver went off to examine from the end of a rope the snow on the western slopes and the rest of us toiled through knee-deep snow up the North Ridge. Warren tried the closed type oxygen apparatus with unlooked for results. It seemed bent on suffocating him, and he did not wear it long. In addition to two of the closed type apparatus in which pure oxygen is breathed by means of a mask over mouth and nose, and which weighs 35 lb., we had two of the simpler open type with which one obtains oxygen by a tube in the mouth and also whatever air is available through the nose. Professor Finch was alone in recommending this type, the comparative success of which was instructive.

I pushed on with a Sherpa to about 24,500 feet, but it was obviously no use trying to occupy Camp V yet, and when more snow fell that day we beat a retreat. A suggestion that two of us should go down by the west side was not accepted owing to Oliver's account of the snow. On 1 June we were at Camp I, whence, next morning, Oliver and I walked up to Lake Camp to see Shipton, Smythe and Lloyd, who were on their way to the western approach. The camp is a pleasant spot by a tarn on the right moraine of the main glacier some 2 miles above Camp I. A change had come over the weather and for the last forty-eight hours a strong west wind had been driving low clouds before it. Through breaks in the flying scud we could see snow being whirled off the face of the mountain in a most encouraging manner, but while the wind might clear the snow off it might also form windslab on the east or lee side slopes; we therefore bowed to Smythe's reiterated warnings, and decided to concentrate on an approach from the west. I joined Shipton's party, which we reinforced to a strength of seventeen porters, and the others were told to follow as soon as some necessary loads had been brought down from Camp III. After making an intermediate camp on 4 June on the main glacier (Corner Camp), we marched up the short glacier lying between the North Face of the mountain and the North Peak, leading to the foot of the west side of the col. Mist caused some difficulty amongst the crevasses of the icefall, but by 2 p.m. we were in camp (West Side Camp) on the snow terrace at the foot of the slope. The height must be about the same as Camp IV (21,500 feet). Snow was still blowing about on the col and the Yellow Band looked fairly free from snow, but we were about to learn that appearances from below were deceptive.

Our way next morning led up the debris of a large avalanche which had apparently fallen recently. In consequence the first 500 feet of the slope was bare ice, and after cutting steps up this we had to cut steps across it in order to get on to snow that was still in place and which at that early hour might be expected to remain there. On the whole the parties who left this route alone in previous years seem to have had reason. We reached Camp IV at 11 a.m. after a long plug up bad snow on which even the feeble sun there was had no good effect. The sky had a curious glassy look through which the sun peered wanly surrounded by a double halo.

Next morning, 6 June, we started with fifteen porters for Camp V. Lloyd was wearing the open type apparatus. The snow slope at the foot of the North Ridge up which we had ploughed so heavily a week ago had now been swept hard by the wind. Approaching 25,000 feet two porters succumbed to altitude and most of the others were unhappy, while yet 300 feet below the Camp V site (25,800 feet) a sudden snowstorm further demoralized them and there was talk of dumping the loads and going down. In the end however better feelings prevailed, and by 4 p.m. everybody was up. Leaving Shipton, Smythe and seven porters there, Lloyd and I took the rest down. Two of those seven actually went down several hundred feet that evening and brought up the two abandoned loads – a very fine piece of work.

Wind prevented the Camp V party doing anything next day, but on the 8th they moved up to Camp VI (27,200 feet), finding it hard work making a track up fairly steep rocks that in many places were snow-covered. The climb of 1,400 feet took eight hours, and the seven porters, who stuck nobly to their task, only got back to Camp V very late and very tired. On the 9th Shipton and Smythe started, but, like Lloyd and me later, they were out too early and had to go back to the tent to warm up. Finally, after leaving the little patch of scree on which Camp VI was pitched, they struck diagonally upwards, but almost at once got into deep powder snow. Realizing the futility of persevering under those conditions, they returned to the tent and thence down to the North Col.

Meantime Lloyd and I had a day off at Camp IV, took three sick men down by the west side, and then, on the day Shipton and Smythe were returning, he and I started up with six porters. As we were going up to Camp V we saw Odell, Warren, Oliver and two porters coming up to Camp IV from the west side camp. Farther up we passed the seven porters returning from Camp V, and in that camp, which we reached at 3 p.m., we met Shipton and Smythe also on their way down. After hearing their report of conditions higher up, we agreed that the summit was out of the question and decided to reach if possible the summit ridge and to work along it to the second step. Two of our porters were persuaded to stay, the rest went down.

A gale in the night made the double-skinned Pyramid tent flap so furiously that sleep was impossible. Leaving at 8 a.m. we reached Camp VI soon after midday. Lloyd, wearing the oxygen, led and I followed, roped to the two porters. He got in some half an hour ahead of us evidently feeling more benefit from the oxygen as we got higher. For the short distance we went next day he also moved faster than I did, but perhaps under the circumstances that was no criterion. What I did expect was that the oxygen would give him sufficient extra "kick" to climb the rocks which so easily defeated us next day;

but Lloyd's opinion is that less effort was required when moving and consequently he was merely less fatigued. We sent the men down, collected snow for cooking and turned in, for the wind was already rising. We ate pemmican soup for supper. At night it blew hard and we slept little.

Starting at 8 a.m. on 11 June in a very gentle breeze we had not been going ten minutes before my hands were numb and Lloyd complained that his feet were in almost the same state. We returned to the tent and waited until 10.30 before trying again. As our first objective was the summit ridge immediately west of the north-east shoulder, we had to climb a steep rock wall some fifty feet high, just above the camp. Not liking the look of this from closer up we turned half-right towards an upwards sloping snow corridor, but there a few thigh-deep steps quickly drove us back to our first choice. There were three or four possible lines up the rock, all of which we tried with an equal lack of success. Each looked simple enough, but the smooth outward-sloping rock easily defeated our irresolute attacks. As I was inspecting the fourth and last possibility, Angtharkay and another man whom we had told to come up were seen approaching the tent. Here was an excuse for going down, had we been in want of one, so down we went. If we had gained the summit ridge then some 200 feet above us we should have been a mile distant from the summit and 1,500 feet below it, and 1,200 yards from the second step. The ridge looked difficult and the second step would almost certainly have defeated us, but it will be a lasting regret that we were unable to try.

We descended to Camp V in a storm and reached Camp IV that evening in calm weather. Only Odell, Oliver and a few porters remained on the col, the others having gone down by the old route that morning. Ongdi, one of our best men, had developed pneumonia, which obliged Warren to go down with him. Pasang, another Camp VI man, was lying paralysed. Oliver was keen to go to Camp VI, but having a sick man on our hands, no hope of climbing the mountain, and some anxiety about the descent, the prudent course was to go down. The ice traverse put the western route out of court for getting a helpless man down, and on 12 June we descended by the old familiar way. Three men were kept back to look after Pasang, and after some difficulty we got him down to the glacier and thence to Camp III.

Thus ended the 1938 attempt. We halted at Rongbuk until 20 June, but in the interim the weather gave us no encouragement to stay. There was talk of returning in the autumn, but none of the party was available, and the chances of finding favourable conditions in October are, in my opinion, exceedingly remote. Assuming the unlikely fact that by then the wind has cleared the snow away, the wind and cold are increasing instead of diminishing, the days getting shorter and the North Face receiving less and less sun.

To sum up, I think we have shown that a small party costing less than £2,500 is as likely to reach the top as a large one costing £10,000. Two parties of two were in position at 27,200 feet, fit and ready to make a serious bid for the summit had conditions allowed. It would have been more convincing to have reached the top, but I believe enough was done to satisfy candid people that our methods are sound.

We learnt, as had already been learnt twice before, that it is impossible to climb the last 2,000 feet if there is snow on the rocks. Siege tactics are impracticable at that height, but even if the labour of ploughing through powder snow was not insuperable there is the danger of the snow sliding off. Though wind seems capable of impacting snow up to about 25,000 feet it seems to have no such effect on snow above that.

The fact that we took no wireless equipment seems to have caused some surprise, but I do not see how even a small receiving set would have benefited us this year, and why a mountaineering party should wish to take a transmitting set is difficult to understand. This year we might have been told in the first days of May that a disturbance was approaching, but the news would not have caused us to alter our plan of making the attempt at the end of the month, because at the time no earlier attempt was possible. Even supposing some omniscient being had told us that from 5 May onwards monsoon conditions would prevail (as they did) we should certainly have been well informed but unable to do anything about it except, perhaps, pack up.

Something has been learnt about oxygen, but my own

belief is that the mountain could and should be climbed without it. The opinion of a representative body of mountaineers has not been taken, but my feeling is that a successful oxygen attempt would merely inspire a wish to do it without. No finality would be reached, and the ultimate result would be another long-drawn series of attempts to climb the mountain in a normal way.

To conclude: the weather is all-important, and for success conditions on the last 2,000 feet must be perfect. In 1936 and 1938 there was great hope that the mountain would be climbed, and yet in neither year was a bid for the top ever possible. Whether with a system of attempts at haphazard intervals the dice are not too heavily loaded is a question that will have to be decided.

Everest 1947

Everest Unofficial

Earl Denman

Denman was a Canadian maverick who tried a clandestine attempt on Everest in 1947. He lacked, together with the small matter of the necessary permit, any high-altitude climbing experience, proper equipment and adequate funds. Such, however, was his obvious guts and determination that he persuaded the Sherpas Tenzing Norgay and Ang Dowa to accompany him.

Denman was not the only "outsider", to use Walt Unsworth's phrase, who attempted Everest solo and on the sly. In 1934 the eccentric Englishman Maurice Wilson perished on the North Col*; in 1951, the Danish adventurer Klaus Becker-Larsen was forced back down Everest's slopes by a rockfall.

We set off for Everest on the morning of Thursday, 10 April. From then onwards we had to be our own beasts of burden, though I carried only a haversack and the small lightweight tent. Tenzing and Ang Dowa packed a large kitbag apiece, and suspended them from their foreheads by broad bands of cloth. I had thought they might obtain porters to carry the loads as far as the base of the mountain, but for some reason or other they did not do so. Perhaps no assistance could be gained from the monastery, or Tenzing did not want to arouse suspicion by requesting it, for we were supposedly going only as far as the base to make a survey and take photographs.

There was a distance of between twelve and fifteen miles of practically level ground to be covered. The mountain lay directly ahead of us in the rubble-strewn Rongbuk Valley. The

---

* see Appendix II

great North Face, with its massive, pyramidal formation, rose almost vertically in an impregnable wall of rock. A climber could have all the pitons and ropes in the world, but he would never be able to progress anywhere near the top in a vertical assault. If the mountain could be sliced through at the level of Rongbuk monastery and placed at sea-level it would represent a difficult but not impossible task. But rising as it does from the height of Rongbuk to 29,000 feet it is an impossible climb. The head of the main Rongbuk Glacier could be seen glistening white, but elsewhere there was surprisingly little snow and ice. An arête and a sloping face to the west held a fair amount of snow, but the North Face, too steep to retain snow readily, stood out grey and sombre. A thin, white streamer – the renowned plume of Everest – was being driven away to the east, and extended for a considerable distance from the mountain peak. (The Houston Mount Everest Expedition had reported that, at a most moderate estimate, the plume at the time of their flight over the summit on 3 April 1933 could not have been less than six miles in length.)

The various bands in which the North Face terminates stood out boldly. An oblique line running at a slight inclination to the east cut off what is known as the "Yellow Band" from the great mass of the mountain. What appeared as a distinct black band came next and, above that, the untrodden "final pyramid". This gave me my idea for establishing proof of reaching the summit, if we should succeed in doing so. My normal habit of collecting small pieces of rock from mountain heights could be put to useful effect. Successive pieces of rock obtained from the various strata comprising the summit block would give reasonable proof of having been that far. I could think of no better proof, and still cannot, for the types of rock from which the different bands are made up must be of very different nature to be shown so clearly from a distance.

We passed nothing of note on the way except occasional hermits' dwelling places, none of which were occupied. It made me smile to think of the imaginative but far from accurate advertisements depicting Everest surrounded by coniferous trees. The scene was in decided contrast with the approaches to many African mountains, where relays of men are needed to go ahead and clear a track through dense forest and undergrowth.

It would be difficult to perceive beauty in Everest. It is no more than a massive upthrust surmounted by snow and ice and blasted by strong winds. N. E. Odell, of past Everest fame, once made the suggestion that expeditions to the mountain should be looked upon primarily as scientific ventures, with an attempt to reach the summit only if conditions proved favourable. No doubt his suggestion was made at a time when there was talk of the Royal Geographical Society withdrawing its support because of an alleged lack of scientific value attaching to the undertaking. Certainly, in my opinion, there is very little of scientific importance to be gathered on Everest. It is essentially a mountaineering project pure and simple. It is wholly a matter of man pitting himself against the highest mountain in the world. Nothing grows there, nothing lives there and the only thing manufactured in the vicinity is intensely bad weather. Everest is sufficient in itself, and should be accepted as it is – a challenge to man's resourcefulness and inquisitiveness.

As we closed upon the mountain, I could not help wondering why the original reconnaissance party of 1921 had tried to find a way, as I think they did, to the west before attempting to penetrate the eastern approaches. The long arête above the main Rongbuk Glacier probably tempted them, but to me the difficulties appeared insuperable in that direction.

We followed round the base of the mountain, proceeding beyond an open patch where camp is established by large expeditions which need to keep a base camp in operation – a thing we could not do, even had we wished to. It provided something of a thrill – the only pleasurable thrill I was to experience – when erecting the two silvercloth tents against a background of Everest for the first time. The weather could not have been better, and so we did not hurry. The ground was extremely rocky, but at least it was not volcanic rock as in the Virungas, for the Himalayas came into being as the result of a fracturing and uplifting of the earth's surface. There was no volcanism accompanying the action.

The tents stood firmly and were good to look at. I took some photographs and entered a few words in my diary while Tenzing darned a pair of stockings and Ang Dowa dozed at his side. It was so warm that I even sunbathed for a few minutes without a shirt. Our camp might have been a picnic scene far remote from the Himalayas. Everest was in generous, almost inviting mood. It lulled me into a false sense of well-being. What had passed, had passed. I did not look back and count my blessings. I felt no more than a mild satisfaction, if any at all, with recent accomplishments. It had not yet dawned upon me that what we had already done was about as much as we could do. To have penetrated so far into a barren, inhospitable, closed territory had been no mean feat. But at the time I thought nothing of it. I did not think to give praise for blessings already received, or to take stock of the series of near-miracles which had served to take me so far from Bulawayo in as little as fifty-three days of hard travelling.

The precious remains of our petrol – what had not seeped out or otherwise gone to waste – had been poured into an aluminium flask, and from this we filled the Coleman stove. Water was near at hand in a small stream and in patches of snow. Our entire supply of tea had already vanished, despite the use of Tibetan tea during part of our journey. This was the result of a bad under-estimate on my part, and it meant that we had to rely solely upon Oxo and Ovaltine. The stove, when set going, fascinated Ang Dowa, who took his cookery seriously, and together we prepared a meal.

Whatever complacency I had felt was banished when a bitterly cold wind swept upon us with breathtaking suddenness. The sun sank low and we crept into our separate tents, Tenzing and Ang Dowa sharing the larger one, in which we had done the cooking. I was alone, cramped in the very low, wall-less tent, which I wanted to try for size and serviceability. As night drew on, the wind increased and the cold penetrated every nook and cranny. Darkness fell and the hours dragged by, but I could not sleep because I could not derive any warmth from my sleeping-bags. Now and then, during the midnight hours, I could hear the others in their tent labouring for breath and moaning softly as they slept between bouts of wakefulness. More than once I thought of going to join them, but I would not disturb their rest. I was too numbed in mind and body to realize the truth, but this first night was really the beginning of the end.

In the morning there was fresh snow on the ground, and some water left in the tent overnight had frozen into a solid block. I lit some candles for the slight warmth they would give, and as soon as it was sufficiently light outside, I joined Tenzing and Ang Dowa in their tent, where we lit the stove and prepared a meal. Then, without any waste of time, we took down the two tents and moved off to our second camp. There was no need to hang around, for we were already well acclimatized after our journey through Tibet, which had been made at considerable altitudes without a return to lower country.

The going was very rough, over and around hills of loose rocks among which it would have been easy to rick an ankle. It was unpleasant enough for me, but how Tenzing and Ang Dowa fared with their heavy loads was something to marvel at. Another thing that amazed me was their almost unhesitating certainty of the route, which is not by any means easy to follow without mistake as it twists and turns through the Lhakpa La. Also, neither man had been on the mountain since 1936 – an interval of more than ten years.

The mountain was utterly barren, and there was so much rubble about that I could easily imagine a mass of scree at this point in years to come. Give the frosts and melted snow a few more decades in which to split and wear away the tumbling, crumbling rock and there will be a vastly different scene. There is nothing I hate more on mountains than fine scree, but Everest will have its share of this in time. There are immense changes taking place at present. It does not require much knowledge of geology to tell that Everest, like all other Himalayan peaks, is young in geological terms. It is even said that the mountain is still growing, and this is quite likely.

Poets of all ages have done much to create a vision of immutability by extolling the "immortal mountains" and "changeless hills", but this is all imaginary. There is no immortality in nature. As with civilization, there is constant modification, alteration and even revolution. Change is not always progressive – advancement and building up – it is also regression and decay. Evidence of change surrounds us in our daily lives: only, because of a natural desire for immortality in some shape or form, we like to believe that the mountains are eternal, indestructible masses. They are not, however, and we who set out to climb them would do well to remember this; it is a sobering thought.

The weather, all-important, remained good throughout the day.

At our second camping site, with a minor peak and tall, fluted seracs forming a background, we decided to erect only the larger of the two tents, in which we could all be accommodated without being too cramped for space. I did not mind sleeping with the others if they did not mind sleeping with me. In fact this joining of forces was entirely agreeable to me, being in line with my desire to make our undertaking a joint venture in which there was no distinction apart from that of employer and employee, which could not be avoided. It had the effect of breaking down the last surmountable barrier between us.

Tenzing and Ang Dowa were acting as porters, but I never thought of them in this way, for a climber can only go as far on Everest as the porters, by their own efforts, will permit. Thus there was an ideal bond between us. We were all porters and we were all climbers. Beyond that we were just three men who were striving to give some meaning to a life which otherwise remains meaningless. What *were* we striving for if not for immortality? Most people are content to leave their own progeny as emblems of their own striving. To others this is not sufficient. The name of an individual or of any group of people will be as nothing in the end. It is only deeds that satisfy, and men and women are only remembered for their deeds, whether they be good or bad.

The sole evidence of the progress of previous expeditions on the mountain was provided by the many rusty sardine tins scattered along the route. There was never a jam tin, or a tin of fruit or vegetables – only sardines. Why these should have survived seemed just as unaccountable as a preference for what always strikes me as a most disagreeable kind of food to take on any high mountain.

That we did not encounter wildlife in any form whatever

was not surprising in view of the absolute barrenness of the scene, but there is no reason why a little problem of wildlife should not be introduced at this stage by discussing the likelihood or otherwise of discovering some mysterious mammal in the vicinity of Everest. To put the question bluntly, does such a creature as the Himalayan "yeti" or "abominable snowman" exist?

Much of the news concerning this subject is of recent origin. It seems that a wild man of the Himalayas was brought to the notice of the Western world by Col L. A. Waddell, who wrote *Among the Himalayas*, published in 1898. But this was only a small start and it was not until the beginning of exploration in the Everest region that attention was again drawn to the possible existence of a wild Himalayan creature as yet unknown to science. It is said that Col Howard Bury, leader of the 1921 reconnaissance, noticed some strange footprints on the Lhakpa La and referred to them in a message as being those of a Wild Man of the Snows. Then – in the following year, I believe, or perhaps in 1924, when the second climbing party went to Everest – the English-speaking lama of Rongbuk mentioned to Gen. Bruce that there were five wild men living on the slopes of the Rongbuk Glacier.

It was left to a Mr Henry Newman, of Darjeeling, to popularize the animal. He did this by taking the Tibetan name of *Metch kangmi* and translating *Kangmi* as "snowman" and *metch* as "abominable," thus arriving at the astonishingly apt and captivating name of "abominable snowman". The English-speaking world now had a name of tremendous appeal with which to conjure.

The Mount Everest Reconnaissance Expedition of 1951, with its widely publicised photographs of footprints, did most of all to add to the growing legend, though there were some sceptics who derided the idea of an "abominable snowman" and looked for signs of retouching in the reproductions of the alleged footprints of the animal. Then, scepticism was increased by a highly feasible explanation which appeared in the *Glasgow Herald* and was subsequently reported in many other newspapers. The writer believed the "footprints" to be water blobs caused by condensation and precipitation under the effect of freakish warm air currents. He also suggested "that the study of the formation of these marks in the snow is a matter for a meteorologist rather than a zoologist or demonologist".

It will be interesting to learn the outcome of an expedition which is now being organized with the object of establishing the existence or otherwise of "the abominable snowman".

What are my own views on the subject?

Firstly, one needs to be very guarded, and there are not many naturalists who will commit themselves in any way. The inclination is to deride the idea out of hand, but there is always the thought that some new species of larger mammal may still await discovery. Certainly Sir Harry Johnston, one of the leading authorities of his time, would not have scorned the likelihood of a Himalayan species unknown to science. For it was he who, on the strength of conversations with H. M. Stanley, went in search of the mythical unicorn and astonished the world of natural history with his discovery of the okapi (*Okapia johnstoni*) at a time when zoologists no longer expected anything new, even from the primeval forests of the Congo basin. Johnston's discovery was made at the beginning of the present century, and as recently as 1913 there was the equally surprising find of the giant sable antelope (*Hippotragus niger variani*) by Frank Varian who came across the animal in Angola, where it has its only habitat. So, quite clearly, there is no reason to ridicule the possibility of another unique species coming to the notice of science in the latter half of the same century.

There is also the strange fact that only in the foothills of the Himalayas have any fossil remains been found of a species of anthropoid ape as near the sub-human form as the gorilla or chimpanzee of equatorial Africa. A form of chimpanzee appears to have been known to early Egyptians, but there have been no living or fossil remains brought to light between central Africa and north-west India, where fossil remains were found in lower Pliocene formations. "From the little we know of it," wrote Sir H. Johnston, "the *Palaeopithecous* of north-west India is rather nearer the human ancestor than any of the anthropoid remains of Europe."

There are greater doubts when considering the nature of habitat. It should not be thought that any large mammal could possibly exist on Everest or any of its satellites. The remarkable photographs of Shipton's "abominable snowman" were taken at a height of about 19,000 feet on one of the glaciers of the Menlung basin, almost twenty miles due west of Everest. Earlier tales of an "abominable snowman" on the Tibetan side of Everest can almost certainly be discounted. The whole question of occurrence or non-occurrence of the larger mammals resolves itself into one of sustenance and remoteness from human interference. The habitat must provide vegetation of the right kind, and also it must afford adequate shelter, especially for mountain-dwelling species. The scientific study of wildlife in relation to its surroundings is known as ecology, and in the entire field of ecology there is no possibility of any chance occurrence as unlikely as that of a large mammal living on Everest.

Some months ago it was reported that a scantily-clad Indian ascetic had been found in good health after spending six months of autumn and winter in an icy Himalayan cave. He, however, had kept himself alive on dried fruits which he had collected during the previous summer.

It has often been suggested that similar ascetics, or men banished from remote monasteries for grave crimes, may be living like wild animals and thereby giving rise to the rumours of an "abominable snowman" or Himalayan "yeti".

In order to uncover the real truth it may be necessary to organize a special expedition in which mountaineers with considerable knowledge of natural history would have to take part. I know from my experiences on the Virunga mountains that one cannot go spooring wild animals while climbing in real earnest. I soon found out that it had to be the one thing or the other, and after that I just kept my eye to the various summits and let everything else go by. And so it is with Everest or any other Himalayan peak.

My second night on the mountain was a repetition of the first, only worse. All night long I tried to pummel some warmth into my cold body, but sleep would not come. My body was numb, and my mind could register nothing but misery. Trying to put my thoughts into words would be as futile as trying to assemble the reactions to death of a drowning man. Each hour seemed a day. Would dawn *never* come?

It did in the end, and we set off early, not because we had to or wanted to, but because inactivity is the killing thing on Everest. One does not have to be on the mountain long to realize this.

Tenzing and Ang Dowa performed prodigies of work in carrying their loads to the next camp. I expected them to complain, but there was never a word of complaint from them. At one time we had to pick our way between numerous tall seracs which rose like giant's teeth from a trough with a flooring of ice and rock. From this trough we turned right, and came later to a glacial pool backed by tremendous pinnacles of ice which were reflected in its mirror-like surface. The North Col was visible and Tenzing said he had never seen it with so little snow.

Beyond the pool we camped at a spot several hundred yards away from the normal camping spot in this vicinity. Tenzing and Ang Dowa, who had hardly rested all the way, put down their loads as though they were only slight encumbrances, like a load of children on a zoo elephant.

There is no praise that can be too high for these men and their kind. They are the real workers, without whose efforts no expedition would have any hope of success. I became convinced more than ever that Everest "belongs" most of all to the Sherpas, and I am delighted that one of them (and one for whom I have such a special affection and admiration) should have been given the first chance of getting to the top.

The weather turned bitterly cold again in the evening, so there was no alternative but to turn in to bed after a few photographs had been taken. The sky had been clear until now, but there was an ominous darkening, and during the night a savage wind, like the breath from a Tibetan mastiff, sprang up. I went to bed in all the clothes I could muster, and this time Tenzing shared his sleeping bag with me, and I realised properly, for the first time, how miserably poor we were and what little chance we stood.

By this time I had not much taste for food, and it was almost too much trouble to prepare anything to eat. Cheese was my real mainstay because its taste still registered on my jaded palate. Otherwise the only food to retain any appreciable flavour was milk chocolate with nuts and raisins, in large slabs. It provided me with a pastime, too. At night I kept some within reach and nibbled it when sleep was out of the question. It was a rather tiring business though, involving the removal of my gloves each time I took a bite. Every movement let in a cold draught as I stole out a hand, took a bite, put on my gloves again and lay sucking until the chocolate melted from the nuts and raisins. It was the only pastime I could think of, and to me the nuts and raisins were treasures which had to be unearthed. Even so, time dragged horribly, and in a few hours I seemed to live a lifetime. Occasionally I heard sharp cracks, like pistol shots, from the pinnacles of ice outside as they contracted in the cold air. I do not recall sleeping for a single minute during the night at this; our third camp.

The wind did not relent in the morning, and we pushed on in the face of it over rough stones to a long rising slope of alternate gravel and ice until finally we entered the East Rongbuk glacier. On one ice slope we came across a broken climbing boot discarded by a previous expedition. The glistening ice of the glacier was made treacherous by a total absence of snow for our nailed boots to bite into. Tenzing used crampons, but Ang Dowa and I carried on without. We all put on goggles.

After the long climb up the glacier, dangerously pitted with crevasses, we swung to the right, where there was a moraine, and ahead, the North Col. Now we faced the wind in all its fury, and near the foot of the col we battled to erect our single tent. The men were tight-lipped, but otherwise their faces remained expressionless. I wondered how they felt, but they said nothing and gave no indication of their feelings. The fact that we had to wear more than one pair of gloves made our task all the more difficult. The wind, as though it had a mind of its own, seemed determined to tear the tent from our grasp as we tried to drive pegs into the frozen ground. We worked for brief spells and then stopped to turn our backs to the wind and slap our hands against our thighs. Some pegs we could drive in but others we could not. Where we could not use them we piled huge stones on top of the guy ropes and hoped for the best. Where pegs could be driven in, we also placed stones on top, as heavy as we could carry, for additional safety.

At last we had the tent as secure as we could make it. Before entering I took a good look at the North Col. It did not look as frightening as I had expected. Its slope was less severe than I had been led to believe. Three men could tackle it in safety, but not in the face of the wind as it was blowing then. It must die down or we would be doomed, one way or another.

That night I prayed. "God help me. Help me to do the right thing. Do not rob me of the chance to go forward, but give me strength to go back if I must."

For myself I cared little. I had dedicated myself to Everest. My whole life was Everest. I did not want to live if we failed. I was not concerned about death. There are a million deaths and a million births. It is easy to die; much easier than to live. But we cannot die without fear: either we must fear to die or we must be afraid of living.

So far we had succeeded in doing on Everest what we had done all the way through Tibet. We had gone from camp to camp without stopping in any one place for more than a single night. This is the great advantage to be gained from having a small, extremely mobile party. The 1933 Everest expedition had taken sixteen to twenty-four days* to do what we had done in four days.

The chronology of their progress from Rongbuk up to this stage is set out below for comparison:

April	16	Arrived Rongbuk.
	17	Base camp established.
	21	Camp I established.
	26	Camp II established.
May	2	Camp III established.
	8	Camp IIIA established.

As can be judged from this progress, there is a considerable lapse of time between the establishment of one camp and

---

* I do not know for certain how their camps corresponded with ours.

another where a large expedition is involved, and a shuttle service has to be run between the base camp and each successive camp. If there are many camps spread out beyond the base of operations one needs a secondary or intermediate base. The result is that, from something easily manageable, an intricate system grows and grows, and the more time that is spent in establishing and servicing a chain of camps, the greater the time lost in other ways.

For instance, it is necessary to be inside a tent by 4 o'clock, and once inside a tent there is nothing to do but get into bed and stay there. This may mean spending fourteen or fifteen hours recumbent at a single stretch, and even ten hours is a long time for a normally active man to be abed. Time can become the great enemy in more ways than one. There have been occasions, in the past, when small-talk has dwindled and arguments have led to petty grievances, and in turn to frayed tempers and hostility.

On the other hand there is the matter of acclimatization to be taken into account. Some may claim that the time spent in establishing camps and stocking them, with intervals between, is all to the good because it provides time for gradual acclimatization. I do not agree with this at all. We never found ourselves in need of time for acclimatizing. Perhaps we might have done so at some point higher than we were able to go, but I do not think so. Or, if we had, a single day would have done much to put us right. Deterioration – both physical and mental – is a worse bogy on Everest than acclimatization.

All through the night the tent had to withstand a howling, piercing blast from the elements. The guy-ropes pulled, tugged, heaved, strained at their fastenings. The sides flapped vigorously and ceaselessly – flap, flap, flap, flap, flap, flap, flap – as quickly as it is possible to repeat the word. Surely no fabric on earth could stand the stress! If it tore, what then? Two pegs were ripped from the ground. If one more went the same way, there would have been no alternative but for me to go outside in an attempt to prevent a total collapse. It was only the construction of the ground sheet and walls all in one piece which saved us from having the whole tent blown away from over our heads.

I rubbed myself, pummelled and kicked, in an effort to relieve myself of the gripping iciness. The only part of my body to retain any of its heat was at the meeting point between my thighs, and I put both hands there in an effort to give them a share of the warmth. Each minute seemed an hour and each hour an eternity. None of us spoke, but we must have known, as the wind slackened but still continued to rage, that we were beaten.

My prayers turned to bitter oaths. And, as this is a faithful record, I confess that I added some words of blasphemy.

With the first glimmer of daylight, I lit the stove and we all had a drink of hot cocoa and a light meal. Neither Tenzing nor Ang Dowa had slept much, and I had not slept at all. We had no programme mapped out, and we discussed nothing, but we were unanimous in going outside and starting to take down the tent. Then we packed as best we could, our hands numbed with cold. Whatever happened we could not stay where we were. We had to go elsewhere, either up or down, to escape from the full force of the wind. We would not give in so easily, so we went on.

The snow on the col was not at all as I had seen it in photographs. The wind, no doubt, had blown much of it away, baring the col to an unusual extent. There were no sweeping, rounded mounds, and not much fine snow. At about the centre of the trough leading to it there was an even, gentle slope to a large pyramid of ice which appeared to have a square base. Beyond this, but diverging at right angles (in the direction of the mountain summit) was a slightly steeper slope, which continued to the top. The obstacle that faced us was, in itself, nothing insuperable – in fact it was not the giant that I had expected it to be. But no sooner had we set upon it than the wind, which until then had relaxed somewhat, gathered up its forces and howled at us with renewed fury. The sky, which on previous days had been clear, was an unrelieved dark mass, almost black. We turned from the height of about 23,500 feet that we had reached and went back as quickly as we could to the site of our fourth camp on the mountain, but it was obvious that we could not set up our tent there. For one thing, our hands were almost useless. They were on the verge of frostbite.

We held our consultation, if it could be called a consultation. We had played our hand.

I had been critical of large expeditions, but now the scales were turned. No expedition, large or small, could have battled on in the face of the prevailing conditions. But a large expedition would have had a chain of camps, or at least a base camp, to retreat to, there to wait and to try again when conditions had improved. We, for our part, had no reserves. Even if we could have retired to a lower camp, we could not have stayed there for any length of time because we had insufficient food to stand siege. We were a spent force.

Another consideration was that of safety. We had no margin whatever between survival and non-survival. A twisted ankle, a broken leg, frostbite or snowblindness – if any of these had happened to any one of us, the entire party would most likely have been doomed. We had known this from the beginning, of course. It was one of the risks we had been willing to take.

My bitterness was like an open wound as we hastened down, almost running. I refused to consider myself vanquished as a mountaineer by a technical difficulty. There were greater forces, or more elemental ones, to take into account, and I felt deprived by them of the opportunity to demonstrate my capabilities to the utmost.

Had I ever been capable of reasoning, I would have known that my material resources were too slender for the tremendous task that I had set myself and my two Sherpa companions. We had attempted more than was humanly possible. There could be no disgrace in such a defeat, but I felt humiliated because I had been spurred on originally by high aspirations.

I suppose it is all a matter of the store we set on things. To some mountaineers, who go as one of a large party, Everest is no more than a glorious adventure. They do not have to pay for anything out of their own pockets, and failure, when it comes, is shared with others, many others: there is nothing personal about it. To me, however (and I am sure, to Tenzing, and probably to Ang Dowa as well), the physical adventure counted for very little in relation to the underlying motives. I thought I saw in the vision of success a wonderful meaning to life – my triumph over the gross materialism into which our civilization as I knew it has been plunged. Then, when success did not come, I thought I saw in failure the final crumbling away of anything that was not strictly material. I had always, since childhood, held to my own religion, a very personal sort of religion, elastic and meant for myself, not for whole groups of people who try to bridge their differences; a religion that I found good because it embraced nothing but the good from all religions, and discarded from them all that is stupid or merely pageantry or idolatry. In short, it was the religion of the high mountains. With failure, I saw a world that was not the world as I wanted it to be. I could never become entirely atheistic, but I tried hard at this time to deny the gods of all religions. Yet, even in my defeat, I struggled blindly, groping for a sustaining truth as I groped with my ice-axe, searching with the others for a way down the mountain, stumbling, cursing, hurrying away, trying to hate what I really loved. Seeking to convince myself that life meant nothing and would end in nothingness.

At Rongbuk we stayed only a day, leaving on the 16th with two tiny donkeys which had been brought in from Chö Dzong. The state of my body was deplorable. My skin had a sickly pallor and was flaking off. It may have been a touch of scurvy caused by a lack of vegetables in my diet. It worried me for a while, but it cleared up by itself. Tenzing and Ang Dowa were taking everything in their stride. There was never a rankling word or a sign of discontent from either of them. I came to like them better than ever because they seemed to understand the things that I could not understand, and they remained staunch at a time when I needed their help desperately.

I caught my last glimpse of Everest as we turned a corner in the trail leading to Chö Dzong. It was snowing at the time, and as I looked back with Tenzing and Ang Dowa there was little of the mountain to be seen. The greater part of it was shrouded in dense masses of grey and black clouds. In my thoughts was the certainty that no one could have survived there under such appalling conditions, and I knew by their looks that Tenzing and Ang Dowa were thinking the same. If

we had not come away when we did, we should have perished.
There could be little doubt about that, and it helped to soften
the blow of defeat somewhat. Even so, I cursed, but as I did
so I knew that if the chance came I would go again to the
mountain. That was why I was going away. It was why I had
not persisted in a suicidal attempt to remain on the mountain
beyond the utmost limit of endurance. One more night on
Everest and there would have been no return, but there would
also have been no defeat to live through, no more striving, no
more fruitless searching, wondering, waiting, yearning, and
no more unhappiness.

The long trail back! It was a journey without a horizon.
There was nothing behind but defeat, and nothing ahead but
emptiness. To the one side there was a desert of loneliness and
to the other a morass of despair. There was nothing to look up
to, and so my eyes remained downcast. I did not want to live,
and yet I could not die. A flood of hot tears would have relieved
the pent-up feeling deep within me, but I could not even cry.
There was no relief of any sort, neither death nor tears, and
because there was no escape I went blindly on, aware of the
wind and cold, but impervious to them.

Often on the way back and in later years I wondered if it
would not have been better to die on Everest. Was I so weak
that I could not give my life, or so regardless of posterity that I
would not? Or is it true that we only meet death when death is
ready to meet us? When we have done our best or worst and
can do no more?

If there has ever been a worse journey, then who has undertaken it? Who, if he were mortal, *could* undertake it?

I recalled the time when, on the outward journey, I had given
thought to a return under conditions of defeat, and had considered it impossible. And so it might have proved if I had not
learned to mellow my bitterness and to catch a glimmer of
hope. Would not another opportunity come? Was it, for
instance, entirely out of the question to hope for inclusion in
some future expedition under the joint sponsorship of the
Alpine Club and the Royal Geographical Society? Having
gained experience of actual Everest climbing, there was now a
likelihood, which did not exist before, but it would mean

forsaking my principles in the choice of a small party rather than a large one. Well, I could but try, and in doing so I would not be the first to forsake a principle. On the other hand (and this was more to my liking) there was the slender possibility that I might get the opportunity of going to Everest again with my present companions under more favourable circumstances at a later date. This was only a slight hope, but I clung to it. For is not hope the last thing we have to lose before life itself? Is it not true that when hope vanishes we die?

It is not my intention to tell in full of the long journey back. It was just a hard, wearying slog, but a few of the incidents are worth recording.

We did not stay at Chö Dzong. We arrived there shortly after two o'clock and left half an hour later with three horses. By means of these, which we rode occasionally, we reached a village called Pemay (short "a"). We arrived long after dark, and I was sore after my first experience of a Tibetan saddle, made of two wooden rungs set about six inches apart. Also, Tibetans make use of exceptionally short stirrup leathers, and I had been forced to ride with my knees nearly touching my chin. I was horribly cramped, and so cold that, after I dismounted, I could not stand erect. I climbed as best I could to an upper-storey room which Tenzing had managed to obtain for the night. At the top of the stairs, which were made of round logs that revolved in a most awkward manner as soon as a foot was set on them, I stumbled blindly into a room in which there was a fire. An old woman sat there, and I squatted by her side to warm myself. A man of about the same age came in, and presently a taper was lit in a small container of oil. The old couple smiled and offered me some tea, which I accepted. I was not aware of the fact that I had intruded into their own living-room until Tenzing came to tell me of my mistake.

I would have left at once, but the two old people smiled understandingly, bidding me to stay and warm myself. It was the first time such consideration had been shown to me in Tibet, and I felt a deep sense of gratitude. It was a humble home, but there was friendliness as well as dirt about the place. The words of Mahatma Gandhi came to my mind: "They were burning huts," he had said (speaking of some religious disorders which had taken place while I was in India), "which to the dwellers were as precious as palaces to the princes." These words, ordinarily, would not have conveyed much meaning to me, but in my predicament of the moment they took on a tremendous significance. I did not wish for a mansion or a palace, but my whole being cried out for comfort, warmth and friendliness. I had these, in a humble Tibetan home, dirty beyond description. The homes of the wealthy may be more elaborate and costly than the slums of the poor, but can they always offer as much?

We used two more donkeys between Pemay and Tsa. Tsa seemed to be deserted by everyone but extraordinarily vicious dogs, but at length we chanced upon the fine house of Kasang Chola La, who obviously was the most wealthy Tibetan we came across. He was not unhandsome, except when he smiled and showed his uneven teeth. His features were hardly Mongolian at all, and he was taller and slimmer than most of his countrymen. His two children, whom I photographed with him, were markedly similar in looks and build. They were, I should say, about eight and ten years of age. He was a deeply religious man, always fondling his string of holy beads, and every time he entered or left his house, he gave the three prayer wheels, set in the wall near the entrance, a gentle spin. I never saw him fail to do this. He wore a double-piece garment, and from his left ear dangled a large turquoise stone. He took snuff, and occasionally I saw him mix it with a pinch of ashes from a fire. He owned five horses, and he offered us three of these for our journey as far as Lachen. Tenzing said we would be nearly seven days in reaching there, so the charge of Rs. 105 was reasonable and I accepted the offer.

The next stage of our journey was to Congrung Laprang, where we made the river crossing in a biting gale. We stayed again with Nombi, who was disappointed to find that we had already obtained horses and would not be requiring any of his as we had previously arranged. However, he treated us well, and I left him a fifty-foot climbing rope with which he was immensely pleased.

I had never thought it possible, but from Congrung Laprang we went to Tarnak in a single day, missing Cojak. Thus we covered two of our outward stages in a single day, during which we had to withstand extreme cold and snow. It was incredibly quick going, but completely exhausting. There was aconite, a poisonous plant, along part of the route, and the horses had to be muzzled. We stayed in the same room as before at Tarnak, but the headman (who had hung a knife over my bed and warned us of bandits on the previous occasion) was away at the time, paying a call at another village. Here Ang Dowa had to crack a mastiff on the head to keep it at bay. We saw nothing of the "six horsemen" who had accosted us on the way out, and we made no attempt to be secretive about our movements. No one was likely to prevent us from *leaving* the country. Kasang Chola La's horses went splendidly over the pass leading to Sar, making light of the steep gradient at which the dzos had baulked. At the top of the pass, the Tibetan who accompanied us left a piece of an old *Bulawayo Chronicle* fluttering with the praying flags. I wonder if it is there today?

We bypassed Sar, as we had done before, and also Tashidzom. Beyond the ravine with its five separate streams, we kept too far over to the left, floundering and nearly sticking in the bog. I had a particularly bad time here, and was pleased to reach Lungma, which I recognised as a village at which we had only halted briefly for lunch when journeying in the opposite direction. Between Muk and Gombolo we again saw a small herd of wild asses, which may have been the ones we had seen earlier. At Gombolo we had the same room as before, and again we arrived after dark and left before dawn. It was best, at this stage, not to take any avoidable risks.

The morning sun was trying, the afternoon winds cruelly penetrating, and we arrived cold and tired at every destination. There was barely time to keep my diary up to date. I half expected a warrant for my arrest to be awaiting me at Darjeeling, and I was anxious to get the whole business over and face whatever consequences there were to be faced. Tenzing and Ang Dowa, for their part, wished to be back with their families as quickly as possible and perhaps to be in time to go out with other expeditions before the climbing season was over.

We went via the Kongra La to Donkung, where we stayed, for a change, in a room with a chimney leading from the roof.

We heard the disturbing rumour that a large party of Englishmen were at Thang-gu. Whether this was true or not, I never knew, for we left Donkung very early, travelling the first few miles over frozen ground by torchlight. We passed Thang-gu and did not stop until reaching Lachen, where there were still no apples on the trees. Here we had to part with the horses and the Tibetan who had come with them all the way from Tsa. This man had never been across the border into Sikkim before. It was a totally new experience for him, and I often wondered what he thought of the dense forests, grasses, flowers and other vegetation. He had a pleasant disposition and never complained about our hurried rate of progress. Often he walked along with one sleeve of his long garment dangling loose, while at other times, when warm enough, he tied both sleeves round his middle. At night, like others of his race, he simply pulled the whole garment over his head and round his feet.

Tenzing arranged with the Sikkimese herdsman who had come with us from Gangtok to Lachen to take us in the reverse direction for Rs. 62, using a mule and a donkey. I was pleased to have him with us again. Like the Tibetan from Tsa, he was pleasant company and a willing worker. He wore his black hair parted in the middle and arranged in a number of small pigtails at the sides. His skin had a coppery colour.

An incident that took place between Lachen and Chungthang stands out in my memory. Other people may think little of it, but to me it typified the monstrous selfishness of our age, and indicated that all is not well with those who profess to be followers of one religion or another.

I was looking forward with eager anticipation to my first meeting with a white man, for I had seen no one with whom I could converse freely since leaving Darjeeling. We were following the west bank of the Tista at a particularly narrow part of the trail when we came face to face with a white man mounted on a large grey mare. There was only room for one horse, so we stood aside to let him and his Sikkimese porter pass. I expected some recognition for our courtesy if for no other reason, but the man brushed past with head held high and a look of complete self-satisfaction on his face. He gave no sign of recognition whatever, and left me wide-mouthed with astonishment. Perhaps he was a missionary, which would make the sin of omission more odious than ever. Tenzing gave a quick glance in my direction, without speaking, but I knew what was in his thoughts.

With our Sikkimese muleteer we reached Gangtok on Sunday, 27 April. Here our trails had to part. The muleteer had to return with his animals to Lachen, while we others had to go on to Darjeeling where we arrived during the afternoon of the following day. I went again to my bleak little boarding-house, where there were no questions asked, and where I kept out of sight as much as possible.

We finished in the same bedraggled manner as we had started. There had been no send-off, and there was no welcome back. We were of no consequence except to ourselves. We did not wish it to be otherwise: indeed, we considered ourselves fortunate to be left in freedom. Only a lack of communication between Tibet and the outer world made this possible, as we were to find out later.

At my last meeting with Tenzing and Ang Dowa, I asked for a few details of Tenzing's adventurous career. He informed me on this occasion that he had accompanied four Everest expeditions.

"But I understood you to say only three when I asked you previously," I remonstrated.

"1935, 1936, 1938 – and Everest 1947," he replied.

I was deeply grateful to him.

Everest 1952

The Longest Day

Raymond Lambert

After pioneering a route into the Western Cwm up the Lhotse Glacier, the Swiss 1952 expedition prepared its final assault. Departing Camp V on 24 May, the Swiss intended to establish Camp VI on the South Col, Camp VII at 27,500 feet, from which two men would make a dash for the summit.

24 May

The day towards which all our efforts had been tending for so many months had come. This was the hour of assault upon the summit. Behind us were all the preparations in Geneva and Zürich and the cities of India, the endless approach, the successive camps, and the agonising crossing of the séracs; the whole past gave place to the final question which now faced us. When we came down again, we should know the answer.

At dawn the sky was clear and the weather calm. Nevertheless, I was distrustful. We had been so brutally trounced for two days that I was still filled with vague anxieties. I am not, I believe, a nervous person, but in those thirty-six hours of raging gale, curled up in my sleeping-bag and listening to the shrieking gusts, in a sort of waking nightmare I had seen myself trapped by such weather at the South Col or even higher, and I had the feeling that at 26,000 feet there would be no mercy. At Camp V there had not been more than forty-five degrees of frost (F.); at the South Col or higher there must have been seventy, and I still had about me the bitter taste of those five bivouacs in a February storm on Mont Blanc. My feet would remind me of them even if my memory was bad.

"What are we going to do?" I asked Dittert, who had come to have breakfast with me.

"You're going up," was all he replied.

Dittert, who had been suffering from sinusitis for a few days, and absorbing penicillin like a sponge, had recovered with surprising rapidity. He had become once more the one we called "le gosse" despite his grey hairs, which must have increased in number in the last month, since he had carried alone the formidable burden of organising the camps. Yet he was still his droll self, lively – too lively sometimes – but quick to recover after his first over-brisk reactions, happy to be alive, happy to be there, completely absorbed, concentrated and thinking of nothing but the expedition: a leader with whom one does not argue. This was my first expedition to the Himalaya and to him I entirely surrendered the responsibility of command. I said to myself more than once: "You will try to do the best you can and what you are told to do." So I concealed my anxieties about the weather and contented myself with pointing to the small thin clouds of ice that were passing across Nuptse and the great foggy masses like cotton wool that were clinging to Pumori.

"Isn't that a bad sign?" I asked.

"No, that's nothing. The wind has gone. Everest is without its plume. You can start."

"Good!" was all I replied.

The preparations were longer than desirable, but at nine o'clock we started off. Aubert and Flory were with me, and six Sherpas were climbing with us; three of them were to stay at the col and these three would only load up at the depot.

We took the Eperon route once more. But not for long. My fears were confirmed, for the sky was quickly veiled, the clouds of ice drew together over our heads and the ceiling gradually descended. We watched it approach anxiously. The summits were swallowed up first – Everest, Lhotse, Nuptse – in order of height, then the South Col. Just as we reached the slope that leads to the rock islet below the Eperon, the wind began to blow again, not very hard but cold, and it began to snow.

We halted and discussed what we should do. Having been made pessimistic by two days of hurricane, our heads being

still filled with the roar of the gusts that would have carried
away anyone on the Eperon or the South Col, we lost courage.
The thought of being involved in the unknown region of the
South Col, where no one had yet been even in good weather,
frightened us. The prospect of being blocked there, and of
being frozen where we stood, or carried off by avalanches on
the return, filled us all with fear. The flanks of Everest are one
of the places of the earth where one is not ashamed of occasional fear. However, as usual we gave our fear the good name
of prudence and turned round.

We made a rapid retreat and met with a cold reception at the
camp. Our comrades did not seem to have found the weather
as bad as we did. Dittert was not pleased and did not hide it
from me. I bent my back to the storm and hoped that the sky
would justify us. But it went against us. Blue troughs appeared,
the cloud ceiling broke up, the snow stopped falling and the
wind ceased to blow. At noon the sky was unclouded and the
weather magnificent.

"One day lost and we haven't too many. You will have to
begin again tomorrow and push on to the end. There is no
more time to lose," the *gosse* said to me. It was not the first time
in our mountaineering life that the weather had taken a mali-
cious pleasure in smiling after threatening us. How many
defeats have been due to these morning storms that have
panicked us and made us retreat, and then dispersed like
smoke in the middle of the day! Never is it so fine as when one
has given up!

Hofstetter arrived and a good meal in the sun softened the
ill-humour that prevailed in Camp V, though I was still a little
rancorous about the ironical sky and about myself and I felt
my will harden, determined not to allow myself to be overcome by illusory anxieties and to put all my energy into the
scales. Like the waves of the sea that do not subside when the
hurricane is over, the human heart has need of a few hours'
respite in order to calm down after it has been troubled. Our
revenge upon the mountain and ourselves would come
tomorrow.

25 May

Fine weather, a slight wind and thirty-six degrees (F.) of frost. At 8.15 I set out again with Aubert, Flory, Tensing and the Tigers Pasang Phutar, Phu Tharke, Da Namgyal, Ajiba, Mingma Dorje and Ang Norbu. Once more we made for the main couloir of the South Col where the ice was now breaking through everywhere. The Sherpas laboured behind us with their loads of from 22 to 26 lbs, but their pace was regular; they kept together and gave a great impression of security. A slip would have been fatal, for the upper lip of the *bergschrund*, immediately below the rock islet, overhung the glacier by at least 130 feet. Ajiba seemed in a bad way; at the end of about an hour, he put down his load and stopped. Despite the cold he was covered with sweat and was shaken from head to foot with convulsive shivers. These sudden attacks of malaria were startling. Luckily we had not gone so far that he could not return alone. We watched him depart while the other Tigers shared out what he had been carrying and we resumed our direct ascent to the first rocks of the Eperon des Genevois.

The steps we had cut had resisted the hurricane and we gained height quite quickly. The snow that was torn from the ridges made our efforts more difficult and we felt the cold severely as we dragged ourselves along the fixed ropes to the depot of food and oxygen which we had set up on a rock platform at about 24,600 feet. Here everyone loaded up again with what he thought he could carry – oxygen canisters, meta, food and tents. At 12.30 the heavy column moved off and progressed slowly along the Eperon before engaging on a flank traverse to the right in the old tracks of Chevalley and Asper, which were still visible though a week old. Small seams of rock followed the sheets of snow. We rose gradually although we were short of breath; our halts were more frequent and they were longer. Time passed rapidly by and the sun drew near to the crests of Nuptse, which were at about our own height. The obligation to surmount the 3,250 feet between the upper Khumbu glacier and the col in one stage is still a trial for those who wish to attack Everest from the Nepalese side.

It was 4.00 p.m. We had been on the move for eight hours and the shoulder still eluded us. The sky was always quite close, at 100 to 150 feet above our heads; but when we had climbed these 100 to 150 feet, the sky was still a little higher up. The cold and the wind were now so unbearable that two more porters, Ang Norbu and Mingma Dorje, fearing frost-bite, stopped, refused to go on and declared that they were going to descend. How could we prevent them? Had we the right to do so? In adventures of this kind, a man should remain free and the sole judge of what he can do and what he wants to do.

We helped them unload and saw them off. Three Sherpas out of seven had gone. For those who continue such an abandonment is always difficult to bear. Here the blow was hard because, in order to succeed, we needed the contents of their sacks at the South Col. After a fashion we moored what we could not carry where it was; we should have to come back and get it. Our already too-heavy sacks were weighted still more. Flory took a tent; I took one too but during these manoeuvres, which were tricky on so steep a slope, we let Aubert's sleeping-bag slip. The wind seized it and it disappeared.

We resumed the endless climb, hauling ourselves up from one rock to another and from one step to another with great difficulty. We looked grotesquely like smugglers at the North Pole in our wadded jackets, with our fur caps down to our eyes and our Lapland boots. We had twenty-day beards and our lips were covered with cream. But it is only after the event that we see the comic side of things; for the time being it was as much as we could do to endure.

The sun sank, the cold became almost unbearable despite our efforts and our clothing. It was 7.00 p.m. We had been climbing for nearly ten hours. At last the slope eased off a little. It was time. Darkness was falling quickly. We would not reach the South Col that day. Without a word, we worked at improvising a bivouac. We dug two platforms with our axes. Strength was needed to wield the axes; we had not got it and the work was slow. Night had fallen when the two tents were up, two little high-altitude tents which are good enough for one man alone, or for two if tightly packed together. But we were three and the Sherpas four.

Frozen, with our ropes still tied and our crampons still on our feet, we went into these precarious shelters. Thinking that a particularly fierce gust of wind might take both us and our shelter to the foot of the col, I had thrust my axe into the snow up to the hilt and to it I had firmly tied the end of the rope. In this fashion Everest would hold us on a leash throughout the night!

We were packed too closely to get into our sleeping-bags; motionless, pressed one against the other, not daring to move for fear of pulling away the badly secured tent ropes, we listened to the moaning of the wind, to the rustle of the snow, the slapping of the tent-cloth and the chattering of our teeth. Suddenly the flap opened and the indefatigable Tensing, he who always thinks of others, brought us something to drink. He had succeeded in heating some soup in the neighbouring tent. "*Merci!* Tensing. Go and sleep."

The night was endless, like the slope to which we were moored, like all dimensions in this terrible land. We endured, we waited in patience, we breathed deeply in order to control our hearts and we suffered the cold, which at first froze our skins and then penetrated slowly to take up its abode in our flesh. Without speaking of it, we thought that this supplementary and unforeseeable fatigue would rob us a little of the strength we would need above the col.

But all nights come to an end. "Fine day, sahibs!" Once again it was Tensing, bringing us chocolate.

Dawn was breaking, driving the shadows from the summits of Nuptse and Pumori. Everest was still no more than a shapeless mass, dark and as if crouching. On our left was the Lhotse glacier, of an indefinable melancholy tint in the last moments of the night. We had no desire to stay abed. We tried to warm ourselves up by exercise, but at 25,600 feet one does not exercise for very long, even for this purpose. It took us more than an hour to take down the tent – we abandoned one of them – to fold it and reload the sacks. At last the slanting sunlight licked the slopes and with it came the courage and confidence that the night had taken away.

The Sherpas were scarcely in good shape, which was not surprising after the night they had just experienced. Nevertheless, Phu Tharke and Da Namgyal wanted to go down several hundred feet to fetch the rest of the loads abandoned by Ang Norbu and Mingma Dorje. Pasang would wait for them. The things we were forced to leave we would come and fetch from the col or the shoulder, which could not be more than about 600 feet above us.

We resumed the ascent to the South Col, which had put up an eleventh-hour defence. Our muscles were frozen and our limbs were stiff; each step cost us dearly. Nevertheless, we gained height. Nuptse, the height of which had terrified us when we looked at it from the lower camps, was now lower than ourselves. We were approaching 26,250 feet; everything about us told us so, even our lungs. We were coming close to Lhotse, where my eyes instinctively sought to discover a way up, as if they were beginning to form new plans for the future. But the present occupied me entirely, more than I desired.

At last, at ten in the morning, we came out on the hump of ice above the South Col. It was a sudden revelation. In two perfect curves, the South Ridge rose to the acute angle that it formed with one of the ribs of the west face: this was the south summit. Eagerly we examined this terminal ridge and its means of access. Everest had now ceased to be the shapeless and monstrous mass we had seen until then. It was a new mountain, still massive, but powerful, and pointed at its summit, which pierced the sky. To the left was the black mass which overlooked the Khumbu, striped with channels of ice; to the right were snow couloirs, rocky islets and the white ridge disclosed for the first time to the eyes of men who were overtaken by desire, despite their fatigue.

This emotion was intense but brief, for it was no place to dream. The day was not ended. Tensing gave us his sack to take down to the col and himself returned to the bivouac site to fetch the equipment and ascend with the other three Sherpas. On the col the wind was violent. There was not a trace of snow: nothing but stones welded together by the frost; a desert in miniature. One would have to be as hard as rock or ice to resist the gusts that had been passing across the col for millennia and seemed in a rage to prevent us from putting up the two tents. On all fours, clinging to the earth like insects, we at last succeeded in bringing sense to the refractory cloth. It took us two hours, and then came the waiting. It is difficult to imagine what these hours of waiting mean for an expedition in the Himalaya.

Tensing returned, escorting our three Sherpas, who were all in bad condition. Pasang declared that he wished to die where he was; Phu Tharke zigzagged like a drunken man; Da Namgyal was suffering from migraine and held his head in his hands. They were out of action. Perhaps they would be usable after a night's rest, but one does not rest above 26,000 feet, where the system deteriorates whether one moves or does nothing. Tensing himself was in extraordinary condition. Twice more he was to return to the bivouac site and reascend with loads.

Aubert and Flory were lying down while I went from one place to another, taking photos. A sea of cloud covered the high plateaus of Tibet. Only the enormous pyramids of Kangchenjunga (28,150 feet) and Makalu (27,790 feet) broke through it. But my eyes ceaselessly returned to the ridge along which we were to go the next day to try our luck in bad conditions for, from all the evidence, the Sherpa party was finished with the exception of Tensing. Tensing at last returned and we went together to sleep.

The next day, despite a better night, the altitude continued to wreck the constitution of the Sherpas and they left us.

"That's another trump card gone," said Flory, watching them depart. Indeed, how would we be able, without using up our last strength in the process, to carry the equipment, food-stuffs and tents necessary for four men to 27,500 feet? Between 23,000 and 26,000 feet the strength of an assault group thins out like the point of a pencil: but our will remained intact. It had been with us for so long, anchored at the bottom of our spirits, which it moved obscurely, almost unconsciously, despite our fatigue.

At ten in the morning, after the three Sherpas had vanished beyond the hump above the col, we set out on two ropes of two men each, Aubert and Flory, Tensing and myself, carrying one tent and food for one day. As soon as we left the zone of ice and stone, we broke into sheets of crusted snow. We made towards the base of the South-East Ridge, at the foot of a large rock buttress. The weather was clear, the intensity of the wind had diminished, as if it concentrated its anger upon the col itself.

Having reached the foot of the buttress, we were disillusioned. It was too steep. The rocks that overlooked us were undoubtedly negotiable at 13,000 feet, but not at 26,000 feet. Flory and Aubert pushed on a further hundred yards to make sure that the eastern face offered no way out, and they ran up against a slope of more than sixty degrees, which vanished into the sky.

So we returned in our steps, moved along the base of the large buttress and attacked the couloir that runs down it. The snow was good and the ascent easy. We made steps between the snow and the rock. We constantly relieved each other in the lead, we gained height quickly and the tents on the col already seemed small. Soon we reached the top of the couloir but the dry rocks allowed us to continue by moving over to the right. We waited for Aubert and Flory while taking oxygen like some precious liqueur; then we continued the climb straight up.

Suddenly I emerged on to the ridge above the large buttress and there discovered a new world, the whole eastern face of the mountain, plunging for more than 16,000 feet to the Karta valley and Tibet. And in the mist, on the far horizon, other chains of mountains broke through. Behind us the summit of Lhotse had fallen away; it was now no more than three or four hundred feet above us. We were at about 27,500 feet.

It was fine and there was no wind. Both of us were fit. Should we sleep there without a Primus and without sleeping-bags? Perhaps the next day . . . ? Tensing interrupted my reflections.

"Sahib, we ought to stay here tonight!" He indicated the tent he had been carrying since the start. I smiled, for our thoughts had been pursuing the same course.

Flory and Aubert joined us. Like us they were in good shape. They too might stay and try their luck the next day. This is doubtless what they desired. But there was only one tent and very little food. We had only set out to make a reconnaissance and to fix the site of Camp VII. In an undertaking like that, the party matters more than the individual; the individual is nothing without the party. In order that the privileged pair should have not only a chance of success but a possibility of returning, it has to be supported at the last camp by the second pair. Though its task might appear to be less brilliant, it needs men who are just as determined and in equally good physical shape – perhaps in better shape, since they should be capable of going to seek and bring back, whatever the risk, those who have taken their lives in their hands.

To all who are familiar with the history of the Himalaya, the effort put up by Odell all by himself, in supporting Mallory and Irvine, seems more extraordinary than the legendary exploit itself. Alone at Camp V at 26,280 feet, because he had had to send back his sick porter; alone at Camp VI to which he had climbed on 8 June, taking food for those who were never to return; going beyond that camp in squalls of wind, hoping to make contact with those whom he had glimpsed for a moment before they vanished into cloud; descending again to Camp V to leave room for Irvine and Mallory, who would have no need of it, and ascending the next day with porters to Camp V, where he slept, and then going on alone the next day to Camp VI, which he found as empty as he had left it; and then, having signalled with the sleeping-bags according to an agreed code that all hope was lost, he took Mallory's compass from the tent and descended. The energy expended by Odell during these three days never ceased to cause wonder among those who understand what it entailed. Of all those who have attacked Everest so far, Odell the geologist was, I believe, the best equipped.

Between the four of us there was no argument. Aubert, who was one of those who found and saved me in the Combe Maudite in 1938, and Flory, reliable, cautious and determined, agreed to leave us. "You two stay. We will wait for you at the col."

We watched them move off, growing smaller and ever smaller down the slope, until they reached the col an hour later. Now we were only two! How many men and how much

effort had been necessary to bring us to this farthest point of
the expedition!

We pitched our tent with great difficulty. The altitude and
the wind made our movements awkward. Our legs would not
obey us and our brains scarcely functioned. Our hands were
more skilful without gloves, but to take them off would cost us
dear. The sun had gone down behind Nuptse and the temperature fell instantly. We took a last look towards Kangchenjunga
and Tibet. Tensing extended an arm westwards, pointing to a
disquieting sea of clouds. The horizon reddened.

In this improvised bivouac there were no sleeping bags, no
equipment, no Primus. Only a tent which slapped in the wind
like a prayer-flag. It was a glacial night. The whole being curled
up as if seeking to create a mattress of air between its skin and
itself. Our muscles stiffened and those of the face became
fixed as if from an injection of anæsthetic. Slowly the cold
penetrated the bones themselves. There was no question of
sleep; the wind and the growling avalanches kept us awake.
Which was just as well.

We were overtaken by a consuming thirst, which we could
not appease. There was nothing to drink. An empty tin gave us
an idea; a fragment of ice and the candle-flame produced a
little lukewarm water. The gusts of wind made our heads whirl;
it seemed to us that we took off with them into space, like those
houses one thinks one sees moving when watching clouds in
flight. To resist this vertigo, I tried to fix my thoughts on the
next day's attack, and I mused on those who at all the stages
were thinking of us: Aubert and Flory at the col, Dittert at
Camp V, Wyss at the base camp. In a state of semi-hallucination
the entire expedition seemed to me to be a stretched bow and
ourselves the arrow. A poor blunted arrow at that. Could it
reach its target?

This was the boundary between waking and sleeping. I
dared not sleep, must not sleep. Tensing shook me and I awoke,
and I shook him in my turn. Amicably we beat one another
and pressed close together throughout the night. In the sky the
stars were so brilliant that they filled me with fear.

The shadows became clearer. The shape of Tensing, rolled
up like a ball, began to stand out from the background of the

tent-cloth, which gradually grew lighter. Dawn entered the half-open tent and with it came anxiety. The wind hurled a handful of ice-needles into my face. Nevertheless, we had to open our eyes. The weather was not reassuring, for the sky was clear to the north, but very dark to the west and south. The summits of Lhotse and Nuptse were hidden in a mass of dark clouds, and the valley was drowned in fog.

What should we do? We looked at each other, undecided, but once more we understood each other without speaking. I indicated the ridge with a wink and Tensing answered by nodding his head. We had gone too far to give up. Our preparations were quickly made, for we had worn everything, except the crampons, from fear of frostbite. They took long to put on again, for our numbed hands were clumsy and bending over literally took our breath away. Laden with the last three canisters of oxygen, sufficient for six hours, we set off below the ridge on sheets of snow broken by bands of rock. One step, three breaths, one step . . . when we rested for a moment, we slobbered at the inhaler; it could only be used during a halt because the resistance of the valves was too great for our lungs when the effort of moving was added. At about every twenty yards we relieved each other in the lead to economize our strength and in order to inhale while letting the other pass. When the slope steepened we advanced like dogs following a scent, sometimes on all fours.

But the weather grew worse. Waves of mist passed, carried along on the south-west wind. Showers lashed at us in passing, leaping over the crest. Then the sun reappeared and reassured us. We rose slowly, terribly slowly. Nevertheless, we still rose. In the clear intervals Lhotse emerged from the storm clouds and it was already below us. The whole landscape and all the summits fell away. The peaks which had seemed monstrous from the lower camps had lost their splendour; they became hills, like the Verte or the Jorasses, seen from Mont Blanc. But the clear intervals did not last; the dense fog, filled with a drift of frozen snow, enveloped us again. All our vital functions were slowed down. There was a confused impression of being on some other planet. Asphyxia destroyed our cells and our whole beings deteriorated.

At about eleven o'clock we came out again on to the ridge, sinking deeply into the wind-crusted snow. There were no technical difficulties; the slope was rather easy and not too steep. We were rather fearful of the cornices to our right and we instinctively kept our distance.

Our pace became still slower. Three steps, a halt, oxygen. Three steps, a halt. Then came a clearing and we saw that the South Summit was at least two hundred metres (*c.* 650 feet) above us. Three steps, oxygen. I watched Tensing. He seemed well but at moments he swayed a little, trying to find his balance. I tried to keep a watch on myself and asked myself: "How do you feel? All right, quite all right." This was euphoria, the worst of all dangers. I remembered the fifth and last bivouac on the Aiguilles du Diable: there, too, I felt well. How did Mallory and Irvine feel when they dissolved into the rarefied air of the North Ridge? Was this not the reason why they did not return?

Granulated snow struck our left cheeks increasingly hard. The wind became more evil. The South Summit was so close: just this band of rock where we were now engaged, the last; just that snow crest. But no; it was impossible to go on. This was the end. We had taken five hours to gain two hundred metres (*c.* 650 feet).

Once more the decision was taken without words. One long look and then the descent. Was it an altitude record? No. Failure. That is what we thought. But did we think? Our bodies were of lead, almost without spirit. There was no trace of automatism, for our muscles no longer obeyed our orders. Pick up your left foot and put it in front; now the other. Our tracks had almost entirely vanished. We stopped as often as on the ascent.

We passed the tent. The wind had begun to do its work, it was torn in two places. Would it last till the others could occupy it?

"Leave it there. Perhaps they will have better luck than us."

And we went on, kept in motion only by the will to resist the lethargy that was invading us. We crouched as we dragged along, descending the couloir and the slope towards the col.

From the col to the tents there were a dozen yards uphill, an insignificant hummock of snow. We could do no more. Flory and Aubert dragged us into our tents, inert, at the limit of exhaustion Tensing sank into a deep sleep and did not move until the hour of departure. For us the adventure was ended. The next day we were to take the road for Europe.

Everest 1953

The Face

Wilfred Noyce

A year after the Swiss failed on Everest, the British led by John Hunt were back on the mountain. Forcing a route up the Khumbu glacier and icefall, all went well until the Lhotse Face. For days the British attack failed. Then, on 21 May, it came the turn of Wilfred Noyce and Anullu to blaze the trail.

I arose at 6.30. The great face, the two swinging slopes of ice enclosing that cut-about line of outcrop, still looked impassably huge. Away against the blue the Geneva Spur jutted beside the grey-black cone of Everest, a triangle whose right side supported a snow banner streaming far out of sight. As so often happened, I was stamping to be off by eight; only to find the Sherpas settling down to an endless enjoyment of their huge *tsampa* cakes. I continued to stamp, meditating the virtues of patience. It was 8.35 before we started up the trail, powdered, but not excessively, by a small fall yesterday.

We were on three ropes, I leading the first and wearing my oxygen. A word or two about this vital feature of "The Plan". No oxygen could be spared for the work of preparing the face; but Charles Wylie and myself leading parties up it would use oxygen, for it was vital that the loads arrive, and leading Sherpas can be an exhausting job. Thus I would now benefit in my double rôle of pioneer and carry-leader. For all except the two assault or summit pairs, the open-circuit apparatus consisted of the portly black cylinder supplied by the RAF and weighing 21 lbs, which needed to be pushed and fiddled into its holder in the very light aluminium carrying frame. The assault set consisted of two or even three light alloy cylinders weighing 11 lbs each, having the advantage that they could be discarded one by one after use. We had all practised oxygen on the acclimatization period. The awkwardness of the set, on a morning like this, lay in the bitingly cold business of screwing up connecting valves; then the swing on to the back, mask on, and the connection of face-tube with the tube from the set. When you were with another sahib, each fixed the other's, switched on the oxygen and watched the dial for the pressure. But with Sherpas this was impossible, because I did not trust them to read the figures and could not read them myself with the apparatus on. Finally there was the problem of resting. The set could remain on your back while you rested on some fairly level space; but if you had nobody who could switch off for you, it was impossible either to switch off yourself or, however elastic you might be, to read the dial just over your right shoulder without removing the whole thing. And that meant unhitching, swinging the weight, made even more heavy by a rucksack on top, off the shoulders, at the risk of following it down whichever steep bit of mountainside you happened to be climbing. Having, at great cost to breath and temper, at last got it off, you must rest it somewhere. If you set it upright, its top-heaviness made a catastrophic crash probable. If you laid it horizontally, it was with the uneasy feeling that the delicate machinery must be catching on every rock splinter.

Experts may tell me that I am making absurdly heavy weather. But to one who is unscientific enough for the whole thing to be clearly magic, every scrape or slither spells possible disaster to the magic box. However, when all is said, and when it is agreed that our apparatus will look prehistorically clumsy in twenty years' time, the result was a plain miracle. When, after all the struggles, the switch was at last turned on, a taste or breath of metallic new life seemed to slip through mouth to lungs, mocking every disadvantage and making life seem good once again.

On the long upward traverse below VI the weight above the shoulders seemed to be trying to swing me at every step down into the Cwm. New snow had blown over all the tracks. Sometimes I stopped to chip again, more often the angle was just easy enough to take a cramponed foot, if only there were a well-balanced body above it. That proposition the oxygen cylinder and rucksack disputed; the look down at the Cwm beyond the green bulge was alarming. A heave, with right hand on fixed rope, a few steps, then a halt. Below me the Sherpas doubled up and gasped, making me feel uncomfortably luxurious in my oxygen. In an hour and three-quarters we had reached Camp VI.

We spent over an hour at the bare site. In the first place the Sherpas were appalled at the extra load of six Dræger cylinders and other oddments that they were expected to take on. In the carefully calculated list of loads we had not, I suspect, allowed for the full weight of Li-los, sleeping-bags and personal gear, which must have made up 20 lbs. Moreover, I had said to Anullu, my sirdar, that we would be travelling light to VI and there picking up further stores. But the Sherpas, living in a childlike present, saw only that they were lightly laden. Therefore there was room for the odd extra comfort. I had been anxious on the face, seeing how bulky their loads appeared to be already. Now I could positively feel the uneasiness with which they were regarding new burdens. They sat down, shifted, felt the cylinders and sat again; entangling the rope more hopelessly with each movement.

The second reason for our long halt was the oxygen supply. I was astounded to find that in this brief ascent my oxygen pressure had sunk from 2,700 to 1,000 p.s.i. A leak. I seemed to hear a faint sizzle from the big nuts at the oxygen bottle's neck. But alas, I had no spanner large enough to tighten these. There were, however, two bottles up here in the snow, both, as I hoped, full. Unfortunately with these black RAF cylinders there was no way of telling the oxygen pressure but by fitting and connecting them, at least none simple enough for me. Both cylinders I fitted slowly, cumbrously, spannered one by one into position. Neither was very much better than my own. There was nothing for it but to try what I might find at VII, which on two litres a minute with my present cylinder I ought to reach. But it was a melancholy little party which finally disentangled itself from the ropes.

I always found climbing with Sherpas three times more tiring than with sahibs. As I dragged along I was heartily envying those lucky ones like Tom Bourdillon, who from the nature of their jobs had less to do with bear-leading. At the time I had no pity for what others might miss. And now the moral tug on the rope was so strong that it almost pulled me from my steps: a dead weight of doubt, dismay and reluctance which the Sherpas themselves could never have explained, had they been blessed suddenly with the gift of tongues. We climbed very slowly; the halts were very frequent. "*Aram* (rest), sahib," and the whole caravan would plump panting down in the snow. I found the whole business so much more tiring than the ascent with George without oxygen, that I risked all and increased my flow rate to four litres a minute.

Just below the final serac we met George's party of three descending. Terrible conditions these last two days on the upper part had prevented further advance, and George, after nine full days on the face, was overdue for a rest. The only solution was Mike's "Go down lower", and down they were going. They warned me that frostbite had affected Mike's hands and George's feet; also, a far more grave problem at the moment, of the shortage of kerosene at VII. Now kerosene was one of the loads I had not thought to take on from VI, believing it to be sufficient above. "You'll have to take some out of the South Col cookers," George said, but in an unconvincing voice. I knew that these South Col tins were sacred. I looked at the dragging ropes of Sherpas; among whom there was only one as untired as ever. Ang Norbu had done fine work for the Swiss last year, but in the autumn had been operated on, in the neck, by Dr Chevalley, and might not go high. He was a local man, and his sister, the elder "Auntie", was our best carrier. Both equally square and solid, undemonstrative and utterly dependable. I had noted him already.

"Ang Norbu and Ang Dawa II, you will go down to Camp VI. Bring up the kerosene." (This was a second Ang Dawa.)

Ang Norbu was ready in a moment, Ang Dawa had no choice but to follow his example. I changed the ropes round, to give them a length to themselves. They started bravely down, with George's party.

"See you soon at Lobuje," Mike called back.

We toiled on, slower than ever. The traverse across the

pinnacle face upset the balance of heavy loads. A few steps and
a halt, bodies doubled up. Fortunately the steps were now
bigger, but the fixed rope they found no help at all. For myself,
I was at last fully enjoying the oxygen, taking proper belays,
looking at my watch, even exhorting the troops, forgetful that
I must sound to them like a muffled elephant. It was 1.45
before we reached camp. There remained still the extra Meade
and the pyramid tent to pitch: a shuffled, jumbling job, thankfully disposed of by all, so that all could flop exhausted inside.
To make tea I poured kerosene out of one of the sacred South
Col cookers, and got one Primus going. In my own tent I
found the remains of a blessed Thermos of lemonade. But
alas, as the tent was now end-on with another Meade occupied
by Sherpas, and therefore very public, I had to share it. The
higher one goes, the lower drops the moral tone of thought
and inclination. It was drink that revived us. Kancha told me
that they were all exhausted from lack of food, since they had
not eaten between 8 a.m. and 3 p.m. But considering their
performance of the day after tomorrow, I believe food shortage was not to blame. The cause was partly thirst and heat,
partly the unexpectedly heavy loads: 50 lbs for the first time to
24,000 feet.

Myself I ate, very slowly and with immense pleasure, a whole
tin of sardines which somebody had carelessly left in a side-
pocket of the tent. To dry lips and empty stomach it seemed
the best thing of the expedition, and I was delighted that there
were not enough to share with the Sherpas. I was doing everything very slowly. That tin must have taken twenty minutes.
How right George had been about the dilemma up here! The
more work you do, the more food you need. The more you eat,
the more you want. A last lick of the lips. Then I climbed out
into the sunshine. The indomitables were labouring up the last
slope, our kerosene tied to their backs. Otherwise there were
no signs of life, all were prostrate inside tents. I went plodding
round, stooping to pull back flaps. "*Thik hai?*" (All right?),
"*Bahut bimar sahib!*" (Very ill). I distributed all the helpful-
looking pills that I had. Then I asked Anullu to come out.

Anullu was the younger brother of Da Tensing. Returning
last year from the Cho Oyu expedition to Darjeeling, he had

cut off his Sherpa pigtail and become the sophisticated man about town. He must have shared the cigarette record with Ang Nyima, and yet these were probably our best two Sherpas. There was about the amount that he smoked and drank, as well as the general reserve of the puckered eyes, a veneer of westernism contrasting strongly with his rugged brother. At the same time there was also in the smooth round face, when it smiled, something that gave confidence; he knew his job and he was fit, though he too had carried his load today. I explained what that job would be, for tomorrow. We must sort the stores, what was to go up, and I must fit Anullu's oxygen set together. He tried George's mask, it was well enough. He, wearing oxygen, must lead one party, I the other. We had six Sherpas intended for the col, specially selected by Charles Wylie. But because of our weight of loads all must go up who could. I had no illusions about the difficulties of combining the two oper-ations of store-lifting and route-making. If none could go, Anullu and I must concentrate on that second job, if only the cylinders would work.

I turned to the cylinders. Twenty-pounder upon twenty-pounder I wriggled in, connected, tried. Not one but seemed to leak, from the big nut at the neck of the bottle. What to do? I had the whole tent outside in a search for a large spanner. In despair, at the appointed hour, I advanced upon the wireless. A few mundane messages. Then: "I've turned all the cylinders on and they all seem to leak." Alas, it was a capricious crea-ture, our wireless. At this critical point a "break in transmission" caused a sleepless night for Tom Bourdillon, down at IV. The mechanic in him had spotted that I omitted to say that I turned them *off*. Knowing me to be far from mechanically inclined, he suspected at once that I had failed to do that operation. I was told later that John spent the rest of the even-ing hopping around with the wireless set. "Come out from behind that serac, Wilf!" – and doubtless stronger expressions such as my informant was too kind to repeat. Fortunately they were not justified.

Oblivious of the panic I was causing, I meanwhile was tuck-ing into a supper of soup, lemonade in quantity, biscuits, cheese, chocolate and condensed milk, which we either sucked

from the tube or spread like jam on Ryvita. An immaculate
Anullu did the cooking, squatted over the Primus next door
and seeming to know exactly where everything was. At
sundown it became very cold. I had been writing my diary,
poetry even, but despite mittens this became impossible. I
spent too much time rubbing hands inside the bag to allow any
for thought. By eight I was climbing out for the last time, into
the moonlight and merciless stars. Everest was still and huge,
peaceful and yet mocking "our miserable tents". Only over the
South Col a faint boom announced wind. I felt very much
alone, oppressed by the impossibility of that star-crowned
black pyramid.

Compelled to rise at 5 a.m. for a journey to the distant
lavatory, which meant tottering leftward beyond the curve of
our sentinel serac, I was astonished at the wild golden light
already splashing upon Pumori and the peaks down the
valley; so astonished that even in my dazed state of sleep I felt
a longing to perpetuate this, and tottered back to pull out my
camera. The painful stoop, the fumble and search and the
heave back to the upright position, show how strong the urge
must have been. I had told Anullu that we would not start too
early, for fear of frostbite; therefore I now snuggled back with
a good conscience.

Tea appeared from the cook's clockwork hands at 6.30.
Then another lie, in that suspense which precedes the tearing
of a man from peaceful horizontal ease to the painful gasps of
the vertical. I must kneel, must pull off the sleeping-bag, must
wriggle lumpishly on all fours into the cold air. The eye
wandered round the tent roof, seized every excuse, a scrap of
paper to be read, a film to be looked at or even the stitching of
the tent; anything to delay the moment! It was long before I
was out, feet clumsy in the big boots whose laces seemed to
catch at every step. The time was 7.45. One or two Primuses
were going, but there were no other signs of life, except a
number of groans and Pasang quietly being sick. Everything
was *not* well, and I pushed in more medicine.

At eight Anullu called across. He had produced miraculous
porridge, putting the oats of several Assault Rations together.

That breakfast made a great difference later, for the most lively deed is prosaically founded on food. Then more uncertainty. Anullu shrugged his shoulders. Groans resounded from the tents. Some had dragged themselves out; one or two were looking at the loads with an eye which could only be called "wan". I asked who was well enough to come on up, and a stocky figure came forward. "*Jaega* sahib" (I'll go). It was Ang Norbu. But who would go with him? For it was impossible that Ang Norbu, without oxygen, should attach himself to our rope. "Ang Dawa *hai* sahib," he said. I was delighted. Two loads at least would go up. But as I was preparing them, Ang Dawa came up, coughing badly. He could not come after all. It was a sad moment. The alternative plan must take the field. The two sickest Sherpas must go down with a note for John, the rest would wait and acclimatize that day, adding their strength in numbers to Charles's party the next. I felt sorry for Ang Norbu after his gallant offer, and he looked disappointed. It was after 9.30 before all these discussions had finished; before Anullu and I, cramponed and using oxygen at the low flow-rate of two litres a minute, stepped out towards the first snow bridge.

The couloir passed, I led at a not too high speed over the first short traverse, which had packed down a lot since the 17th. In three-quarters of an hour, breathing that invigorating flow, we had reached our highest point of that day. Just beyond it we rested, swinging the heavy cylinders gently off our backs, careful not to capsize after them. Mask off, set balanced against a slope. Then rest, that absurd peacefulness of another world. In movement, in camp, the triviality of day to day is heightened by the extra exertion of each thought and twist. It is the succession of life's burdens magnified through a distorting mirror. But rest is different. All that lurked in our hinterland now comes forward. The mind is at ease, that is to say willing to receive and register. At the time it may not even appear to register, but remains like a painting that waits for the overlying daub of tiredness, some day, to be removed. And then perhaps, in an evening of future years, the picture will show more clear than it ever showed through the mists of reality.

After rest we went on. Yes, the route did still keep to the left, as an obvious fixed rope showed; but the start looked steep. Not knowing we made for this rope's bottom, and were soon floundering in fathomless snow. We should have joined the rope (left by George's party) some way up, from the right. A little farther on a great half-moon of wall confronted us. Right or left? Right, Anullu suggested knowingly, and we started over to where a wide slant of snow seemed to lead back and to above us, over the wall's top, between this and the next wall. The slant was of nastily hard snow. I chipped and chipped. But no, the snow was going to peter out on ice. There was nothing for it but to come down and not waste time. I was glad that there were no Sherpas being held up behind us. The less promising-looking line to the left did lead, after a minor steep wall, on to easier, leftward-slanting slopes. I noted an aluminium piton with a great coil of thick rope. It appeared later that this was the highest point reached by George's party and that Da Tensing had left the rope.

We were keeping towards the left-hand side of our Lhotse glacier, but with no prospect of getting off it; though sometimes temptation beckoned on the shining, straight slopes that separated us from the great spur. A zigzag course in heavy snow now took us to the bottom of another rope, left by the Swiss. None of these ropes did we dare to use, not knowing how the attachment had weathered. I cramponed up beside it to a small platform, really the beginning of a long ledge running to the right across the face. Along the line of flat we edged, painfully aware of the dangling temptation of rope above us, and of the view down the overhang that seemed to push us out and away; and below, almost between the legs, the toy tents of V dotting the plain. It looked as if the structure of the wall was altering rapidly; now a jump would land us among our friends 3,000 feet below.

It was well that we had not trusted the rope. This particular one hung down, I have said, temptingly. We found on arrival that it dangled from a piton stuck in a little plateau; and the piton, more than half out, waited precariously on another pull, before it joined the ice-fragments capering down towards V. At the time I was too occupied with other things, with mask and movement forward, to be thankful. First, the way. The plateau top was really the top of a narrowing slice, bounded by space on the side overlooking the Cwm, by a crevasse on the mountain side. Let's try again, in the hope of a bridge. Some way along the crevasse deepened, widened; now I must return. There was no choice but to the right, to regain the parent mountain wall beyond our slice by a step on to narrow uprights of ice-sliver. A few more steps led us finally beyond the line of crescent walls, typical feature of this Lhotse Face of ours. Looking up I could see ever-subsiding hummocks; and then, a few hundred feet beyond again, the ugly black towers of Lhotse rising from polished snow. It looked as if we were up.

I was stepping along, feeling how alert, how full of life I was with the oxygen, now the depressing intricacies of putting on and taking off were over. How different I should have felt without it! Quite suddenly I was looking down one of the most impressive crevasses I have seen, a gash in the soft snow cheek up which we were striding. But it was still a crevasse, and we were accustomed to crevasses. One walked some yards right or left, and there would be a snow bridge. This time therefore we walked left. No bridge. Right then; but there was no bridge here either. The thing clearly crossed the whole snow face. I looked at Anullu, and Anullu, behind his mask, looked back at me. He was pointing. Where he pointed, the crevasse, some eight feet wide, had narrowed to perhaps three. The cause of narrowing was the two lips, which had pushed forward as if to kiss over the bottle-green depths below. The lips were composed, apparently, of unsupported snow, and seemed to suspend themselves above this "pleasure-dome of ice", into whose cool chasms, widening to utter blackness, it would at other times have been a delight to peer. I walked right once more, then left. Nothing. I signed to Anullu that he should drive his axe well in and be ready for me. Then I advanced to the first unsupported ledge. I stood upon this first ledge and prodded. Anullu would have held me, had one ledge given way, but he could not have pulled me up. As the walls of the crevasse were undercut to widen the gap, I would have been held dangling and could not have helped myself out. It would be silly to face such a problem in the Alps without a party of three. But I cannot remember more than a passing qualm.

Altitude, even through oxygen, dulled fears as well as hopes. One thing at a time. Everest must be climbed. Therefore this step must be passed. I prodded my ice-axe across at the other ledge, but I could not quite reach deep enough to tell. I took the quick stride and jump, trying not to look down, plunged the axe hard in and gasped. The lip was firm. This time the Lhotse Face really was climbed.

Only lying in my sleeping-bag that night did I realise the implications of one step.

Perhaps a hundred yards up, one last small cleft barred our path, but this time a bridge offered itself at once. On the almost level ground beyond we had our first proper halt. I switched off Anullu's apparatus, swung my own clumsily off and switched that too. I dangled my mask from the ice-axe head to dry, and rejoiced in fresh air on the face. We sat and ate a little, but we needed drink most of all. Anullu had a specially large and welcome water-bottle filled with lemonade. He himself seemed to prefer smoking to eating, and had reeled off two cigarettes by the time I had finished three biscuits and some cheese. We were now at the apex, as it were, of the Lhotse glacier; nothing barred us from the smooth sweep of slope that bounded the spur, now seen as a fine jutting eminence, bald-topped and dropping steeply towards the Cwm in an edge of mixed rock and snow. This half-obscured the great rocky cone of Everest, distinguished by the snowdrift racing from it. We had halted at 12.15. At 12.50 we set off again, after the delays of putting on and adjusting sets.

I put Anullu in the lead. A little below our level, at a rock ribbon crossing the face toward the spur, one Swiss rope could be seen dangling disconsolately. Too low, I thought. Anullu set off at what seemed the pace of a fast Swiss guide (though it can have been no more than half that): a performance more remarkable, since there was still an ankle-deep surface layer. Sometimes drifts had crusted over with wind, and here steps must be cut, to my secret inward relief. Just time to bend and gasp. The word "traverse" is a misnomer; this traverse must rise diagonally across the slope. At last, after an hour's move-ment upward, we had reached the wide gully almost in the shadow of the spur, where some slight rock intrusions gave a relief; downward sloping, half-buried little shelves. It was the first step on rock since Base Camp; a welcome change, though a scrapy business in crampons.

How were we to get on to the spur? I had been told, keep to the right and cross it at its top, whence a 600-foot drop to the col. But look, there was a snow gangway slanting gently up under a rock band on to the very crest. If one could reach that, it might be possible to skirt round to the col without having to descend on to it. We made for the gangway. It was of steeper snow than it looked, and hard. Pecks with the axe, then a pause. Strange how breathless I could feel, even on four litres a minute. Anticipation was breathless too as the crest drew near, backed by the shadow of Everest's last pyramid, now a floating right-handed curve from which snow mist blew. I was leading again, and hacked the last steps on to the crest. Still no view, and no easy traverse; we must go on up to the widening top. First boulders, up which we stumbled easily, then more snow, the broad forehead of the Geneva Spur, and then suddenly nothing was immediately above us any more. We were on a summit, overlooked in this whole scene only by Lhotse and Everest. And this was the scene long dreamed, long hoped.

To the right and above, the crenellations of Lhotse cut a blue sky fringed with snow cloudlets. To the left, snow mist still held Everest mysteriously. But the eye wandered hungry and fascinated over the plateau between: a space of boulders and bare ice perhaps four hundred yards square, absurdly solid and comfortable at first glance in contrast with the sweeping ridges around, or the blank mist that masked the Tibetan hills beyond. But across it a noisy little wind moaned its warning that the South Col, goal of so many days' ambition, was not comfortable at all. And in among the glinting ice and dirty grey boulders there lay some yellow tatters – all that remained of the Swiss expeditions of last year.

We were soon descending the drop to the plateau, only some 200 feet down after all. But first I took out the 500-foot length of nylon line from my sack and started laying it down, from a piton driven in. This was to be a moral lifeline for weary Sherpas returning from the long carry. As we approached, I remember very clearly my wonderment at being here, at walking so easily and comfortably down to this place which held the Swiss prisoners for three days in the spring; which in the autumn they had described as "having the smell of death about it". To me, with one Sherpa and an oxygen mask in a stiff breeze, it bore a strong resemblance to parts of Scafell Pike in winter. A week later the tale was different. But I had no forebodings.

We crunched down to the last of the wind-crust, myself still unwinding the rope. Then the flat. The yellow rags lay in dead little heaps, or flapped forlornly from metal uprights that still stood. Round about was spread a chaos of food, kitbags, sleeping-bags, felt boots. Whenever people talk of the "conquest" of Everest, I close my eyes and see that ghost-ridden scene. Our tents must now look like that. Meanwhile Anullu, who had enjoyed no such romantic reflections, was suddenly to be seen fastening a fine Swiss rucksack containing felt boots on to his back. "Hey, the other people will need that." But to my every suggestion he returned the laconic reply that Tenzing had told him that if he reached the col first, he was to have the first spoil. Arguing from behind an oxygen mask is not easy. "What about your oxygen?" No, he would rather leave his oxygen. Foolishly, perhaps affected by the altitude, I failed even to realize that George might need his mask after all, and we left that too. All this, with my photographs, took some time, and the South Col is no place upon which to linger idle. I was wearing only one sweater, and no down clothing, for it had been comparatively warm on the face. I picked up some matches, a tin of sardines and a box of Vita-Weat, a candle and cheese. I took a photograph. Then we turned to go.

Oxygen helped me, I know, up those 200 feet to the spur. To make sure that it worked, we tried out our handrail. On the top the wind blew less cold than on the col, and I must tell what I was wearing: string vest, flannel shirt and thick sweater, thick pyjama trousers and windproof suit over all. Two pairs of gloves. Not very warm clothing for over 26,000 feet, I can hear you say, but the truth is that up to the spur, in the noonday, it was often warm. But not always.

On the crest I stopped, amazed at the swing of the ridge of Nuptse, now below us, with its myriad ups and downs. On each side the cloud billows foamed gently, but the ridge itself, its furrowed sides and dazzling ice edge, sparkled up into a pure sky. So elating was the effect of oxygen, I even pointed out its beauties to Anullu: who doubtless thought me quite mad.

Halfway back across the traverse we halted. I swung my cylinder heavily into the snow, Anullu produced his large flask. It was drink that above all we needed, not food, and neither of us ate. I thought, "Going down I ought not to need my oxygen." I would switch off. It would now be easier, and it was an awkward job reading the pressure without a companion able to help. The perilous crevasse we jumped merrily from its upper lip. Then on, down to the intricacies. But I had been spoilt. I was not going so well. I thought, "Well, I'll put it on again, I won't be so tired and I'll drain the last drop." The heavy swing off, the switch on, the fatigue of the swing of the cylinder back. The fastening of the tubes. Then, at last, the metallic breath. But, oh dear, with oxygen on I can never keep my goggles clear. There they were, misted up again. I peered and rubbed, they were still misted. We were coming down unearthly terraces dimly seen, the circles of Dante's Purgatorio, into the declining sun. Strange shapes seemed to rise towards me. At the shaft left by George we halted to cut a length of the rope, which I took on to fix in the bottom couloir. At last we were crossing the last slope above camp, and there were confused cries from below. It was the reality of Charles's party, and they seemed even to be cheering. However I had an *idée fixe* about this bottom couloir. We were not going to hurry it. I hammered in the spike with axe-head, and knotted two lengths of rope together. Then we dangled them down the couloir and on to the bridge. We crossed the crevasse as the sun tipped Nuptse, then dragged along the flat in an ecstasy of anticipation. Before six we were drinking tea beside the very crowded tents.

The Dream Comes True

Tenzing Norgay

After Noyce's solving of the Lhotse Face problem (see preceding pages), the British were in a position to establish a camp on the South Col; it was from there that the summit assaults would be launched. Charles Evans and Tom Boudillon tried first and reached the South Summit on 26 May – the highest point reached on Everest thus far – but exhaustion and oxygen problems prevented them from gaining the true summit a mere 300 feet above them. The next to have their chance were Ed Hillary, a New Zealand beekeeper, and Tenzing Norgay, the Sherpa. On 28 May Hillary and Tenzing Norgay made their bid. It was Norgay's second attempt at the top; only the year before he had tried for the prize with the Swiss climber Lambert.

May the 28th . . . It had been on the 28th that Lambert and I had made our final effort, struggling up as far as we could above our high camp on the ridge. Now we were a day's climb lower; a day later. A year later.

When it first grew light it was still blowing, but by eight o'clock the wind had dropped. We looked at each other and nodded. We would make our try.

But a bad thing had happened during the night: Pemba had been ill. And it was clear that he could not go higher. The day before we had lost Ang Tempa, who had been one of those supposed to go up to Camp Nine, and now, with Pemba out of it, only Ang Nyima was left of the original Sherpa team of three. This meant that the rest of us would all have to carry heavier loads, which would make our going slower and harder; but there was nothing we could do about it. A little before nine

Lowe, Gregory and Ang Nyima started off, each of them carrying more than forty pounds and breathing oxygen, and about an hour later Hillary and I followed, with fifty pounds apiece. The idea of this was that our support party would do the slow, hard work of cutting steps in the ice, and then we would be able to follow at our own pace, without tiring ourselves . . . Or perhaps I should say without tiring ourselves *too much*.

We crossed the frozen rocks of the col. Then we went up the snow-slope beyond, and up a long couloir, or gully, leading towards the South-East Ridge. As had been planned, the fine steps cut by the others made the going easier for us, and by the time they reached the foot of the ridge – about noon – we had caught up with them. A little above us here, and off to one side, were some bare poles and a few shreds of canvas that had once been the highest camp for Lambert and me; and they brought back many memories. Then slowly we passed by and went on up the ridge. It was quite steep, but not too narrow, with rock that sloped upward and gave a good foothold, if you were careful about the loose snow that lay over it. About 150 feet above the old Swiss tent we came to the highest point that Colonel Hunt and Da Namgyal had reached two days before, and there in the snow were the tent, food and oxygen-tanks which they had left for us. These now we had to add to our own loads, and from there on we were carrying weights of up to sixty pounds.

The ridge grew steeper, and our pace was now very slow. Then the snow became thicker, covering the rocks deeply, and it was necessary to cut steps again. Most of the time Lowe did this, leading the way with his swinging axe, while the rest of us followed. But by two in the afternoon all of us, with our great loads, were beginning to get tired, and it was agreed that we must soon find a camping-place. I remembered a spot that Lambert and I had noticed the year before – in fact, that we had decided would be our highest camp-site if we had another chance at the top – but it was still hidden above us, and on the stretch between there was no place that could possibly have held a tent. So on we went, with myself now leading – first still along the ridge, then off

to the left, across steep snow, towards the place I was looking for.

"Hey, where are you leading us to?" asked Lowe and
Gregory. "We have to go down."

"It can't be far now," I said. "Only five minutes."

But still we climbed: still we didn't get there. And I kept
saying, "Only five minutes . . . Only five minutes."

"Yes, but how many five minutes are there?" Ang Nyima
asked in disgust.

Then at last we got there. It was a partly level spot in the
snow, down a little from the exposed ridge and in the shelter
of a rocky cliff, and there we dropped our loads. With a quick
"Goodbye – good luck" Lowe, Gregory, and Ang Nyima
started down the col and Hillary and I were left alone. It was
then the middle of the afternoon, and we were at a height of
about 27,900 feet. The summit of Lhotse, the fourth highest
peak in the world, at which we had looked up every day
during the long expedition, was now below us. Over to the
south-east Makalu was below us. Everything we could see for
hundreds of miles was below us, except only the top of
Kangchenjunga, far to the east – and the white ridge climbing on above us into the sky.

We started pitching the highest camp that has ever been
made. And it took us almost until it was dark. First we
chopped away at the ice to try to make our sleeping-place a
little more level. Then we struggled with frozen ropes and
canvas, and tied the ropes round oxygen-cylinders to hold
them down. Everything took five times as long as it would
have in a place where there was enough air to breathe; but at
last we got the tent up, and when we crawled in it it was not
too bad. There was only a light wind, and inside it was not too
cold to take off our gloves. Hillary checked the oxygen-sets,
while I got our little stove going and made warm coffee and
lemon juice. Our thirst was terrible, and we drank them down
like two camels. Later we had some soup, sardines, biscuits
and tinned fruit, but the fruit was frozen so hard we had first
to thaw it out over the stove.

We had managed to flatten out the rocks and ice under the
tent, but not all at one level. Half the floor was about a foot

higher than the other half, and now Hillary spread his sleeping-bag on the upper half, and I put mine on the lower. When we were in them each of us rolled over close against the canvas, so that the weight of our bodies would help hold it in place. Mostly the wind was still not too bad, but sometimes great gusts would come out of nowhere, and the tent would seem ready to fly away. Lying in the dark, we talked of our plans for the next day. Then, breathing the "night-oxygen", we tried to sleep. Even in our eiderdown bags we both wore all our clothes and I kept on my Swiss reindeer-boots. At night most climbers take off their boots, because they believe this helps the circulation in the feet; but at high altitudes I myself prefer to keep them on. Hillary, on the other hand, took his off and laid them next to his sleeping-bag.

The hours passed. I dozed and woke, dozed and woke. And each time I woke I listened. By midnight there was no wind at all. God is good to us, I thought. Chomolungma is good to us. The only sound was that of our own breathing as we sucked at our oxygen.

May the 29th . . . On the 29th Lambert and I had descended in defeat from the col to the cwm. Down – down – down . . .

At about three-thirty in the morning we began to stir. I got the stove going and boiled snow for lemon juice and coffee, and we ate a little of the food left over from the night before. There was still no wind. When, a little while later, we opened the tent-flap everything was clear and quiet in the early-morning light. It was then that I pointed down and showed Hillary the tiny dot that was the Thyangboche Monastery, 16,000 feet below. "God of my father and mother," I prayed in my heart, "be good to me now – today."

But the first thing that happened was a bad thing. Hillary's boots, lying all night outside his sleeping-bag, had frozen, and now they were like two lumps of black iron. For a whole hour we had to hold them over the stove, pulling and kneading them, until the tent was full of the smell of scorched leather and we were both panting as if we were already climbing the peak. Hillary was very upset, both at the delay and at the danger to his feet. "I'm afraid I may get frostbitten, like

Lambert," he said. But at last the boots were soft enough for him to put on, and then we prepared the rest of our gear. For this last day's climbing I was dressed in all sorts of clothes that came from many places. My boots, as I have said, were Swiss; my wind-jacket and various other items had been issued by the British. But the socks I was wearing had been knitted by Ang Lahmu. My sweater had been given me by Mrs Henderson, of the Himalayan Club. My woollen helmet was the old one that had been left to me by Earl Denman. And, most important of all, the red scarf round my neck was Raymond Lambert's. At the end of the autumn expedition he had given it to me and smiled and said, "Here, perhaps you can use it some time." And ever since I had known exactly what that use must be.

At six-thirty, when we crawled from the tent, it was still clear and windless. We had pulled three pairs of gloves on to our hands – silk, wool, and windproof – and now we fastened our crampons to our boots, and on to our backs slung the forty pounds of oxygen apparatus that would be the whole load for each of us during the climb. Round my axe were still the four flags, tightly wrapped. And in the pocket of my jacket was a small red-and-blue pencil.

"All ready?"

"*Ah chah*. Ready."

And off we went.

Hillary's boots were still stiff, and his feet cold, so he asked me to take the lead. And for a while that is how we went on the rope – up from the campsite to the South-East Ridge, and then on along the ridge towards the South Summit. Sometimes we found the footprints of Bourdillon and Evans and were able to use them; but mostly they had been wiped away by the winds of the two days before, and I had to kick or chop our own steps. After a while we came to a place I recognized – the point where Lambert and I had stopped and turned back. I pointed it out to Hillary, and tried to explain through my oxygen-mask, and as we moved on I thought of how different it was these two times – of the wind and the cold then and the bright sunshine now – and how lucky we were on this day of our great effort. By now Hillary's feet were feeling better, so we changed places on the rope; and we kept doing this from then on, with first one of us leading the way and then the other, in order to share the work of kicking and chopping. As we drew near the South Summit we came upon something we had been looking for – two bottles of oxygen that had been left for us by Bourdillon and Evans. We scraped the ice off the dials, and were happy to see that they were still quite full. For this meant that they could be used later for our downward trip to the col, and meanwhile we could breathe in a bigger amount of what we were carrying with us.

We left the two bottles where they were and climbed on. Until now the climbing – if not the weather – had been much the same as I remembered from the year before – along the steep, broken ridge, with a rock precipice on the left and snow cornices hiding another precipice on the right. But now, just below the South Summit, the ridge broadened out into a sort of snow-face, so that the steepness was not so much to the sides as straight behind us, and we were climbing up an almost vertical white wall. The worst part of it was that the snow was not firm, but kept sliding down, sliding down – and we with it – until I thought, next time it will keep sliding, and we will go all the way to the bottom of the mountain. For me this was the one really bad place on the whole climb, because it was not only a matter of what you yourself did, but what the snow under you did, and this you could not control. It was one of the most dangerous places I had ever been on a mountain. Even now, when I think of it, I can still feel as I felt then, and the hair almost stands up on the back of my hands.

At last we got up it, though, and at nine o'clock we were on the South Summit. This was the highest point that Bourdillon and Evans had reached, and for ten minutes we rested there, looking up at what was still ahead. There was not much farther to go – only about 300 feet of ridge – but it was narrower and steeper than it had been below, and, though not impossible-looking, would certainly not be easy. On the left, as before, was the precipice falling away to the Western Cwm, 8,000 feet below, where we could now see the tiny dots that were the tents of Camp Four. And on the right were still the snow cornices, hanging out over a 10,000-foot drop to the Kangshung Glacier. If we were to get to the top it would have to be along a narrow, twisting line between precipice and cornices – never too far to the left, never too far to the right, or it would be the end of us.

One thing we had eagerly been waiting for happened on the South Summit. Almost at the same moment we each came to the end of the first of our two bottles of oxygen, and now we were able to dump them here, which reduced the weight we were carrying from forty to only twenty pounds. Also, as we left the South Summit, another good thing happened. We found that the snow beyond it was firm and sound. This could make all the difference on the stretch that we still had to go.

"Everything all right?"

"*Ah chah*. All right."

From the South Summit we first had to go down a little. Then up, up, up. All the time the danger was that the snow would slip, or that we would get too far out on a cornice that would then break away; so we moved just one at a time, taking turns at going ahead, while the second one wrapped the rope round his axe and fixed the axe in the snow as an anchor. The weather was still fine. We were not too tired. But every so often, as had happened all the way, we would have trouble breathing, and have to stop and clear away the ice that kept forming in the tubes of our oxygen-sets. In regard to this, I must say in all honesty that I do not think Hillary is quite fair in the story he later told, indicating that I had more trouble than he with breathing, and that without his help I might have suffocated. In my opinion our difficulties were about the same – and luckily never too great – and we each helped and were helped by the other in equal measure.

Anyhow, after each short stop we kept going, twisting always higher along the ridge between the cornices and the precipices. And at last we came to what might be the last big obstacle below the top. This was a cliff of rock rising straight up out of the ridge and blocking it off, and we had already known about it from aerial photographs and from seeing it through binoculars from Thyangboche. Now it was a question of how to get over or round it, and we could find only one possible way. This was along a steep, narrow gap between one side of the rock and the inner side of an adjoining cornice, and Hillary, now going first, worked his way up it, slowly and carefully, to a sort of platform above. While climbing he had to press backward with his feet against the cornice, and I belayed him from below as strongly as I could, for there was great danger of the ice giving way. Luckily, however, it did not. Hillary got up safely to the top of the rock, and then held the rope while I came after.

Here, again, I must be honest and say that I do not feel his account, as told in *The Ascent of Everest*, is wholly accurate. For one thing, he has written that this gap up the rock-wall was about forty feet high, but in my judgement it was little more than fifteen. Also, he gives the impression that it was only he who really climbed it on his own, and that he then practically pulled me, so that I "finally collapsed exhausted at the top, like a giant fish when it has just been hauled from the sea after a terrible struggle." Since then I have heard plenty about that "fish", and I admit I do not like it. For it is the plain truth that no one pulled or hauled me up the gap. I climbed it myself, just as Hillary had done; and if he was protecting me with the rope while I was doing it, this was no more than I had done for him. In speaking of this I must make one thing very clear. Hillary is my friend. He is a fine climber and a fine man, and I am proud to have gone with him to the top of Everest. But I do feel that in his story of our final climb he is not quite fair to me: that all the way through he indicates that when things went well it was his doing, and when things went badly it was mine. For this is simply not true. Nowhere do I make the suggestion that I could have climbed Everest by myself; and I do not think Hillary should suggest that he could have, or that I could not have done it without his help. All the way up and down we helped, and were helped by, each other – and that was the way it should be. But we were not leader and led. We were partners.

On top of the rock-cliff we rest again. Certainly, after the climb up the gap, we are both a bit breathless, but after some slow pulls at the oxygen I am feeling fine. I look up; the top is very close now; and my heart thumps with excitement and joy. Then we are on our way again. Climbing again. There are still the cornices on our right and the precipice on our left, but the ridge is now less steep. It is only a row of snowy humps, one beyond the other, one higher than the other. But we are still afraid of the cornices, and, instead of following the ridge all the way, cut over to the left, where there is now a long snow-slope above the precipice. About a hundred feet below the top we come to the highest bare rocks. There is enough almost level space here for two tents, and I wonder if men will ever camp in this place, so near the summit of the earth. I pick up two small stones and put them in my pocket to bring back to the world below. Then the rocks too are beneath us. We are back among the snowy humps. They are curving off to the right, and each time we pass one I wonder, Is the next the last one? Is the next the last? Finally we reach a place where we can see past the humps, and beyond them is the great open sky and brown plains. We are looking down the far side of the mountain upon Tibet. Ahead of us now is only one more hump – the last hump. It is not a pinnacle. The way to it is an easy snow-slope, wide enough for two men to go side by side. About thirty feet away we stop for a minute and look up. Then we go on . . .

I have thought much about what I will say now – of how Hillary and I reached the summit of Everest. Later, when we came down from the mountain, there was much foolish talk about who got there first. Some said it was I, some Hillary. Some that only one of us got there – or neither. Still others, that one of us had to drag the other up. All this was nonsense. And in Kathmandu, to put a stop to such talk, Hillary and I signed a statement in which we said "we reached the summit almost together". We hoped this would be the end of it. But it was not the end. People kept on asking questions and making up stories. They pointed to the "almost" and said, "What does that mean?" Mountaineers understand that there is no sense to such a question; that when two men are on the same rope they are *together*, and that is all there is to it. But other people did not understand. In India and Nepal, I am sorry to say, there has been great pressure on me to say that I reached the summit before Hillary. And all over the world I am asked, "Who got there first? Who got there first?"

Again I say, "It is a foolish question. The answer means nothing." And yet it is a question that has been asked so often – that has caused so much talk and doubt and misunderstanding – that I feel, after long thought, that the answer should be given. As will be clear, it is not for my own sake that I give it. Nor is it for Hillary's. It is for the sake of Everest – the prestige of Everest – and for the generations who will come after us. "Why," they will say, "should there be a mystery to this thing? Is there something to be ashamed of? To be hidden? Why can we not know the truth?" . . . Very well: now they will know the truth. Everest is too great, too precious, for anything but the truth.

A little below the summit Hillary and I stopped. We looked up. Then we went on. The rope that joined us was thirty feet long, but I held most of it in loops in my hand, so that there was only six feet between us. I was not thinking of "first" and "second". I did not say to myself, "There is a golden apple up there. I will push Hillary aside and run for it." We went on slowly, steadily. And then we were there. Hillary stepped on top first. And I stepped up after him.

So there it is – the answer to the "great mystery". And if, after all the talk and argument, the answer seems quiet and simple I can only say that that is as it should be. Many of my own people, I know, will be disappointed at it. They have given a great and false importance to the idea that it must be I who was "first". These people have been good and wonderful to me, and I owe them much. But I owe more to Everest – and to the truth. If it is a discredit to me that I was a step behind Hillary, then I must live with that discredit. But I do not think it was that. Nor do I think that, in the end, it will bring discredit on me that I tell the story. Over and over again I have asked myself, "What will future generations think of us if we allow the facts of our achievement to stay shrouded in mystery? Will they not feel ashamed of us – two comrades in life and death – who have something to hide from the world?" And each time I asked it the answer was the same: "Only the truth is good enough for the future. Only the truth is good enough for Everest."

Now the truth is told. And I am ready to be judged by it.

We stepped up. We were there. The dream had come true . . .

What we did first was what all climbers do when they reach the top of their mountain. We shook hands. But this was not enough for Everest. I waved my arms in the air, and then threw them round Hillary, and we thumped each other on the back until, even with the oxygen, we were almost breathless. Then we looked round. It was eleven-thirty in the morning, the sun was shining, and the sky was the deepest blue I have ever seen. Only a gentle breeze was blowing, coming from the direction of Tibet, and the plume of snow that always blows from Everest's summit was very small. Looking down the far side of the mountain, I could see all the familiar landmarks from the earlier expeditions – the Rongbuk Monastery, the town of Shekar Dzong, the Kharta Valley, the Rongbuk and East Rongbuk Glaciers, the North Col, the place near the North-East Ridge where we had made Camp Six in 1938. Then, turning, I looked down the long way we ourselves had come – past the South Summit, the long ridge, the South Col; on to the Western Cwm, the icefall, the Khumbu Glacier; all the way down to Thyangboche, and on to the valleys and hills of my homeland.

Beyond them, and around us on every side, were the great Himalayas, stretching away through Nepal and Tibet. For the closer peaks – giants like Lhotse, Nuptse and Makalu – you now had to look sharply downward to see their summits. And, farther away, the whole sweep of the greatest range on earth – even Kangchenjunga itself – seemed only like little bumps under the spreading sky. It was such a sight as I had never seen before and would never see again – wild, wonderful, and terrible. But terror was not what I felt. I loved the mountains too well for that. I loved Everest too well. At that great moment for which I had waited all my life my mountain did not seem to me a lifeless thing of rock and ice, but warm and friendly and living. She was a mother hen, and the other mountains were chicks under her wings. I too, I felt, had only to spread my own wings to cover and shelter the brood that I loved.

We turned off our oxygen. Even there on top of the world it was possible to live without it, so long as we were not exerting ourselves. We cleared away the ice that had formed on our masks, and I popped a bit of sweet into my mouth. Then we replaced the masks. But we did not turn on the oxygen again until we were ready to leave the top. Hillary took out his camera, which he had been carrying under his clothing to keep it from freezing, and I unwound the four flags from around my axe. They were tied together on a string, which was fastened to the blade of the axe, and now I held the axe up, and Hilary took my picture. Actually he took three, and I think it was lucky, in those difficult conditions, that one came out so well. The order of the flags from top to bottom was United Nations, British, Nepalese, Indian; and the same sort of people who have made trouble in other ways have tried to find political meaning in this too. All I can say is that on Everest I was not thinking about politics. If I had been, I suppose I would have put the Indian or Nepalese flag highest, though that in itself would have been a bad problem for me. As it is, I am glad that the U.N. flag was on top. For I like to think that our victory was not only for ourselves – not only for our own nations – but for all men everywhere.

I motioned to Hillary that I would now take his picture. But for some reason he shook his head; he did not want it. Instead he began taking more pictures himself, around and down on all sides of the peak, and meanwhile I did another thing that had to be done on the top of our mountain. From my pocket I took the package of sweets I had been carrying. I took the little red-and-blue pencil that my daughter, Nima, had given me. And, scraping a hollow in the snow, I laid them there. Seeing what I was doing, Hillary handed me a small cloth cat, black and with white eyes, that Hunt had given him as a mascot, and I put this beside them. In his story of our climb Hillary says it was a crucifix that Hunt gave him, and that he left on top: but if this was so I did not see it. He gave me only the cloth cat. All I laid in the snow was the cat, the pencil and the sweets. "At home," I thought, "we offer sweets to those who are near and dear to us. Everest has always been dear to me, and now it is near too." As I covered up the offerings I said a silent prayer.

And I gave my thanks. Seven times I had come to the mountain of my dream, and on this, the seventh, with God's help, the dream had come true.

"*Thuji chey, Chomolungma*. I am grateful . . ."

Everest 1960

Onwards, and Onwards!

Wang Fu-chou and Chu Yin-hua

The announcement by Communist China that it had succeeded in placing men on Everest's summit in 1960 was greeted with scepticism in the West: there was no photograph, and the official account by summitteers Wang Fu-chou and Chu Yin-hua was longer on Party ideology than it was on the nitty-gritty of the climb. Time, however, has tended to favour the Chinese claim.

The Chinese ascended via the North Col, thus succeeding where all the British pre-war expeditions had failed.

In the evening of 23 May, after six days of exhausting march, we thirteen members of the Chinese mountaineering expedition, led by deputy leader Hsu Ching, reached the Final Assault Camp at 8,500 metres above sea-level. That night we ate very little food. The decision made at the Party meeting to launch the final assault on the summit was like a bugle call for front-line soldiers to push forward against the enemy. We could not suppress our excitement. The thought that we would make the final assault on Mount Chomolungma the next day kept us awake almost the whole night.

On the morning of the 24th, the sky over Chomolungma was clear and serene. According to the weather forecast, it was an ideal day for the ascent. The four team members assigned for the final assault – Gonpa, Liu Lien-man and the writers – after drinking plenty of water and putting rucksacks on our backs, were all set for the task. However, we were confronted with serious difficulties right away. We discovered that we had not sufficient oxygen left. Furthermore, deputy leader Hsu Ching could not be with us, as he had to stay at the Final

Assault Camp to direct the whole operation as well as make all necessary arrangements to call for assistance in case of need. During the acclimatization marches, he had always been in the lead to make reconnaissance or open up roads, but now he was in a state of exhaustion. He obviously felt sorry that he could not go along with us and tears came down his cheeks. With a warm heart he said encouragingly, "I'll stay here to welcome your successful return!" With tears in our eyes, we also assured him that we would not fail the Party and the people's expectations and would conquer the highest peak of the world. Then with a deep feeling we set off to climb the last 350 metres of Chomolungma.

Soon, all four of us reached the famous Second Step, which is 8,600 metres above sea level. No wonder the British adventurers were stopped short here, and described it as the last hundredweight blow. The step is a sheer cliff of some thirty metres high, with an average gradient of sixty to seventy degrees. We cleverly skirted around the slope in a direction parallel to the base. But near the top of the step a three-metre-high vertical rock slab suddenly stood in our way. Liu Lien-man blazed the trail but failed in all his four attempts to open up a way. After each fall, it took him ten to fifteen minutes to get up again. Now he was completely exhausted. This made Chu Yin-hua impatient. He took off his heavy cramponned boots and thick woollen socks. Gripping the crevice with his hands and stepping on the rock surface with his feet, he tried to climb up. But twice he failed and fell down. Then snow began to swirl in the air, which made the climbing all the more difficult. What was to be done? Turn back like the British climbers had done before? No! Certainly not! The whole Chinese people and the Party were watching us. The moment we thought of the big send-off we got at the Base Camp with the beating gongs and drums and loud cheers, the solemn pledge we had taken before we started out, and the national flag and the plaster bust of Chairman Mao which we took along, we felt all-powerful again. After taking some oxygen and a short rest, we were determined to climb to the top. This time, Liu Lien-man made use of his experience as a fireman. The short ladder method was employed. He crouched and let Chu Yin-hua step on his shoulders, and with great effort he stood up. Good! Chu Yin-hua got on the rock slab, and then Gonpa too. All of us were overjoyed at the success. It took us three full hours to get on top of this three-metre-high rock slab.

After walking about 100 metres on top of the Second Step, Liu Lien-man fell down. With great exertion he managed to stand up and march forward again. But after a few steps, he fell again. He did not utter one word, so the rest of us didn't pay any attention. But when he fell for the third time, we began to realize that this veteran mountaineer was completely exhausted and couldn't go any further. And the oxygen he had brought along seemed to be exhausted too. It was then seven o'clock in the evening, and we had another 180 metres to cover before reaching the summit. The oxygen reserves we brought along were also running low. Liu Lien-man is an experienced and skilful climber and a staunch Party member. Without him our ascent to the summit would be much more difficult. On the other hand, how could we leave him at an altitude of 8,700 metres with such thin air? It was too dangerous! Of course, we could sacrifice our personal interests and leave the little oxygen we had to him. But that would endanger our successful assault on the summit. In this dilemma, we did not know what to do. Then the three Communist Party members, Liu and the writers, held an emergency meeting on the highest peak of the world. At the meeting, Liu was still full of hope of our success. He said, "Press on. Be sure to finish the job! I'll be alive here to welcome you back." It was also decided at the meeting that we should get on top of the peak even without oxygen. Liu was then helped to a safe shelter below a cliff, and we said goodbye to him with tears in our eyes. Though he wasn't with us his noble spirit gave us great strength to score the final victory.

In front of us, at 8,700 metres, there was another ice and snow slope. We laboured forward painstakingly in knee-deep snow. For every few steps we had to halt to catch our breath. In scaling a one-metre rock in our way, all three of us slipped several times. It was almost midnight when we got through this stretch of ice and snow.

It was getting darker and darker and we were getting weaker and weaker for every inch we made forward. Then we were confronted with another sheer icy cliff. We were forced to trudge along the northern slope and circle around the cliff westward towards the ridge in the north-west. We were just about to ascend when we discovered our oxygen reserves were all out! At that moment, we remembered the decision made at the Party meeting and Liu Lien-man's words of encouragement, which filled us with confidence to plant our national flag on the summit. We had already reached 8,830 metres above sea-level and nothing would make us turn back! But our legs refused to carry us any further, so we had to go on all fours. Gonpa took the lead, and we two followed closely behind. Onwards, and onwards! We forgot time and cold. Suddenly we noticed Gonpa had disappeared. With a great surprise we looked upward. We spotted a shadow on top of the towering peak just a few metres away. It was Gonpa himself! We were overjoyed with excitement. Immediately, we forgot our fatigue, and great strength seemed to come back to us. When we went up to the top, we found there was another peak, still a few metres higher than the one we had just surmounted. That was the highest point of Chomolungma. Then we made our final assault with still greater exertion. Breathing became so difficult that each inch forward meant tremendous efforts. The last few metres of ascent took us no less than forty minutes.

At this time, we saw the star-studded sky above us on the top peak of Chomolungma. To the south of the crest was gleaming white snow, and to the north was nothing but dull grey rocks. We stood on an oval-shaped space, the boundary line between snow and the rocks.

We stayed upon the crest for about fifteen minutes. We placed the Chinese national flag and a plaster bust of Chairman Mao Tse-tung separately on a great rock to the north-west of the summit and covered them with small stones. Then in accordance with international usage, we pencilled a note with our signatures and placed it under a heap of rocks. We were speechless, but our hearts were filled with joy and excitement. We had successfully completed the task the Party and Chairman Mao Tse-tung had entrusted to us.

After a short stay on the summit, we started to descend. The great excitement overshadowed our extreme fatigue. We were

worried about our comrade Liu Lien-man. The day was breaking when we came down from the snow-covered slope. In the
distance we could see Liu Lien-man still there alive. We learned
that after we had departed, Liu found out that he still had
some oxygen left, but he didn't take any for himself. He
thought of his comrades battling towards the summit of
Chomolungma, and wrote in his diary that the oxygen was
reserved specially for them. Finally he fell into a state of semi-
consciousness. As soon as we found out what he had done, and
as he offered us his breathing apparatus and a piece of candy
which he had saved for a long time, we were all moved to tears
by his noble character and embraced him and kissed him.

Soon the red sun rose slowly from the east behind the mountains, and shed its shining rays upon us. Ah, it was the shining
light of our motherland! It was the shining light of the Party
and Chairman Mao Tse-tung who gave us boundless strength
and wisdom.

The Shoulders of Giants

Gyan Singh

Singh led the first Indian attempt on the summit. An army officer, he was also Principal of the country's Himalayan Mountaineering Institute, at which Tenzing (an Indian national, despite being a Sherpa born and bred in Nepal's Sola Khumbu region) was chief instructor.

The Himalayas have been for centuries a region of pilgrimage and worship for millions of devout Indians. Equally, traders and missionaries have for generations braved the Himalayan hazards to enter Tibet over some of the highest mountain passes in the world. Among the early explorers and surveyors of this rugged mountainous terrain were some Indians, who, though ill-equipped and untrained in climbing techniques, performed some incredible feats of mountaineering in the execution of their tasks.

Till about ten years ago there were scarcely any Indians who went to the Himalayas for sport. The real impetus to mountaineering in India came from the ascent of Everest in 1953 when, teamed with Sir Edmund Hillary, Tenzing Norgay stood on the roof of the world. The spark of enthusiasm ignited by Tenzing's feat has already developed into a torch to light the path of those who seek adventure and excitement among the Himalayan heights. Indian youth's response to the call of the mountains is yet another sign of national awakening.

Thus, the Himalayan Mountaineering Institute came into being in 1954 to commemorate Tenzing's great achievement. With Tenzing himself as the director of field training, the Institute has trained young men on basic and advanced courses and has also helped in organizing expeditions to lesser peaks in the Himalayas. The sport, however, grew fast and barely four years after the Himalayan Mountaineering Institute was started, an Indian team successfully climbed Cho Oyu, the sixth highest mountain in the world. Encouraged by this success, the sponsoring committee booked Everest for 1960, and also for 1962 in case it was not possible to make an attempt in 1960.

By all standards, an attempt on a mountain of the magnitude of Everest is an ambitious project requiring thorough planning and preparation over a long period. For one reason or another very little work was done in 1958 and, in fact, the first half of 1959 also went by without achieving much in the way of preparation.

During July and August 1959 I had gone to Europe on the invitations of the French Mountaineering Federation and the Swiss Foundation for Alpine Research to attend some international mountaineers' meetings. When I returned to India in September, I was surprised to find that the sponsoring committee offered me the leadership of the expedition. It was a pleasant surprise, and indeed an honour, but I was diffident about accepting the task. However, after some thought I found it impossible to decline.

Once the decision had been made, two immediate tasks confronted us; first the selection of a team, and second the procuring of equipment. The selection of the team was not difficult because at the Himalayan Mountaineering Institute we were able to organize a special pre-Everest course in the Kabru region of western Sikkim in October and November 1959. Twenty-five mountaineers responded to the invitation, and after the course, on Tenzing's recommendation and mine, the sponsoring committee finalized the team. We were happy to find that there were more qualified aspirants than places in the expedition, so several worthy men were unfortunately turned down.

In the end we selected thirteen men, all with considerable Himalayan experience. First there were the three Sherpa instructors from the Mountaineering Institute: Da-Namgyal, Ang Temba and Gombu, all of whom had been on Everest before. Then Keki Bunshah, Captain Narinder Kumar of the Kumaon Regiment, Sonam Gyatsho (who was one of the two who reached the summit of Cho-Oyu in 1958), Flight-Lieutenant Chaudhury, Rajendra Vikram Singh, B. D. Misra, C. P. Vohra, Captain Jungalwalla of the Gorkha Rifles, Instructor-Lieutenant M. S. Kohli of the Indian navy and myself. In addition, we had two doctors, Flight-Lieutenant N. S. Bhagwanani and Captain S. K. Das of the Army Medical Corps; a Films Division camera man C. V. Gopal; and a transport officer, Flight-Lieutenant A. J. S. Grewal. Our small signals detachment was led by Captain S. G. Nanda. Meteorologist K. U. Shankar Rao, and the Secretary of the Indian Mountaineering Federation, Sohan Singh, also accompanied us.

The second problem was far more difficult because it had been decided that as much of our equipment as possible should be manufactured in India, and imports should be restricted to specialized items only. In the past most expeditions to Himalayan peaks, including Indian expeditions, had to use European equipment. But we knew that we could rely on the skill and ingenuity of our own countrymen. In nearly all cases the indigenous equipment stood the severe test very well indeed. This in itself is perhaps one of the expedition's major achievements. It will perhaps be possible in the near future for Himalayan expeditions to obtain reliable equipment and stores in India, thus reducing expenditure on transportation, and delays and irritations at arrival ports.

While we knew that India could make the equipment, the time factor was against us. We had barely five months in which to train and select the team, obtain prototypes of equipment and test them, place final orders for stores and equipment and ensure delivery in time for us to start packing on 20 February 1960.

The attempt on a major Himalayan peak is, to a large extent, a logistical problem of great magnitude, the planning and preparation for which must begin the day the project is conceived. If success on a mountain like Everest is to be assured, a team of ten to twelve climbers and over forty Sherpas must first be properly equipped and transported with adequate supplies to the base of the mountain. To achieve this, many of the resources of modern technology must be mobilized. It was very gratifying to find that Indian industry and ordnance factories cooperated in a magnificent manner. Under Tenzing's personal supervision, Sherpas and Nepali women of Darjeeling worked long hours knitting excellent woollen wear for the expedition. The Swiss Foundation for Alpine Research in Zurich gave us unstinting support and handled the supply of oxygen apparatus and other essential imported items. For three months the members of the team and many friends, as well as our sponsors, worked almost round the clock collecting the nineteen tons of equipment and stores which began to arrive at the Central Vista Mess in New Delhi towards the middle of February 1960. Now everyone worked eagerly sorting out the gear, classifying it and packing it in sixty-pound loads. Finally, on 27 February, we passed our first big hurdle. We laid out the packages on the lawns of the mess ready for transportation by road to Lucknow on the first lap of our journey to Everest.

When we arrived in Jayanagar on 4 March, most of our Sherpas and over 700 porters were already waiting for us. We had only one day in which to register the porters, pay them advances, allot them loads and divide them into two parties, as it was not convenient for so many to march in one train. Here Tenzing's help in handling the Sherpas and porters proved invaluable. The first party entered Nepal on schedule on 6 March, after a heart-warming farewell from the people of Jayanagar and many friends who had come to see us off.

Our two weeks' journey to the acclimatization training camp near Thyangboche Monastery took us through terai jungles, lush padi-fields and over beautiful alpine meadows. Apricot and cherry trees in blossom and blooming rhododendrons and magnolias dotted the landscape along our route. Often local villagers would bring eggs, milk and fruit, all as a friendly gesture, expecting nothing in return. Our long caravan arrived in Namche Bazar on 21 March. This sleepy-looking village, with about a hundred houses, is in the heart of Sherpa country, not far from Everest, and is an important landmark for all expeditions going to East Nepal. That night a heavy and much-needed snowfall blanketed the surrounding country.

Three days later we reached Thyangboche, where we were given an audience by the incarnate lama in a simple but solemn ceremony. The Lama promised to offer prayers for the safe return of the expedition. That same day we reached our acclimatization training camp at Pangboche at a height of 13,200 feet. Based on this camp, for the next three weeks we carried through a programme which entailed climbing peaks of 16,000 to 19,000 feet. We climbed in different groups and in different areas, carrying varying loads in our rucksacks. We also used this period for familiarizing ourselves with our oxygen and other specialized equipment. Physiologist Das and Doctor Bhagwanani kept a careful watch on our performance and conducted certain physiological tests. But so far no one required much medical attention, for we were all in excellent health and enormously enjoyed the good food with which the expedition had been provided. This was also a sure sign of the fact that we were acclimatizing well.

In the second phase of our acclimatization programme, we had divided ourselves into three parties each of four members, and each with a team of ten high-altitude Sherpas. Each party was self-sufficient in equipment and stores and had selected its own area for its climbing activity. The plans of all three parties were ready by 30 March.

The first party, consisting of Keki Bunshah, Kohli, Jungalwalla and Ang Temba, moved in the direction of the base of Everest. They did their climbing exercises on the way. This party had been given the task of establishing the base camp and exploring the route through the Khumbu ice-fall.

The second party, consisting of Kumar, Misra, Vohra and Da-Namgyal, went over to the Amadablam area, where they indulged in some interesting rock scrambles. This party climbed the lower slopes of Amadablam and spotted fixed lines and rope-ladders put up by the ill-fated British expedition to that great mountain in 1959. The party also climbed a relatively difficult rock feature, the Yellow Tower, so named by the Swiss expedition to Everest in 1956.

The third group, consisting of Sonam, Gyatscho, Chaudhury, Rajendra Vikram and the photographer Gopal, went towards Taweche. They found the mountain very difficult from the southern slopes, but did some useful training climbs on ice and rock faces for three days, after which they moved to the Chukhung glacier.

By the end of the first week of April we had received the welcome news from Grewal that he would join us with oxygen equipment in the following week. Thus, all forces could now rapidly converge on the base camp. Our exciting task was about to begin. We had our equipment, and what is more, we were in good training and excellent health and our morale was high.

Our route towards the summit of Everest lay along the Khumbu glacier, through the Western Cwm, across the Lhotse face to the South Col and finally along the South-West Ridge to the top. This was the route followed by the earlier parties because it is the only feasible approach from the Nepalese side of the mountain.

On reaching the base camp we could not see the summit of Everest, but the western shoulders of Everest and Nuptse enclosed the entrance to the Western Cwm above the Khumbu Glacier. Down these faces we could see and hear avalanches thundering intermittently into the valley.

Even without reconnaissance we were aware of the three main hurdles that had to be overcome before reaching the top of Everest. First, the Khumbu ice-fall, an awe-inspiring mass of ice which cascades nearly 2,000 feet down a steep gradient. In its downward plunge, this enormous slab of ice is broken up into gaping crevasses, massive ridges and ice-towers, forming a complicated labyrinth. The ice-fall in some respects is the most difficult obstacle and is constantly changing. Yet throughout our stay on the mountain we had to negotiate it every day. In order to establish higher camps it was also necessary to transport nearly two tons of stores and equipment over this treacherous and dreaded portion of the glacier.

The second hurdle was the Lhotse Face, a very long and steep slope of granite-hard ice and rock rising to 26,000 feet from the Western Cwm at about 22,400 feet. We knew this would tax our energy in cutting steps and fixing rope lines. Here we would also enter the so-called deterioration zone with its extremely rarefied atmosphere. Finally, there was the summit pyramid where, in addition to the technical difficulties, the effects of weather and high altitude were even more pronounced.

By the time all the parties assembled at the base camp on 13 April, the first party, consisting of Ang Temba, Keki, Kohli, Jungalwalla and Bhagwanani, had already established Camp I on 10 April at a height of 19,000 feet. They had also probed forward and made the route a part of the way towards the site of Camp II, but had to return somewhat short of their goal.

In accordance with our prearranged plan, the first team had to come off the mountain for a well-earned rest. The second party, composed of Da-Namgyal, Kumar, Vohra and Nisra, took over from the advance party.

I accompanied the second party up the ice-fall and spent the night at Camp I, established in an excellent location by Ang Temba and Kohli. Early next morning we started climbing towards the top of the ice-fall. After nearly three hours we arrived at the point reached by the earlier party. Here the Khumbu Glacier is compressed into a narrow gorge by the massive walls of Everest and Nuptse. Ahead of us, beyond several huge crevasses lay the Western Cwm and Lhotse. At this point we stopped on an ice ridge with Misra and my Sherpa companion, Lakpa. I contemplated the chaotic scene for some time. Looking back down the ice-fall I marvelled at the track-building ability of our climbers. The trail was marked with over 200 multicoloured silk flags; ropes and ladders were fixed on vertical ice faces and there were many wide crevasses over which bridges had been made with baulks of timber lashed together. Many sections of light aluminium ladders were used for bridging other obstacles. We could see hundreds of feet of rope firmly fixed to the vertical ice ridges to assist the climbers and Sherpas traversing those dangerous sections.

Hours passed. Around three o'clock, Da-Namgyal and the four Sherpas who had gone ahead returned to inform us modestly that Camp II had been established. With a little more work, we could now start ferrying supplies through the ice-fall into the Western Cwm. Thus, with the establishment of Camp II at 20,000 feet, the first obstacle had been overcome; we had found our way through the Khumbu ice-fall.

In spite of a few incidents, we plodded uphill steadily. For example our liaison officer, Dhanbir Rai, fell ill from acute acclimatization failure. Captain Das, our doctor physiologist, saved Rai's life by prompt administration of oxygen and medicine. Yet we went on. On the ice-fall one of the teams supervised the movement of supplies to Camp II, sometimes using plastic explosives to demolish tottering seracs. Further ahead, in the Western Cwm, Da-Namgyal and Kumar plodded forward, going round crevasses and dodging the artillery of avalanches hurtling down the near-vertical slopes of Everest and Nuptse. They established Camp III on 17 April at a height of 21,200 feet. Although fairly tired, they pressed on towards the Lhotse face and at a height of 22,400 feet marked a site for Camp IV with a flag. Exhausted by their continuous and strenuous march, they handed the task over to the third team. Now Gombu, Sonam and Chaudhury formed the vanguard while the second party went down to Labuje, at 16,000 feet, to recuperate.

We had now reached the high-altitude zone where one had not only to guard against the deteriorating effects of reduced oxygen, but to cope with strong prevailing westerly winds beating relentlessly against the Lhotse face. Under such conditions upward progress is agonizingly slow and a man's efficiency and performance drop considerably because his capacity to think and act rationally is reduced to a confused blur. In the face of these heavy odds, after fully establishing Camp IV, Gombu, Sonam and Chaudhury began their work on the formidable Lhotse Face on 20 April.

Past expeditions had explored different routes from the Western Cwm to the South Col. The most practical route, however, was up the steep Lhotse Glacier a part of the way, followed by a high traverse towards and over the Geneva Spur to the South Col at nearly 26,000 feet. Sir John Hunt and Albert Eggler's teams were lucky to find fairly long stretches of firm snow in which they were able to kick steps. Unfortunately for us the previous winter had been very mild and there was not much snow on the Lhotse Face. Thus we had to hack our way laboriously over the very long ice slope of the Lhotse Face.

In addition to these technical difficulties, we now faced very definite logistical problems. Our line of communication was stretched from the base camp at 18,000 feet through the ever-changing Khumbu ice-fall up to Camp IV at 22,400 feet. So far it had not been possible to stock the intermediate camps adequately. Thus, while Gombu, Sonam and Chaudhury were inching their way up the Lhotse Face, all remaining available hands were busily engaged in ferrying supplies to Camp III. They succeeded in keeping a small trickle of essential stores and equipment to the forward team. Camp III, which was our advance base camp and the second firm base, was now steadily growing in size.

The Lhotse Face was a tough nut to crack. Gombu and Sonam had made good progress on 20 April and nearly reached the site of Camp V, but had expended all their manilla rope and most of their energy. A day or two later Ang Temba and his team took over but, in the face of icy winds, made little headway. One of the Sherpas suffered frostbite on his fingers. On 28 April, however, the indomitable Da-Namgyal succeeded in pitching a tent at Camp V at an altitude of nearly 24,000 feet. The western disturbances had already set in and the strong winds reduced the temperature to −22°C. Da-Namgyal and Kumar had worked against heavy odds and this herculean effort took its toll; both the climbers were thoroughly exhausted and had to descend to base and later to the rest camp to recover from their ordeal.

As we could not afford to expend much oxygen at this stage we worked in short shifts and a succession of climbers now took over the lead. Gombu succeeded in passing the Yellow Band and traversed towards the Geneva Spur up to a height of about 25,000 feet before he returned exhausted. Vohra and Chaudhury went next and climbed up to 25,500 feet on 6 May. Finally, on 9 May, without using oxygen, Ang Temba and Jungalwalla, with a party of six Sherpas, reached the inhospitable South Col after crossing the 26,000-feet level. After leaving a tent, a few oxygen cylinders and some stores they climbed down to Camp V and descended to base camp the next day. While exploring the South Col, Ang Temba recovered a diary of Dr Hans Grimm, who was a member of the 1956 Swiss expedition to Lhotse and Everest.

During these hectic days we had our share of casualties.

There were a few cases of minor illness and some early stages of frostbite. All the same we kept up the momentum of our advance for the final bid. While a continuous succession of loads was being transported through the ice-fall and the Cwm to Camps III and IV, Lieutenant Nanda was at work setting up a telephone line from Camp II to the advance base in the Western Cwm, perhaps the highest telephone link ever established.

It would appear logical that, having reached the South Col, we should have maintained the momentum and begun the final and crucial phase of our task at once, but weather conditions frustrated our hopes. Severely cold and strong westerlies permitted no more than two small ferries to be pushed to the South Col. Then, after 13 May, the weather started deteriorating rapidly and snow began to fall intermittently. Faced with these conditions, we had no option but to withdraw to lower camps.

The pre-monsoon lull can generally be expected any time after the middle of May and on average should last for a fortnight. It was, therefore, still not too late, but when the weather showed no signs of clearing up, even after 16 and 17 May, we were a little anxious.

About this time, at the advance base, I was not too well and the doctor, Flight-Lieutenant Bhagwanani, suggested that I should go down. The weather continued bad and I had no option but to descend to the base camp on the 19th. But before leaving the advance base I was able to call a conference and announce my summit teams. I had to make a few difficult decisions. First, our most experienced and reliable member, Da-Namgyal, had to be dropped because of illness. Secondly, I had to detail Jungalwalla to the important assignment of supporting the summit teams from the South Col, which I had hoped to do myself. He would otherwise have been considered for one of the summit teams. Finally, I decided on the first summit team: Gombu, Sonam and Kumar. The second party was made up of Ang Temba, Kohli and Vohra. All these climbers possessed the required stamina, determination and experience to tackle the task.

After keeping us in great anxiety for over a week the weather suddenly cleared up on 20 May. We wondered: had the pre-monsoon lull arrived? The met forecast on All-India Radio indicated the monsoon's steady advance up the Bay of Bengal, but there was no mention of the lull.

Although it was clear and bright on 20 and 21 May and there was hardly any wind, we could not send our men up the steep Lhotse Face immediately after a heavy snowfall because of the avalanche hazard. After allowing two days for the fresh snow to consolidate and become first on the slope, the first team set out from Camp III on 22 May. In order to save time they went from Camp III to Camp V, where the three climbers and nine Sherpas spent the night. By the afternoon, accompanied by Jungalwalla and his support party, the team had reached Camp VI on the South Col.

24 May was a day of good weather and absolute calm. At seven that morning Gombu, Kumar and Sonam, supported by seven of the best high-altitude Sherpas, left the South Col in high spirits and carried with them a tent, butane gas fuel, food, sleeping bags and the indispensable oxygen cylinders. Using oxygen, the party made good progress and set up Camp VII at 27,600 feet. Here the Sherpas wished the climbers Godspeed and good luck and trudged slowly back to the South Col.

Gombu, Kumar and Sonam settled down for the night. Despite the altitude the three ate well that evening and crawled, fully clothed, into their sleeping bags. In a tent intended for only two, they were somewhat cramped. Excitement and the high altitude prevented sound sleep. They slowly crawled out of their bags at three in the morning and prepared to start.

Till the previous evening everything seemed to be going very smoothly and they were very optimistic about the final outcome. Luck, unfortunately, was no longer with them. The calm atmosphere of the day before had given way to a strong stormy wind which started whipping their tent at ten the night before. The three climbers waited hopefully for wind to abate. At seven there was still no sign of the wind velocity decreasing. There was no time to waste. They decided to take their chance and they set out.

The wind was strong and the going was heavy, but they were fresh and rested and at first made steady progress. The three climbers on one rope moved slowly, haltingly, up the South-East Ridge, keeping slightly below the crest. Soon the condensed and frozen moisture from exhaled air blocked the valves of Kumar's oxygen mask. He rapidly changed the mask and bladder, but this incident was an ominous portent of what might happen later when the climbers were obliged to expose themselves on the ridge to the full fury of the gale.

That moment soon arrived, and it became obvious that progress towards their goal was going to be painfully slow. Powder snow, carried by the wind, lashed at the climbers' faces with such force that they had to turn their faces sideways to advance at all. Twice the party halted while Sonam rectified the frozen valves of his mask. The wind was showing no signs of abating. Instead, it increased and particles of drift snow restricted vision. To make matters worse the climbers' goggles were filled with powdered snow, blown in through small ventilation holes. Visibility was practically nil at this stage.

About midday they halted for a little rest. They checked their height and found that they had reached 28,300 feet. They were barely 700 feet from the summit. The temptation to go on was great but the possibility of reaching the summit and returning safely was remote. Fortunately Kumar, Gombu and Sonam were mountaineers of sufficient experience to realize that, unlike a military operation, lives should not be risked unduly on a sporting adventure, no matter how worthy the goal. After a brief consultation they took the wise but difficult decision to retrace their steps.

This was the climax of the expedition. Next day the monsoon reached the Everest region, a week earlier than anticipated. The second team, which had in the meantime moved up to the South Col, waited throughout 26 May for the weather to clear while the weary first summit team descended to the advance base camp. On 27 May the weather was worse and the second summit team was also asked to withdraw from the mountain as fast as it could. Under those conditions further efforts would have been suicidal. Despite dogged determination, the supreme effort had failed. The climbers and Sherpas had done their best; and when you have done your best you can do no better.

We were turned back not by the mountain but the "autocratic element", the weather, over which man has no control.

By 29 May, the anniversary of the first ascent of Everest, everyone was back in base camp. It was willed that we should not succeed that year.

If we were disappointed, we also had reasons to be proud. Mountaineering is, for Indians, a relatively new sport. It was heartening to find that our young climbers were fit to challenge the world's loftiest peak. We had organized and conducted a major expedition, solved seemingly impossible logistical problems, and had reached a point higher than any other mountain in the world except Everest itself. What was most important was the fact that every member and Sherpa returned safely. It was also proved that India could make mountaineering equipment that could stand the test of the highest mountain.

Not the least achievement of the expedition was the stimulus to mountain climbing given by our attempt. More and more young Indian men and women are now going out to seek the vigour, health and happiness which only a sojourn in the high mountains can provide. Nearly a dozen Indian expeditions went to the Himalayas during 1961, the hard core and leadership for which was provided from among the seasoned Everesters of 1960. More than half a dozen peaks have been climbed. Everest is always there, waiting for our successors. These will come and, standing on our shoulders, will one day succeed where we so narrowly failed.

The 1960 Indian bid failed. So did the 1962 one, but the 1965 Indian expedition put no fewer than nine climbers on the summit.

Everest 1963
The Final Frontier

Tom Hornbein

In 1963 the Americans went to Everest. While most of the expedition's resources were directed at the British South Col route, Tom Hornbein and Willi Unsoeld wanted to forge a new route to the crest, via the West Ridge.

At four the oxygen ran out, a most effective alarm clock. Two well-incubated butane stoves were fished from inside our sleeping-bags and soon bouillon was brewing in the kitchen. Climbing into boots was a breathless challenge to balance in our close quarters. Then overboots, and crampons.

"Crampons, in the tent?"

"Sure," I replied. "It's a hell of a lot colder out there."

"But our air mattresses!"

"Just be careful. We may not be back here again, anyway. I hope."

We were clothed in multilayer warmth. The fishnet underwear next to our skin provided tiny air pockets to hold our body heat. It also kept the outer layers at a distance which, considering our weeks without a bath, was respectful. Next came Duofold underwear, a wool shirt, down underwear tops and bottoms, wool climbing pants and a lightweight wind parka. In spite of the cold, our down parkas would be too bulky for difficult climbing, so we used them to insulate two quarts of hot lemonade, hoping they might remain unfrozen long enough to drink during the climb. Inside the felt inner liners of our reindeer-hair boots were inner soles and two pairs of heavy wool socks. Down shells covered a pair of wool mittens. Over our oxygen helmets we wore wool balaclavas and our parka hoods.

The down parka lemonade-muff was stuffed into our packs as padding between two oxygen bottles. With camera, radio, flashlight and sundry mementos (including pages from Emerson's diary), our loads came close to 40 lb. For all the prior evening's planning it was more than two hours before we emerged.

I snugged a bowline about my waist, feeling satisfaction at the ease with which the knot fell together beneath heavily mittened hands. This was part of the ritual, experienced innumerable times before. With it came a feeling of security, not from the protection provided by the rope joining Willi and me, but from my being able to relegate these cold grey brooding forbidding walls, so high in such an unknown world, to common reality – to all those times I had ever tied into a rope before: with warm hands while I stood at the base of sun-baked granite walls in the Tetons, with cold hands on a winter night while I prepared to tackle my first steep ice on Longs Peak. This knot tied me to the past, to experiences known, to difficulties faced and overcome. To tie it here in this lonely morning on Everest brought my venture into contact with the known, with that which man might do. To weave the knot so smoothly with clumsily mittened hands was to assert my confidence, to assert some competence in the face of the waiting rock, to accept the challenge.

Hooking our masks in place we bade a slightly regretful goodbye to our tent, sleeping-bags and the extra supply of food we hadn't been able to eat. Willi was at the edge of the ledge looking up the narrow gully when I joined him.

"My oxygen's hissing, Tom, even with the regulator turned off."

For the next 20 minutes we screwed and unscrewed regulators, checked valves for ice, to no avail. The hiss continued. We guessed it must be in the valve, and thought of going back to the tent for the spare bottle, but the impatient feeling that time was more important kept us from retracing those forty feet.

"It doesn't sound too bad," I said. "Let's just keep an eye on the pressure. Besides if you run out we can hook up the sleeping T and extra tubing and both climb on one bottle." Willi envisioned the two of us climbing Everest in lockstep, wed by six feet of rubber hose.

We turned to the climb. It was ten minutes to seven. Willi led off. Three years before in a tent high on Masherbrum he had expounded on the importance of knee-to-toe distance for step-kicking up steep snow. Now his anatomical advantage determined the order of things as he put his theory to the test. Right away we found it was going to be difficult. The couloir, as it cut through the Yellow Band, narrowed to ten or fifteen feet and steepened to fifty degrees. The snow was hard, too hard to kick steps in, but not hard enough to hold crampons; they slid disconcertingly down through this wind-sheltered, granular stuff. There was nothing for it but to cut steps, zigzagging back and forth across the gully, occasionally finding a bit of rock along the side up which we could scramble. We were forced to climb one at a time with psychological belays from axes thrust a few inches into the snow. Our regulators were set to deliver two litres of oxygen per minute, half the optimal flow for this altitude. We turned them off when we were belaying to conserve the precious gas, though we knew that the belayer should always be at peak alertness in case of a fall.

We crept along. My God, I thought, we'll never get there at this rate. But that's as far as the thought ever got. Willi's leads were meticulous, painstakingly slow and steady. He plugged tirelessly on, deluging me with showers of ice as his axe carved each step. When he ran out the 100 feet of rope he jammed his axe into the snow to belay me. I turned my oxygen on to "2" and moved up as fast as I could, hoping to save a few moments of critical time. By the time I joined him I was completely winded, gasping for air, and sorely puzzled about why. Only late in the afternoon, when my first oxygen bottle was still going strong, did I realize what a low flow of gas my regulator was actually delivering.

Up the tongue of snow we climbed, squeezing through a passage where the walls of the Yellow Band closed in, narrowing the couloir to shoulder-width.

In four hours we had climbed only 400 feet. It was 11 a.m. A rotten bit of vertical wall forced us to the right on to the open face. To regain the couloir it would be necessary to climb this sixty-foot cliff, composed of two pitches split by a broken snow-covered step.

"You like to lead this one?" Willi asked.

With my oxygen off I failed to think before I replied, "Sure, I'll try it."

The rock sloped malevolently outward like shingles on a roof – rotten shingles. The covering of snow was no better than the rock. It would pretend to hold for a moment, then suddenly shatter and peel, cascading down on Willi. He sank a piton into the base of the step to anchor his belay.

I started up around the corner to the left, crampon points grating on rusty limestone. Then it became a snowploughing procedure as I searched for some sort of purchase beneath. The pick of my axe found a crack. Using the shaft for gentle leverage, I moved carefully on to the broken strata of the step. I went left again, loose debris rolling under my crampons, to the base of the final vertical rise, about eight feet high. For all its steepness, this bit was a singularly poor plastering job, nothing but wobbly rubble. I searched about for a crack, unclipped a big angle piton from my sling, and whomped it in with the hammer. It sank smoothly, as if penetrating soft butter. A gentle lift easily extracted it.

"Hmmm. Not so good," I mumbled through my mask. On the fourth try the piton gripped a bit more solidly. Deciding not to loosen it by testing, I turned to the final wall. Its steepness threw my weight out from the rock, and my pack became a downright hindrance. There was an unlimited selection of handholds, mostly portable. I shed my mittens. For a few seconds the rock felt comfortably reassuring but cold. Then not cold any more. My eyes tried to direct sensationless fingers. Flakes peeled out beneath my crampons. I leaned out from the rock to move upward, panting like a steam engine. Damn it, it'll go; I know it will, T, I thought. But my grip was gone. I hadn't thought to turn my oxygen up.

"No soap," I called down. "Can't make it now. Too pooped."

"Come on down. There may be a way to the right."

I descended, half rappeling from the piton, which held. I had spent the better part of an hour up there. A hundred feet out we looked back. Clearly we had been on the right route, for above that last little step the gully opened out. A hundred feet higher the Yellow Band met the grey of the summit limestone. It had to get easier.

"You'd better take it, Willi. I've wasted enough time already."

"Hell, if you couldn't make it, I'm not going to be able to do any better."

"Yes you will. It's really not that hard. I was just worn out from putting that piton in. Turn your regulator clear open, though."

Willi headed up around the corner, moving well. In ten minutes his rope was snapped through the high piton. Discarding a few unsavoury holds, he gripped the rotten edge with his unmittened hands. He leaned out for the final move. His pack pulled. Crampons scraped, loosing a shower of rock from beneath his feet. He was over. He leaned against the rock, fighting for breath.

"Man, that's work. But it looks better above."

Belayed, I followed, retrieved the first piton, moved up, and went to work on the second. It wouldn't come. "Guess it's better than I thought," I shouted. "I'm going to leave it." I turned my oxygen to four litres, leaned out from the wall and scrambled up. The extra oxygen helped, but it was surprising how breathless such a brief effort left me.

"Good lead," I panted. "That wasn't easy."

"Thanks. Let's roll."

Another rope-length and we stopped. After six hours of hiss Willi's first bottle was empty. There was still a long way to go, but at least he could travel ten pounds lighter without the extra cylinder. Our altimeter read 27,900. We called base on the walkie-talkie.

Willi: West Ridge to Base. West Ridge to Base. Over.

Base (Jim Whittaker, excitedly): This is Base here, Willi. How are you? How are things going? What's the word up there? Over.

Willi: Man, this is a real bearcat! We are nearing the top of the Yellow Band and it's mighty tough. It's too damned tough to try to go back. It would be too dangerous.

Base (Jim): I'm sure you're considering your exits. Why don't you leave yourself an opening? If it's not going to pan out, you can always start working your way down. I think there is always a way to come back.

Willi: Roger, Jim. We're counting on a further consultation in about 200 or 300 feet. It should ease up by then! Goddammit, if we can't start moving together we'll have to move back down. But it should be easier once the Yellow Band is passed. Over.

Base (Jim): Don't work yourself up into a bottleneck, Willi. How about rappeling? Is that possible, or don't you have any Reepschnur [a thin cord tied to a thicker rope for rappeling] or anything? Over.

Willi: There are no rappel points, Jim, absolutely no rappel points. There's nothing to secure a rope to. So it's up and over for us today . . .

While the import of his words settled upon those listening 10,000 feet below, Willi went right on:

Willi (continuing): . . . and we'll probably be getting in pretty late, maybe as late as seven or eight o'clock tonight.

As Willi talked, I looked at the mountain above. The slopes looked reasonable, as far as I could see, which wasn't very far. We sat at the base of a big, wide-open amphitheatre. It looked like summits all over the place. I looked down. Descent was totally unappetizing. The rotten rock, the softening snow, the absence of even tolerable piton cracks only added to our desire to go on. Too much labour, too many sleepless nights and too many dreams had been invested to bring us this far. We couldn't come back for another try next weekend. To go down now, even if we could have, would be descending to a future marked by one huge question: what might have been? It would not be a matter of living with our fellow man, but simply living with ourselves, with the knowledge that we had had more to give.

I listened, only mildly absorbed in Willi's conversation with Base, and looked past him at the convexity of rock cutting off our view of the gully we had ascended. Above – a snowfield, grey walls, then blue-black sky. We were committed. An invisible barrier sliced through the mountain beneath our feet, cutting us off from the world below. Though we could see through, all we saw was infinitely remote. The ethereal link provided by our radio only intensified our separation. My wife and children seemed suddenly close. Yet home, life itself, lay only over the top of Everest and down the other side. Suppose we fail? The thought brought no remorse, no fear. Once entertained, it hardly seemed even interesting. What now mattered most was right here: Willi and I, tied together on a rope, and the mountain, its summit not inaccessibly far above. The reason we had come was within our grasp. We belonged to the mountain and it to us. There was anxiety, to be sure, but it was all but lost in a feeling of calm, of pleasure at the joy of climbing. That we couldn't go down only made easier that which we really wanted to do. That we might not get there was scarcely conceivable.

Willi was still talking.

Willi: Any news of Barry and Lute? Over.

Jim: I haven't heard a word from them. Over.

Willi: How about Dingman?

Jim: No word from Dingman. We've heard nothing, nothing at all.

Willi: Well listen, if you do get hold of Dingman, tell him to put a light in the window because we're headed for the summit, Jim. We can't possibly get back to our camp now. Over.

I stuffed the radio back in Willi's pack. It was 1 p.m. From here we could both climb at the same time, moving across the last of the yellow slabs. Another 100 feet and the Yellow Band was below us. A steep tongue of snow flared wide, penetrating the grey strata that capped the mountain. The snow was hard, almost ice-hard in places. We had only to bend our ankles, firmly plant all twelve crampon points, and walk uphill. At last, we were moving, though it would have appeared painfully slow to a distant bystander.

As we climbed out of the couloir the pieces of the puzzle fell into place. That snow rib ahead on the left skyline should lead us to the summit snowfield, a patch of perpetual white clinging to the North Face at the base of Everest's final pyramid. By 3 p.m. we were on the snowfield. We had been climbing for eight hours and knew we needed to take time to refuel. At a shaly outcrop of rock we stopped for lunch. There was a decision to be made. We could either cut straight to the North-East Ridge and follow it west to the summit, or we could traverse the face and regain the West Ridge. From where we sat, the ridge looked easier. Besides, it was the route we'd intended in the first place.

We split a quart of lemonade that was slushy with ice. In spite of its down parka wrapping, the other bottle was already frozen solid, as were the kippered snacks. They were almost tasteless but we downed them more with dutiful thoughts of calories than with pleasure.

To save time we moved together, diagonalling upward across down-sloping slabs of rotten shale. There were no possible stances from which to belay each other. Then snow again, and Willi kicked steps, fastidiously picking a route between the outcropping rocks. Though still carting my full load of oxygen bottles, I was beginning to feel quite strong. With this excess of energy came impatience, and an unconscious anxiety over the high stakes for which we were playing and the lateness of the day. Why the hell is Willi going so damned slow? I thought. And a little later: he should cut over to the ridge now; it'll be a lot easier.

I shouted into the wind, "Hold up, Willi!" He pretended not to hear me as he started up the rock. It seemed terribly important to tell him to go to the right. I tugged on the rope. "Damn it, wait up, Willi!" Stopped by a taut rope and an unyielding Hornbein, he turned, and with some irritation anchored his axe while I hastened to join him. He was perched, through no choice of his own, in rather cramped, precarious quarters. I sheepishly apologized.

We were on rock now. One rope-length, crampons scraping, brought us to the crest of the West Ridge for the first time since we'd left Camp 4 West yesterday morning. The South Face fell 8,000 feet to the tiny tents of Advance Base. Lhotse, straight across the face, was below us now. And near at hand 150 feet higher, the South Summit of Everest shone in the afternoon sun. We were within 400 feet of the top! The wind whipped across the ridge from the north at nearly sixty miles an hour. Far below, peak shadows reached long across the cloud-filled valleys. Above, the ridge rose, a twisting, rocky spine.

We shed crampons and overboots to tackle this next rocky bit with the comforting grip of cleated rubber soles. Here I unloaded my first oxygen bottle though it was not quite empty. It had lasted ten hours, which obviously meant I was getting a lower flow than indicated by the regulator. Resisting Willi's suggestion to drop the cylinder off the South Face, I left it for some unknown posterity. When I resaddled ten pounds lighter, I felt I could float to the top.

The rock was firm, at least in comparison with our fare thus far. Climbing one at a time, we experienced the joy of delicate moves on tiny holds. The going was a wonderful pleasure, almost like a day in the Rockies. With the sheer drop to the cwm beneath us, we measured off another four rope-lengths. Solid rock gave way to crud, then snow. A thin, firm knife-edge of white pointed gently towards the sky.

Buffeted by the wind, we laced our crampons on, racing each other with rapidly numbing fingers. It took nearly twenty minutes. Then we were off again, squandering oxygen at three litres per minute, since time seemed the shorter commodity at the moment. We moved together, Willi in front. It seemed almost as if we were cheating, using oxygen; we could nearly run this final bit.

Ahead the North and South Ridges converged to a point. Surely the summit wasn't that near? It must be off behind. Willi stopped. What's he waiting for, I wondered as I moved to join him. With a feeling of disbelief I looked up. Forty feet ahead, tattered and whipped by the wind, was the flag Jim had left three weeks before. It was 6.15. The sun's rays sheered horizontally across the summit. We hugged each other as tears welled up, ran down across our oxygen masks, and turned to ice.

Everest 1971

The Death of Harsh Bahuguna

Murray Sayle

The 1971 international expedition was a baby of its idealistic times. Under the leadership of Norman Dyhrenfurth the expedition brought together climbers of ten nations in the belief that they could work harmoniously together in common purpose – even in the extreme conditions of Everest. Faced with an abundance of stellar climbers, Dyhrenfurth decided to occupy them by two simultaneous ascents of the mountain: via the West Ridge; and via the unclimbed South-West Face. Unfortunately, the expedition became morassed in personal and national rivalries. Yet the climbers did unite once: when an accident befell the Indian Harsh Bahuguna during a descent of the West Ridge in a blizzard. A scratch international team set out to rescue him. That they failed does not divert from the courage and altruism of their effort. Murray Sayle reported the expedition for the Sunday Times.

Since we set off on this expedition, I considered Harsh Bahuguna one of my closest friends among the climbers. We often walked together on the march in, and talked about all sorts of things: his wife and two small daughters, his obsession with Mount Everest and his career in the Indian Army.

Harsh – which in Sanskrit means "happiness" – came from an Indian tribal group, the Garhwali, who are famous as soldiers and hill climbers (they are first cousins of the Gurkhas of Nepal). His uncle, Major Nandu Jayal, died in 1958 while attempting another Himalayan giant, Cho Oyu.

Harsh himself came within 800 feet of the summit of Everest as a member of the successful Indian Army expedition of 1965. His own attempt was delayed to the last of the

Indian groups because of stomach trouble, and then a sudden break in the weather robbed him of his chance of the summit.

I was not alone in thinking that Harsh was a special friend – after his death, I found that at least two-thirds of the climbers were sure they were particularly close to him. But, if he had a special companion on the expedition, it was undoubtedly the Austrian Wolfgang Axt. They ate together, shared a tent on the march in and another at Base Camp, shared much of the dangerous work of forcing a passage up the icefall (where they were outstanding) and they spent the last five days of Harsh's life together in a tiny tent perched high on the West Ridge of Everest.

They made odd, but clearly close friends. Axt is 6 feet 3 inches, beautifully built, and his approach to people, to life itself, is in terms of physical strength and endurance. He is married to the former Austrian women's sixty-metre sprint champion; and no one has ever heard him discuss any other subjects but health diets, fitness, climbing mountains and related topics. He often told us how much he enjoyed climbing with Harsh.

The sequence of events which ended with Bahuguna's death and the subsequent dissensions began on the evening of 17 April, when a deputation called on Norman Dyhrenfurth, our Swiss-American joint leader, in his tent at the advance base camp in the Western Cwm (Camp II, 21,700 feet), and presented something like an ultimatum. The visitors were Carlo Mauri, the Italian mountaineer and adventurer (he was a member of the Ra voyage), Pierre Mazeaud, the member of the French National Assembly who hopes one day to be Minister for Youth and Sport and other members of the ridge team.

They said what everyone knew: that, largely because of the weather, the face route was looking hopeful and the ridge route, for which the deputation had opted, was lagging behind. Unless more Sherpa porters were switched to ferrying supplies to the ridge, they said, then the whole ridge group should turn their efforts to the classical, "easy" route – up the South Col.

Dyhrenfurth is a genial man who prefers discussion and

consensus to giving orders. He was severely hampered by a bad case of high-altitude laryngitis, which he was trying to treat by inhaling steam from a pan of melted snow; but he did his best to explain that both he and the British joint leader, Colonel Jimmy Roberts (directing the Sherpa lift of supplies up the icefall from Base Camp), were also disturbed about the supply situation. The icefall, much trickier than usual, was absorbing a lot of Sherpa labour, and a logjam of supplies was building up at Camp I, perched on an ice-cliff at the top of the fall. The answer, said Dyhrenfurth tactfully, was for the sahibs themselves to start carrying up some supplies.

The deputation had touched on a sore spot which, sooner or later, was bound to disturb an expedition like ours. No one enjoys the dull work of carrying supplies in support – climbing thousands of feet with a reel of rope, a couple of oxygen cylinders and a box of food, then dumping it and climbing down again. And at those altitudes, everyone seems to have a definite stock of energy, no more and no less, although the amount varies with individuals. Ambitious people who conserve their energies for the glamorous summit push are being no more than human.

Still, a story going around the expedition is that one eminent climber by mistake picked up the rucksack of another during a "support" climb and found he could easily lift it with his little finger. And, when our chapter of calamities began, there were only two oxygen bottles in the high camps on the face, only one on the ridge.

Not that all work on the two routes up Everest had ceased for lack of supplies. The same day as the deputation, Odd Eliassen of Norway and Michel Vaucher of Switzerland (Yvette's husband) completed a fixed-rope traverse across a steep ice-slope near the foot of the ridge, cutting out an unnecessary 300-foot descent before the final crossing of the glacier to advance base camp. And, far up the ridge, Bahuguna and Axt had spent four days together moving Camp III, the first on the ridge, 1,000 feet nearer the summit.

That night the All-India Radio forecast bad weather for the Everest area. As we supply some of the data for this forecast, we assumed that the Indian broadcast was telling us about the unsettled weather we already had. In fact, the forecast well understated what was coming.

Next morning, 18 April, Norman Dyhrenfurth, reasoning that one good example is worth any amount of ordering or exhortation, set off alone to walk down the Western Cwm from Camp II to. Camp I and collect a symbolic load of two cylinders of oxygen, and walk back.

I enter the story, very peripherally, at this point. About the same time, I set out from Base Camp to ascend the icefall and examine the supply situation in the Western Cwm for myself. We were three on a rope: our sirdar (boss) of the Sherpas, Sonam Girme, obligingly guiding two duffers, Dr Harka Gurung, the eminent Nepalese geographer, determined to do a bit of fieldwork on his subject, and my clumsy self.

It started to snow as we strapped on our crampons. By halfway up, at a piece of ice we call "The Dump", it was snowing hard, and by good luck I declined a suggestion that I should stay there overnight without food, fuel or a sleeping-bag.

We passed the final maze of ladders, ropes and log bridges in a freshening blizzard. The racing clouds descended until we could no longer see the tops of the ice-cliffs we were climbing; once, an avalanche of stones as big as barrels crashed out of the clouds 100 yards to our right. Snow smothered the trail a foot deep in an hour; towards the end, even our sirdar started to lose his way. I got one leg up to the hip in a crevasse; the other two pulled me out.

After a six-hour ascent we arrived, not a moment too soon, in the middle of a ring of red tents – Camp I (20,500 feet), set on a thousand-ton ice-block entirely surrounded by crevasses fifty feet deep. As it happened we were the last people through the icefall for more than a week. We found the two Americans, doctors David Isles and Dave Peterson, in charge of the camp, and they treated my frost-nipped toes. We were told that Norman Dyhrenfurth had just left for Camp II with his two symbolic bottles of oxygen.

We sat down in our madly flapping tents, powdery snow driving in through every crack, to wait out the blizzard. Only later did we learn something of the tragic events taking place a mile and a half up the cwm.

Dyhrenfurth's route took him close under the 5,000-foot face of Nuptse on his right, and already the mountain was beginning to growl with incipient avalanches as the blizzard plastered thick snow on the face. A small avalanche clipped his heels as he hurried towards advance base (Camp II), the snow obliterating the trail before his eyes (there are small but nasty crevasses all the way up the cwm). Then, away on his left, he heard a man shouting. The wind whipped the words away, but to Dyhrenfurth it sounded like a cry for help. He redoubled speed to Advance Base.

About the same time, Wolfgang Axt plodded exhausted and alone into Advance Base. His blond hair and beard were stiff with ice. The first person he met was Antony Thomas, a BBC director who is making a documentary on the climb. Axt's first words were, "Harsh is in difficulties up there."

A concerned knot quickly gathered – Odd Eliassen of Norway, Michel Vaucher of Switzerland, Carlo Mauri of Italy, Pierre Mazeaud of France, Don Whillans and Dr Peter Steele of Britain. While Axt related, as well as his tired condition permitted, what had happened, they began preparations for a rescue attempt. Through the swirling snow, they could occasionally hear the same muffled shouts Dyhrenfurth had heard.

Both men were very tired. Bahuguna especially, said Axt, so at about 3.30 pm when the weather began to deteriorate seriously, they had decided to come down to Advance Base from Camp III.

All had gone well with the descent, Axt leading, until they reached the horizontal fixed rope traverse. Neither of them had seen it before, as Vaucher and Eliassen had installed it only the previous day.

These rope traverses are common in the Alps, where Axt has done most of his climbing, but less so in the Himalayas, where Bahuguna had gained most of his experience. A rope, slung horizontally between a series of ice pitons, enables a climber to cross an ice-wall, going sideways. The climber clips a carabiner (a sort of snap link) over the rope; this is in turn fastened to a harness round his body. He then propels himself along by using his hands on the rope, and digging the front points of his crampons into the ice at his feet.

The tricky part is where the rope, which is not completely taut, passes a piton: the last bit of rope is uphill and the climber must unclip, pass the piton without support and clip on again.

Axt said that he had gone first along the rope traverse and round a corner where his companion was out of sight, then across an easier second section of the rope. At the end of the traverse he waited about twenty minutes; but then, feeling his feet beginning to freeze and the storm getting worse, he returned to Advance Base to get help.

As this was being told, Dr Steele called for a Sherpa volunteer to come with him and bring his resuscitation gear, and Ang Parba at once stepped forward, while Don Whillans collected as many ski sticks as he could lay hands on to mark a new path over the glacier moraine. The forlorn rescue effort set out through the blizzard at 5.15 pm, Michel Vaucher and Odd Eliassen in the lead, Whillans, Dr Steele, Ang Parba, Carlo Mauri and Pierre Mazeaud close behind.

Vaucher and Eliassen found the dying man still clipped to the traverse rope, at a point where he should have unclipped to pass a piton. He had lost a glove, his hands were frozen, his face was coated with ice and his protective clothing had been pulled up by his harness to expose his midsection to the driving storm.

Asked by Eliassen, "Are you okay?" he appeared to mumble an affirmative. The Swiss and the Norwegian were unable to move Bahuguna sideways, so they tried to lower him on a 130-foot rope which Eliassen had brought for the purpose. Meanwhile, at the foot of the ice-slope, Dr Steele, Mazeaud and the Sherpa were trying to find a level and sheltered spot for a resuscitation attempt. But the rope was thirty-five feet too short, as near as they could judge in the snow and darkness.

Whillans, who had been following the unsuccessful lowering operation, decided to try a last forlorn hope. Without an ice-axe or a protective rope, he clawed his way on the front points of his crampons across the steep ice-slope to where Bahuguna hung upside down by his harness from the end of the rescuers' rope. Whillans managed to right him. His face was blue; he was unconscious, with wide staring eyes. He was barely alive, and could not have lasted more than half an hour.

Whillans, clinging by his crampon points to the ice-cliff, had no way of getting the dying man up or down, and in a blizzard at night at 22,000 feet, had only one decision to make – although he said later it was probably the hardest of his life.

"Sorry, Harsh old son, you've had it," he muttered, in a north-countryman's gruff farewell, and scrambled back over the ice.

Next morning, the climbers struggled through the storm to a breakfast of sorts in the "Indian" tent – ironically, an Indian army bell tent very like the ones used on the Everest expeditions in the 1920s. Major Bahuguna had borrowed it for our expedition. Rations were short and everyone deeply depressed. Axt came in, refreshed from his sleep. "How is Harsh?" he asked cheerily. "*Ist tod*," someone said in German – "He is dead." Axt was thunderstruck, a pitiable spectacle. Grimfaced, Dyhrenfurth announced there would be an inquiry in the Indian tent, and directed Bill Kurban of the BBC to tape-record the brief proceedings.

Those concerned related what they knew in their own languages, except Odd Eliassen, who spoke English. Axt, normally bursting with self-reliance, had difficulty in enunciating his statement. Dyhrenfurth asked Axt only two questions, both in a hoarse whisper, difficult to hear against the raging storm.

"Why were you not roped together?"

"We had run out of rope in establishing the way to Camp III."

"Why did you not go back along the traverse to look for Harsh after you had waited twenty minutes for him?"

"I was getting cold, I thought I had better fetch help."

The blizzard raged a full week after that, and by the time it ended it was apparent to most of us that even the South Col route was no longer possible. If the supply lines can be re-established, if the weather holds, if morale can be restored then there is just a chance that something can be saved from the disasters we have faced.

The 1971 international expedition failed to place any climbers on the summit. The highest point achieved, by Don Whillans and Dougal Haston, was 27,400 feet/8,352 metres on the South-West Face.

Everest 1975

The Hard Way

Doug Scott and Dougal Haston

In 1975 a British expedition led by Chris Bonington tried its luck on the South-West Face, with its daunting rock band at 26,000 feet/7,925 metres. This was eventually penetrated by Tut Braithwaite and Nick Estcourt, leaving Doug Scott and Dougal Haston to make a summit bid on 23 September.

Dougal Haston

. . . Shortly after first light I moved out into blue and white dawn to continue the upward way, leaving Doug wrapped in all the down in the tent mouth, cameras and belays set up for action. There was a rock step lurking ahead that had seemed reasonably close in the setting afternoon sun of the previous day. Now in the clear first light, a truer perspective was established as I kept on thrusting into the deep-powdered fifty-degree slope, sliding sideways like a crab out of its element reaching for an object that didn't seem to come any closer. One hundred metres of this progress it was, before I could finally fix a piton and eye the rock step. It wasn't long, seven or eight metres, but looked difficult enough. Downward-sloping, steep slabs with a layer of powder. Interesting work. Grade 5 at this height. Much concentration and three more pitons saw a delicate rightwards exit and back, temporarily thankful, into deep snow to finish the rope length and finally give Doug the signal to move.

Doug Scott

I traversed across on his rope and up the difficult rocks to his stance. I led out another 400 ft over much easier ground, parallel with the top of the rock band. We gradually armed to the task and began to enjoy our position. After all the months of dreaming, here we were cutting across that upper snow field. Dougal led out the next reel of rope.

Dougal Haston

The conditions and climbing difficulty began to change again. Kicking through with crampons I found there was no ice beneath. Rock slabs only, which have never been renowned for their adherence to front points. A few tentative movements up, down, sideways proved it existed all around. It seemed the time for a tension traverse. But on what? The rock was shattered loose and worse – no cracks. After I had scraped away a large area a small movable flake appeared. It would have to do. Tapping in the beginnings of an angle, which seemed to be okay to pull on but not for a fall, I started tensioning across to an inviting-looking snow lump. Thoughts flashed through my mind of a similar traverse nine years before, near the top of the Eiger Direct. There it would have been all over with a slip, and suddenly, as I worked it out, things didn't look too good here, if you cared to think in those directions. Not only didn't I care to, I also didn't dare to think of full consequences, and chasing the dangerous thoughts away, I concentrated on tiptoeing progress. Slowly the limit of tension was reached and my feet were on some vaguely adhering snow. This will have to do for the present, were my thoughts as I let go the rope and looked around. A couple of probes with the axe brought nothing but a sense of commitment.

"No man is an island," it is said. I felt very close to a realization of the contrary of this, standing on that semi-secure snow step in the midst of a sea of insecurity. But there was no racing adrenalin, only the cold clinical thought of years of experience. About five metres away the snow appeared to deepen. It would have to be another tension traverse. Long periods of excavation found no cracks. Tugs on the rope and impatient shouting from Doug. Communication at altitude is bad in awkward situations. One has to take off the oxygen mask to shout. Then when one tries to do this, one's throat is so dry and painful that nothing comes out. Hoping that Doug would keep his cool, I carried on, looking for a piton placement. A reasonable-looking crack came to light and two pitons linked up meant the game could go on. This time I felt I could put more bearing weight on the anchor. Just as well. Twice the tension limit failed, and there was the skidding movement backwards on the scraping slabs. But a third try and a long reach saw me in deep good snow, sucking oxygen violently. The way ahead relented, looking reasonable. My voice gained enough momentum to shout to Doug, and soon he was on his way. Following is usually monotone – sliding along on jumars. This one was not so. I could almost see the gleam in Doug's eyes shining through his layers of glasses as he pulled out the first tension piton with his fingers.

"Nasty stuff, youth."

I had to agree as he passed on through.

Doug Scott

I continued across further, using up one of our two climbing ropes, before dropping down slightly to belay. We had probably come too high, for there was easier snow below the rocks that led right up towards the South Summit Couloir. However, avalanches were still cascading down the mountain, so we climbed up to the rocks in an effort to find good peg anchors for the fixed ropes. We didn't want to return the next day to find them hanging over the rock band. Dougal led a short section on easy snow, then all the rope was run out and we turned back for camp.

I sat in the snow to take photographs and watched the sun go down over Gaurishankar. What a place to be! I could look straight down and see Camp II 6,000 ft down. There were people moving about between tents, obviously preparing to camp for the night. Mounds of equipment were being covered with tarpaulins, one or two wandered out to the crevasse toilet, others stood about in small groups before diving into their tents for the night. A line of shadow crept up the face to Camp IV by the time I was back to our tent. I again sorted out loads and pushed in oxygen bottles for the night, while Dougal melted down snow for the evening meal.

We discovered over the radio that only Lhakpa Dorje had made the carry to Camp VI that day. He had managed to bring up vital supplies of oxygen, but unfortunately the food, ciné-camera and still film we needed had not arrived. Anyway they were not essential, so we could still make our bid for the summit next day. There was also no more rope in camp, but I think we were both secretly relieved about this. Chris had always insisted that whoever made the first summit bid should lay down as much fixed rope as possible so that if that first attempt failed the effort would not be wasted. This made good sense, but it did take a lot of effort up there and we all longed for the time when we could cut loose from the fixed ropes. It was a perfect evening with no wind at all as we sat looking out of the tent doorway sipping mugs of tea. Finally the sun was gone from our tent and lit up only the upper snows, golden turning red, before all the mountain was in shadow. We zipped up the tent door and built up quite a fug of warm air heating up water for corned beef hash.

Dougal Haston

Five hundred metres of committing ground was a good day's work on any point of the mountain. The fact that it was all above 27,000 feet made our performance level high and, more to the point, we hadn't exhausted ourselves in doing it. This was crucial because deterioration is rapid at such altitudes. Over tea we discussed what to take next day. I still reckoned deep down on the possibility of a bivouac. Doug seemed reluctant to admit to the straight fact, but didn't disagree when I mentioned packing a tent sac and stove. The packs weren't going to be light. Two oxygen cylinders each would be needed for the undoubtedly long day, plus three fifty-metre ropes, also various pitons and karabiners. Even if a bivouac was contemplated we couldn't pack a sleeping bag. This would have been pushing weight too much. The bivouac idea was only for an emergency and we would have hastened that emergency by slowing ourselves down through too much weight – so we tried to avoid the possibility by going as lightly as possible. The only extra I allowed myself was a pair of down socks, reckoning they could be invaluable for warming very cold or even frost-bitten feet and hands. There was no sense of drama that evening. Not even any unusual conversation. We radioed down and told those at Camp II what we were doing, ate the rest of our food and fell asleep.

Doug Scott

About one in the morning we awoke to a rising wind. It was buffeting the tent, shaking it about and pelting it with spin-drift, snow and ice chips. I lay there wondering what the morning would bring, for if the wind increased in violence we should surely not be able to move. At about 2:30 we began slowly to wind ourselves up for the climb. We put a brew on and heated up the remains of the corned beef hash for break-fast. The wind speed was decreasing slightly as we put on our frozen boots and zipped up our suits. Dougal chose his down-filled suit, whilst I took only my windproofs, hoping to move faster and easier without the restriction of tightly packed feathers around my legs. I had never got round to sorting out a down-filled suit that fitted me properly.

Because of the intense cold it was essential to put on cram-pons, harnesses, even the rucksack and oxygen system in the warmth of the tent. Just after 3:30 we emerged to get straight on to the ropes and away to the end. It was a blustery morning, difficult in the dark and miserable in the cold. It was one of those mornings when you keep going because he does and he, no doubt, because you do. By the time we had passed the end of the fixed ropes the sun popped up from behind the South Summit and we awoke to the new day. It was exhilarating to part company with our safety line, for that is after all what fixed ropes are. They facilitate troop movements, but at the same time they do detract from the adventure of the climb. Now at last we were committed and it felt good to be out on our own.

Dougal Haston

There's something surrealistic about being alone high on Everest at this hour. No end to the strange beauty of the experience. Alone, enclosed in a mask with the harsh rattle of your breathing echoing in your ears. Already far in the west behind Cho Oyu a few pale strands of the day and ahead and all around a deep midnight blue with the South Summit sharply, whitely, defined in my line of vision and the always predawn wind picking up stray runners of spindrift and swirling them gently, but not malignantly, around me. Movement was relaxed and easy. As I passed by yesterday's tension points only a brief flash of them came into memory. They were stored for future remembrances, but the today mind was geared for more to come. Not geared with any sense of nervousness or foreboding, just happily relaxed, waiting – anticipating. Signs of life on the rope behind indicated that Doug was following apace and I waited at yesterday's abandoned oxygen cylinders as he came up with the sun, almost haloed in silhouette, uncountable peaks as his background. But no saint this.

"All right, youth?" in a flat Nottingham accent.

"Yeah, yourself?"

A nod and the appearance of a camera for sunrise pictures answered this question, so I tied on the rope and started breaking new ground. The entrance to the couloir wasn't particularly good, but there again it was not outstandingly bad by Himalayan standards, merely knee-deep powder snow with the occasional make-you-think hard patch where there was no snow base on the rock. On the last part before entering the couloir proper there was a longish section of this where we just climbed together relying on each other's ability, rope trailing in between, there being no belays to speak of.

The rope length before the rock step changed into beautiful, hard front-pointing snow ice but the pleasure suddenly seemed to diminish. Leading, my progress started to get slower. By now the signs were well known. I knew it wasn't me. One just doesn't degenerate so quickly. Oxygen again. It seemed early for a cylinder to run out. Forcing it, I reached a stance beneath the rock step. Rucksack off. Check cylinder gauge first. Still plenty left. That's got to be bad. It must be the system. Doug comes up. We both start investigating. Over an hour we played with it. No avail. Strangely enough I felt quite calm and resigned about everything. I say strangely because if the system had proved irreparable then our summit chance would have been ruined. There was only a quiet cloud of disappointment creeping over our heads. Doug decided to try extreme unction. "Let's take it apart piece by piece, kid. There's nothing to lose." I merely nodded as he started prising apart the Jubilee clip which held the tube onto the mouthpiece. At last something positive – a lump of ice was securely blocked in the junction. Carving it out with a knife, we tentatively stuck the two points together again, then shut off the flow so we could register oxygen being used. A couple of hard sucks on the mask – that was it. I could breathe freely again.

Doug started out on the rock step, leaving me contemplating the escape we'd just had. I was still thinking very calmly about it, but could just about start to imagine what my feelings of disgust would have been like down below if we'd been turned back by mechanical failure. Self-failure you have to accept, bitter though it can be. Defeat by bad weather also, but to be turned back by failure of a humanly constructed system would have left a mental scar. But now it was upward thinking again. Idly, but carefully, I watched Doug. He was climbing well. Slowly, relaxed, putting in the odd piton for protection. Only his strange masked and hump-backed appearance gave any indication that he was climbing hard rock at 28,000 feet.

Doug Scott

At first I worked my way across from Dougal's stance easily in deep soft snow, but then it steepened and thinned out until it was all a veneer covering the yellow amorphous rock underneath. I went up quite steeply for thirty feet, hoping the front points of my crampons were dug well into the sandy rock underneath the snow. I managed to get in three pegs in a cluster, hoping that one of them might hold, should I fall off. However, the next thirty feet were less steep and the snow lay thicker, which was fortunate seeing as I had run out of oxygen.

I reached a stance about a hundred feet above Dougal, and with heaving lungs, I started to anchor off the rope. I pounded in the last of our rock pegs and yelled down to Dougal to come up. While he was jumaring up the rope I took photographs and changed over to my remaining full bottle of oxygen. I left the empty bottle tied on the pegs.

We were now into the South Summit Couloir and a way seemed clear to the top of the South-West Face. We led another rope length each and stopped for a chat about the route. Dougal's sporting instincts came to the fore – he fancied a direct gully straight up to the Hillary Step.[1] I wasn't keen on account of the soft snow, so he shrugged his shoulders and continued off towards the South Summit. I don't know whether the direct way would have been any less strenuous, but from now on the route to the South Summit became increasingly difficult.

Dougal Haston

The South-West Face wasn't going to relax its opposition one little bit. That became very evident as I ploughed into the first rope length above the rock step. I had met many bad types of snow conditions in eighteen years of climbing. Chris and I had once been shoulder-deep retreating from a winter attempt on a new line on the North Face of the Grandes Jorasses. The snow in the couloir wasn't that deep, but it seemed much worse to handle. In the Alps we had been retreating, but now we were trying to make progress. Progress? The word seemed almost laughable as I moved more and more slowly. A first step and in up to the waist. Attempts to move upward only resulted in a deeper sinking motion. Time for new techniques: steps up, sink in, then start clearing away the slope in front like some breaststroking snow plough and eventually you pack enough together to be able to move a little further and sink in only to your knees. Two work-loaded rope lengths like this brought us to the choice of going leftwards on the more direct

---

1 A vertical step of about eighty feet which is the final serious obstacle to the summit of Everest.

line I had suggested to Doug in an earlier moment of somewhat undisciplined thinking. By now my head was in control again and I scarcely gave it a glance, thinking that at the current rate of progress we'd be lucky to make even the South Summit.

It seemed that conditions would have to improve but they didn't. The slope steepened to sixty degrees and I swung rightwards, heading for a rock step in an attempt to get out of this treadmill of nature. No relief for us. The snow stayed the same, but not only was it steeper, we were now on open wind-blown slopes and there was a hard breakable crust. Classic wind slab avalanche conditions. In some kind of maniacal cold anger I ploughed on. There was no point in stopping for belays. There weren't any possibilities. I had a rhythm, so kept the evil stroking upwards with Doug tight on my heels. Two feet in a hole, I'd bang the slope to shatter the crust, push away the debris, move up, sink in. Thigh. Sweep away. Knees. Gain a metre. Then repeat the process. It was useful having Doug right behind, as sometimes, when it was particularly difficult to make progress, he was able to stick two hands in my back to stop me sliding backwards. Hours were flashing like minutes, but it was still upward gain.

Doug Scott

I took over the awful work just as it was beginning to ease off. I clambered over some rocks poking out of the snow and noticed that there was a cave between the rocks and the névé ice – a good bivvy for later perhaps. Just before the South Summit I rested while Dougal came up. I continued round the South Summit rock while Dougal got his breath. I was crawling on all fours with the wind blowing up spindrift snow all around. I collapsed into a belay position just below the frontier ridge and took in the rope as Dougal came up my tracks. After a few minutes' rest we both stood up and climbed onto the ridge, and there before us was Tibet.

After all those months spent in the Western Cwm over this and two other expeditions now at last we could look out of the Cwm to the world beyond – the rolling brown lands of Tibet in the north and north east, to Kangchenjunga and just below us

Makalu and Chomo Lonzo. Neither of us said much, we just stood there absorbed in the scene.

Dougal Haston

The wind was going round the South Summit like a mad maypole. The face was finished, successfully climbed but there was no calm to give much thought to rejoicing. It should have been a moment for elation but wasn't. Certainly we'd climbed the face but neither of us wanted to stop there. The summit was beckoning.

Often in the Alps it seems fine to complete one's route and not go to the summit, but in the Himalayas it's somewhat different. An expedition is not regarded as being totally successful unless the top is reached. Everything was known to us about the way ahead. This was the South-East Ridge, the original Hillary/Tenzing route of 1953. It was reckoned to be mainly snow, without too much technical difficulty. But snow on the ridge similar to the snow in the couloir would provide a greater obstacle to progress than any technical difficulties. There were dilemmas hanging around and question marks on all plans.

My head was considering sitting in the tent sac until sunset or later, then climbing the ridge when it would be, theoretically, frozen hard. Doug saw the logic of this thinking but obviously wasn't too happy about it. No other suggestions were forthcoming from his direction, however, so I got into the tent sac, got the stove going to give our thinking power a boost with some hot water. Doug began scooping a shallow snow cave in the side of the cornice, showing that he hadn't totally rejected the idea. The hot water passing over our raw, damaged throat linings brought our slide into lethargic pessimism to a sharp halt.

Swinging his pack onto his back Doug croaked, "Look after the rope. I'm going to at least try a rope length to sample conditions. If it's too bad we'll bivouac. If not we carry on as far as possible."

I couldn't find any fault with this reasoning, so grabbed the rope as he disappeared back into Nepal. The way it was going quickly through my hands augured well. Reaching the end Doug gave a "come on" signal. Following quickly, I realized that there were now summit possibilities in the wind. Conditions were by no means excellent, but relative to those in the couloir they merited the title reasonable. There was no need to say anything as I reached Doug. He just stepped aside, changed the rope around and I continued. Savage, wonderful country. On the left the South-West Face dropped away steeply, to the right wild curving cornices pointed the way to Tibet. Much care was needed, but there was a certain elation in our movements. The Hillary Step appeared, unlike any photograph we had seen. No rock step this year, just a break in the continuity of the snow ridge. Seventy degrees of steepness and eighty feet of length. It was my turn to explore again. Conditions reverted to bad, but by now I'd become so inured to the technique that even the extra ten degrees didn't present too much problem.

Doug Scott

As I belayed Dougal up the Hillary Step it gradually dawned upon me that we were going to reach the summit of Big E. I took another photograph of Dougal and wound on the film to find that it was finished. I didn't think I had any more film in my rucksack, for I had left film and spare gloves with the bivvy sheet and stove at the South Summit. I took off my oxygen mask and rucksack and put them on the ridge in front of me. I was seated astride it, one leg in Nepal, the other in Tibet. I hoped Dougal's steps would hold, for I could think of no other place to put his rope than between my teeth as I rummaged around in my sack. I found a cassette of colour film, that had somehow got left behind several days before. The cold was intense and the brittle film kept breaking off. The wind was strong and blew the snow Dougal was sending down the Nepalese side right back into the air and over into Tibet. I fitted the film into the camera and followed him up. This was the place where Ed Hillary had chimneyed his way up the crevasse between the rock and the ice. Now with all the monsoon snow on the mountain it was well banked up, but with snow the consistency of sugar it looked decidedly difficult.

A wide whaleback ridge ran up the last 300 yards. It was just a matter of trail-breaking. Sometimes the crust would hold for a few steps and then suddenly we would be stumbling around as it broke through to our knees. All the way along we were fully aware of the enormous monsoon cornices, overhanging the 10,000-foot East Face of Everest. We therefore kept well to the left.

It was while trail-breaking on this last section that I noticed my mind seemed to be operating in two parts, one external to my head. It warned me somewhere over my left shoulder about not going too far right in the area of the cornice, and it would urge me to keep well to the left. Whenever I stumbled through the crust it suggested that I slow down and pick my way through more carefully. In general it seemed to give me confidence and seemed such a natural phenomenon that I hardly gave it a second thought at the time. Dougal took over the trail-breaking and headed up the final slope to the top – and a red flag flying there. The snow improved and he slackened his pace to let me come alongside. We then walked up side by side the last few paces to the top, arriving there together.

Afterwards Haston and Scott survived the highest bivouac yet, at 28,750 feet/8,763 metres. On 26 September Peter Boardman and Pertemba also reached the top of Everest. During their descent they encountered Mick Burke at the South Summit, who was making a solo effort (see "The Skies Were Already Darkening" by Peter Boardman on the following pages).

The Skies Were Already Darkening

Peter Boardman

Descending from the top of the world after his successful attempt with Pertemba, British climber Peter Boardman was astounded to meet Mick Burke, the British expedition's cameraman, on his way up in a solo attempt. The three agreed to regroup at the South Summit. For Boardman and Pertemba it proved a fruitless wait.

All the winds of Asia seemed to be trying to blow us from the ridge. A decision was needed. It was four in the afternoon and the skies were already darkening around the South Summit of Everest. I threw my iced and useless snow-goggles away into the whiteness and tried, clumsily mitted, to clear the ice from my eyelashes. I bowed my head into the spindrift and tried to peer along the ridge. Mick should have met us at least three-quarters of an hour before, unless something had happened to him. We had been waiting for nearly one and a half hours. There was no sign of Doug and Dougal's bivouac site. The sky and cornices and whirling snow merged together, visibility was reduced to ten feet and all tracks were obliterated. Pertemba and I huddled next to the rock of the South Summit where Mick had asked us to wait for him. Pertemba said he could not feel his toes or fingers and mine too were nailed with cold. I thought of Mick wearing his glasses and blinded by spindrift, negotiating the fixed rope on the Hillary Step, the fragile one-foot windslab on the Nepal side and the cornices on the Tibetan side of the ridge. I thought of our own predicament, with the 800 feet of the South Summit Gully – guarded by a sixty-foot rock step halfway – to descend, and then half of the 2,000-foot great traverse above the rock band to cross before reaching the end of the fixed ropes that extended across from Camp VI. It had taken Doug and Dougal three hours in the dawn sunshine after their bivouac to reach Camp VI – but we now had only an hour of light left. At 28,700 feet the boundary between a controlled and an uncontrolled situation is narrow and we had crossed that boundary within minutes – a strong wind and sun shining through clouds had turned into a violent blizzard of driving snow, the early afternoon had drifted into approaching night and our success was turning into tragedy.

A mountaineer when he is climbing is doing, seeing and feeling and yet on his return home from the hill he often baulks at recollection in public of these experiences because he treasures the privacy and intensity of his memories. And yet, as Hornbein remarked after being asked to write about his ascent of the West Ridge:

> I soon learned, Everest was not a private affair. It belonged to many men.

The stories of man's adventures on Everest have almost reached the stature of myth in the popular imaginations of the twentieth century. The full record of our expedition will eventually appear to add to these stories. I do not aspire here to document the planning and events of the expedition, nor to presume to evaluate its achievements, nor to predict the future of climbing on Everest. I fear that at such a cold touch the pains and charms that are my memories of Everest will fly.

My memories are of a keen apprehension that turned into a living nightmare. Even on the leech-infested walk-in we dreamt about the climb to come – one morning Tut and Doug confessed, with gallows humour, "I keep getting stranded above the rock band" and, "Dougal got severe frostbite last night". While Nick and Tut were tackling the Rock Band I wrote:

> Everyone is very optimistic that we'll crack it soon, but it's still early days. We've been lucky with the weather and there could easily be a storm at any time to curtail or even set back all movement.

"Think upwards" always seems to be a good dictum for
success in climbing and the Everest summit was in my mind
night and day all the time I was moving up the face into
position for the second attempt. Aside from the physical effort
and practical judgement and worry there is a dreamlike quality
in the climbing on Everest. At Camp V I wrote:

> The face is a strange unreal world. All dressed up in one-
> piece oversuits and six layers on the feet, oxygen mask and
> goggles one seems distanced from where one is and what
> one is doing, like a sort of moonwalk.

This half-glimpsed quality was preserved far back in my mind.
As a child I used to daydream over a painting in a big picture
book, *Adventure of the World*, which depicted the tiny bold
figures of Hillary and Tenzing on the top of a summit that
thrust out of a sea of clouds.

As Pertemba and I crossed the traverse above the rock band
in the early dawn of our summit day it felt as if we were on that
highest peak above the clouds, as if the sight of the endless
cloud sea was joining hands with the dreamland of the past.
The weather was changing and the cloud layer was up to
27,000 feet, covering Nuptse and everything beyond it. Only
the top of Lhotse peeped out below us, whereas above us the
sun sparkled through the snow smoking over the summit ridge.
For three days I had been jumaring up fixed ropes, counting
steps and trying to keep in front of some Sherpas coming up
to Camp IV, gasping up to Camp V, and then following Nick
and Tut's intricate route through the rock band. But now I felt
free and untrammelled, and exhilarated as if I had just become
committed on the start of a climb in the Alps. Pertemba and I
moved, unroped, steadily away from the end of the fixed line
and kicked away the spindrift from the tracks that Doug and
Dougal had made two days before. Everest, the myth, with its
magic and history, seemed to make me feel strong, thinking
upwards. Invincible together.

The snow was only a few feet deep on top of the rocks and
the route wavered around spurs and over rock steps. The
South Summit Gully was steep but there was a fixed line

hanging over the rock step halfway up it. As I reached the South Summit, Pertemba dropped behind and I waited for him. His oxygen mask had stopped working. One and a half hours and several cold fingers later we had slit open the tube and cleared the two inches of ice that were blocking the airway, and patched the mask back into working order. We changed to fresh oxygen cylinders and moved, roped now, along the ridge towards the summit of·Everest. Its red ribbons were fading in the strong light and fluttering prayers from the other side of the mountain. The Chinese tripod was catching drifting snow and leaning defiantly in the wind. Its presence was strangely reassuring. Pertemba attached a Nepalese flag to it and I hung a Deadman snow anchor from it. We ate some chocolate and mint cake and I burbled into a tape-recorder. We started down.

We were amazed to see him through the mist. Mick was sitting on the snow only a few hundred yards down an easy angled snow-slope from the summit. He congratulated us and said he wanted to film us on a bump on the ridge and pretend it was the summit, but I told him about the Chinese maypole. Then he asked us to go back to the summit with him. I agreed reluctantly and he, sensing my reluctance, changed his mind and said he'd go up and film it and then come straight down after us. He borrowed Pertemba's camera to take some stills on the top and we walked back fifty feet and then walked past him while he filmed us. I took a couple of pictures of him. He had the Blue Peter flag and an auto-load camera with him. He asked us to wait for him by the big rock on the South Summit where Pertemba and I had dumped our first oxygen cylinders and some rope and film on the way up. I told him that Pertemba was wanting to move roped with me – so he should catch us up fairly quickly. I said, "See you soon" and we moved back down the ridge to the South Summit. Shortly after we had left him the weather began to deteriorate.

A decision was needed. I pointed at my watch and said "We'll wait ten more minutes." Pertemba agreed. That helped us – it gave some responsibility to the watch. I fumbled in my sack and pulled out our stove to leave behind. The time was up. At first we went the wrong way – too far towards the South Col. About 150 feet down we girdled back until we found what we thought was the South Summit Gully. There was a momentary lessening in the blizzard, and I looked up to see the rock of the South Summit. There was still no sign of Mick and it was now about half past four. The decision had been made and now we had to fight for our own lives and think downwards.

Pertemba is not a technical climber, not used to moving away from fixed ropes or in bad conditions. At first he was slow. For three pitches I kicked down furiously, placed a Deadman and virtually pulled him down in the sliding, blowing powder snow. But Pertemba was strong and adaptable – he began to move faster and soon we were able to move together. Were we in the gully? I felt panic surge inside. Then I saw twin rocks in the snow that I recognized from the morning. We descended diagonally from there and in the dusk saw Dougal's oxygen cylinder that marked the top of the fixed rope over the rock step.

We abseiled down to the end of the rope and tied a spare rope we had to the end and descended the other 150 feet. From there we descended down and across for 1,000 feet towards the end of the fixed ropes. During our traverse we were covered by two powder snow avalanches from the summit slopes. Fortunately our oxygen cylinders were still functioning and we could breathe. It was a miracle that we found the end of the fixed ropes in the dark, marked by two oxygen cylinders sticking out of the snow. On the fixed rope Pertemba slowed down again and I pulled him mercilessly until he shouted that one of his crampons had fallen off. The rope between us snagged and in flicking it free I tumbled over a fifteen-foot rock step to be held on the fixed rope. At one point a section of the fixed rope had been swept away. At half past seven we stumbled into the "summit boxes" at Camp VI. Martin was there and I burst into tears.

The storm pinned the three of us to Camp VI at 27,600 feet for thirty-six hours. Pertemba and I shared one of the two boxes and were completely dependent on Martin. Pertemba was snow-blinded and I was worried about my feet. Martin had a good supply of gas and he kept us supplied with tea and oxygen cylinders. Our box was becoming buried in snow every four hours and Martin kept on dragging himself out to clear [the boxes], damaging his fingers from frostbite. It was miserable inside the box, the snow was pressing the walls and it felt like that medieval dungeon cell known as "the little ease" – maddeningly too short to stretch out, too low to sit up. Pertemba lay back, his eyes closed and lips moving in silent incantation. I felt isolated from my friends lower down the mountain by a decision and an experience I could not share.

During the second night the wind and snow ceased but their noise was replaced by the roar of avalanches sweeping past either side of the snowy crest on which we were perched and plunging over the edge of the rock band. Dawn came – clear and cold, sad and silvery. We looked across the traverse and up the gully to the South Summit but there was no sign of Mick. We turned and began the long repetitive ritual of clipping and unclipping the piton brake and safety loop and abseiling, rope-length after rope-length, 6,000 feet down to the Western Cwm.

As we emerged from the foot of the gully through the rock band we could see tiny figures outside the three boxes of Camp V, 1,000 feet below us. It took a long time to reach them, for many of the anchors on the fixed ropes had been swept away. Ronnie, Nick, Tut and Ang Phurba were waiting for us and helped us down into the living air and warmth of the Western Cwm and the reassuring faces of Camp II.

Everest 1978

Only the Air That We Breathe

Peter Habeler

Oxygen was first used in Himalayan climbing as early as 1907, and many climbers considered that the "thin air" of Everest would only be overcome by its use. Some pioneers, however, considered the use of oxygen unsporting, even unethical. In the event, the 1922 expedition was equipped with the gas, and thereafter it was regarded as imperative by all Everest-bound mountaineers for half a century. In the 1970s, a new breed of purist climber decided to forgo oxygen at high altitude on "sport-ethical" grounds, prime among them Reinhold Messner from the Italian Tyrol and Peter Habeler from the Austrian Tyrol. After an oxygenless ascent of Gasherbrun I (8,068 metres) in 1975 the pair decided to decided to try Everest without bottled air. Their summit push came on 28 May.

After four hours, towards half past nine, we stood in front of the tents of Camp V at an altitude of 8,500 metres. Mallory and Irvine, too, had managed to get this far. From now on we would be entering completely new territory. We were left totally to our own resources. If anything happened to us now, no rescue team would be able to come up to help us, no helicopter – nothing. The smallest accident would mean certain death.

Reinhold and I had often spoken together about the fact that, in this last phase, it would be impossible to help each other should anything untoward occur. Although we were incredibly close to each other, and formed an indivisible unit, we were agreed on one thing. If one of us should get into difficulty, the other would have to try at all costs to find safety for himself alone. The small amount of strength that remained to each of us was hardly enough for one; any attempt to rescue, or even to recover the other, would be doomed to failure.

I sat in front of the small tent, which was half-covered by snow, while inside Reinhold tried desperately to get a cooker going to brew up tea. I snuggled up to the side of the tent in order to rest in the lee side, and stared out into the fog. Occasionally the wall of fog would lift for a moment, and I could see deep below me the Valley of Silence. I could see Lhotse, and again and again I looked up to the South Summit where an enormous trail of snow signified that up there a far more violent storm was raging than down here in Camp V. The weather would undoubtedly worsen. The fine weather period was over.

Perhaps our attempt on the summit was finally over too, our Everest expedition wrecked once and for all. Of one thing I was convinced: I would never come up here a second time. Already the desire to turn back was almost overpowering. To bivouac here in Camp V, and perhaps to wait for the weather to improve, was also completely out of the question. We would probably never have got out of the tent at all again, and in no event would we have had the physical or mental strength to climb any further. Our energy would have lasted at the most for the descent and no more. Yet climbing on was, under these circumstances, also a "way of no return".

In 1956, two Japanese had mastered the route from the South Col to the summit in one go. This had taken them a whole day, and having therefore reached the main summit late in the afternoon, they were forced to bivouac on the way back. Consequently, in spite of carrying oxygen, they had suffered terrible injuries through frostbite. But neither Reinhold nor I had time to think of these dangers. The will to push on blotted out everything else, even the wish to turn back or at least to sleep. We wanted in any case to go on up, even if we could only reach the South Summit, which is 8,760 metres high. After all, to conquer even the South Summit without oxygen would have been a tremendous success. It would have proved that one day it would be possible to reach the main summit by human strength alone.

It took exactly half an hour for Reinhold to prepare the tea.

My deliberations were also shared by him; we exchanged them wordlessly. We were completely united in our determination to continue the assault on the summit.

Once again we set off. The tracks of our predecessors, which could still be seen in the snow, served as an excellent orientation guide. The clouds were moving over from the south-west, from the bad-weather corner of the Himalayas. We had to push ourselves even more because that promised bad news. We found ourselves in the lower area of the jet stream, those raging winds of speeds up to 200 kilometres per hour, upon which the enormous passenger planes are carried from continent to continent. We had traversed the troposphere and were approaching the frontier of the stratosphere. Here cosmic radiation was already noticeable and the intensity of the ultra-violet radiation had multiplied. Only a few minutes without our snow-goggles sufficed, even in the fog, to diminish our powers of vision. In a very short space of time direct insolation would lead to snow-blindness and painful conjunctivitis.

Reinhold and I photographed and filmed as often as we had the opportunity. To do this, we had to take off our snow-goggles and we also had to remove our overgloves. Each time it became more difficult for us to put the gloves back on again. But losing them would have led to the very rapid paralysis and frostbite of our hands.

Since it was no longer possible to go on in this deep snow, we had made a detour towards the South-East Ridge. Here the wall dropped 2,000 metres down to the south-west. One false step and we would have plunged down into the Valley of Silence. The exposed and airy climb on brittle rock without any rope demanded extreme concentration. Reinhold was right behind me. I took the lead to the South Summit. Completely without warning, we suddenly found we had passed through the clouds and now stood on the last stage before our goal.

At this point the storm attacked us with all its might. However, in spite of the storm and the fatigue, my fear of the mountain had dissipated with the clouds. I was quite sure of myself. Over there lay the main summit, almost near enough to touch, and at this precise moment I was sure we were going to do it. Reinhold, too, told me later: "This was the moment in which I was convinced of the success of our adventure."

A sort of joyful intoxication overcame the two of us. We looked at each other – and shrank back. From Reinhold's appearance I could only conclude that my own was very similar. His face was contorted in a grimace, his mouth wide open while he gasped panting for air. Icicles hung in his beard. His face was almost without human traits. Our physical reserves were exhausted. We were so utterly spent that we scarcely had the strength to go ten paces in one go. Again and again we had to stop, but nothing in the world could have held us back now.

We had roped ourselves together because the Summit Ridge, as Hillary has already described it, was densely covered in cornices. It is true, however, that in an emergency a rope would not have helped us.

We crawled forwards at a snail's pace, trusting to instinct alone. The sun glistened on the snow, and the sky above the summit was of such an intense blue that it seemed almost black. We were very close to the sky, and it was with our own strength alone that we had arrived up here at the seat of the gods. Reinhold signified to me with a movement of his hand that he wanted to go on ahead. He wanted to film me climbing up over the ridge, with the bubbling sea of clouds below.

To do this he had to take off his snow-goggles in order to focus the camera better. It occurred to me that his eyes looked inflamed, but I thought nothing more of it, no more than he did. Our altitude was now 8,700 metres, and we had obviously reached a point at which normal brain functions had broken down, or at least were severely limited. Our attentiveness and concentration declined; our instinct no longer reacted as reliably as before; the capacity for clear logical thinking had also apparently been lost. I only thought in sensations and loose associations, and slowly I was overcome by the feeling that this threatening fearful mountain could be a friend.

Today I am certain that it is in these positive and friendly sensations that the real danger on Everest lies. When one approaches the summit, one no longer perceives the hostile, the absolutely deadly atmosphere. I have probably never been so close to death as I was during that last hour before reaching the summit. The urgent compulsion to descend again, to give in to fatigue, which had overcome me already in Camp V, had disappeared. I was now feeling the complete opposite. I had been seized by a sense of euphoria. I felt somehow light and relaxed, and believed that nothing could happen to me. At this altitude the boundaries between life and death are fluid. I wandered along this narrow ridge and perhaps for a few seconds I had gone beyond the frontier that divides life from death. By a piece of good fortune I was allowed to return. I would not risk it a second time, my reason forbids me to gamble with my life in such a way again.

In spite of all my euphoria, I was physically completely finished. I was no longer walking of my own free will, but mechanically, like an automaton. I seemed to step outside myself, and had the illusion that another person was walking in my place. This other person arrived at the Hillary Step, that perilous 25-metre-high ridge gradient, and then climbed and pulled himself up in the footsteps of his predecessors. He had one foot in Tibet and the other in Nepal. On the left side there was a 2,000-metre descent to Nepal; on the right the wall dropped 4,000 metres down towards China. We were alone, this other person and myself. Although he was connected to me by the short piece of rope, Reinhold no longer existed.

This feeling of being outside myself was interrupted for only a few moments. Cramp in my right hand bent my fingers together, and tore me violently back to reality. I was attacked by a suffocating fear of death. "Now I've had it." This thought went through my head, "Now the lack of oxygen is beginning its deadly work." I massaged my right forearm and bent my fingers back, and then the cramp eased.

From then on I prayed, "Lord God, let me go up right to the top. Give me the power to remain alive, don't let me die up here." I crawled on my elbows and knees and prayed more fervently than I have ever done in my life before. It was like a dialogue with a higher being. Again I saw myself crawling up, below me, beside me, higher and higher. I was being pushed up to the heights, and then suddenly I was up again on my own two feet: I was standing on the summit. It was 1.15 on the afternoon of 8 May 1978.

And then suddenly Reinhold was with me too, still carrying his camera and the three-legged Chinese surveying instrument. We had arrived. We embraced each other. We sobbed and stammered and could not keep calm. The tears poured from under my goggles into my beard, frozen on my cheeks. We embraced each other again and again. We pressed each other close. We stepped back at arm's length and again fell round each other's necks, laughing and crying at the same time. We were redeemed and liberated, freed at last from the inhuman compulsion to climb on.

After the crying and the sense of redemption, came the emptiness and sadness, the disappointment. Something had been taken from me; something that had been very important to me. Something which had suffused my whole being had evaporated, and I now felt exhausted and hollow. There was no feeling of triumph or victory. I saw the surrounding summits, Lhotse, Cho Oyu. The view towards Tibet was obscured by clouds. I knew that I was standing now on the highest point in the whole world. But, somehow, it was all a matter of indifference to me. I just wanted to get home now, back to that world from which I had come, and as fast as possible.

Habeler made the descent to the South Col in a record one hour.

Everest 1979

"Tone, We Are At The Top"

Nejc Zaplotnik

In 1979 the Yugoslavians attempted the "West Ridge direct" route to the top of Everest. Two summit bids were forestalled, then Nejc Zaplotnik and the Stremfelj brothers, Andrej and Marko, reached Camp V at 26,640 feet on 12 May for their attempt to reach the top of the world.

The wind tugged at the strings of the tent. The anticipation of a great day filled our hearts. I had lived for this moment and now I was ready. It was clear to me that it was going to be a matter of life and death. Long ago I had decided that Everest was worth my toes. Fingers and hands, I had thought, should be spared. But now I was suddenly convinced that no sacrifice could be big enough.

The oxygen had thinned my blood, making it spread pleasant warmth throughout my body, and I fell asleep again. It was two o'clock and Andrej was busy clattering with the dishes. I knew it was my turn to do the cooking, but I was reluctant to abandon the cosiness of my sleeping-bag.

We forced ourselves to drink, but not with much success. We tied our laces and prepared two oxygen cylinders each. The flags for the summit had long been put in the rucksack, along with the best wishes – our own and those of friends in lower camps. Two pairs of gloves were put on and we were ready. It was five o'clock. We crawled out of the tent and shouldered our gear. The highest summits all around were just becoming tinged with the early sunshine. Apart from Cho Oyu they were all below us, far below!

The lower part of the route was somewhat familiar to us, as

it had been described well by our companions. Easy rock interspersed with snow extends towards a gully coming down from
the ridge. I was fairly high up when Marko called to me saying
that his oxygen valve had gone. He had already replaced it
once and did not have another spare. Oh, damn it! I felt tears
of wrath rise to my eyes. Marko could do nothing more than
wave his hand in farewell. Angrily I dashed with my ice-axe
against the rock. I would have damned well like to have
smashed them all – axe and rock and valve and everything else.
But no! My task was to climb. I turned my thoughts to the
rocks ahead. Exposed traverses brought us into the gully. We
were making quick progress, with Andrej following close after
me. But then suddenly I heard an ominous "pshshshshsh . . ."
Andrej's valve had gone too. "Oh, cursed be all the devils and
every cloven-footed creature in the world!" But I knew that the
situation was critical and I forced myself to calm down. I gave
him my spare valve. And then crack and p-shshshsh again! I
unscrewed the bad valve and hurled it down the precipice. I
would have liked to have hurled the oxygen bottles after it, too.
And what now?

"Andrej, take my valves and bottles. You will lead the ascent,
as you will have the oxygen, and I will follow you without."

But Andrej did not agree. He knew very well that climbing
without oxygen in that awful cold and severe terrain, at a
temperature of minus 40 °C and a wind of 120 kilometres per
hour would cripple me for life. I fastened Andrej's rotten valve
back to his bottle and, by spitting on it, tried to find out how
badly damaged it was. To my great joy the hissing lessened.
The frozen saliva had stopped the little hole in the security
valve. I fell to licking that damned cold metal like one obsessed
until the hissing was stopped completely. A patch of the skin of
my tongue got torn off and remained glued to it, too, but it
held right up to the top!

On we went. The gully is blocked by a vertical smooth chimney. Over the slabs on the left was dangling a white rope, which
had been fastened there by Marjon and Viki. My jumar bit into
the frozen rope, my crampons scratched on the smooth granite slabs. I had set the valve at four litres per minute, and yet I
gasped for breath while working up the rope with my heavy

gear on my back. Andrej was standing below shooting pictures. All right, we would need documents. How often had we said that truly nice things were only to come later, when back at home we would be sitting at table and looking at the Himalayas on the screen. No cold any more, just an inexhaustible teapot on the table. No ferocious wind, but just the familiar swirling of the cigarette smoke rising towards the ceiling. A room full of friends, all married to the mountains for good like ourselves, and the screen full of the Himalayas, sweet and kind and homely. There would be slippers on our feet instead of crampons, the wine would loosen our tongues and make the hearts swell with memories and alluring new plans.

I often slipped on the rope but was careful not to be left hanging. The harness would then have choked me. Even so I could hardly breathe. When after hard labour I had reached the top of the rope I waited for Andrej. I took off my set and switched off the oxygen.

The gully is split into two branches. The previous day Romi and Dule had chosen the one to the right and missed the route. They had landed on a gendarme, from where further progress along the ridge seemed extremely problematic, so they had come back to try the left couloir. But they had lost too much time. At 3 p.m. they had only reached the ridge, and retreat was inevitable. By following their route we came up to a steep rock step just below the ridge. The edge of the step was smooth and verglassed, offering no holds at all. Should we take the rope and belay? No! Speed was the only security. Fortunately we were both used to soloing, as we had done no end of solo climbs in the Alps and trusted each other completely.

I rammed the spike of the axe into a smooth granite crack, pulled myself over the edge and landed on the ridge, face to face with a wind that almost swept me away into Tibet. Andrej joined me, but it was only with our four limbs dug deep in the snow that we could resist the onslaught of the huge current of air dashing against us. The rocks around us droned like a big organ. Far below we could see the big river of ice winding its way through the Western Cwm and over the debris of the icefall. Nuptse and its slanting ridge did not obstruct the view to the southern horizon any more. I gazed to the east where Makalu should have been but Lhotse still blocked the view.

The wind caused our goggles to become constantly coated with ice. We cleaned them every minute, but it helped little. Whenever we dived back into shadow, we simply took them off, even at the risk of incurring snow-blindness. We hoped it wouldn't affect us before we reached a camp. Afterwards we would cope with it somehow. The ridge was sharp and snowy, interspersed with rock steps, which allowed no breather. Then we reached the Yellow Band. Actually, we found ourselves in the middle of it. Layers of yellow granite slope down from under the top of Everest and enliven the dark flanks of Changtse, finally to be drowned in dry, brown Tibet.

Now I forget so many things. All less remarkable details on our way to the summit have escaped my memory. When after a few days at Base Camp Andrej and I tried to recall the exact route and make a diagram, we found that it was beyond us to explain how we had passed from the Yellow Band on to the Grey Step. All we could remember was that the passage was not so hard as the band below and the step above, that there were snowfields interspersed with smooth windblown slabs and now and then a steep wall. We did remember, however, that the Grey Step had been looming large above us, virtually overhanging, and that the wind did its best to blow us off the ridge. And that it was all like a nightmare. We had been so bent on reaching the summit that anything less important was drowned in oblivion for good.

We reached the foot of the Grey Step. A hundred metres of repulsive, vertical and overhanging rock. I was about to go straight ahead, just a few metres to the left of the ridge, where a system of cracks offered a possibility. I was taking off my gloves as part of the preparation for taking off my crampons when Andrej turned right, round an edge, on to the South Face. The initial pitch on that side is harder than these cracks, but the wall eases off sooner. We took the South Face – one single drop of 2,500 metres down into the Western Cwm. A tiny brittle ledge took us into the magnificent exposure above the precipice. Entranced we climbed up, climbed as we do at home, in the Alps! I dug out a little stance in the snow and drove a weak peg into the brittle rock. I finally took off my gloves and roped myself up, with Andrej belaying, while I tackled an overhanging crack. The cold of the rock bit immediately and ruthlessly into my bare fingers. After a few more moves and touching more rock they became frozen hard and totally numb. I had set the oxygen valve to the maximum supply, but there was nothing that could help to ward off the cold. The fifteen-kilogram burden on my back threatened to pull me down. There was no time to test the holds, or the frozen fingers would have let go. Suddenly, with a broken-off piece of rock in my hands, I landed in the snow below, held by the rope thanks to Andrej's presence of mind. Knee-deep in the snow I waved my hands to make blood come back to my fingers. The blood obeyed, but, oh, how it hurt! I would have howled with pain if I had had any breath left. Andrej was silent. His faith in me was not shaken. So I tackled the overhang again. A bit higher a foothold broke off. I remained hanging on my fingers for a while, but having lost all support for my feet I slipped again. Bloody hell! What is the time, Andrej? A quarter to twelve. We are damned late! Shouldn't we go back? Andrej asked. No answer. We would talk it over on top of the Grey Step.

I tackled the overhang now slightly more to the left. It was even more arduous there, the rocks hanging even farther out beyond the vertical, but the strain would be limited to a shorter section. I made a loop on the rope, then climbed as high as I could and passed the loop round a hump of rock. But when I stepped into the loop I found that the hump was too small to hold the rope and I started slipping down again. My fingers were fast losing strength, and yet I kept pulling myself up. Somehow I managed to catch a tiny hold with one of my feet, but at the same time I pressed the little tube for the oxygen supply against the rock with my knee and pulled it out of my mask. Oh, God help me! I'll choke! I rallied the last of my will power and dragged myself on to a snow-covered miniature ledge. The tube was pushed back in its place and I paused to take some oxygen. The fingers had long stopped hurting, they were totally numb again. But Andrej, we will win! We will win the battle! Not the battle against the mountain, but against ourselves and our shortcomings. You can't fight against the mountain. There you can only survive or die. There are no more alternatives, and the choice is yours. We two will survive, we two must survive . . .

I followed a narrow ledge leading as far as the crack on my right-hand side which I had attempted before. It was easier there now, but still impossible with gloves on. At the end of the pitch I hammered in a piton. The crack was shallow, two centi-metres only, but I had no choice. I switched off the oxygen. The first bottle was empty. Cloud suddenly descended upon us. But it did not matter. I did not think of Makalu any longer, I did not long to see it any more. I only wished we would escape from this hell safe and sound. While Andrej was climb-ing, the piton was bending under his weight. We both were literally hanging on it. Would it break off? I did not feel any fear but trusted in my good fortune. Andrej was swinging in mid-air on one jumar, half-choked by the rope and harness. He thought he would never do it.

Finally he touched the rocks and found some support for his feet. Memories of previous hard training in domestic hills crossed my mind. How often had we been running, as if for life, in heat and rain, in snow and mud, with tongues dangling down to our knees, day after day, every day. Now we reaped what we had sown. I was glad that we were together on the hill. Friendship means more than the greatest success.

By now we had used up one bottle of oxygen each. We let the empty shells slip into the abyss. Andrej took over the lead in the following pitch. It was decidedly easier. Belayed by the rope from above I advanced quickly. We were now on top of the Grey Step. The wind had grown into a hurricane. The rope, however, was put back into the rucksack, and only then did we remember to switch on the radio. What impatient moments they must have gone through in the camps below, and we never bothered so much as to come on the air.

"Hello, Tone, come in, please."

"I'm on the air."

"We've just managed to climb the Grey Step. It looks easy ahead of us. Three more hours and we reach the top."

"Bravo, boys!"

"Tone, what's the time? We're late, aren't we?"

"Not at all. It's only twelve. Over and out for now. We'll be continually on the air."

How was that? At a quarter to twelve we had been at the foot of the Grey Step, it had taken us three hours to climb it, and now it was twelve. Andrej dug out his watch from under his gloves and down jacket – it was truly no more than twelve o'clock. How was that possible? It must have been nine before, but Andrej, upset by my falls, must have mixed up the hands and read it as a quarter to twelve. So we were not late – we would manage without a bivouac. Then I realized that my hands were still numb. The fingers were as white as wax, and I did not feel them at all. I panicked. I had been so preoccupied with climbing that I'd had no eye for anything but hard passages we had had to negotiate. Now I fell to rubbing my fingers, but I could not bring any life back to them. I swung my arms at their full length like a windmill. Finally there was the first trace of pain, the herald of the more severe pain to come. With the blood streaming again through the cramped veins, I calmed down. The skin remained white, though. But that was harmless.

The cloud settled down, totally obstructing our view. Gentle snow-slopes gradually narrowed up into a gully, which rose steeper and steeper towards the final step below the summit. We were now 8,600 metres high. The ridge soared steeply again, vanishing somewhere in the cloud. We did not have to take our gloves off any more. We helped each other now and then on awkward spots, which saved us the trouble of taking out the rope. The ridge assumed the form of a knife-edge, but the rock was firm. I held on to the crest of the ridge with my hands and let the crampons scratch along a vertical slab on the South Face side. Oh, the passion of rock-climbing! We forgot where we were. We strove to reach a goal just a few metres ahead, and once that was reached we fixed a new one a few metres higher. We had to take off the ice-coated goggles, as we could not see the little footholds on the smooth rock any more. And then we surmounted the very last steep step. What followed was a gentle slope with black gravel where the wind had swept off all the snow. Then a sharp crest of snow, and then we made out the aluminium tripod. The Chinese pyramid! I waited for Andrej and let him go first. A matter of friendship, nothing else. At that moment I felt tears rising to my eyes. On Gasherbrum I had been in front, and now it was Andrej's turn. At first he did not want to accept, but then he did and was the first to make the final step . . .

The summit!

We hugged and clapped each other on the shoulders. Tears . . . We had reached the highest point of our terrestrial globe.

We took off the oxygen sets along with the masks. A feeling of terrible freedom overwhelmed me, I felt like hovering in mid-air. It was a freedom acquired through hard work, won by myself, dependent on myself. We sat down together by the Chinese pyramid, with hardly any thought coming to our minds, but immensely happy because the strain was over. With the aim reached, I felt utterly empty. With a trembling hand I took the radio out of the rucksack.

"Hello, Camp I, hello, Tone, come in please."

"I'm on the air."

"Tone, we are on the top!"

Everest 1980

Grim Nights

Joe Tasker

Although the notorious West Ridge of Everest had succumbed to Hornbein and Unsoeld in 1963, its variants and possibilities continued to entrance. There was the "direct" west ridge ascent by the Yugoslavians in 1979, and in the following year a British eight-man expedition sought its conquest in winter. Joe Tasker was among them.

The site for Camp II had been reached. Twenty-eight rope lengths, over 4,000 feet of rope fixed in place, stretched up from the plateau of the Lho La to a twisting rib of rock a thousand feet below the crest of the West Shoulder. That distance was quite far enough between camps, any further would have produced a diminishing return in that so much effort was being expended in just reaching the top of the ropes that if the camp was located any higher, a day's rest might have become necessary to regain strength after reaching Camp II.

Pete and Ade had run out the final rope lengths, but there had been some conflict over the roles of those active on the hill, as I learnt on reaching Camp I. Ade and John had climbed together one day and intended to do so on the next day. Brian and Pete were carrying loads in support. Pete was annoyed at the assumption that he would play a supporting role on two days running, and he protested strongly that he was not only a doctor but also a climber and that there was no point in his being on the mountain if he was not to have his share of the more interesting business of leading.

John and Ade had been working on the assumption that it was better for those who were fittest to do the work that demanded most effort and since Pete had been a long way behind them while they were leading it seemed most efficient to continue in the lead themselves.

John has a preference for avoiding confrontation, for withdrawing from an argument to preserve the peace even though he is not convinced of the other view. When Pete maintained that he was climbing as well and as fast as anyone, John stood down and let Pete partner Ade next day.

This disagreement typified the difficulties of a democratically organized expedition; we all had differing views and opinions. Ade did not like to see decisions being made out of, as he saw, a sense of personal pique and he bluntly told Pete that he did not expect to be kept waiting. If Pete was as fit as anyone, he should reach the high point at the same time as Ade himself.

Pete was the least known to anyone on the trip. He had an individualist streak in him, preferring to walk on his own and to go off for solitary excursions. So far I had not been impressed with his performance; in comparison to the twins, in spite of the charts he kept of everyone's movements, he had done considerably less. It came as a disturbing surprise to hear of his forceful demands when the twins were characterized by a selfless application to whatever task arose.

On the day they set off together, Ade arrived at the top of the ropes long before Pete and, since it was relatively easy ground, laid in place another 300 feet of rope before Pete arrived. They completed together another 600 feet of climbing before finding a place suitable for a camp.

John and Ade descended to Base Camp as I came up. Al and Paul had gone up to pitch a tent at Camp II and Ade suggested that Alan and I did the same. After a comfortable night at Camp I, in the now familiar caves, Alan and I set off for Camp II. Brian and Pete were going to carry a load up and then descend to Base Camp for a rest while we continued with the route.

I like to be either at the back of a group or well ahead. When every step is an effort it is difficult to match one's pace to another person's and if I am in front I tend to assume that those behind could move faster but for my holding them up. If at the back I can make my own pace. On this occasion I got well ahead, counting off each rope as I left it. Twenty-eight rope lengths seemed endless, but the first fourteen were the worst – 4,000 feet of slow, upward trudging, facing away from the wind. I expected to arrive in mid-afternoon at Camp II. The weather was not fine. Clouds covered the sky, streaming rapidly from the crest of the West Shoulder. The wind sometimes threw me off balance and I looked forward to settling into a tent when I reached the campsite.

Paul and Al were surprised when I arrived, being convinced that the weather was too foul for anyone to think of coming up. Consequently there was no platform dug ready for a second tent. I took it for thoughtlessness and told them so. They had had a bad night in the coffin-like confines of the box tent. Paul and Al were both big and broad-shouldered; in the tent they were too squashed against each other to rest properly. There was only one door, which opened directly onto the outside, and to cook they had the choice of keeping the door zipped closed and suffocating from the fumes from the stove or leaving it open and being covered in snow from the icy blasts of the wind.

Even if the weather had been better, both Al and Paul were suffering too much from lack of sleep and the constant buffeting they had felt from the wind through the tent walls. The only virtue of the tent was that it had very thick poles and seemed proof against the wind.

I set to with some annoyance to dig a platform out of the slope directly above the box tent. Paul cursed me and explained, with common-sense arguments, that I was knocking down great chunks of snow and ice, which were building up behind his tent and forcing it off its platform. I was frantic at the thought of being caught by nightfall without a well-erected tent; long icicles hung from my moustache and beard and my hands were numb. Clouds concealed even the cheering brightness of the sun and snow stung my face.

Paul came up to help me erect the tent, one I had used in ferocious weather on K2 and had every confidence in. Now I could not manage it at all. The savage wind kept grabbing at the tent; I tried and failed many times to locate the poles in the necessary places. Paul held on but I was the only one who had used these tents, had sung their praises and now could not expect more than minimal help as the method of erecting it was too complicated to be passed on when every shouted word was snatched away by the wind. I bent one of the aluminium tubes into place to form an arc from which the tent would hang. The pole snapped. I felt a fool for advocating the use of this tent. The weather on K2 had been terrible, but the quality of the cold on Everest was much more severe. My useless hands fumbled with other poles as I tried various ways of botching up my blunder. Paul watched with mute, helpless interest. With the poles finally in place I suspended the light inner tent from the arcs formed and turned to pulling the orange outer tent over the framework. It is the outer tent which gives the structure strength. When properly in place the arcs hold the outer skin in tension and a stable dome is formed. The last manoeuvre of pulling the outer tent over the end of the pole is hardest and in my struggles, with the tent lifting in the air, another pole snapped. I was furious but allowed my fury to rage without stopping my movements for a moment. Brian appeared, dropped his load, and grabbed the tent too.

It was not a perfect job, but when we had finished the tent was upright and, for the moment, withstanding the wind. We drove stakes into the snow to anchor the tent and buried the edges with blocks of ice and more snow. I dived inside, Paul scuttled off to his own tent and Brian hurried back down to Camp I. These slopes were no place to linger needlessly, and tears were already forming in my eyes at the pain of frozen fingers returning to life.

Alan arrived late in the afternoon and settled into the tent with me. The icy platform beneath the groundsheet was uneven, and near the edge it was insubstantial. The useable floor space of an already tiny tent was much reduced. We both shuffled into sleeping bags and, pressed close against each other, tried to impose some sort of order onto the chaos of food and gear strewn inside the tent. If it was not done before dark we would have no hope of locating anything we needed.

An icy layer began to form on the inside surface of the tent fabric as the condensation from our breathing came into contact with the cold material and froze. It was 5 p.m. and almost dark before we were reclining in uncomfortable readiness to prepare the evening meal. Suddenly we heard the slow, rhythmic crunch of footsteps outside and the sound of Pete coughing; he had just arrived.

"Pete, it will be dark soon, what are you doing up here?"

He had set off with a load, as we knew, but, instead of descending in time to regain Camp I before dark, had continued. There was no sleeping bag for him and no room. He had on his down suit, the normal clothing up here, but it was so cold that a sleeping bag as well was necessary to survive the night.

"Oh, I'll be all right."

He seemed unconcerned and passed by to visit Al and Paul at the other tent. I was amazed when he did not leave for another half hour. There were ropes all the way down to the level plateau of the Lho La but in the dark it is so easy to make a fatal mistake.

"Have you got a torch?"

"Yeah, I'll be all right," he repeated and crunched off. Alan looked at me with incomprehension and shook his head.

The tent we were in differed from the box tent occupied by Al and Paul in that there was an inner tent and outer shell. The outer shell came right down to floor level and had a flap on which we had placed blocks of ice and snow. We could thus open the doors on the inner tent without the wind blowing in. This enabled us to collect snow to melt and allowed us to ventilate the tent while cooking.

Hoar-frost formed a thickening layer on every surface; a dangling piece of nylon cord grew to three times its usual size with the accumulation of ice crystals on it. Outside the wind swept ceaselessly across the ice slope into which we had cut a slot for the tent.

Each gust that shook the tent sent down showers of ice, and undermined any confidence in it surviving the night. One of us had to be attentive to the stove the whole time to prevent it overturning and soaking clothes and food. It was a wretched, squalid scene.

I was too uncomfortable to sleep easily and the noise

from the wind banging at the tent kept me in a state of nervous anticipation. The box tent was twenty feet below but communication was impossible. Alan has the enviable ability to relax and sleep in the most painful circumstances, an accomplishment that he attributes to his drunken youth at Cambridge when he frequently spent the night where he fell. I needed a sleeping pill to block out the discomfort and anxiety.

The whole of the next day was spent enlarging the tent platform and building a protective wall of snow blocks as a windbreak. There was no let-up in the ferocious buffeting of the wind and stinging snow flurries; no opportunity for consultation; each person did what he thought best. Al felt ill after two successive nights of disturbed sleep and insufficient food. He shuffled off down.

Our purpose in being at Camp II was to continue upwards but until we had a comfortable camp we could do little and against this wind there was no hope of progress. All efforts were focused on merely surviving the savage, inescapable cold. The tents seemed like flies against the massive wind that battered the mountain. I was incapable of undressing sufficiently to relieve myself, the cold was so severe.

In the midst of another wretched night I awoke in terror feeling snow on my face and in the bewilderment between nightmare and wakefulness shook Alan and asked if he was all right. It was the recurring nightmare which had troubled me ever since the avalanche high on K2. The sensation I had experienced on waking to find snow pouring remorselessly down and crushing me under a black, soundless blanket before losing consciousness, had left a lasting mark on my psyche.

Alan reassured me that nothing had changed. The tent was still shaking in the wind and a torch, shone inside, showed the constant showers of hoar-frost which fell from a layer a quarter-inch thick, which covered the walls and roof.

Alan had a rough night, which left him listless and weary next day. He descended to Camp I to escape for a while from the horror of life at Camp II. Paul came by a little later. He too felt dreadful after a third night spent in the path of the winds. Even though the wind did not penetrate the tents, the noise wore on the nerves and there was the ever-present anxiety that the fabric of the tent would tear or the poles would break. Inside the tents the air temperature varied between −30°C and −40°C. A stove did not seem to make any difference, we had to wear gloves the whole time, and rather than raise the temperature a stove only increased the depth of hoar-frost that formed inside the tent.

I shared a drink I had ready with Paul, who described the discomfort of the box tent before descending to the secure caves of Camp I, and I was left alone.

Alone again on this hostile mountain. I wrote in my diary, which had become little more than a series of notes to mark the passage of time: "On most mountains there is some respite; once on the Lho La there is a constant battering of the psyche and body by the wind and cold. It really is grim waking up here to a tent coated with rime."

A weak sun made a pale appearance through the clouds but the rime never left the tent all day. I wondered what I could do. Camp II was at 22,500 feet; I considered going on my own to survey the ground above or dropping back to bring up some rope and equipment that had accumulated at various points on the way. Being left alone took the urgency out of doing anything, and since each time I opened the tent door a swirling cloud of snow blew in, I let the day slip away completely without stirring outside.

There was no radio at Camp II and no means of guessing the movements of anyone else. The cold and altitude had a numbing effect on my sensitivity as well as my flesh. I did not stir from my sleeping bag all day, welcoming the extra space now that Alan had gone, and drifted periodically in and out of sleep, like someone in a hospital bed. No one else arrived that day and as dark came on I prepared a solitary meal, which I ate as a duty.

I took two sleeping pills to wipe out my stark surroundings but was woken at 10 p.m. by the crash of wind against the tent. I lay for the rest of the night listening and worrying whether the tent would hold. Morning was welcome for the arrival of light but the wind did not lessen; I was too fatigued to make any progress outside, and reluctant to undergo the chore of stowing all the gear strewn inside the tent and face the unpleasantness of descending to Camp I.

I can no longer remember the experience of being alone; I find it hard to comprehend that I spent three days without stirring above the tent at Camp II. Like the gum anaesthetized by the dentist's needle, insensitive but not dead, I performed the minimum necessary to survive but languished in comatose inactivity whenever possible. Three days and no possibility, no thought of upward movement. I did not miss the company of others but noticed the passage of time in which I had not said a word. Sometimes I did think aloud but cut off any philosophical musings which probed the sense of what I was doing.

By early afternoon, having glimpsed the mental lassitude that can induce the physical paralysis leading to death, I had resolved to escape downwards. I packed gear into rucksacks, which I placed outside into a maelstrom of snow, found the lifeline of rope and headed down. My legs, unaccustomed after my confinement to exercise, collapsed under me as I slid down the ropes and my hands fumbled weakly at each knot. When I reached the level plateau of the Lho La, standing freely for the first time in days, I dropped one of my ascendeurs, which slid down a slight incline for fifty feet. I was too tired to go after it. Stumbling and falling, I made my way back against the wind to the snow caves.

Innumerable accidents occur when people become separated or isolated on a mountain. In the prevailing wild weather, Paul and Alan were anxious lest I should try to fight my way down alone or remain trapped for days if no one else could get up.

"It's all right leaving someone on his own if you want an exciting story to take back," said Alan, "but not if you want to climb a mountain safely."

I relaxed into the security of the cave as Alan prepared endless drinks and food, which he passed over to Paul and me. We had done no more than spend a few days at 22,500 feet but we felt as if we had survived a traumatic ordeal and could luxuriate in the relative comfort of this cave of Camp I. The temperature inside was only −10°C.

Later in the afternoon John arrived and the sight of the three of us languishing in sleeping bags brought on a torrent of recrimination from him. He was highly critical of the lack of progress above Camp II, and censorious of the amount of food we were consuming while lying inactive at Camp I.

With the slow deliberation of the self-righteous I explained to him the conditions we had experienced, and gradually it sank into John that the sunny days he had been enjoying at Base Camp bore no relation to the brutal life on the mountain. Contrite and apologetic, John agreed that he was "sounding off a bit" without sufficient awareness of our situation.

Ade was also meant to be coming up with Mike, the cameraman; John had last seen them doing some filming in the overhanging groove. Mike had done some rock-climbing in Britain but even though we had ropes in place all the way to the cave now we preferred that one of us should be with him on the mountain as much as possible. The amount of camera equipment which was accumulating at the Lho La was alarming; it clearly showed the differences of emphasis between the climbers and the film crew. I felt strongly that not a single day should be lost in climbing the mountain through attention to the film.

By dark the fierce winds still ripped across the slopes outside and there was no sign of Ade and Mike. The never distant unease surfaced. I left the warmth of my sleeping bag, fastened on my harness and crawled out into the night. I could not stand in the wind. I clipped some ascendeurs to the anchored rope and pulled myself up the incline. After 100 feet the ropes crossed the slope horizontally but still I could not stand. I crawled on all fours, my harness fastened to the rope by the ascendeur, which allowed me to pull myself forward without sliding back. I could not see in the dark, I could not look up into the wind without my face being stung with snow and numbing instantly. It was only 300 feet to the rocks at the far side and three times I was picked up and thrown up the slope by the force of the wind. I felt idiotic and presumptuous against such power. I descended to the top rim of the amphitheatre and peered into the dark; no sight, no sound above the wind. I shouted uselessly and turned back.

At the far side of the traverse across the slope a shadowy

figure, cowled and ominous, stood waiting. It was Paul, his back to the wind, waiting to make sure I was safe. No word passed, we descended to the cave and in the calm inside I told them I had found nothing.

A radio call at 6 p.m. to Base Camp revealed that they had not arrived back. We arranged a re-call at 7 p.m. and with relief heard that Ade and Mike had appeared ten minutes earlier. I always have a slight sense of foolishness as if I have been over-reacting in such situations, but to wait until one is sure that something has gone wrong is to invite tragedy.

We spent a restless night; the roof of the cave seemed to lift with the force of the wind, eardrums popped with the sudden pressure changes as the wind hammered at the entrance, the thump of the blasts kept everyone's nerves on edge.

Morning brought no change. We concocted a meal from freeze-dried scrambled egg mixed with chunks of tinned ham. It tasted almost like real food.

By 1 p.m. we were too tired and dispirited to stay up any longer. The weather showed no signs of improvement and I radioed down our decision.

Once at the top of the corner I slid down away from the constant roar that had been with me for days; it was like a climatic deconditioning process. A thousand feet lower and a parting in the clouds let sunlight filter through and warm my body. I began to relax and the tension of the last few days ebbed away; these walls of rock which had taken all our efforts were now reassuring and pleasant to pass over. I realized that I had not relieved myself for three days and a sudden overwhelming urge forced me to rip open my harness, down suit and under-clothes to release three days of constipation just in time.

Everest 1980

Solo

Reinhold Messner

Having scaled Everest without oxygen in 1978, Messner came back to the mountain two years later for the ultimate climb: the first solo ascent. Once again, he disdained the use of oxygen.

As the sun struck the tent in the morning and licked the hoar-frost from the inside wall. I packed everything again, leaving behind two tins of sardines and a gas cartridge as well as half the soup and tea. I must make do with the rest of the provisions. The weather was good, next day I had to be on the summit.

For the first fifty metres I was slow, then I found my rhythm again and made good progress. I was climbing now somewhat to the right of the North Ridge and the ground became steeper and steeper. I stuck fast in the snow and progressed dreadfully slowly until I came to a place where an avalanche had broken away. To the right on the North Face I saw my chance. The whole slope was one big avalanche track. There I would be able to move fast enough and reassured myself that after two weeks of fine weather there was no danger of avalanche, that the snow had consolidated up above. The weather would still hold for a couple of days.

So I began a long, easily rising traverse, with many pauses, but regular. What with the exertion and concentration, I had not noticed that the weather had turned bad. My surroundings were shrouded in mist. The peaks below me had flattened out and I moved with the feeling of no longer belonging to the world beneath. When I looked at the altimeter at three o'clock in the afternoon near the Norton Couloir I was disappointed.

It showed only 8,220 metres. I would gladly have gone on further but there was no bivouac site. Besides, I was too tired, so there I stayed.

An hour later, my tent stood on a rock outcrop. I had given up taking pictures. It took too much energy to screw the camera on the ice axe and set it, to walk away ten paces and wait for the click of the delayed action release. It was much more important that I make myself something to drink.

The snow had turned to ice at the edge of the rocks. I was sure it thawed in high summer when it was windless and misty, even on the summit of Everest. Nevertheless I must not be careless because at this height a few degrees of frost could cause frostbite. What should I do in the morning if the thick mist had not dispersed? Should I wait and see? No, that was crazy. At this height one only deteriorated. The day after tomorrow I would have been so weakened that I would have been no longer capable of a summit assault. I had to either go up or go down. There was no other choice. Twice while melting snow I took my pulse. Way over 100 beats per minute. The night lasted a long time. I kept my clumsy double-layered boots on so that they did not cool down.

The morning of 20 August I left everything behind; even my rucksack stayed in the tent, but after a short while I missed it like a true friend. It had been my conversation partner, it had encouraged me to go on when I had been completely exhausted. Lack of oxygen and the insufficient flow of blood to the brain were the cause of these irrational experiences, which I had got to know on my solo ascent of Nanga Parbat. Up here, the British climber Frank Smythe had shared his biscuits with an imaginary partner in 1933.

The rucksack had been my companion but without it I got along much better. And my second friend, the ice axe, was still there.

The way up the Norton Couloir was not too difficult. A snow gully led to a steep step shot through with brightly coloured rock. In the middle there was a narrow ribbon of snow which made the ascent easier. An avalanche had gone down here not too long before, so the snow bore my weight. But then it became softer and my speed decreased. On hands and knees I climbed upwards like a four-legged creature, completely apathetic, the route never-ending. By the time I was standing on a ledge below the summit the mist was so thick that I could scarcely orientate myself. A dark, vertical rock wall above me barred the way but something in me drew me to the left and I made a small detour around the obstacle.

The next three hours I lost all track of time. Every time blue sky appeared through the thick clouds I thought I saw the summit and yet I was still amazed and surprised when suddenly the aluminium tripod, the summit indicator of Everest, stood before me, barely still sticking out above the snow. The Chinese had anchored it to the highest point in 1975 in order to be able to take exact measurements but now, in the monsoon period, everything was different up here. Snow cornices, which towered up to the south, seemed to be higher than I was. I squatted down, feeling as heavy as lead. A scrap of cloth wrapped round the tripod point was frozen. I must take some pictures, I told myself, as if repeating a formula. But I could not rouse myself to it for a long time.

At the time I was not disappointed that, once again, I had no real view. For the second time I was on the highest point on earth and could see nothing. It was completely windless and the clouds welled around me, as if the earth were pulsating underneath. As yet I did not know how I had done it but I knew that I could do no more. I could only stand up to go down.

Everest 1982

Lost Somewhere High

Chris Bonington

Bonington led the British 1982 attempt on the unclimbed North-East Ridge, one of the most coveted prizes left on Everest. It was during the assault on the ridge's forbidding pinnacles that Peter Boardman and Joe Tasker lost their lives.

The following morning, 4 May, Pete, Joe and I set out for the pinnacles. Dick was dropping back down the ridge a hundred metres or so to pick up some rope we had left there. Stimulated by a sense of exploration, I found that the strength-sapping tiredness I had experienced the previous day had vanished, but even so, I was unable to keep up with Pete who strode ahead, seemingly effortlessly, picking his way across the airy crest that joined the snow dome to the foot of the first pinnacle. From there the ridge soared in an upthrust that led to a mini-peak that, as we came closer, masked the continuation of the ridge. It was as if that first pinnacle was the summit we were trying to attain.

Pete, who had reached the bottom of the pinnacle three-quarters of an hour or so in front of Joe and me, had already uncoiled the rope and was about to start climbing. There was no discussion about who should take the lead. He was going so strongly, with such confidence. I was all too glad to belay myself and sit crouched on a rock, whilst he cramponed up the steepening slope leading to the base of a rocky buttress split by an icy groove. He could not find any cracks in which to place a piton anchor for a belay, and so carried on, bridging precariously on smooth, slaty shelves on either side of the groove. The rope ran out slowly through my fingers, came to an end and I knotted another rope on to it. If he fell there was nothing that could save him and he'd probably pull me off as well.

At last he reached the top, managed to hammer in a good piton anchor and I followed him up the rope. He had set out on the next pitch, trailing a rope behind him, before I had reached the top. I followed on. The afternoon slipped by, with cloud swirling around the crest of the pinnacles, engulfing us in a close grey-white world. But he was determined to reach the crest and was running out yet another length of rope, as I, the portable belay, stamped and shivered and wished he'd come down.

Next day it was the turn of Dick and Joe to lead. Pete and I were to carry loads of rope and tentage behind them. My own strength had oozed away once again. Pete just walked away from me. Dick and Joe were already at our high point of the previous day. By the time I had reached the foot of the rope we had fixed, Pete had caught them up. Hardly thinking, I dumped the tent and ropes on the boulder at its foot and fled back down the ridge to our snow cave. I watched their progress through the rest of the afternoon. And it was so slow. That day they only pushed the route out for two more rope-lengths, but at what a cost.

On their return that evening I learnt that Dick, who had climbed the penultimate pitch up the corniced ridge in frightening bottomless unstable snow, had experienced a strange sensation of numbness spreading down one side of his body. By morning the sensation had worn off, but we were all worried by its implications, though we didn't know the cause. We talked it out. Pete, as always, wanted to press on but, quite apart from Dick's mysterious ailment, I was worried about the time we were spending at very nearly 8,000 metres – Dick and Pete had been at this altitude for four nights. We were making so little progress for so much effort, it seemed much better to get back down for a rest, and then go for the summit alpine-style, without any more of this exhausting to and fro. We finally decided to drop back.

I had been having increasing doubts about my ability to go much further, and yet, as if to commit, perhaps con, myself, I left not only my sleeping-bag but also my camera equipment in the snow cave when we started down. It was a slow, nerve-stretching descent, for the weather had broken and half a metre of fresh snow covered a hard base. It took all day to get back down to Advance Base. Charlie commented that we looked like four very old infirm men as we plodded back across the glacier. He didn't give Dick an examination that night, telling him it would be better to do it at base the following day, but as we walked down he told me of his fears that Dick had suffered a stroke and would almost certainly have to head for a lower altitude and probably go all the way home.

I, also, was coming to a decision. The doubt had been present throughout the expedition, indeed from the earliest stages of planning. I knew, both from my age and performance at altitude, that my chances of getting to the top of Everest without oxygen were slim. Yet I hadn't been able to resist the lure of the North-East Ridge. I don't think it was egotistical ambition, since I knew all too well that our chances of success were scant, particularly for a small team who would not be able to use oxygen, even if we wanted to, since we could never have ferried it to where it was needed. I should have been as happy to go for the original North Col route, which would have given a much higher chance of success, but I knew that the others wanted to try the great unknown of the North-East Ridge. I enjoyed climbing with them, for their company and ability as mountaineers. Because of this I was happy to accept the possibility that I couldn't keep up.

Now I was faced with the reality. I could never keep up with Pete and Joe and so would either have to force their retreat, or descend by myself. I doubted if I any longer had the strength or the will even to reach our high point.

Back at base we confronted our change in circumstance. Charlie diagnosed that Dick had had a stroke and felt that he would have to escort him all the way back to Chengdu. I told the others of my decision not to return to the ridge but that I wanted to give them all the support I could. I suggested that Adrian and I should climb up to the North Col, so that we could meet Pete and Joe there, giving them a safer line of retreat once they had crossed the pinnacles and reached the line of the old route.

We returned to Advance Base on 13 May. I felt no regret or disappointment about my decision, for now I had a role that I could fill effectively. Adrian and I were a little expedition of our own with an objective that we could realistically attain.

Pete and Joe were undoubtedly subdued by the scale of the challenge but, all the same, their plan was realistic. There remained less than 300 metres of height gain, but very nearly a mile in horizontal distance, most of it above 8,200 metres, to where the North-East Ridge joined the original route. I thought they had a reasonable chance of making this and then, if they were exhausted, as I suspected they probably would be, they could just drop down to the North Col where we would be awaiting them. We could see that the route back down to the North Col looked comparatively straightforward. If they managed to do this, they would have achieved an amazing amount, even if they didn't reach the summit, which once again, I felt, would be beyond their reach – it was another 500 metres in height, a mile in distance. You can only spend a very limited time above 8,000 metres without using oxygen, at least for sleeping. Reinhold Messner's formula for success in his solo ascent of Everest had been to spend only two nights above 8,000 metres on his way to the top. But he had chosen a very much easier route in 1980. It would all depend on how quickly Pete and Joe could cross those pinnacles.

The 15th of May dawned clear though windy. Pete and Joe fussed around with final preparations, packing their rucksacks and putting in a few last-minute goodies. Then suddenly they were ready. I think we were all trying to underplay the moment.

"See you in a few days."

"We'll catch you tonight at six."

"Good luck."

Then they were off, plodding up the little slope beyond the camp through flurries of wind-driven snow. They were planning to move straight through to the second snow cave. Adrian and I set out shortly afterwards for the North Col, though that day we barely got started on the bottom slopes. It was all much steeper and more complex than I had anticipated. We returned the following day and by six that evening were about a hundred metres below the col, our way barred by a huge crevasse. Pete and Joe had reached the third snow cave and came up on the radio. They sounded cheerful and confident, were going for the pinnacles the next day. We arranged our next radio call at three o'clock the following afternoon and then again at six.

It was after dark when we got back to Advance Base. We had been on the go for twelve hours and were very tired. Adrian had never been on snow slopes that were so steep and consequently it had taken even more out of him. We were too tired to cook and just crawled into our sleeping-bags.

It was always difficult getting up before the sun warmed the tent, which happened at about nine. Even then I lay for a long time in a stupor before thirst and hunger drove me from out of the warmth of my sleeping-bag. It was a perfect day without a breath of wind. I immediately went over to the telescope and started scanning the ridge. I looked at the snow shoulder, behind which hid the third snow cave. No sign of them there. I swung the telescope along the crest of the ridge leading to the First Pinnacle. Still no sign. Could they have overslept? And then I saw them, two small distinct figures at the high point they had previously reached on the First Pinnacle. They had certainly made good progress. They must have set out before dawn and were still moving quickly. But now they were on fresh ground and their pace slowed.

We spent the rest of the day taking turns at watching them work their way gradually across the First Pinnacle, but now their progress was almost imperceptible. They were moving one at a time and the going must have been difficult. Three o'clock came and I tried to reach them on the radio, but there was no reply. Perhaps they were so engrossed in their climbing, they had no time to respond to our call. Six o'clock. Still no reply. Could there be a fault in the radio? We kept calling them every half hour.

At nine that evening, when the sun was already hidden behind Everest, we looked up at them for the last time and called them yet again on the radio. One figure was silhouetted against the fading light on the small col immediately below the Second Pinnacle, while the other figure was still moving to join him. They had been on the go for fourteen hours, still had to dig out a ledge for their tent and would then have a night out at over 8,250 metres. I couldn't help wondering what shape they would be in the following morning.

There was no sign of them next day. They had presumably bivouacked on the other side of the ridge and, because of the steepness of the flank that we could see, it seemed likely they would be climbing for some distance out of sight. That morning, Adrian and I set out for the North Col, reaching it the following day. We spent the next three days gazing across at the ridge, waiting, hoping, willing Pete and Joe to reappear. But they never did. We were sure that they could not get beyond the point where the unclimbed section of the ridge joined the original route without us seeing them and, as the days went by, our hopes faded. Unless something had gone catastrophically wrong, they would have either retreated or have come into sight. They couldn't possibly spend four nights above 8,200 metres without supplementary oxygen and keep going.

Meanwhile Charlie had returned and was at Advance Base. On 21 May Adrian and I abandoned the North Col and joined him. We could come to only one conclusion, that either they had had a fall or had collapsed from exhaustion. My first impulse was to try to climb the ridge to see for myself, but I had to abandon that idea immediately. Neither Charlie nor Adrian had the experience even to reach our previous high point. And if we did get to the third snow cave, it is very unlikely we could have seen anything.

Then Charlie suggested that we should go right round the mountain into the Kangshung valley to examine the other side of the ridge through the telescope. The chances of seeing anything seemed slight but at least we would have done everything we possibly could. But someone had to keep the north side under observation as well. It was just possible that they were still alive and could be on their way back. We decided that Adrian should stay in lonely vigil at Advance Base while Charlie and I went round to the Kangshung valley.

A week later we were at the head of the Kangshung Glacier gazing up at the huge face, the biggest and highest in the world, a gigantic hanging glacier clad in snow, contained on its right-hand side by the North-East Ridge. The ridge looked even longer, even more inhospitable than it had from the East

Rongbuk Glacier, with steep fluted snow dropping down from bulging cornices, and the only glimpses of rock high up near the crest. We gazed at each tiny black patch but came to the conclusion that these were rocks, sticking out of the snow. There was no sign of life, no tracks, nothing that could be a human body. It was silent in the early morning sun at the head of the Kangshung Glacier but cloud was beginning to form below the summit of Everest and was slowly drawn like a gossamer veil across the face, hiding features but leaving the shape of the mountain just discernible.

We turned away, still no wiser as to what had happened to Pete and Joe, and started back down the long valley. I still couldn't believe that they were dead and, as the truck took us on the final stage of our journey back round to Base Camp, fantasized that Pete and Joe would be waiting for us, laughing at all the fuss we had made, keen to go back up and finish off the climb.

But I knew that that couldn't be. Adrian, as arranged, had now evacuated Advance Base with the help of some Tibetans with their yaks, and was waiting for us at Base. We had to accept that Pete and Joe were dead, lost somewhere high on that North-East Ridge of Everest. Charlie, perhaps more realistic than me, had each evening been quietly chipping out a memorial plaque. We placed it on a plinth of stone just above our camp, alongside several memorials to others who had died on the north side of Everest.

Two Eagles Hovered High Above Us

Maria Coffey

Maria Coffey was the girlfriend of Joe Tasker, whose vanishing on the North-East Ridge is described by Chris Bonington in the previous pages. On learning of Tasker's death, Coffey journeyed to the mountain that had taken his life. With her was Hilary Boardman, Peter Boardman's widow.

Chomolungma kept her eastern face shrouded for the next two days as we moved closer to the mountain across dramatically changing terrain. Moonlike landscapes on the high plains transmuted to muddy trails through lush vegetation in the valleys. We pressed on, crossing and recrossing rivers by rickety bridges or by precariously hopping from stone to stone, trudging through mud, willing the clouds to lift. I remembered Charlie's and Chris's prediction that there would be little chance of good weather on the east side of the mountain, but I was still convinced we would be lucky. The feeling of drawing so close was intense. Hilary was voluble in her grief: she talked and cried openly. I became increasingly withdrawn, conscious of tension building inside me. If Chris was right, if Joe and Pete had fallen down the Kangshung Face, then they were not far away, they were somewhere in the crevasses at the foot of Chomolungma. I immersed myself in an awareness of Joe's proximity, allowing it to override my loneliness and the reality of the loss. Asleep and awake I dreamed of somehow getting to his body, wrapping myself around his frozen form and breathing warmth and life back into him. It was an illusion, born out of hopeless desperation.

Drying out round the stove at the end of the fourth day of trekking, we made a group decision to turn back. Going further towards the face meant crossing a glacial moraine that could be unstable after so much rain, and there was no indication of the weather clearing. Early the next morning Hilary and I walked up to a rocky knoll to make our private goodbyes. The Kangshung Face was ahead of us, hidden by the heavy mist that clung to it so resolutely, but I could feel its presence. Joe could be nearby, held somewhere within its folds. Perhaps this was as close to him as I would ever be again. With that thought the illusion snapped. There were no miracles to be had, the relationship was over, except for what I could cling to in memory. Chomolungma could not give him back to life. I sat down and began to weep, heaving sobs which bent me double as in the early days of grief. Hilary held me until I quietened and then I leaned on her and tried, brokenly, to express my thoughts. She looked over my head.

"Zhiang is coming."

He walked slowly by, placed something on the cairn at the very top of the knoll and then stood and looked towards the cloud-covered mountain. When he returned his face was set tight as if holding in feelings, and he did not glance in our direction. We went up to the cairn. Two cans of beer were set there, and a small posy of flowers lay between them. An offering to the mountain and a sign of respect of Joe and Pete.

"That was more apt than any church service," said Hilary.

It was a gesture which helped me to walk away from the knoll towards the waiting yaks.

Halfway down, much to my surprise and bewilderment, there was a familiar tugging at my bowels.

"Hilary. I've got to stop for a shit."

"OK, I'll wait for you."

"Christ, I feel embarrassed."

"Why?"

"I don't know. It doesn't seem like a very suitable thing to do. I mean, here. Now."

"I'm sure Joe will think it's funny. And Pete won't look: he's very considerate that way."

I couldn't wait any longer, and, despite my tear-soaked face and the outpouring of grief that had left me weak and wobbly, I imagined I could hear amused laughter.

We retraced our steps, back through the dense vegetation, up the muddy slopes and onto the windy plain. As night fell the mist rolled in around the campsite. In the big wigwam I chopped vegetables, drank whisky and tried to socialize, but I couldn't concentrate on conversation. My mind was outside, out in the mist and heading towards the mountain. After dinner I walked through the fog until I was out of earshot of the camp and away from its light. Squatting on my haunches, I felt the cloud close in and I imagined Joe walking towards me with his relaxed, loping stride, dressed in his usual garb of jeans, boots and sweater, which varied little with the seasons. Had his ghost emerged from the mist I would hardly have been surprised, but nothing moved, there was no sound. I remembered an American girl I had met years before, in Patagonia. I had just arrived at Fitzroy National Park and she and her team of Italian climbers were preparing to leave. Her boyfriend had died on a nearby mountain the previous year, and she had travelled to South America to find his body and bury it. One of the climbers was a priest. They had reached the point on the glacier where her boyfriend and his companion had landed after the fall, said Mass and lowered the bodies into crevasses. She was young, in her twenties. As we talked she was using an ice axe to hammer nails into the wall of the wooden hut that was at the "road head" of the park.

"This was his," she said, waving the axe.

"You mean . . ."

"We found it beside him. I may as well use it. These nails will be good for hanging stuff on. And who knows, I might come back some time."

"Are you glad you came?"

"Sure I am. Now I can believe he's really dead. Now I have a picture of him. Now . . ." she stopped for a second, her voice caught. "It was good to at least be able to say goodbye."

That girl . . . I couldn't remember her name, or what part of America she was from, or why she was with Italian climbers. But the feeling I had had on that day came back clearly, my admiration of her composure and my wonder at her strength. I could never have foreseen it back then, but now I was envious of her, for her chance to say goodbye.

My legs had begun to cramp, and I was cold and damp. I stirred, stretched and returned to our tent, which was aglow with the light of several candles.

Crawling in I discovered Hilary in the middle of a full-scale nosebleed. Her red thermal underwear was matched by the mounds of bloody tissues scattered around the sleeping-bags, and she was distraught with a mixture of grief and frustration at not being able to stop the flow of blood. I calmed her and the bleeding ceased, but her confusion carried through to her sleep. During the night her anguished cries woke me.

"No! No! Pete! *Pete!*"

She sat bolt upright, suddenly awake. In the dream she had relived her avalanche experience, but I and her two nieces were with her and Pete was trying to dig us all out. For a while, then, we lay awake and she talked about the real avalanche, which happened when Pete and Joe were on Everest, six weeks before they disappeared. She wrote to Pete about it and he replied, "What is important is that you are alive and so am I."

The sharp frost of the morning gave us hope the mountain would appear. The clouds were playing a teasing game, allowing a glimpse of a peak and then covering it up again. Makalu appeared for a time and there was confusion over whether or not it was Chomolungma. We ran up a slope for a better view, our lungs heaving and burning in the thin, cold air. The face we saw was massive, spectacular and terrifying, but it was not the Kangshung.

Jacques was weak and despondent, so we took turns at walking with him and giving him encouragement. As I plodded up snow-covered slopes behind a yak, past tiny blue lakes, with the sun breaking through and snow peaks appearing, the loveliness would send a shiver through me and I would be glad to be alive and to be there. Hilary and I hung back at the Langma La Pass, watching the clouds around Chomolungma, willing the curtain to open and show us the awesome vista behind. Three times the mists rolled back to reveal the summit, but the Face stayed shrouded. Zhiang was hovering anxiously, wanting us to leave and follow the others, but we needed the steadying of those minutes, letting our thoughts settle before heading down from the mountain. It occurred to me that perhaps it was no coincidence that the Kangshung Face was not being revealed to us. Perhaps it was, after all, easier for us this way. I blew a kiss towards the east side of Everest and turned away.

Verdant hillsides pungent with juniper, and the gentle colours of irrigated fields and villages; after the landscapes of the high passes I felt I was seeing the lower Kharta Valley with new eyes. And as we began the drive to the northern side of Chomolungma I was calm, almost happy. Two eagles hovered high above us on the air currents. Joe and Pete, I thought, watching us leave. It was a fine place to spend eternity.

Leaning precariously out of the truck, I craned my neck to look up at the steep, fluted, colourful walls and down to the tumbling river rushing through waterfalls and rapids. The gorge opened out onto a wide plain, so flat it must once have been a lake. Villages rolled by, cornfields splattered colour across the aridity and cows tethered to stakes grazed hopefully among the windswept, stunted grasses. Denny became agitated in the back of the truck, his photographic desires frustrated by the relentless movement of the bumpy vehicle. Despite his periodic banging on the cab roof, Tele, encouraged no doubt by Dong who was anxious that we reach Rongbuk before dark, drove purposefully on. I sympathized with Denny, who needed photographs for a travel brochure, but for myself I didn't mind. The images forming and transforming before us, day after day, were being imprinted on my memory. And it felt right to be pressing onwards, skirting the mountain in a long loop to reach the northern side before the light faded.

We stopped briefly at a dusty village where Zhiang tried to bargain for a sheep. I was dumbstruck to realize that he planned to put the live animal in the back of the truck and slaughter it at Base Camp. My relief was great when the deal fell through, but Zhiang had been delighted by my dismay and from then on would bleat at me regularly.

Pieces of a bridge recently washed away lay scattered along the banks of a wide, meandering river. Zhiang leaned forward for a rapid discussion with Dong and Tele in the cab, and the truck plunged in. I watched water rise almost to the top of the tyres and recede again as we began to climb the far bank, before the unmistakable sound of wheels spinning in mud signalled a sudden halt. We clambered over the cab roof, across the bonnet and stone-hopped to land. Tele, his feet bare and trousers rolled up, lowered his skinny legs into the icy water. He threw ropes to us and we heaved on them as he revved the engine until the truck came free and mounted the bank, dripping from its undersides. Tele climbed down again, still shoeless, folded his arms and smilingly surveyed the river, obviously delighted by the manoeuvre and its success.

"Like a rock-climber looking at a route he's just done," laughed Hilary.

Late in the afternoon, as light was fading, we reached the Rongbuk Valley. It is windswept, stark and cold, and totally dominated by the vast bulk of the mountain at its head. Chomolungma, silent and majestic, seems to emanate an ancient power. I imagined what Joe must have felt on this approach, seeing the scale of the challenge he had taken on. I remembered how the yak drivers and porters in the Kharta Valley stopped to pray and leave offerings to the mountain.

"Can you see?" said Hilary, as we balanced against the cab in the back of the truck and scanned the East-North-East Ridge through binoculars. "They were almost at the part where it levels out. They'd done the hardest stuff. It would have been a long slow plod to the summit."

There were no clouds on that side of the mountain: it stood hard and clear against the sky. Seeds of understanding were slowly, slowly germinating in me. I had been tortured by unanswered questions – why were they so drawn to this mountain, why did they push the limits instead of turning back and coming home? But, little by little, the puzzle was beginning to fit. Le Grand Combin had begun it and now, the closer I drew to Chomolungma, the more I began to feel that perhaps their deaths were not as senseless as they had seemed.

He is a portion of that loveliness
That once he made more lovely.

Familiar words slightly adapted and carved on a granite bench stop the windy hill behind Chris Bonington's house in Cumbria. They are there in memorial to a local boy, Mick Lewis, who died at sixteen in 1944. The first time I walked up High Pike with Hilary, Chris, Wendy and the dogs, and we rested on the bench and read the words, I had been moved; now, in the Rongbuk Valley, the sentiment seemed right for Joe and Pete. As the sun was dipping out of sight and an orange glow spread over the mountain, we arrived at Base Camp.

Joe had described the site to me in letters and once enclosed a photograph: he posed against a backdrop of grey, moraine hillocks with Changtse and Everest beyond, and held onto his hat to prevent the wind whipping it away. "This is a desperate place," he wrote. We pulled up outside a large tent where a small group of Dutch climbers and Chinese officials stood waiting to greet us. There was a pile of trunks and cardboard boxes full of tinned food. A generator hummed and two trucks, identical to ours, stood next to it. One-man tents were dotted about the flat, dusty site. It was an orderly scene, set in a wilderness. Mr Wang, the Chinese liaison officer, made the introductions and insisted that we eat with them in their food tent. Hilary and I quickly withdrew to erect our tent before the light was gone, choosing a spot next to the wide and shallow glacier river that formed a boundary on one side of the Base Camp. Close by was a hillock, another boundary.

"Ladies on left, gentlemen on right!" Mr Wang had said, referring to the large boulders, on either side of the rocky outcrop, which afforded a little privacy. And on the top of the hillock stood memorial cairns for climbers who had lost their lives on the mountain. I smiled at the intimacy of the connection.

There was barely any soil to catch the tent pegs, and we paused from hammering to watch the last rays of the sun on the ridge. I hugged Hilary; it seemed a long time since the morning she had suggested the journey to Everest Base Camp, and our friendship had grown deep and enduring along the way, through all the highs and lows.

Our names were being called, a meal was ready. Inside the spacious tent a circle of picnic chairs was illuminated by a single lightbulb, and several propane stoves formed the kitchen area. Porters lounged in the darker recesses, resting and eating. We were ushered in, seated and served with delicious food. Mr Wang talked kindly to us of Pete and Joe, whom he had met earlier in the year. But it was not an easy evening for us to socialize and we soon thanked him and left. Night had fallen and the outline of Chomolungma was just visible against the brightly starred sky.

"It's strange to think of them here, Hilary."

"Pete described it so well. It's exactly as I imagined."

"How do you feel?"

"Close to Peter."

"I wish . . . I wish Joe had got my last letters. And my birthday cards." I had sent him two, one funny, the other romantic. They, and the three letters, had been returned unopened.

"You must stop worrying about that, Maria. It doesn't matter now."

"It's horrible to regret so much. You're lucky in that way."

"No, I'm not. I regret that Peter's baby isn't growing inside me."

We were nearly at the tent. I knew she had begun to cry.

"In one letter he joked about sending frozen sperm. I was sure I was pregnant before he left. I had to write and tell him I wasn't. I wish I was pregnant, I wish I had been left with a part of Peter."

"Hilary, Hilary." I soothed her. "It's cold. Let's get inside."

We crawled into the small nylon shell that had become a familiar home. Two insulation mats were laid out to give some protection against the cold, stony ground and at night we made an extra layer with our clothes. On top were the voluminous feather-filled sleeping-bags. At the end of the tent stood two rucksacks and along the sides, in the limited space next to the sleeping-bags, were diaries, water bottles, tissues, washbags, towels. Hilary's belongings were organized, but I still tended towards a frenzied scramble of unpacking whenever I needed something. With the onset of darkness the temperature, at 17,500 feet, was dropping rapidly and we wriggled into the sleeping-bags still wearing thermals and socks and drew the hoods tightly around our faces.

"Let's go up to the cairn in the morning."

"Yes. At first light."

My sleep was disturbed by dreams and I tossed and turned until the alarm finally startled me fully awake. We dressed quickly and gathered together the things we had brought to leave at the cairn. Hilary had a piece of gritstone, the Derbyshire rock Pete had loved to climb on, and some poppy seeds to scatter in the hope that they might germinate and bloom. Joe's family had given me a religious medal and a prayer card to leave there, and I had brought pressed flowers and the translation of a Chinese poem. Suddenly I was reluctant to leave the tent and my stomach knotted with tension. As two mourners we were about to take offerings to a grave, to perform one of the rituals of death, and this had an air of finality that I still resisted. Angry, frustrated tears fell on what I held, the papers, the flowers and a round of metal. This was all that was left, memories and flimsy representations.

"Come on, Maria," urged Hilary. "We must go before everyone gets up."

The morning air was sharp and frosty and rocks crackled under our boots as we climbed the hillock. They had not been the only ones to perish on the mountain – there were several mounds of stones holding memorial plaques. We found the granite slab on which Charlie Clarke had chiselled their names:

"In Memory of Peter Boardman and Joe Tasker May 1982."

I traced the letters and numbers with my finger, wiping away ice crystals, and thought back to 17 May, four months before. I had been taking my course then; I walked to the college and called in for a friend on the way. We sat outside in the morning sun of that unusually warm spring, waiting for classes to begin. My thoughts must have drifted during a lecture because in my diary page for that day there is a complicated doodle of snow-capped mountains with the sun setting behind them.

Three days later, while spending a weekend in the Lake District with Sarah, I had had a vivid nightmare. I was running down the windswept streets of Ambleside, rain was washing over my upturned face and I was screaming. She remembers me sitting up in bed, rubbing my eyes and saying, "I dreamt that Joe is dead."

There had been no way that I could allow myself to dwell on

the possible implications of that dream. It had to be a manifestation of the fears and worry I had been tamping down into my
subconscious for weeks. Or so I had assured myself, and Sarah.
And maybe it was. Or perhaps I did pick something up, some
disturbance through the realms of time and space that are not
yet understood. Because, as far as we know, the dream had
been accurate. By then he was already dead.

Hunkered before the cairn, looking beyond it to Chomolungma,
I felt no more anger and frustration but simply a great sadness.
On 17 May I had been so excited about Joe coming home. The
house was almost finished, he would be delighted by the transformation, he could retreat there while his building work went on.
We had a whole summer ahead of us . . . But it was over, everything was over. I missed him so much. Hilary was planting poppy
seeds; it was time for my private ceremony. I stood up and quietly
read the prayer, and then the poem:

> . . . Oh that I had a bird's wings
> And high flying could follow you . . .

Papers, flowers, metal; I slipped them into a plastic envelope
and dropped it inside the cairn. A breeze blew up, lifting my
hair and raising a little dust. No other movement, no sound, no
bird cries.

"Are you finished?"

The question pulled my gaze away from the memorial cairn.
Hilary was standing very close, and speaking in a low voice.
Our ritual was over.

*In 1992 Boardman's body was discovered near the second pinna-
cle. It is surmised that Tasker fell to his death, and Boardman died
of exposure during a solo descent.*

Everest 1988

Escape

Stephen Venables

Venables was the lone Briton in an American expedition that forced a new route up the Kangshung Face. Only Venables – who climbed without oxygen – reached the summit. He did so hours behind schedule, and an open bivouac at 27,900 feet/8,500 metres followed that night of 12 May. The next morning he met up with teammates Robert Anderson and Ed Webster, but the descent took an ominous turn as the effects of altitude, frostbite and exhaustion gripped.

I knew that this was all wrong. It was now the afternoon of 14 May and we had spent almost four days above 8,000 metres. We had broken the rules and we were asking for trouble. We should have left early that morning to descend all the way to Camp I, but now we would be pushed even to reach Camp II before dark.

It was nearly 4 p.m. when we eventually left. A combination of laziness and the intention of glissading most of the way down meant that we did not bother to rope up. We did not have the strength to take the tents we had carried up from Camp II and left them standing on the bleak plateau; we would have to manage without them when we got down to the flying wing. I left my Therma-Rest, my spare mittens, my down sleeping boots and the windsuit which had saved my life two days earlier. I could manage without it now and I had to keep weight to a minimum. Before he left, Ed asked, "What shall we do with this?"

"Ah – the mail packet. Perhaps the Australians will wander over here and pick it up, if they're still on the mountain."

"I'll leave it here in the tent. You never know, even if no one picks it up now, the tent might still be standing in the autumn, when the next lot comes up here. Right, I'm going. Make sure you and Robert come soon." He left quickly, determined to escape to a safer altitude.

Robert was still nurturing his last few ounces of gas, making one final brew of tepid water. I concentrated on my crampons. When they were safely on my feet I sat drinking half a pan of water, watching Robert staggering over to the edge of the plateau to start down the East Face. About ten minutes later I managed to stand up, put on my rucksack, pick up my ice axe, fit its safety loop over my wrist, put one foot forward and start walking.

I did not get very far before sinking to my knees to rest. That was better than sitting down, because it required less effort to stand up again from a kneeling position.

The afternoon had closed in, it was snowing and the South Col seemed even more forlorn than usual. I knew that if I failed to follow the other two I would die, but still I dallied, stopping to rest every few steps. When I reached the brink of the plateau and looked down the East Face Robert was resting far below. I saw the furrow where he had slid down and yelled, "Is it all right?" I took his garbled shout to mean "Yes" and jumped over the edge, landing in a sitting position and glissading off down the slope.

It was steeper than I remembered and I accelerated rapidly. I leaned hard over to one side, braking with the ice axe, but it made little difference. I was sliding faster and faster, then suddenly I hit submerged rocks. The ice axe skidded on the rocks; then it was plucked up in the air. I felt a sharp crack on my hipbone, I bounced faster and faster and then I was flung up in a rag doll somersault, spinning over and landing on my back to accelerate again. I was shooting down the slope, but now I was on snow again and could dig in my heels, braking desperately and finally coming to a gasping halt, coughing and spluttering in a shower of powder snow.

I lay there, battered, bruised and helpless, almost succumbing to terror before finding the courage to stand up. Luckily I had broken no bones but my one ice axe had been wrenched off my wrist, almost taking the Rolex with it, and now I had no tool to safeguard my descent. I was blinded by snow and frantically took off mittens to wipe clear my glasses, irretrievably dropping one mitten in the process. Now I had to split the remaining double mitten, wearing the flimsy down mitt on one hand and the outer on the other.

Robert was still a long way below watching impassively and Ed was far ahead, out of sight. Again I felt weak and helpless and in a fit of terror I yelled down, "Robert, wait. Please wait! Don't go without me." Then I started to kick shaky steps down towards him, holding my useless penguin arms out to the side.

Robert waited patiently and when I reached him he explained that he had also slid out of control. "I never saw those rocks at all. Then the snow below avalanched, carrying me all the way down here."

"Can I borrow your spare tool?" I asked. "You had two tools with you, didn't you?"

"Sorry, I've lost both of them. The ice axe was ripped off my wrist and the spare ice hammer fell out of my holster. Now I just have this ski stick. I could break it in half . . ."

"No, it's all right."

We carried on down, Robert leaning on his ski stick, I holding out my mittened hands for balance. Dusk was falling as I followed the others' tracks across the big slope above the Flying Wing. That traverse seemed an interminable purgatory. Robert and Ed were now out of sight and I was sitting down every few steps, finding it harder and harder each time to stand up again. Snow was still falling and everything was cold and grey.

I suddenly remembered a winter evening in 1976, in Italy, returning exhausted to the roadhead after an abortive climb above the Val Ferret. I longed to be back there, taking off snowshoes and walking into the little bar where I had sat on a high stool and made myself gloriously dizzy with a tumblerful of dark sweet vermouth and a cigarette. Then I thought about skiing in bad weather, succumbing to temptation and ordering an overpriced Swiss glühwein. Which took me back to the soft green twilight of an evening in January 1986, camping among the primeval tree heathers of Bigo Bog in the Ruwenzori Mountains of East Africa. It had been a long wet day and after changing into dry clothes we had lit a fire to make mulled wine. Soon the air had been infused with the hot steam of wine, lemons, Cointreau and spices, sweetened with heaped spoons of sugar.

Darkness fell and there was no restorative hot drink. I wanted help to remove my sunglasses and I shouted out to Ed and Robert; but they were too far ahead, so I had to manage on my own, fumbling with wooden fingers to take off sunglasses, open the zipped lid of my rucksack and take out clear glasses and headtorch. Now I could see where I was going but I still felt lonely and frightened that I would not make it to Camp II. I kept shouting "Robert! Ed!" as I trudged laboriously over the little crevasse, past the marker wand, down into the dip, then back right, following the shelf under the Flying Wing, longing for warmth and rest and the reassuring company of my friends.

At last I saw their lights at the site of our Camp II. They had already fitted one of the cached gas cylinders to the burner Robert had carried down and the first brew was on the way. The instant coffee and milk which they had found in the Asians' tent two nights earlier tasted disgusting but we drank it anyway, hoping that it would give us some strength. For an hour I just lay in the snow, too feeble to get into my sleeping bag. When I eventually made the effort I kept boots and overboots on my feet, deciding now that it would be best to disturb the frozen toes as little as possible. I had left my inflated Therma-Rest on the South Col but my down sleeping bag kept me warm enough in the snow. Robert produced one or two more brews before we all fell into a deep sleep.

Thirst and a croaking cough woke me at dawn on 15 May. For ages I lay inert, coughing up foul lumps of phlegm from my throat. Then I tried to rouse Robert and Ed, begging them to light the stove. I tried several times but there was no response. In the end I had to do it myself. It was a big effort, leaning up on one elbow, scooping snow into the pan, setting the stove upright and struggling with my slightly frostbitten right thumb to work the flint of the lighter. Fifteen minutes later I had to replenish the snow, then I dozed again. Eventually we had a full pan of dirty tepid water but the stove fell over and we lost it. I started the laborious process again, forcing myself to repeat the whole exhausting routine, but after about forty-five minutes the stove fell over again.

The day was now well advanced. The weather was fine again and the open cave under the Flying Wing was a blazing suntrap. The heat was appalling, pressing down on us and intensifying our thirst. I managed to haul myself out of my sleeping bag and unzip the legs of my down bibs but I could not find the energy actually to take them off.

The third attempt to make a drink was successful. Then Robert's slurred zombie voice suggested that we should eat some food. The bag we had left here five days earlier contained chocolate, freeze-dried shrimp and clam chowder and potato powder. "No – I couldn't," croaked Ed. "Not the chowder."

"Can you make some potato then, Stephen?" Robert asked.

He managed to eat a reasonable helping, and I forced down a few spoonfuls but Ed could not face it. He was more concerned about getting off the mountain and kept urging, "We must go down! Soon we won't be able to move." We knew that he was right, but each of us was lost in his own private world of dreams, sprawled helpless in the stultifying heat, powerless to face reality.

"We should signal to the others."

"Yes, we should stand up so that they can see us."

"Maybe they saw our lights last night. Anyway, they'll see us when we start moving."

"We should go soon."

"But I want to sleep."

"We'll go soon."

"We need another drink. It's so hot!"

The heat grew worse as the East Face was covered by a layer of cloud, thin enough to let the sun through, but also just dense enough to reflect the white heat back onto the snow. We were imprisoned in a merciless shimmering glasshouse and it was only in the afternoon, when the cloud thickened and snow started to fall, that we felt cool enough to move.

Ed urged us on as usual. His frostbitten fingers had now ballooned into large painful blisters, but he still managed to be ready first. Again we had wasted nearly a whole day and it was after 3 p.m. when Ed set off, wading through the deep heavy snow below the Flying Wing. I followed last, nearly an hour later. It was snowing and visibility was bad. After I had descended about 150 metres I heard Ed's voice further below, shouting up through the cloud to Robert.

"This is scary – I can't see a thing and I've just slipped over a cliff. We're not going to make it to Camp I tonight. If we try and continue we're just going to get lost. We'll have to go back up to Camp II, where we've got shelter and gas. We'll just have to spend another night there and make sure we leave early in the morning."

I knew that Ed was right but groaned with despair at the horror of having to force my body uphill. It was a slow painful battle to climb back up that slope and Ed quickly overtook me. He had our one remaining ice axe and moved alongside me as I balanced my way up a fifty-degree bulge of ice that we had slipped over on the way down, sweeping off the snow. Ed would drive his pick into the ice as high as possible, then I would use it as a handhold to step up higher, before letting go and balancing on my tiptoe crampon points, with the mittened palms of my hands just pressed to the ice, while Ed moved up alongside and placed the axe higher. Robert was approaching the bulge from below and shouted gloomily, "What am I supposed to do?"

"I'll leave it here – halfway up!" Ed shouted encouragingly.

"Thanks a lot. How am I meant to reach it?"

"Jump – I suppose."

It was dark by the time Robert eventually joined us under the Flying Wing. Ed and I were sprawled once again in our sleeping bags and I was starting to melt snow. We had no tea, coffee, Rehydrate or sugar – nothing to flavour our water except the remains of the potato powder. After the first cup of water I promised to produce another solid meal of potato, knowing how desperately our bodies needed fuel, but the meal never materialized for I fell too soon into an exhausted sleep.

When we woke at dawn on 16 May, we knew that this was our last chance. If we stayed another night at this altitude with virtually no food we would probably become too weak to move. It was now five days since Paul had left us on the South Col. We knew that he and the others would be worried, but once again we were too apathetic to take advantage of the cloudless morning and stand up to wave; instead we lay hidden under the Flying Wing, reasoning that the others would see our tracks of the previous evening and realize that we were on the way down.

Ed's blistered fingers were now agonizing and Robert's fingertips, though less badly damaged, were also painful, so I prepared the morning water. Everything smelled and tasted disgusting and the other two refused to eat the chocolate-coated granola bars that I had found. However I managed to sit up and eat two bars, concentrating stubbornly on the unpleasant task and swilling them down with sips of dirty melted snow. All this took time and we failed to leave before the sun hit us. This time I found it even harder to struggle out of the stifling oven of my sleeping bag and the down bibs. Beside me, Ed looked like an old man. His face was lean and haggard, his hair hung lankly and the light had gone out of his eyes as he stared in horror at his swollen blistered fingers. His voice too was the dry croak of an old, old man, repeating over and over again, "We've got to go down. We *must* go down. If we don't go down today we're going to die."

Robert, like me, was almost silent, fighting his own private battle against lassitude, building himself up for the great effort of departure. Ed, the most sensitive member of the team, seemed more deeply affected by the trauma of our descent and actually said that it was going to take him a long time to get over the psychological shock of this experience. However, because he was so sensitive to the danger threatening us and because he so urgently needed to reach Mimi's medical help, he had become our leader.

The only help Ed could give us was his insistent croaks of

encouragement. We were powerless to help each other physically and I thought with detachment how our situation was
starting to resemble the 1986 tragedy on K2, when the storm
finally cleared, allowing the Austrian climbers, Willi Bauer
and Kurt Diemberger, to bully their companions into fleeing
the hell of Camp IV, after eight days at nearly 8,000 metres
had reduced them all to emaciated wrecks. Julie Tullis had
already died in the storm. Alan Rouse was only semi-
conscious, incapable of moving, pleading deliriously for
water. Diemberger and Bauer could do nothing and had to
leave him lying in his tent. The other two Austrians, Immitzer
and Wieser, collapsed in the snow soon after leaving the
camp. The Polish woman, "Mrufka" Wolf, managed to keep
going but died later that day on the fixed ropes. Only Bauer
and Diemberger, both large heavy men with enormous bodily
reserves, crawled down alive.

Our experience had not approached the horror of K2: we
had only spent four days, not eight, above 8,000 metres; we
had been hindered slightly by poor weather, but we had
experienced nothing to compare with the horrendous storm
on K2; we had failed to make adequate brews but we had at
least been drinking something, our gas at Camp II was still
not finished and there were further stocks at Camp I; nevertheless we were now in danger of re-enacting the K2 tragedy
and as I lay flat on my back, delaying feebly the moment of
departure, I realized how easy and painless it would be just to
lie there until I died.

"Come on, you guys, we've got to move! It's clouding
over already." Ed was right: it was only 9 a.m. and the clouds
had arrived earlier today with their crippling greenhouse
effect. I reached out for the things I wanted to take –
cameras, torch, down bibs and jacket. The sleeping bag
would have to stay here, like Ed's and Robert's. It seemed
monstrous to litter the mountain with $1500 worth of sleep-
ing bags, but they weighed two and a half kilos each and the
less weight we carried the greater chance we would have of
reaching safety.

At 10 a.m. Ed was ready. Again he urged me to move.
"Don't wait long, Stephen. You've got to get up and move: if

you don't get down alive you won't be able to enjoy being famous." Then he left.

Robert made his final preparations, and I fitted my crampons. Everything was now ready but I wanted another rest so, while Robert set off, I sat on my rucksack. I sat there for nearly an hour, bent over with my elbows on my knees and my head cupped in my hands. My eyes were shut and I swayed slightly, almost falling asleep as I dreamed of life after Everest. Ed was right: life would be fun when I returned to earth. People would be surprised and pleased by our success. I would be so happy and everything would be so easy. I would be able to eat delicious food and I would have that sweet red vermouth, with great crystals of ice and the essential sharpness of lemon. And I would drink orange juice, cool tumblers full of it, sitting in the green shade of a tree. That life was so close, so easily attainable; all I had to do was reach Advance Base – just one more day of effort and then the others would take over.

I tried to stand up and failed. It was a feeble attempt and I told myself that next time I would succeed. After all, I *wanted* to descend, didn't I? I was just being a little lazy. I would have to concentrate a little harder on the task: lean forward, go down on my knees, shoulder the rucksack, stand up and away! Easy. Let's try now.

Nothing happened.

I began to worry. It was nearly an hour since Robert and Ed had left and I knew that they would not have the strength to climb back up for me. It was 11 a.m. and I had to leave now and catch up with them. I just had to take that simple action to save my life but I was finding it so hard. I was also frightened now that when I stood up my legs might be too weak to remain standing.

There was only one way to find out and with a final concentrated effort I started to move. This time it worked. I went down on my knees, reached round behind me and pulled the rucksack onto my shoulders. Now came the hardest part. I pressed a mittened hand to one knee, pushed up with the other knee, held out both hands for balance and stood up. I managed to stay upright and took a few wobbly penguin steps to the edge of the shelf under the Wing. It was so tempting to sink back down onto the shelf and fall asleep, but I forced my mind to concentrate on directing all energy to those two withered legs. The effort succeeded and I managed six faltering steps down the slope, sat back for a rest, then took six steps more, then again six steps. It was going to be a long tedious struggle, but I knew now that I was going to make it.

Everest 1993

On Top of the World

Rebecca Stephens

Stephens's introduction to Everest came in 1989 when she reported the Anglo-American assault on Everest's then unclimbed North-East Ridge for the Financial Times. *With some borrowed climbing kit she made her first ever ascent of a mountain – and set a height record for a British woman on Everest. Years later, with Mont Blanc, Kilimanjaro, Kenya and McKinley under her boots, she went back to Everest, with the DHL British 40th Anniversary Everest Expedition, determined to become the first British woman to reach the top. As "Becks" moved up the mountain on 16 May, however, the weather reports worsened.*

I had one thing to do before Tcheri Zhambu and I had a rest and that was to call John, at Camp II, on the radio. "Peter has the weather forecast in detail for you," he said. "It's a different forecast, and I'm afraid, gorgeous, a worse one than you originally had."

"Becks?" It was Peter. "The weather isn't as good as we want to have for you. We've spoken to Bracknell at length and they've given us some intermediate windspeeds for, literally, now, five o'clock local time. They say that it's gusting to thiry-three knots. The forecast then, for eleven o'clock, local time, tonight, is the wind picking up thirty-five to forty knots and then tomorrow, going up to forty-five knots." He went on, all depressing news. "It's not great," he said. "It's really not great. And tomorrow they're talking about thundery showers, so if you go up you've really got to get down fast before the really nasty weather comes in. Over."

"Thanks, Peter. Over."

All we could do was continue as planned. 7 p.m., and we put

our heads down for two or three hours. The windward side of the tent had collapsed almost completely, so that we were sandwiched with the ground beneath and the canvas flapping around our knees. I couldn't sleep, just rested.

"Tcheri Zhambu," I whispered, after a little time had passed. He stirred.

"Tcheri Zhambu, there's no wind." I could hardly believe it: the forecast was as wrong as it was possible to be.

Tcheri Zhambu sat bolt upright. It was 10 p.m., we planned to leave at 11 p.m. He lit the stove for a brew. It takes a while, as I had discovered, to collect and melt snow, but an hour or so passed and I got the distinct impression that something was up. The Sherpas, Ang Passang and Kami Tchering in the other tent, and Tcheri Zhambu with me, were talking among themselves in Nepali.

"What's going on?" I asked Tcheri Zhambu.

"Weather's not good."

"But there's no wind," I retorted. I stuck my head out of the tent: the mountain was as clear as a bell, the sky crowded with stars.

"Ang Passang says black cloud in valley. Too dangerous."

"Well," I mused, "the perfect excuse." A large part of me thought: I can go back to bed, put my head down, forget the whole bloody thing. I could live with failure, I thought, if it was the weather not I that dictated it. But another part of me still wanted that summit. There was only one thing left to do.

"Ang Passang?"

"Black cloud," he said. "We're young."

"Ang Passang, pass the radio, please." John and Sandy had said to me that they would be sleeping in the cook tent that night, by the radio, so I could call them at any time. I was touched. The boys at Base Camp were doing the same.

I explained. "John, Ang Passang just keeps saying it's dangerous. He says the cloud is too black, we may not find our way, and there's lightning. You have a view on that?"

"I don't know, Becks." This was desperate. "The weather's going to get worse, not necessarily in the next two hours, but it's going to build up. Whether it will hold off long enough I wouldn't like to say," said John.

The discussion went round in circles: Camp IV to Camp II, Camp II to Base Camp, and back to Camp IV. Everyone threw in their bit. Everyone was up, it seemed: John, Noel, our *sirdar* Ang Phurba, the Sherpas at Base Camp. It was snowing lower down the hill – might be the edge of the storms on the North Indian Plain, it's monsoonish, they said. Yes, black clouds are thunderclouds, and thunderstorms often strike ridges. But it was clear up there now, black only in the valley. "Talk it over very gently with Ang Passang and let him make the final decision," said John. "It's his life too."

The message that I was receiving from my teammates was thunderingly loud and clear: "We want you to succeed, Rebecca. We want, desperately, for you to get to the top, but we don't want to be responsible if you die." And who could blame them? John displayed remarkable courage that night. He is a leader. He has led all his life, in the Royal Marines, at Plas y Brenin, on mountains. This time he was leading on the largest mountain of all, but not from the front, as he would have liked, and as he was used to, but from 4,000 feet down the hill. I knew, of course, that I wouldn't die: I felt this with the assurance a seasoned traveller feels when boarding a plane. But the reality of the situation was disquieting. Three people had died in the two months we had been on Everest, each one where we were about to go – at above 26,000 feet, in the Death Zone. How on earth would John feel if he encouraged us to go and we did not return?

We waited an hour. The wind did not pick up and the stars still crowded the sky. Then I saw three little head-torches making their way up the hill from the col. I remembered now: I had seen three figures far behind, as we climbed the Lhotse Face. Must be them. I don't know how the decision was made, but one thing was sure: if those three people thought there might be even the slimmest chance of making the summit, I could not go back to bed.

It was 12.30 a.m. and we were ready to go: water-bottles full, chocolate, gloves, glasses, radio, crampons on, ice-axe in hand, oxygen on back, mask on face. "Get on those ropes," said John. "Get onto the South Summit. Reassess the situation there. And good luck. I think you're going to be OK. Over."

I heard him switch to Base Camp. "The beauty of fixed ropes," he said, "is that you can't get lost. If the worst comes to the worst they can just turn round and rattle down the ropes back to the tent."

Kami Tchering, Ang Passang, Tcheri Zhambu and I walked into the darkness, one behind the other. I was the lucky one. Each of the Sherpas carried a large British oxygen bottle and I had a little Russian one. They switched on to only one litre per minute, for fear, I think, of running dry, while I, with plenty, afforded three litres per minute. The extra oxygen and the lighter weight more than compensated for my feebleness compared with the Sherpas, and I kept pace, even felt relaxed, as we puffed a rhythmic breath the hundred yards or so across the rocky, snow-encrusted plateau towards the icy band that lay between it and the gully that rose, awesome, above.

From afar, the icy band, convex, bulbous, looked like glass. It had an inauspicious blue sheen that spelt hard, brittle ice, and indeed it was, but it was impregnated in places with little pebbles that made the going easier. A keen eye could pick out boot-sized steps in the otherwise steepish ground, pricked with the traces of numerous pairs of crampons that had passed this way before us. These we followed, Kami Tchering and Ang Passang at a steady pace, Tcheri Zhambu, behind, more slowly. I hung back. He was coughing, on and on, as if a fish-bone was stuck in his throat. "Tcheri Zhambu?" Still he coughed. "I go back," he said. It was agonizing just listening to him. "But not here!" I cried. We were slap in the middle of a particularly nasty slippery bit. "Climb to the top of the ice, where it's safe, and we can talk."

But when we were safe, there was little need for discussion. He was going, he said, there was no way that he could carry on. He dropped his rucksack so that we could transfer the spare Russian bottle from his sack into mine. "Thank you, Tcheri Zhambu, thank you for everything," I said, and waved him goodbye, a lonely figure in the darkness.

I wonder if John would have been happy to let us go on if he had known what we were to discover as the ground steepened and we entered the foot of the gully that led straight up the face, and to the right, onto the South-East Ridge. There were no fixed ropes – or if there were, we didn't find them. They must have been buried under the snow. It was very dark. And to add to the fun I had let my head-torch batteries run flat, as had Ang Passang. Kami Tchering led, turning his head every few paces so we could follow.

It was much steeper than I had imagined and icy in patches. In other places rock lay camouflaged under the thinnest powdering of snow. Crampons scraped, and slipped. I wondered at times how the hell we were going to get down again. But for the moment we were heading up. Kami Tchering took a few steps; Ang Passang followed him, and I went behind him. We rested, leaning on our ice-axes, like old men bent over walking-sticks. Once when we were in this position we looked eastward, and saw in the night sky a brilliant yellow light, flickering mysteriously like a candle-flame. I watched, intrigued, as it grew larger and larger; and then realized, rather stupidly, that what we were gazing at was the moon: a plump, sickle moon. And in the valleys far below us in Tibet, lightning flashed.

On we went. The three lights ahead were a little closer now, and I could see, above, in the shadows, a snowy passage between rocks leading diagonally to the right, towards the ridge. We're doing rather well, I thought. We're making progress. But the Sherpas, I learnt, felt otherwise. It was about 4 a.m., still dark, and they sat down in the snow on a precarious shelf by a large rock and refused to budge.

"What's the matter, guys?"

They were chatting away on the radio in Nepali. I took the radio. "Becks?" It was John. "Nawang says you've got two cold scared Sherpas." Well, perhaps. Thin cloud now engulfed us and the stars were no longer visible. "Maybe if you can persuade them to keep going until dawn, that might do the trick," he said.

Maybe. "Look, Ang Passang, let's just keep climbing until we catch up with the three ahead. We can discuss it with them." I tried everything. "Take my jacket." (I carried a spare one in my sack.) "If you get to the top? Yes, of course you can come to London."

They were reluctant, but eventually they – we – moved on.

We never did discuss it with the three climbers ahead. We caught up with them, for they, without oxygen, were climbing slowly, said hello and climbed on past.

It was hard work, harder for the Sherpas than for me on only one litre of oxygen per minute. The gradient was a little kinder on the traverse to the ridge, but the snow was a little deeper. I couldn't take more than six or seven steps in succession. I tried – ten steps, I promised, next time – but I never did, except for once, without oxygen. The tubing that ran from the oxygen bottle to the mask had a little valve, encased in a transparent shell so that you could see at a glance if the gas was flowing or not. It was a device designed to show when a change of bottle was required, and was totally superfluous. My oxygen didn't run out on a flat bit of ground, cushioned with a soft blanket of snow, or even where it was gently sloping, where I could have taken off my rucksack and changed the bottle relatively easily. It happened on the steepest bit of mixed rock and snow we had yet encountered on that traverse from snow-gully to ridge. I was fighting for breath instantly as if my face had been smothered with a pillow. Looking up, a few yards above, I saw my salvation: a platform of snow. In a panic, ice-axe swinging, crampons flying, I scurried up to it with the speed of the devil. I landed in a heap, gasping for every breath as if it was my last, thinking my ribcage would implode.

Bottle changed and sunglasses on, for flat morning light now pervaded the valley, and we climbed on, up steep but easier ground, onto the ridge. We stopped to rest for a while, and gazed down on the South Col, far, far below. Looking up, we were able to see the South-East Ridge for the first time from the eastern side, sweeping high and gently to our right. It was at once breathtaking and daunting, for it looked a hell of a way to climb.

The snow was deep and fresh on the ridge, and lacking any hint of footsteps left by climbers who had passed this way before us. It was a high, beautiful wilderness, and we were alone.

We took it in turns to kick steps in the snow, Kami Tchering leading, and when he was tired, Ang Passang, and when he was tired, it was down to me. A light snow blew in our faces. The whole of Tibet was one ominous snowcloud, nothing but an ethereal wall of pale grey; and I worried a little that the cloud might blow over and visibility deteriorate. The nagging doubt that afflicts all mountaineers from time to time – should we climb on or should we turn back? – haunted me every step of the way, but we climbed on, until somewhere along the South-East Ridge leading to the South Summit the Sherpas' attitude changed. No words were spoken, but I knew, as if by osmosis, that they, too, wanted to climb to the summit.

It took an age to climb that ridge, hour after hour, and I didn't know when it would come to an end. Whereas six, maybe seven steps in succession had been possible lower down, here the snow was deeper, the altitude higher, the air thinner, and it was impossible to take more than one, some-times two steps, without bending over double from the waist, to recover breath, and rest. Each step was a monumental effort of will, requiring a kick, and another kick, to secure a footing and ensure you didn't slide with the soft snow down again to where you had started.

"Up there, South Summit," the Sherpas pointed. On we went. Where it was particularly steep, the underlying rock lay exposed and, half on this rock, half on snow, we trod carefully, slowly picking a route up the ridge, until finally the gradient eased and the rock once again lay hidden deep under the snow, and the going became a little less precarious.

At this point I was leading, and made my way round and up a snowy knoll to the top of what I knew to be the highest point we had viewed from the South Col, far below: the South Summit, 28,750 feet up in the sky. It was a marvellous moment. The snowy summit was comfortably large, and flat. I felt no fear, no worry of some careless, fatal slip. I could sit in the snow, as I did, and gaze upon the world stretched beneath me. And I was alone, quite alone. For a few moments the view, down into my beloved Western Cwm, to Nuptse's crenellated ridge, to the monster that was Lhotse, and beyond, to Pumori, to Cho Oyu, far in the west, was all mine.

I rootled in my rucksack, and called John. "It's warm!" I cried. Well, it wasn't warm exactly, but not cold either, with oxygen, swaddled in layer upon layer of fleece and down. "There are sort of little whirlwinds of snow, but the wind isn't strong. I can put my gloves down without worrying about them." In a fit of extravagance I had just switched up my oxygen to four litres per minute; I thought I could afford it, just for the final push. "So," I said, "I'm feeling fine, I'm feeling great! But I feel sorry for the Sherpas; they're on two litres per minute now. Over."

"Becks, we heard that perfectly. That's great news. I suppose the Sherpas can't turn theirs up any, can they? Over."

"They've only got one British cylinder each. Over." And this was a dilemma, for their British masks were incompatible with my Russian bottles.

We chatted a while, John and I, about ridges, snowy bumps and Hillary's Step. It was the most elevated conversation I'm ever likely to have! "How far behind you are the Sherpas?" he asked.

"Well, I can't see them now, but there's a ridge not very far away. Over."

He went on, "Peter's got a telephone conversation lined up with your mum when you're on the top, if you've got the energy and the time."

This threw me. "If – ah, here come the Sherpas – if I have a conversation with Mum, do I need the New Zealand radio? Over."

"Yes, course you do, you dope. Over."

"Well, I hope the Sherpas have got it. It wouldn't work last night. Over."

"OK, well your mum will never forgive you, but we will." And that was that, over.

It was about 11.00 a.m. Together we planted my half-used oxygen bottle in the snow, to be collected on our return, and replaced it with a new, full one so that there would be no need to carry a spare, and walked to the summit ridge. I don't know why: I had read hundreds of books and talked to countless people, and yet when I first set eyes on the view along that final ridge towards the summit, it staggered me. Everything we had climbed thus far had been snow and ice, with just a little smidgen of rock peeping through here and there. What lay ahead was rock, mostly: large angular lumps, falling away abruptly, left and right. To the left it falls sharply away, 6,000 feet into Nepal; and to the right, even more sharply; if that's possible, the 9,000 feet of the Kangshung Face, into Tibet.

"You can go first, Kami Tchering," I said.

"No, you can go."

"No, you go."

Kami Tchering led, down a little gully and onto the ridge. It wasn't difficult by alpine standards; I'd heard it said it was a mere *peu difficile*, but it was about as exposed as you can get. This was Hillary Step territory. I could see it ahead: a large rhomboid boulder standing on its head, complicated with slabs and cornices all about. But first we had to inch our way along the ridge to that point. On closer inspection, it seemed that for most of the way we could follow a passage on snow. On the right, huge cornices, beaten and swept into shape by the prevailing westerly winds, jutted out like great snowy waves over the 9,000-foot drop into Tibet. And from the tips of these waves, the ridge, snow for the most, dropped steeply to join the edge of the rocks atop the western face, falling into Nepal. Along this, we climbed, grabbing a rock hold with our clumsy mittened hands where we could, checking and double checking each step to ensure its stability. Climb too high to the right, stick an ice-axe into the snow for balance, and it would enter in Nepal, to exit the other side of the cornice in Tibet. Climb too low to the left and, well, there was nothing. There were fixed ropes in parts, into which I diligently clipped my harness; but where there were not, one slip and it would all have been over.

Within an hour or so, perhaps less, we were at the foot of Hillary's Step. This, Harry had said, was so nondescript that you could climb it without noticing it. In a pair of plimsolls, perhaps; on a warm summer's afternoon, in shorts, bare-fingered, perhaps. But at nearly 29,000 feet, in heavy boots, hands rendered into useless clubs by vast gloves, ice-axe swinging, goggles steaming up, I beg to differ.

A bunch of old tat hung like a knotted loop of multicoloured spaghetti, from some unseen anchor. I grabbed it, pulled, and with a series of inelegant kicks, tugs, pushes, rams and elbow shoves, jostled and heaved my clumsy self onto a sloping mantel, the top of the rhomboid, I suppose, some two-thirds of the way up the Step. From here it was relatively simple: I planted my axe into a snowy shelf above, and scrambled.

I was glad when we left the rockier part of the ridge behind, for ahead, as before, cornices swept in vast, frozen waves to the right, and steep rocky slopes fell away to the left, into Nepal; the ridge was broader than before, though, more gently inclined, a little kinder. It undulated on, as ridges tend to do, one bump, then another, and another.

But there was an air of confidence among us now and despite fatigue, thin air, the effort required to put one foot in front of the other and the implausibility of us climbing together on the summit ridge of this, Everest, the most majestic mountain of them all, we knew now that we would make it to the summit. And we knew the moment we were about to arrive, for there, ahead, was the highest bump of them all with lots of flags on top. We stood and waited until the three of us were huddled in a little cluster, and together stepped on top of the world. It wasn't very dramatic but the joy on the Sherpas' faces made my heart near burst: "Summit, summit, summit. We make summit!"

Everest 1996

Hope Lost

Anatoli Boukreev

In the late afternoon of 10 May 1996 a sudden killer storm swept up the Himalaya valleys and swallowed Everest in blizzard. Temperatures dropped by as much as fifteen degrees in as many seconds; the windspeed hit 100 kilometres per hour. As bad luck would have it, there were no fewer than ten expeditions on the mountain that day. Soon eight climbers would be dead, in the worst ever Everest tragedy. Boukreev was the high-altitude guide for the commercial Mountain Madness Expedition. On 10 May he not only summitted Everest without oxygen, he went into the storm alone and rescued Charlotte Fox, Tim Madsen and Sandy Hall Pitman from certain death. Meanwhile, the Mountain Madness leader Scott Fischer was collapsed, apparently close to death, on a ledge 1,200 feet above the South Col. Boukreev determined to make a last attempt to save Fischer's life.

I slept like two hours and after seven-thirty that morning Pemba came with tea. And I heard some Sherpas pass by our tent, and I ask Pemba, "What is the situation now? Somebody go to Scott or no?" And he gave some tea and he was just quiet. No answer. I said, "Scott needs help. Please send some Sherpas up." So, he went to the Sherpas' tent and he began to talk. And now I have no power. It would be for me a stupid idea to go again. I needed some recovery time.

At probably eight-thirty I took a look at our climbing route from yesterday, and I can see the storm has lost power. I see some Sherpas going up, and he says, "Okay, father of Lopsang started together with Tashi Sherpa," and I ask, "They carry oxygen?" and he tells me, "Yes."

And then I speak with Neal. "Okay, this is my position. I would like to stay here," and he says Okay and he worked for the clients and took them down.

A strong wind had come up, and I kept myself inside the tent, but around one or two I went out, and I spoke with Todd Burleson and Pete Athans with Alpine Ascents (guides for a commercial expedition), who had come to Camp IV to help with getting climbers down from the trouble we had had. I asked them, "Do you know what is happening?" and they said some Sherpas had returned with Makalu Gau, so I went to the Taiwanese tents.

When I went into the tent, I saw this Makalu Gau, his face and hands all frostbitten, but he was talking a little bit, and I asked him, "Did you see Scott?" and he says, "Yes, we were together last night." And I had hopes that Scott could survive, but with this news I thought, "Scott is finished, dead already," and I got upset about this, but this news is only from the Taiwanese, so I want to talk with our Sherpas who went up.

I go inside the Sherpas' tent, and the father of Lopsang is crying with great sadness, and he says, "We cannot help." And he speak very small, very little bit of English. I don't understand. "What is happening?" And they said to me, "He died." And then I said, "Was still breathing?" and they told me. "Yes, he's still breathing, but no more signs of life."

I asked, "Did you give him oxygen?" and they said, "Yes, we give oxygen," and I asked, "Did you give him some medicine?" and they said, "No." And now I understood, so I went outside the tent and talked with Todd Burleson and Pete Athans, and I asked, "Can you help me go up to help with Scott? People say he is still alive, like 8,350 metres."

Pete Athans, who spoke Nepali, understood the situation, and he said to me, "Actually I spoke with the Sherpas, and they said it's impossible to help Scott." And I said, "Why? Maybe we will try." He says, "But it is bad weather coming. Storm didn't finish. And people try to give him oxygen, but oxygen didn't help him." Todd Burleson was quiet, but Pete Athans talked with me. And he said, "Scott was, yes, able to breathe, but he wasn't able to drink tea, just people put his tea inside of his mouth, but he couldn't swallow."

And Pete Athans said, "Impossible. For this situation, impossible for him." I said, "But maybe, maybe some breathing, if he has some breathing, maybe oxygen will improve, and I go out again."

I went inside the tent again with Lopsang's father and asked him, "Can you say little more information? Did you give him no medicine? When you gave him new oxygen?" He said, "Oh, we gave him one bottle oxygen, put mask, and open oxygen."

And I said okay and got a radio from the Sherpas and radioed to Base Camp, and I spoke with Ingrid and asked her, "This is the situation, what do you advise?" And she is upset also and says to me, "Anatoli, try to help everything that is possible for you; please try to find some possibility." I said, "Okay, I will try everything that is possible, but what is your advice?" She said, "Okay, about medicine, do you have this small packet with the injections?" And I told her, "Yes, I have the injection." And she said for me to try it with Scott, and I promised her I would try everything.

Then, I go to the Sherpas' tent, and see that Lopsang is using oxygen and some other Sherpas are using oxygen. And I said, "Okay, I need some oxygen. I need three bottles of oxygen and a thermal bottle of tea. Can you make it for me?" And people said, "Why you need?" I said, "I will go up." People say, "It is stupid idea."

So, I left the tent and then Lopsang's father came and began to speak with Pete Athans in Nepali, and Pete Athans came and said, "Anatoli, what do you want to do?" I said, "I will go up; I need oxygen; I need thermal bottles of tea." And Pete Athans tried to explain to me that it was a bad idea. He said, "Now the storm has gone down a little bit, and if you go now, you will get this storm again." I said to him, "This is what I need to do."

I knew from my experience; I explained to him my position. This situation with Scott was a slow process; maybe Scott, if he had oxygen, would possibly revive. Scott is just before the Balcony, and he has enough oxygen maybe until seven o'clock. I need some oxygen.

Pete is like the Sherpas, and I understand he thinks it is a stupid idea, but I get some oxygen. I ask for three, but get only two. I think maybe it came from David Breashear's expedition, but I don't know for sure. I began to hurry; I began to prepare myself, but as I prepared, the wind began to come higher. It is just around four o'clock, maybe four-fifteen.

I took my pack and was leaving, and I saw Pete Athans outside of the tent, and I asked Pete Athans, "Maybe you will go up?" He said just, "No." And I said, "How many will try to help?" And just – he got sad, he just cried a little bit. He thinks there is no chance.

I just started from the tents and maybe 150 metres ahead, I saw a small moving point, somebody coming down to me, and I was very wondered. I thought it was like a phantom, a miracle, and I began to hurry. And in a short time I came up on this man, who was carrying his hands without gloves up in front of his body like a surrendering soldier. And I did not know then who this was, but now I understand it was Beck Weathers.

I said, "Who are you?" He didn't speak or answer, and I asked him, "Did you see Scott?" And he said to me, "No one I saw. No one I saw. It is my last time in the mountains. I don't want to come back to these mountains. Never, never . . ." It was like crazy talk.

Just I think my head is broken, and I am thinking, "Anatoli, you need to be able to think if you go up again." And I yell back, "Burleson! Pete! Please help me!" And I asked them, "Can you help with this man? I will go. I will keep my time." And they tell me, "Don't worry, we will take care of him."

Everyone said it was stupid to go for Scott, but I saw this man survived, and this was a push for me. And I took a mask, everything, and I began to move with oxygen, without resting, and I climbed steadily, but darkness started to come, nightfall just began. And also a strong wind began with a blizzard and a difficult time.

And just around seven o'clock, five minutes past probably, I found Scott. Dark also, with a serious storm, and I saw him through the snow, again like a mirage. I saw the zipper of his down suit open, one hand without a mitten, frozen. I opened his face mask, and around the mask face it is frozen, but a different temperature, and under the mask it is like a blue colour, like a big bruise. It is like not life in the face. I saw no breathing, just a clenched jaw.

I lose my last hope. I can do nothing. I can do nothing. I cannot stay with him.

It began to storm again, seven o'clock. Oxygen – I lose my last hope, because I thought when I started, "Oxygen will improve his life." If by now oxygen does not improve, no signs of life, no pulse or breathing . . .

Very strong wind began, I am without power, without power. And for me, just what do I need to do? Actually, I understood this. If I found him like Beck Weathers, it would be possible to help him. He was revived. Like Beck Weathers revived, he would need help and possibly giving him this help, like oxygen, everything would be possible. It would be possible to help Scott. I understand there is no way for me. No way for him. What do I need to do?

And I saw his pack and I roped it around his face to keep away the birds. And with maybe four or five empty oxygen bottles around, I put them on his body to help cover. And just maybe seven-fifteen I started to go down fast. And I understand I lose power, I lose emotion. I can't say how it was. I was very sad.

Storm began, very strong, new blow of fresh snow with strong wind. And I began to use the ropes, and when I finish at like 8,200 metres, visibility is gone. Began just darkness, probably seven-forty, impossible to see. I have my headlamp. I used oxygen a little bit. Then I stopped oxygen because it is not helping my visibility, like two metres, three metres probably, impossible to see. And I found again Kangshung Face, same place, I think, near Yasuko Namba probably. I can see just two metres, but I understood. And then I go some more in a changed direction, and the snow on the ground is finished and I began to see some oxygen bottles. I turn back a little and go up a little, and I saw some tents.

I know these are not our tents, but next will be ours. When I found this place, I began to hear some voices. And I go without visibility, by the noise. And I come to the noise in a tent. I open. I see this man just alone by himself. I saw Beck Weathers, and I don't understand why he is alone, but I lose power, go

for my tent, because I cannot help. Some sleeping bag I have.
Just I crawl inside of my tent and go to sleep.

*Although painted as the "Russian villain" in Jon Krakauer's
account of 10–11 May Into Thin Air, Boukreev's actions on those
days were regarded as sufficiently heroic by the American Alpine
Club for him to be given its highest honour, the David A. Sowles
Memorial Award.*

*Boukreev died in 1997 while attempting a winter assault of
Annapurna.*

Dead Man Walking

Beck Weathers

A Texan pathologist, Weathers was a client with the Adventure Consultants guided expedition on Everest during the killer blizzard of 10 May. Along with another client, Yasuko Namba, he spent the night in the open on the South Col, where they were found the next day by members of Adventure Consultants expedition. So severe was Weathers's and Namba's frostbite that they were judged as good as dead and left where they lay. An official notification of Weathers's death was phoned to his wife.

But Weathers wasn't dead yet.

About four in the afternoon, Everest time – twenty-two hours into the storm – the miracle occurred: I opened my eyes. Several improbable, if not impossible, events would follow in succession. I would stand and struggle alone back to High Camp. Next day I'd stand again and negotiate the Lhotse Face. Then there would be the highest-altitude helicopter rescue ever. Those were the *big* things. The miracle was a quiet thing: I opened my eyes and was given a chance to try.

In my confused state, I at first believed that I was warm and comfortable in my bed at home, with Texas sunlight streaming in through the window. But as my head cleared I saw my gloveless hand directly in front of my face, a gray and lifeless thing.

I smashed it onto the ice. It bounced, making a sound like a block of wood. This had the marvellous effect of focusing my attention: I am not in my own bed. I am somewhere on the mountain – I don't know where. I can't see at any distance, but I know that I am alone.

It would take a while to recapture the previous night in my

mind. When I did, I assumed the others all were rescued and that for some reason I was overlooked, left behind. Was it something I said?

Innately, I knew that the cavalry was not coming. If they were going to be there, they already would have been there. I was on my own.

One mystery still unsolved is why I no longer was lying next to Yasuko. She remained where Stuart Hutchison and the Sherpas found, and left, us that morning. But I awoke from the coma alone and a good distance away that afternoon. I can only surmise that sometime between morning and late day I semi-revived and somehow made my way (perhaps fifty yards) in the direction of High Camp before collapsing again.

Somewhere in the midst of all this came another shock – my epiphany. Suddenly, my family appeared in my mind's eye – Peach, Bub and Meg. This was not a group portrait or some remembered photo. My subconscious summoned them into vivid focus, as if they might at any moment speak to me. I knew at that instant, with absolute clarity, that if I did not stand at once, I would spend an eternity on that spot.

I thought I was inured to the idea of dying on the mountain. Such a death may even have seemed to me to have a romantic and noble quality. But even though I was prepared to die, I just wasn't ready.

I struggled to my feet and took off my pack, discarding it along with the ice-axe. This was going to be a one-shot deal. If I don't make that camp, I'm not going to need equipment, I decided. It would just slow me down. For a fleeting moment I reflected that these likely were my last earthly possessions.

I also realized at just that moment that I had to take a major-league leak. There was no choice but to let fly in my suit. At least that warmed me up, temporarily.

My first idea was to walk in a sort of grid. I started out in a succession of squares, searching for some landmark or way to orient myself. Soon, however, I realized that was getting me nowhere.

Then I recollected that the night before someone had yelled out during the storm, "What direction does the wind blow over High Camp?"

The answer was "It blows up that face, across the camp, across the col." Which meant that if the wind had not shifted, High Camp ought to be somewhere upwind.

So I chose that direction, feeling it was as good as any of the 359 other choices I had. If I fell down, I was determined to get up. If I fell down again, I would get up again. And I was going to keep moving until I fell down and could not stand or I walked into that camp, or I walked off the face of the mountain.

Both my hands were completely frozen. My face was destroyed by the cold. I was profoundly hypothermic. I had not eaten in three days, or taken water for two days. I was lost and I was almost completely blind.

You cannot sweat that small stuff, I said to myself. You have to *focus* on that which must be done, and do that thing.

I began to move in that same repetitive, energy-conserving motion that my body knows so well. The ground was uneven, scattered with little ledges maybe five to eight inches deep that in the flat light of late afternoon were invisible to me.

Each time I encountered one of these hidden ledges, I would fall. At first, I instinctively put out my hands to break the fall, but I didn't want to compound the effects of the frostbite by further damaging my hands, so I held them close to my body and tried to turn on my back, or on my side, each time I slipped and fell. I hit the frozen ground pretty hard. *Blam!* Each time there'd be this little light show in my head from the jolt. Then I'd get up and start again.

Part of me was apathetic, even accepting, a reprise of the previous afternoon up on the Balcony. The sun was going lower and lower, and I knew the second it was gone, I was gone, too. I'd lose the light, and the temperature would come screaming down. I had thoughts of falling one last time and not being able to get up and then just watching that sun set.

What surprised me about that realization was I was not at all frightened by it. I am not a particularly brave individual, and I would have expected myself to be terrified as I came to grips with that moment. But that was not what I felt at all.

No, I was overwhelmed by an enormous, encompassing sense of melancholy. That I would not say goodbye to my family, that I would never again say "I love you" to my wife, that I would never again hold my children, was just not acceptable.

"Keep moving," I said to myself again and again.

I began to hallucinate again, getting awfully close to losing it. Things were really moving around.

Then I saw these two odd blue rocks in front of me, and I thought for one moment, Those might be the tents! Just as quickly I said to myself, Don't! When you walk up to them and they are nothing but rocks, you're going to be discouraged and you might stop. *You cannot do that.* You are going to walk right up to them and you are going to walk right past them. It makes *no* difference.

I concentrated on these blue blurs, torn between believing they were camp and fearing they were not, until I got within a hundred feet of them – when suddenly a figure loomed up! It was Todd Burleson, the leader of yet another climbing expedition, who beheld a strange creature lurching toward him in the twilight.

Burleson later shared his first impressions of me with a TV interviewer:

"I couldn't believe what I saw. This man had no face. It was completely black, solid black, like he had a crust over him. His jacket was unzipped down to his waist, full of snow. His right arm was bare and frozen over his head. We could not lower it. His skin looked like marble. White stone. No blood in it."

Todd Burleson's amazement stemmed in part from my appearance, and in part from the news he'd received that everyone above High Camp, including me, was dead.

He quickly recovered his composure, reached out and took me by the arm to the first tent – the dead Scott Fischer's tent – where they put me into two sleeping bags, shoved hot-water bottles under my arms, and gave me a shot of steroids.

"You are *not* going to believe what just walked into camp," they radioed down to Base Camp. The response back was "That is fascinating. But it changes nothing. He is going to die. Do not bring him down."

Fortunately, they didn't tell me that.

Conventional wisdom holds that in hypothermia cases, even so remarkable a resurrection as mine merely delays the inevitable. When they called Peach and told her that I was not as dead as they thought I was – but I was critically injured – they were trying not to give her false hope. What she heard, of course, was an entirely different thing.

I also demurred from the glum consensus. Having reconnected with the mother ship, I now believed I had a chance to actually survive this thing. For whatever reason, I seemed to have tolerated the hypothermia, and genuinely believed myself fully revived. What I did not at first think about was the Khumbu Icefall, which simply cannot be navigated without hands. I was going to require another means of exit, something nobody had ever tried before.

They left me alone in Scott Fischer's tent that night, expecting me to die. On a couple of occasions I heard the others referring to "a dead guy" in the tent. Who could that be? I wondered as I slipped in and out of wakefulness.

To complicate matters, the storm came roaring back, every bit as ferocious as the previous night. It shook that tent and me in it as if we were absolutely weightless. I remembered how Scott had talked about a new tent he was trying out, how it was an experimental, lightweight model, extremely flexible. I wondered if I was in that tent and, if so, how well it had been secured to the ground. The wind certainly was strong enough to blow me and the tent clear off the South Col.

With each gust it pressed so heavily on my chest and face that I couldn't breathe. In the brief moments between the gusts, I rolled onto my side, eventually discovering that if I lay on my side, I could breathe even as the tent pressed down on me.

My right hand and forearm were less than useless in all this. They started to swell and discolor down to my wristwatch. I tried desperately to bite the thing off, but Seiko makes a darn good watchband, and I failed.

All the commotion and discomfort notwithstanding, I must have lost consciousness repeatedly that night. I don't remember the blizzard blowing out the doors and filling the tent with snow, but it did. I don't remember being blasted out of my sleeping bag, but clearly I was, because that was how I found myself at dawn . . .

Nearly everyone packed up to break camp at daybreak, and they did so very quietly. I didn't hear any of it. Besides myself, only Jon Krakauer, and Todd Burleson and Pete Athans, who were guiding the same expedition together, remained in camp.

I heard a noise outside.

"Hello!" I yelled. "Anybody out there?" Krakauer, who was checking out each tent before he, too, headed down the mountain, stuck his head inside. When he saw me, Jon's jaw dropped right down to the middle of his chest. I was supposed to be dead.

"What the hell does a person have to do around here to get a little service!" I said, then added, "Jon, if you don't mind, would you ask Pete Athans to step over here? I'd really like to talk to him."

Athans, an acquaintance from previous expeditions, looked in and saw that I, in fact, was still alive. I was fully dressed. I had my boots on. (You can't take them off because your feet will swell and you can't get back in them.) So it was a relatively simple thing for me to stand, put my crampons back on with Pete and Todd's help, and drink two litres of tea.

Now the dead guy was ready to head down the Lhotse Face.

After negotiating the Lhotse Face, Weathers was airlifted from Camp II by Lieutenant Colonel Madan K.C. of the Royal Nepalese Army. It was the highest ever rescue by helicopter.

Everest 1996

Nightmare

Matt Dickinson

The Briton Matt Dickinson went to Everest to film others ascending Everest, and ended up scaling the mountain himself, despite being largely bereft of climbing experience. He was accompanied by the professional mountaineer Al Hinkes and three Sherpas. Their climb took place a bare week after the killer storm of 10 May.

I ran through a mental checklist as we put the final touches to the equipment. Ski goggles ready in the pocket of the wind suit. Spare glacier goggles in another pocket. Headtorch ready with two spare bulbs and spare battery. Two one-litre water bottles filled with "isotonic" high-energy glucose drink. Walkie-talkie checked. Food – chocolate and Christmas pudding – ready. Stills cameras loaded with fresh film. Crampon repair kit. Spare carabiner. Figure-of-eight descendeur. Jumar clamps.

"Where's your drink?" Al asked.

"In the rucksack."

"You're better off putting them inside the down suit next to your skin."

I did as Al said, zipping up one of the plastic nalgene bottles into the suit just above the harness. The Sherpas were clearly ready to go. My mind raced through the mental checklist searching for the one missed component, the one small forgotten item that would bring the summit bid to a grinding halt.

There wasn't one. We were ready.

Without a word, we turned away from the tents and started our climb up into the night. Lhakpa led, with Mingma and Gyaltsen behind, then Al and myself at the tail.

After the suspense and tension of the preparation it was a sheer relief to be moving. Those first few steps had, for me, a truly epic quality. I knew we were in an incredibly privileged position – a position thousands of mountaineers would give their eye-teeth (and perhaps a lot more) to share.

We were leaving camp six bang on schedule on as near as the North Face ever gets to a perfect night. We had liquid, food, an adequate supply of oxygen and the assistance of three very strong Sherpas. Our equipment was tried and tested, we were as fit as one can be above 8,000 metres with no major sickness or injury to cope with.

It doesn't get much better than that. The "window" was open. For the first time, I allowed myself the luxury of thinking that we might just make it. If our luck held.

In the precise minutes of our departure from camp six, as we later learned from the Hungarian climber who was with him in the tent, Reinhard died.

The Sherpas set a fast pace up the first of the snowfields lying above the camp. Al kept up easily but I found myself lagging behind. The thin beam of light from the headtorch, seemingly so bright when tested in the tent, now felt inadequate for the task, illuminating a pathetically small patch of snow.

Catching up, I concentrated on watching Al's cramponed feet as they bit into the snow. The conditions were variable with an unpredictable crust. Frequently it gave way, plunging us thigh deep into a hidden hole.

I quickly learned not to trust the headtorch with its tunnel vision effect. It confused the eye by casting shadows of unknown depth. Rocks could be bigger than they seemed. Holes in the snow lacked all perspective. Distances became hard to judge. Was Lhakpa's light ten metres in front of me . . . or fifty? I couldn't tell.

We crossed several old tent platforms, abandoned by previous expeditions. Each one was littered with the usual shredded fabric, splintered tent-poles and empty oxygen cylinders. A foil food sachet got spiked by one of my crampon teeth and dragged annoyingly until I could be bothered to remove it.

At each of these wrecked sites, Al, the mountain detective, would pause for a moment to cast his headtorch around the remains. Even now, on our summit bid, his fascination for them was as keen as ever.

The climb continued, step after step, up the snowfield towards the much more demanding terrain of the Yellow Band. Very conscious of our limited oxygen supply, I tried to concentrate on regulating my breathing; I knew from scuba-diving training how easy it is to waste air.

But the terrain of the North Face is mixed; both in steepness and in composition. Steep ice fields give way to shallower rock slabs. Demanding rock sections end in long traverses. Establishing a breathing pattern is virtually impossible. Mostly I found I was puffing and panting at a very fast rate and there was nothing I could do about it.

After an hour I found I was feeling better. The headache and nausea had faded away with the concentrated physical work of the climb. My feet and hands both felt warm, and the weight of the rucksack was not as bad as I had feared.

Reaching the end of the larger of the two snowfields, we encountered the first bare rock. I watched in horror as the three pinprick lights of the Sherpas began to rise up what seemed to be a vertical wall. Surely it was an optical illusion? I had never heard anyone talk about any actual climbing before the ridge. But, standing at the foot of the rock section, my heart sank. It was steep. Very steep. I was completely inexperienced in night climbing, and fear formed an icy pool in the pit of my stomach.

We were about to tackle the Yellow Band.

Worse, we would have to climb on rock with our crampons on. This is like trying to climb stairs on stilts. The spiked fangs act like an unwanted platform sole, elevating the foot away from any real contact with the rock. Using crampons on rock greatly increases the risk of a misplaced foothold or a twisted ankle. In a tight spot, where the feet have to move in close proximity, they are even more deadly. A spike can snag in the neoprene gaiter of the other foot, a mistake which invariably leads to a heavy fall.

On other mountains we might have stopped to remove the crampons, but here that was not an option. On the North Face of Everest, removing crampons every time you made a transition from snow to rock would waste hours of precious time and risk almost certain frostbite to the hands.

I paused for a brief rest as the others made their way up into the rock band. Turning off my headtorch, I let my eyes adjust to the dark. The sky was mostly still clear of cloud but I could see no sign of the moon. The only illumination came from the stars, which were as dazzling as I have ever seen them. The towering mass of Changtse was now far below us, I could just see the sinuous curves of its fluted ridge.

Further down, thousands of metres further down, the great glaciers were just visible, reflecting the dull metallic grey of the starlight against the darker shadows of their deep valley walls. The whole of Tibet lay beneath us and there was not a single electric light to be seen.

Taking off my Gore-tex overmitts, I reached up to the oxygen mask. Ice was beginning to constrict the intake valve at the front. I carefully broke the chunk away.

Then, my crampons clanking and scraping with a jarring metallic ring against the rock, I began the climb up. The route took a line up a series of ledges, linked by narrow cracks. It was a nasty scramble, involving strenuous leg and arm work to lunge up steps which were often uncomfortably high. More than once I found myself jamming a knee into a crack for support, or squirming up on to a balcony on my stomach.

"This must be the first step," I yelled up at Al. He didn't reply and hours later, when we reached the real first step, I realised how far out I had been.

We came to a platform and took a few minutes' rest before beginning the next section.

The climb was littered with tatty ropes. Some were frayed, some were kinked from unknown causes, others were bleached white from exposure to the intense ultraviolet radiation here above 8,000 metres. Al sorted through them with a professional's eye, muttering under his breath.

Selecting the best of a bad lot, Al attached his jumar clamp and started up, sliding the handgrip of the camming device with each move. I waited for him to gain some height and then followed on. The crampons made every move a nightmare, as they had to be jammed into crevices or rested on protrusions to gain a purchase. Often I found my feet scrabbling frantically for a hold, the metal spikes grinding the flaking rock into granules of grit.

A steady barrage of small stones, and the occasional fist-sized rock, came down from above where the Sherpas were climbing. Normally this is avoidable by all but the clumsiest climber, but here every foothold had the potential to dislodge debris. Our ears rapidly become adept at guessing the size of an approaching missile as it clattered down the rock-face.

"Below!" A flat, briefcase-sized rock slithered down the face and spun off into the dark depths.

After sixty or seventy metres of ascent I made my first mistake. Pushing down to lift my body weight up on a boulder foothold, my crampon slipped away with no warning, unbalancing me and crashing my knee into a sharp ledge. The down suit cushioned much of the blow but it still took me several minutes to regain my composure as a series of sparkling stars did cartoon laps of honour across my field of vision.

On that fall, as at many other times, my entire body weight was suspended on the rope.

Another twenty metres of ascent brought me to the anchor point of the rope I was climbing on. Shining the headtorch on to the fixing point, I could scarcely believe what I was seeing. My lifeline was attached to the face by a single, rusting metal piton which had been ineptly placed in a crack.

Out of curiosity I tested the solidity of the anchor point with my hand. It moved. With one gentle pull, the piton slid right out. I stared at it dumbly for a few seconds, incredulous that my recent fall had been held by this pathetic piece of protection.

Throughout the expedition the knowledge that fixed ropes existed on the more technical rock had been a reassuring notion. "Get to camp six and then you're on the fixed ropes" was a much repeated mantra, implying that they were somehow safe. In that one heart-stopping moment as the piton slid out of its crack, my faith in the fixed ropes was destroyed. I resolved to rely on them as little as I could.

The incline eased off and I found Al and the three Sherpas waiting for me. As I arrived they continued onwards up a series of steps cut into wind-hardened snow. At the next steep section Lhakpa again led the way up the rocks. Climbing strongly and steadily, the light from his headtorch rapidly went out of view.

I had a favour to ask. "Al, can you let me go in front? I'm not happy at the back."

"No problem." Al unclipped his sling from the rope and let me pass. It was a generous gesture that I greatly appreciated.

I started up the next rock section feeling a lot more confident with Al behind me at the tail-end of the rope. This was partly psychological, and partly from the practical help he could give by shining his headtorch on to holds. I found myself moving easier and with more certainty.

As everywhere on Everest, the rock was fragmented and unreliable. Apparently solid handholds came away easily in flakes, boulders trembled under the weight of a leg and a flow of gravel-sized stones seemed to be perpetually on the move.

Just inches from my hand a stone the size of a telephone directory fell out of the night. Impacting hard, it shattered into hundreds of pieces, showering me with splinters of stone. Mingma's warning cry from above came simultaneously. I saw his headtorch flash down the face.

"You OK?"

"OK." We carried on up.

By now I had no idea of our precise position on the face. From the Rongbuk Glacier the distance from camp six to the North-East Ridge does not look great. In fact, as I was discovering, it is a significant climb. It was now many hours since we had left the camp and my body was already feeling as if it had done a substantial day's work.

There was still not the slightest glimmer of dawn. I began to long for the first rays of light.

Now we started what I guessed was the final section of the Yellow Band; more steep slogging up an eroded fault in the rock strata. It began with a stretching high step of a metre or more up on to a ledge; another occasion when there was no choice but to rely on a fixed rope. Then, with the infernal crampons scraping horribly on the rock, we scrambled up for about thirty minutes, pausing every five minutes or so for breath.

Turning back for a moment, I saw that Al was free-climbing the section. He, like me, had no confidence in the fixed ropes, but, unlike me, had the experience to know he could climb the route without a fall.

As the ground evened off, we began another traverse to the right, across a field of dirty snow. A bright red rope had been laid across it – the newest protection we had seen so far. Clipping on, I wondered who had fixed it: the Indians, or perhaps the Japanese?

The line continued up through a crack and then on to a sloping rock plateau the size of a tennis court. Crossing it, I realized we had finished the first stage of the climb.

The horrors of the night climb ended as we took the final steps on to the North-East Ridge. The crumbling cliffs of the Yellow Band had been steeper, more complex and much more committing than I had imagined. Climbing them in the dark, with just the glow-worm light of the headtorch, had been a nightmare.

Now, with the first rays of dawn to light our route along the ridge, I reached up and turned the headtorch off. If all went well now, we could be on the summit within the next six hours.

Everest 1996

The Whole of a Magnificent Planet to Myself

Cathy O'Dowd

*On the morning of 25 May, Ian Woodall and Cathy O'Dowd
reached the highest height, the first South African climbers to do so.
Below, O'Dowd relates the final grind to the summit.*

*Unfortunately, the South African expedition did not escape the
tragedies of 1996. Later in the day of 25 May, a third South
African climber, Bruce Herrod, summitted Everest but died during
the descent.*

I move down the short steep slope to the start of the ridge. I
notice a set of orange oxygen bottles piled by the track. And
something else, a long, blue shape. I realize with shock it is the
body of Rob Hall. But here? From all I remembered of the
events of the storm, I expected him to be lying on the other
side of the South Summit.

But now it is the crossing of the ridge that claims my attention. It is slow, cautious work. The trail runs just to the left of
the knife-edge of the ridge, staying below the cornices that
hang over the Tibetan side, while staying above the unstable
dinner plates of rock a few feet down on the Nepalese side.
The only flat ground is the footprints left by previous climbers. I move up the ridge almost as if I have put on mental
blinkers, seeing only the two footsteps ahead of me. With each
step I sink the shaft of my ice axe into the snow on the uphill
side, using the head of the axe to provide a handhold. It is a
little like walking along an undulating plank. Not particularly
difficult, as long as you ignore the fact that there is

a 2,500-metre drop on one side, and a 3,000-metre drop on the other.

Despite my concentration, other thoughts and memories wander through my head. It is ten years and half a world away from orientation week at Wits University in 1987. I knew then that I hated all physical activity, or what I knew of it in the form of school sport. Nevertheless, I enjoyed the outdoors, although I knew nothing of the sport of climbing. I had spent the week wandering around the university, looking at all the different clubs on offer. I had watched with disbelief the figures in old khaki shorts and shocking pink lycra scaling the library wall, and listened to the pitch from the Mountain Club chairman. I was not convinced, and was more interested in joining the Exploration Society. But on the very last day, with the abandon born of spending my father's money, I decided to join the Mountain Club as well.

Little did I know then where I would be ten years later.

My steady progress along the ridge is broken by the sudden rock wall of the Hillary Step. I stop short, trying to refocus mentally from snow to rock. The first section is relatively easy, involving some cautious scrambling up and round big blocks. Then a careful traverse across loose scree brings me to the foot of an awkward, angled chimney. The floor is unstable rock and snow, the chimney just wide enough to wriggle up with a pack on. I work my way up it, suddenly conscious of the burden of the bulky clothing, the big oxygen set, the enormous boots and crampons. Jammed awkwardly near the top, I contemplate the tangle of ancient fixed rope that hangs down the back of the chimney. The creeper-like mass consists of bits of all sizes and colours, much bleached bone-white from years of extreme weather. Manoeuvring past it without getting it tangled around my rucksack, crampons or ice axe is as much of a challenge as negotiating the wall itself. Finally I grab a huge bundle of it in one hand and pull, wriggle and flop my way on to the summit of the block.

Again, odd memories float through my mind. I remember the first rock climb I ever did, Donderhoek Corner in Upper Tonquani, all of grade 12. A classic chimney thrutch, it was an unprepossessing beginning. The second was Hawk's Eye, a daring 13. Although I coped well with the wall, it took quite some talking to get me to climb over the nose of the Hawk's Eye. I quite enjoyed the climbing, was less impressed by the amount of flaming sambuca being thrown down everyone's throats, and was far from convinced that this was an experience to be repeated. However, I was impressed by a young and handsome blond called Mike Cartwright. And given that the only place he could be found on the weekends was in the kloofs, I decided to give this climbing lark another go.

Once above the Hillary Step the ridge widens slightly, still corniced and very steep on the Tibetan side but slightly gentler on the left, before the steep drop of the South-West Face. I realize with amusement that although the exposure, and the danger, is far greater here than on the slopes lower on the mountain, I feel no fear, only exhilaration. I can see straight down the South-West Face of Everest into the Western Cwm, down to the tiny campsite over 2,000 metres below me, our Camp II. We have come a long way since then, and a longer way still from home.

I've been moving alone along the ridge for some time. Pemba and Ian are out of sight ahead, the other three climbers somewhere behind. Although I mostly concentrate on the few steps in front of me, blocking out the vast empty spaces surrounding the ridge, occasionally I allow myself the luxury of looking out across the myriad of snowy peaks below. With no one else in sight, and no signs of human existence visible below, it is like being the last person alive on earth, having the whole of a magnificent planet to myself.

I feel humbled, aware of how frail and fragile the humans are dotted on the side of this huge edifice of snow and rock. I am also frustrated. The ridge undulates gently. Each crest looks as if it might be the final one, but as I drag my weary body on to the top I find another one slightly higher, slightly further on. The ridge seems to run on interminably in front of me. I feel like the *Flying Dutchman* trying to round the Cape, or as if I might be on a snowy treadmill, a ridge that runs forever with no conclusion, and I am condemned to walk it for eternity.

I've anticipated the false summits, recalling reading about them in Stacey Allison's account of the first American woman's ascent of Everest. I try to suppress all expectations, to deal with the ridge step by step, rather than face the inevitable disappointment expectation of the summit would bring.

My mind wanders once more, seeking escape from the mental boredom of the slow, plodding ascent. I recall my first great pronouncement on my climbing career. It was made halfway up a small, loose and aloe-strewn rock-face in Wilgepoort. I was following the route with a friend, Linda Waldman. I told her that while I liked climbing, I had no interest in learning to lead rock routes. She agreed. Within a few months we were both leading.

My next great pronouncement came after a friend hauled me up a 300-metre rock-face at Blouberg. The first few hours I enjoyed, but then I was ready to go home. Unfortunately we were only halfway up. I announced that I was interested only in walk-ins under half an hour, and climbs of fifty metres or less. Over the next few years I climbed big walls all over the country, from Blouberg, to the Drakensberg, to the Western Cape, and then moved on to 600-metre rock walls in the Alps.

My third great pronouncement was that, although big walls were great, you wouldn't catch me dead mountaineering. Too high, too cold, too dangerous . . . Little did I know.

I move slowly up yet another small rise and on to the top of it. And stop short, aware of two figures and a sudden blaze of colour. Ian and Pemba are seated in the snow with something behind them that to my puzzled gaze looks rather like a ruined tent. After hours in an almost monochrome world of blue sky, white snow and black rock, the medley of red, yellow and green is disconcerting. Then Pemba turns and sees me. A huge grin spreads across his face and I notice his gold tooth glinting in the sunlight. He stands up and begins to wave both arms and his ice axe in the air.

That's it, I think. That is the summit of Everest.

For the second time today I am filled with an incredible sense of excitement. At last I know that not only am I capable of climbing Everest, but that I have actually done it. Only ten more metres. I never imagined it would get to this.

The last slog up the final slope seems interminable. I am very tired, stopping to rest every four or five steps. I clamber slowly towards the dash of colour, which becomes a pile of prayer flags covering a metal tripod.

Ian speaks into the radio: "And then there were three."

Philip's voice comes through in a chatter of excitement.

I sink down on to my knees beside Ian and hug him, barely able to feel the man beneath the piles of clothing we are both wearing. I turn to hug Pemba, acutely conscious of the pleasure of being able to share the moment with friends and teammates. I am glad that I am not here alone.

Everest 1998

Breaking the Ice

Bear Grylls

After surviving the incident in the icefall recounted below, Grylls went on to become – at 23 – the youngest Briton to reach the summit of Everest.

We set off alone. I led the way, feeling still relatively strong. It was wonderful and freeing to be alone here with Mick, climbing together, communicating silently, and working our way up the icefall, where only the Sherpas had been before.

It was good to have that focus of concentration where your mind is uncluttered and thinks only of the job in hand. Our minds felt sharp as we kicked into the ice and secured ourselves to the next rope. The air felt fresh as it filled our lungs. Your body needed all the oxygen it could get from each breath and it seemed to savour the moment as the air rushed in. It felt good.

The route now steepened and a series of ladders strapped together leant against huge forty-feet vertical ice blocks. The overhangs became bigger and more sinister. We were careful to be precise in what we did, and became acutely aware of our surroundings. We didn't talk. At 1.45 p.m. we could go no further. The route ahead had collapsed the night before, and a jumble of vast ice blocks lay strewn across the face. The rope shot vertically down below us, drawn as tight as a cable, as it stretched under the weight of the ice around it. I looked at Mick behind and he pointed at his watch. We were at our time limit and needed to turn around.

I was just ahead, and noticed that I was standing in a particularly vulnerable part of the icefall. I felt suddenly very unsafe and started down towards Mick. Suddenly, 200 metres to my right, I heard a large section of ice break off. The block tumbled, like a dice across a board, down the icefall. I crouched, just staring. As the snow settled behind it, I got to my feet, then hurried my pace down towards Mick. I wanted to get out of here now, I felt too exposed.

The colour of the ice where we were was dark blue, and pinnacles reached over us, 100 feet high. It seemed unstable and flaky, and was beginning to drip from the heat of the sun. It is at this time, in the mid-afternoon, that the icefall is most dangerous, as it melts, and parts begin to collapse.

Racing all in one go under these overhangs that cast menacing shadows was impossible; the body wouldn't allow it. Repeatedly we would be halfway through, then would be forced to stop and recover our breath, still deep within the jaws of the overhang. But there was nothing we could do; the body had to stop and get more oxygen.

Once safely out the other side we would sit and recover and encourage the other to follow quickly. We were new to the icefall and were trying to learn its tricks.

Soon we were out of the nasty section and back among more familiar territory; ahead we could see the plateau where we had left the Sherpas. We passed through the part that they had been repairing. We could be no more than 100 metres from the icefall doctors now. I was looking forward to seeing them, and then getting down. We had been in the ice for almost nine hours now and were tired. Little did I know that the day was far from over.

As I came round the corner of a cornice, I could hear the whispered voices of Nima and Pasang nearby. Energy flooded back and I leapt from ice block to ice block down towards them. Ten yards later I needed to stop and rest; they were close now. I smiled at the sound of their hushed and tentative tones.

I unclipped, and clipped into the next rope down, and leant against the ice, recovering. Suddenly the ground just opened up beneath me.

The ice cracked for that transient second, then just collapsed. My legs buckled beneath me, and I was falling. I tumbled down, bouncing against the grey walls of the crevasse that before had been hidden beneath a thin veneer of ice.

The tips of my crampons caught the edge of the crevasse walls and the force threw me across to the other side, smashing my shoulder and arm against the ice. I carried on falling, then suddenly was jerked to a violent halt, as the rope held me firm. The falling ice crashed into my skull, jerking my neck backwards. I lost consciousness for a precious few seconds. I came to, to see the ice falling away below me into the darkness, as my body gently swung round on the end of the rope. It was eerily silent.

Adrenalin soared round my body, and I shook in waves of convulsions. I screamed, but can't remember what. My voice echoed round the walls. I looked up to the ray of light above, then down to the abyss below. Panic overwhelmed me and I clutched frantically for the walls. They were glassy smooth. I swung my ice axe at it madly, but it wouldn't hold, and my crampons just scraped along the ice. I had nothing to lean against, no momentum to be able to kick them in. Instead the flimsy stabs with my feet hardly even brushed the surface of the ice. I clutched in desperation to the rope above me, and looked up. "Hold, damn you. Hold."

I grabbed a spare jumar device from my harness. (This is a climbing tool that allows you to ascend a rope but won't allow you to slip down.) I slapped it on to the rope as added security. Suddenly I felt strong pulls tugging on the rope above. They wouldn't be able to pull me out without my help. I knew I had to get out of here fast. The rope wasn't designed for an impact fall like this. It was a miracle that it had held at all, and I knew it could break at any point. The pulls on the rope above gave me the momentum I needed to kick into the walls with my crampons. This time they bit into the ice firmly.

Up I pulled, kicking into the walls, a few feet higher every time. I scrambled up, helped by the momentum from the rope. Near the lip, I managed to smack my axe into the ice and pull myself over. Strong arms grabbed my windsuit and hauled me with great power from the clutches of the crevasse. They dragged me to the side, out of danger, and we all collapsed in a heaving mess. I lay with my face pressed into the snow, eyes closed, and shook with fear.

"Don't Leave Me Here To Die"

Cathy O'Dowd

During a failed 1998 push on the North Face Cathy O'Dowd (see the "Everest 1996" section) came across Francys Arsentiev, a dying American climber.

I stared at the body, blinking in disbelief. We were in the shadow of the first step, so the light was dull. The body lay about ten metres from where I stood and was angled away from me. It jerked – a horrible movement, like a puppet being pulled savagely by its strings.

We had been on a well-organised and, so far, successful trail towards the summit of Everest, worrying only about ourselves. Now a stranger lay across our path, moaning. Lhakpa shouted down at me and waved me to move on, to follow him up onto the Step. I looked back at the raggedly jerking figure.

Each team or solo climber did, or should, arrive at the mountain self-sufficient. Anyone who turned up assuming they could borrow food, clothing or tentage would receive short shrift. Similarly, you could not climb yourself to a standstill then expect other teams to risk their lives to save you.

Saving someone was not straightforward. There was no emergency number to call, no mountain rescue to whom the problem could be handed over. We would not be able to walk away, feeling we had done our civic duty and that "the experts" were now in charge. Anyone who becomes immobile on a mountain as large and remote as Everest is probably going to die. On this side of the mountain, we would have to get the victim all the way back to base camp before we could contemplate trying to find a helicopter. If they had to be carried, that would require a number of teams, dozens of people and at least three days climbing.

Whoever it was on the rocks in front of me was so badly incapacitated that they had spent the night out on the mountain rather than crawl down. Life lay in keeping moving, as that generated body heat and, with every metre of descent, moved you into thicker air. I suspected we had virtually no chance of saving this climber.

We stood to throw away an entire expedition: the money, the time, the thousands of vertical feet of physical and mental effort. We had sponsors who expected us to go for the summit. We had personal ambitions that pointed in the same direction. We were only 240 vertical metres from the top, only four or five hours in climbing time. We were so close to fulfilling everything we had set out to do.

Should we throw it all away for some rescue attempt that was doomed? The body was lying in a ghastly inverted V. It looked as if the climber's spine might be broken. If they couldn't walk they were probably condemned. Why waste time, stand around getting cold and demoralised, when the attempt was futile? Why not just turn away and climb on? This all ran through my head in the space of a few seconds. But all the debates, the issues, the logical analysis were useless. I simply could not do it. I could not put the summit of a mountain ahead of a human life. I would not want to live with myself if I could. However hopeless this person's situation might be, I had to try. I walked back to Ian, who was standing with Jangbu, watching Lhakpa climbing the First Step.

"That body's alive. I'm going to have a look." It took him a moment to understand what I was talking about. "We can't just leave," I insisted. He nodded and I stepped down from the trail and walked across the loose shale towards the body. I thought it might be one of the Russian team. The person was lying with their harness clipped to a line of fixed rope, stomach uppermost, head and legs dangling down on either side. I knelt down cautiously next to the body and saw it was a woman.

"Don't leave me," she said. Her skin was milky white, and totally smooth. It was a sign of severe frostbite and it made her look like a porcelain doll. Her eyes stared up at me, unfocusing, pupils huge dark voids. "Don't leave me," she murmured again.

I felt sick. With her long, dark hair, she looked like me. For a shocked second, I felt as if I was glimpsing a possible future for myself. The fact that she was conscious both encouraged and appalled me. It might be possible to save her – or we might yet have to leave her.

"I need to fetch the rest of my team," I said to her. "We have several people here. We will try and help you. I will come back, I promise."

"Why are you doing this to me?" she asked.

Ian and Jangbu came back with me. Lhakpa, Pemba and Ci Luo, seeing the turn events had taken, began to descend towards us. The woman had no visible trauma injuries and her bizarre position turned out to be the result of complete muscular limpness. She was as helpless as a rag doll. It looked as if someone had clipped her harness to the end of a fixed rope, presumably so she would not slip down the slope, and had then left her to go for help. Next to her was an orange bottle of oxygen, of Russian make, and a mask. The bottle was empty.

While Ian and Jangbu pulled her straight, I collected her down gloves, which had been thrown to one side. Her jacket was over her shoulders but her arms were not in the sleeves. Our bodies can react bizarrely to trauma. A fairly common occurrence with severe hypothermia is a sensation of extreme warmth. The victim may start tearing off clothing; it looked as if she had done this.

The men tried to replace her clothing. Her hands were swollen masses, her arms limp. She had no motor control. As Ian tried to get her arms into her sleeves, she gave no resistance and no assistance. Jangbu was trying to give her hot juice from his Thermos. Then they each grabbed her under one arm and tried to pull her into a sitting position against a boulder. She was a dead weight. The two strong men took several heaves to get her sitting, and then both doubled over, gasping for breath. It showed us what it would take to try to actually carry her anywhere, let alone carry her or drag her for days down the mountain.

We had no capacity for giving her oxygen. Her mask would

not fit our bottles. We carried spare bottles but no spare masks. For the oxygen to have any effect, she would have to be put on high flow, and stay on for hours. A few whiffs would have no effect. One of us would have to go off oxygen permanently to give her a mask, which would exhaust our spare supplies very quickly. Until we established that we had a real chance of saving her, the risk was too great.

We had no means of communication with the outside world. Pemba tried calling base camp, but their set was not switched on.

"I am an American. I am an American," the climber suddenly said.

American? But the American team was below us, a full day behind. My mind wandered back to what I had seen the day before; two tiny figures at the foot of the First Step, one still, one moving around.

Could she be Fran, the bubbly American woman who had sat in our ABC kitchen tent one night, passing the hours while she waited for her husband, the Russian climber, Serguei? That might make sense. She and Serguei were climbing as a twosome. They had no Sherpas, no oxygen. They would not be in radio contact with others on the mountain. But that did not explain how she came to have an oxygen bottle lying next to her. Nor did it explain where he had gone. Three Uzbek climbers were approaching.

"Will you help us?" I asked. "This woman is dying. We might be able to carry her down. Would you help?"

The leader of the three looked down at me reluctantly. "We tried to help yesterday. We left her with oxygen. She is too far gone to help."

He spoke into his radio, presumably talking to his base camp. However, they did stay, watching Ian and Jangbu to see what decision they took. Ian had the climber by both shoulders and was speaking directly at her, his face only inches from hers. "You have to help us. If you can help us, we can try and move you down the mountain. If you don't you are going to die." He was staring into her face, looking for some reaction. There was nothing. She knew we were there, but she was not mentally coherent. It was difficult to know what was left in her head.

I noticed her other crampon a few feet below us and took a tentative step down the slope to retrieve it, but immediately thought better of it. The slope was covered in loose rock shards, like a million smashed dinner plates. They were slipping away under my feet, rolling down the slope towards the Rongbuk Glacier 4,300 metres below us. It was like trying to move across ball-bearings. I could see how a climber, having lost their balance, would not be able to stop the downward momentum. Had that happened to Serguei?

Ian and Jangbu had been trying to pull the woman into an upright position. Ian thought that if she could take some of her weight on her feet, even if she could not actually walk, it might be possible to move her down the mountain with a climber at each shoulder. However, her legs simply crumpled under her weight, as useless as strands of spaghetti.

We had been with Fran for nearly an hour, standing still in temperatures of around -30 °C. Perched perilously on the steep, unstable slope, I could not even stamp my feet for warmth. I was beginning to feel profoundly cold. My fingers were almost totally numb. I had full-body shivers and my teeth were chattering behind my oxygen mask.

The decision to leave Fran came upon us without much discussion. The Uzbek climbers and Lhakpa had long been of that opinion. What hope I had faded in the face of her incoherence, her physical incapacity. Now Ian and Jangbu straightened up and turned away. She had stopped talking and seemed to have sunk into unconsciousness. The thought of going on was intolerable. I had lost the will to reach the summit. Besides the physical drain of the cold, I was emotionally shattered. I had never encountered anything like this. I had passed bodies, I had had friends not come back, but I had never watched anyone die. Nor had I had to decide to leave them.

It was harder for me because she was female. It is not that I thought women immune to the risk, but it was such a male-dominated environment. Everywhere you turned, everyone you talked to was male. I climb because I enjoy it. I climb for the pleasure of the activity, of the surroundings. There was no pleasure left. I wanted to be down, to be off the mountain, to have both feet on flat ground.

After abandoning that attempt, O'Dowd went on, in 1999, to become the first woman to reach the summit from both south and north. Francys (Fran) Arsentiev died after O'Dowd's group left her. It later emerged that Fran had made it to the top, becoming the first American woman to do so without oxygen. Her husband Serguei also died on the mountain.

Everest 1999

We Had Found George Mallory

Conrad Anker

When Mallory and Irvine quit their tent on 8 June 1924 for Everest's summit they climbed into myth. No mystery has possessed mountaineering more than that concerning their disappearance and the tantalizing possibility that they reached the top. In 1999 a Mallory and Irvine research expedition set forth to Everest to discover the climbers' fate. Their primary search area was high on the North Face where in 1975 a Chinese climber, Wang Hong-bao, had seen what he thought was the body of an Englishman. The American high-altitude climber Conrad Anker was one of the searchers for Mallory and Irvine.

I had just sat down to take off my crampons, because the traverse across the rock band ahead would be easier without them. I drank some fluid – a carbohydrate drink I keep in my water bottle – and sucked a cough drop. At that altitude, it's essential to keep your throat lubricated.

I looked out over this vast expanse. To the south and west, I could see into Nepal, with jagged peaks ranging toward the horizon. In front of me on the north stretched the great Tibetan plateau, brown and corrugated as it dwindled into the distance. The wind was picking up, and small clouds were forming below, on the lee side of some of the smaller peaks.

All of a sudden, a strong feeling came over me that something was going to happen. Something good. I usually feel content when the climb I'm on is going well, but this was different. I felt positive, happy. I was in a good place.

It was 11:45 a.m. on 1 May. We were just below 27,000 feet on the North Face of Mount Everest. The other four guys were fanned out above me and to the east. They were in sight, but too far away to holler to. We had to use our radios to communicate.

I attached my crampons to my pack, stood up, put the pack on, and started hiking up a small corner. Then, to my left, out of the corner of my eye, I caught a glimpse of a piece of blue and yellow fabric flapping in the wind, tucked behind a boulder. I thought, I'd better go look at this. Anything that wasn't part of the natural landscape was worth looking at.

When I got to the site, I could see that the fabric was probably a piece of tent that had been ripped loose by the wind and blown down here, where it came to rest in the hollow behind the boulder. It was modern stuff, nylon. I wasn't surprised – there are a lot of abandoned tents on Everest, and the wind just shreds them.

But as I stood there, I carefully scanned the mountain right and left. I was wearing my prescription dark glasses, so I could see really well. As I scanned right, I saw a patch of white, about a hundred feet away. I knew at once there was something unusual about it, because of the colour. It wasn't the gleaming white of snow reflecting the sun. It wasn't the white of the chunks of quartzite and calcite that crop up here and there on the north side of Everest. It had a kind of matte look – a light-absorbing quality, like marble.

I walked closer. I immediately saw a bare foot, sticking into the air, heel up, toes pointed downward. At that moment, I knew I had found a human body.

Then, when I got even closer, I could see from the tattered clothing that this wasn't the body of a modern climber. This was somebody very old.

It didn't really sink in at first. It was as if everything was in slow motion. *Is this a dream?* I wondered. *Am I really here?* But I also thought, *This is what we came here to do. This is who we're looking for. This is Sandy Irvine.*

We'd agreed beforehand on a series of coded messages for the search. Everybody on the mountain could listen in on our radio conversations. If we found something, we didn't want some other expedition breaking the news to the world.

"Boulder" was the code word for "body". So I sat down on my pack, got out my radio, and broadcast a message: "Last time I went bouldering in my hobnails, I fell off." It was the first thing that came to mind. I just threw in "hobnails", because an old hobnailed boot – the kind that went out of style way back in the 1940s – was still laced onto the man's right foot. That was another reason I knew he was very old.

We all had our radios stuffed inside our down suits, so it wasn't easy to hear them. Of the other four guys out searching, only Jake Norton caught any part of my message, and all he heard was "hobnails". I could see him, some fifty yards above me and a ways to the east. Jake sat down, ripped out his radio, and broadcast back, "What was that, Conrad?"

"Come on down," I answered. He was looking at me now, so I started waving the ski stick I always carry at altitude. "Let's get together for Snickers and tea."

Jake knew I'd found something important, but the other three were still oblivious. He tried to wave and yell and get their attention, but it wasn't working. At 27,000 feet, because of oxygen deprivation, you retreat into a kind of personal shell; the rest of the world doesn't seem quite real. So I got back on the radio and put some urgency into my third message: "I'm calling a mandatory group meeting right now!"

Where we were searching was fairly tricky terrain, downsloping shale slabs, some of them covered with a dusting of snow. If you fell in the wrong place, you'd go all the way, 7,000 feet to the Rongbuk Glacier. So it took the other guys a little while to work their way down and over to me.

I rooted through my pack to get out my camera. That morning, at Camp V, I thought I'd stuck it in my pack, but I had two nearly identical stuff sacks, and it turns out I'd grabbed my radio batteries instead. I realized I'd forgotten my camera. I thought, Oh, well, if I had had the camera, I might not have found the body. That's just the way things work.

When I told a friend about this, he asked if I'd read Faulkner's novella *The Bear*. I hadn't. On reading that story, I saw the analogy. The best hunters in the deep Mississippi woods can't even catch a glimpse of Old Ben, the huge, half-mythic bear that has ravaged their livestock for years. It's only when Ike

McCaslin gives up everything he's relied on – lays down not only his rifle, but his compass and watch – that, lost in the forest, he's graced with the sudden presence of Old Ben in a clearing: "It did not emerge, appear: it was just there, immobile, fixed in the green and windless noon's hot dappling."

As I sat on my pack waiting for the others, a feeling of awe and respect for the dead man sprawled in front of me started to fill me. He lay face down, head uphill, frozen into the slope. A tuft of hair stuck out from the leather pilot's cap he had on his head. His arms were raised, and his fingers were planted in the scree, as if he'd tried to self-arrest with them. It seemed likely that he was still alive when he had come to rest in this position. There were no gloves on his hands; later I'd think long and hard about the implications of that fact. I took off my own gloves to compare my hands to his. I've got short, thick fingers; his were long and thin, and deeply tanned, probably from the weeks of having walked the track all the way from Darjeeling over the crest of the Himalayas to the North Face of Everest.

The winds of the decades had torn most of the clothing away from his back and lower torso. He was naturally mummified – that patch of alabaster I'd spotted from a hundred feet away was the bare, perfectly preserved skin of his back. What was incredible was that I could still see the powerful, well-defined muscles in his shoulders and back, and the blue discoloration of bruises.

Around his shoulders and upper arms, the remnants of seven or eight layers of clothing still covered him – shirts and sweaters and jackets made of wool, cotton, and silk. There was a white, braided cotton rope tied to his waist, about three-eighths of an inch in diameter – many times weaker than any rope we'd use today. The rope was tangled around his left shoulder. About ten feet from his waist, I could see the frayed end where the rope had broken. So I knew at once that he'd been tied to his partner, and that he'd taken a long fall. The rope had either broken in the fall, or when his partner tried to belay him over a rock edge.

The right elbow looked as if it was dislocated or broken. It lay embedded in the scree, bent in an unnatural position. The right scapula was a little disfigured. And above his waist on a right rib, I could see the blue contusion from an upward pull of the rope as it took the shock of the fall.

His right leg was badly broken, both tibia and fibula. With the boot still on, the leg lay at a grotesque angle. They weren't compound fractures – the bones hadn't broken the skin – but they were very bad breaks. My conclusion was that in the fall, the right side of the man's body had taken the worst of the impact. It looked as though perhaps in his last moments, the man had laid his good left leg over his broken right, as if to protect it from further harm. The left boot may have been whipped off in the fall, or it may have eroded and fallen apart. Only the tongue of the boot was present, pinched between the bare toes of his left foot and the heel of his right boot.

Goraks – the big black ravens that haunt the high Himalaya – had pecked away at the right buttock and gouged out a pretty extensive hole, big enough for a gorak to enter. From that orifice, they had eaten out most of the internal organs, simply hollowed out the body.

The muscles of the left lower leg and the thighs had become stringy and desiccated. It's what happens, apparently, to muscles exposed for seventy-five years. The skin had split and opened up, but for some reason the goraks hadn't eaten it.

After fifteen or twenty minutes, Jake Norton arrived. Then the others, one by one: first Tap Richards, then Andy Politz, then Dave Hahn. They didn't say much: just, "Wow, good job, Conrad," or, "This has to be Sandy Irvine." Later Dave said, "I started blinking in awe," and Tap remembered, "I was pretty blown away. It was obviously a body, but it looked like a Greek or Roman marble statue."

The guys took photos, shot some video, and discussed the nuances of the scene. There seemed to be a kind of taboo about touching him. Probably half an hour passed before we got up the nerve to touch him. But we had agreed that if we found Mallory or Irvine, we would perform as professional an excavation as we could under the circumstances, to see if what we found might cast any light on the mystery of their fate. We had even received permission to take a small DNA sample.

Tap and Jake did most of the excavating work. We'd planned
to cut small squares out of the clothing to take down to Base
Camp and analyze. Almost at once, on the collar of one of the
shirts, Jake found a name tag. It read, "G. Mallory". Jake
looked at us and said, "That's weird. Why would Irvine be
wearing Mallory's shirt?"

We didn't have all that much time to work. We'd agreed on a
tentative turnaround hour of 2:00 p.m., to get back to Camp V
while it was still daylight, and by the time we started excavating, it was past noon. There were clouds below us, but only a
slight wind. As one can imagine, this was hard work at 26,700
feet (the altitude of the body, as I later calculated it). We had
taken off our oxygen gear, because it was just too cumbersome
to dig with it on.

Because the body was frozen into the scree, we had to chip
away at the surrounding ice and rock with our ice axes. It took
some vigorous swings even to dislodge little chunks, the ice
was so dense. We were all experienced climbers, we were used
to swinging tools, so we did the chipping pretty efficiently;
only once did a pick glance off a rock and impale the man's
arm. As we got closer to the body, we put down our axes and
started chipping with our pocketknives.

We were so sure this was Sandy Irvine that Jake actually sat
down, took a smooth piece of shale in his lap and started to
scratch out a tombstone with Irvine's name and dates, 1902–
1924. But then we found the "G. Mallory" tag on the collar,
and shortly after, Tap found another one on a seam under the
arm. It read, "G. Leigh Mallory." We just stared at each other,
stunned, as we realized this wasn't Irvine. We had found
George Mallory.

As we excavated, Tap chipped away on his left side, Jake on
his right. I did mostly lifting and prying. Dave and Andy took
pictures and shot video.

It was good fortune that George was lying on his stomach,
because most of the stuff you carry when you climb is in the
front pockets, so it had been protected by his body for seventy-
five years. It may seem funny, or even pretentious, but we
referred to him as "George", not as "Mallory". All through the

weeks before, we'd talked about Mallory and Irvine so much that it was as if we knew them, like old friends; they had become George and Sandy.

We left George's face where it was, frozen into the scree, but once I could lift the lower part of his body, Tap and Jake could reach underneath him and go through the pockets. The body was like a frozen log. When I lifted it, it made that same creaky noise as when you pull up a log that's been on the ground for years.

It was disconcerting to look into the hole in the right buttock that the goraks had chewed. His body had been hollowed out, almost like a pumpkin. You could see the remains of seeds and some other food – very possibly Mallory's last meal.

We didn't go near George's head. We moved the loose rock away from it, but we didn't try to dig it out. I think that was a sort of unspoken agreement, and at the time, none of us wanted to look at his face.

Of course we were most excited about the possibility of finding the camera. Jake even thought for a minute he'd found it. George had a small bag that was lodged under his right biceps. Jake reached in there, squeezed the bag and felt a small, square object, just about the right size. We finally had to cut the bag to get the object out, and when we did, we found it wasn't the camera after all, it was a tin of beef lozenges!

The clincher that it was Mallory came when Jake pulled out a neatly folded, new-looking silk handkerchief in which several letters had been carefully wrapped. They were addressed to Mallory. On the envelope of one of them, for instance, we read, "George Leigh Mallory Esq., c/o British Trade Agent, Yalung Tibet."

Besides the letters, we found a few penciled notes in other pockets. As we found out later, they were all about logistics, about bringing so many loads to Camp VI, and so on. We read them carefully, hoping Mallory might have jotted down a note about reaching the summit or turning back, but there was nothing of the sort.

One by one, Jake and Tap produced what we started calling "the artifacts". It seemed an odd collection of items to carry to the summit of Everest. There was a small penknife; a tiny pencil, about two and a half inches long, onto which some kind of mint cake had congealed (we could still smell the mint); a needle and thread; a small pair of scissors with a file built into one blade; a second handkerchief, well used (the one he blew his nose on), woven in a red and yellow floral pattern on a blue background, with the monogram G.L.M. in yellow; a box of special matches, Swan Vestas, with extra phosphorus on the tips; a little piece of leather with a hose clamp on it that might have been a mouthpiece for the oxygen apparatus; a tube of zinc oxide, rolled partway up; a spare pair of fingerless mittens that looked like they hadn't been used.

Two other artifacts seemed particularly intriguing. Jake found a smashed altimeter in one pocket. The hand was missing from the dial, but you could see that the instrument had been specially calibrated for Everest, with a range from 20,000 feet to 30,000 feet. Inscribed on the back, in fine script, was "M.E.E. II" – for Mount Everest Expedition II. And in the vest pocket, we found a pair of goggles. The frames were bent, but the green glass was unbroken. It was Andy who came up with the possible significance of the goggles being in the pocket. To him, it argued that George had fallen after dusk. If it had been in the daytime, he would have been wearing the goggles, even on rock. He'd just had a vivid lesson in the consequences of taking them off during the day, when Teddy Norton got a terrible attack of snow blindness the night after his summit push on 4 June.

As we removed each artifact, we put it carefully in a Ziploc bag. Andy volunteered to carry the objects down to Camp V. To some people, it may seem that taking George's belongings with us was a violation. We even had a certain sense that we were disturbing the dead – I think that's why we had hesitated to begin the excavation. But this was the explicit purpose of the expedition: to find Mallory and Irvine and to retrieve the artifacts and try to solve the mystery of what had happened on 8 June, 1924. I think we did the right thing.

As interesting as what we found was what we didn't find. George had no backpack on, nor any trace of the frame that held the twin oxygen bottles. His only carrying sack was the little bag we found under his right biceps. He didn't have any water bottle, or Thermos flask, which was what they used in '24. He didn't have a flashlight, because he'd forgotten to take it with him. We know this not from Odell, but from the 1933 party, who found the flashlight in the tent at the 1924 Camp VI.

And we didn't find the camera. That was the great disappointment.

It was getting late – we'd already well overstayed our 2:00 p.m. turnaround. The last thing we gathered was the DNA sample, to analyse for absolute proof of the identity of the man we'd found. Simonson had received approval for this procedure beforehand from John Mallory, George's only son, who's seventy-nine and living in South Africa. I had agreed to do this job.

I cut an inch-and-a-half-square patch of skin off the right forearm. It wasn't easy. I had to use the serrated blade on Dave's utility knife. Cutting George's skin was like cutting saddle leather, cured and hard.

Since the expedition, I've often wondered whether taking the tissue was a sacrilegious act. In Base Camp, I had volunteered for the task. On the mountain, I had no time to reflect whether or not this was the right thing to do.

We wanted to bury George, or at least to cover him up. There were rocks lying around, but not a lot that weren't frozen in place. We formed a kind of bucket brigade, passing rocks down to the site.

Then Andy read, as a prayer of committal, Psalm 103: "As for man, his days are as grass: as a flower of the field, so he flourisheth. /For the wind passeth over it, and it is gone . . ."

We finally left at 4:00 p.m. I lingered a bit after the other four. The last thing I did was to leave a small Butterfinger candy bar in the rocks nearby, like a Buddhist offering. I said a sort of prayer for him, several times over.

Everest 2014

The Blackest Day

Jon Reiter

Just after 7 a.m. local time on 18 April 2014 an overhanging bulge of ice on Everest's West Shoulder dislocated and caused an avalanche that killed sixteen Nepali guides. It was the worst climbing accident in the history of Everest. Jon Reiter, a 49-year-old climber from California, was on the mountain when the ice hit. Below are his blogs about the tragedy.

Friday, 18 April 2014

Tragedy on the mountain

As some of you have heard by now, there was a large avalanche in the icefall today. It came down off the left shoulder of Everest just as we were entering the "football" field, which is just below camp one. Marcus and I were each pushed down behind large blocks of ice by our Sherpas, which shielded us from the brunt. These guys are truly amazing! They saved our lives! We are shaken but OK. Unfortunately there are some still up there who were not so lucky today. As I write this I feel emotional and don't know what to say. One thought is that we were SO lucky! But the overwhelming feelings are for the poor families of the people that didn't make it. I'm so near to this situation right now that I can't think straight. Of course we are all asking ourselves that serious question of "why are we here?" I don't want to try to answer that question in this state of mind but it is the big question floating over our whole camp today.

I'll close with these thoughts; I feel so grateful! I do know this is part of climbing these big mountains and I'm willing to accept the risk. But I do love and appreciate my family and friends more than this adventure. I have a wonderful life and I'm SO lucky today. If I didn't have all of you in my life none of this would matter. I just wanted you all to know what happened and that I'm OK. Thank you for being part of my life.

As a buddy of mine reminded me in times like this. "Stay calm, say a prayer, move forward."

Peace and Love, Jon

Saturday, 19 April 2014

We're all going to need a few days to figure things out

This picture was taken today as my friend Dawa Sherpa was leaving base camp. Dawa is the man who was by my side when the avalanche struck. He's the guy who spent all day yesterday digging his friends and neighbors out of the snow and sending their limp bodies hanging on a cable from a helicopter down to base camp. After a long sixteen agonizing hours he showed up at my tent, before going to his own, to make sure I was OK. He's an amazing man and I have great respect for him. He's a perfect example of the selfless Sherpa people that we entrust with our lives while on the mountain and who we quickly learn to call our friends.

The Sherpa community here in Base Camp is naturally quite shaken by this event and most of them have decided to step back from this expedition for a few days, trek home to their villages and reassess the situation with their families.

Unfortunately the death toll is still climbing. We have recovered sixteen lost souls as of an hour ago. We're hoping to locate two more of the missing today and get them back down here to BC, one way or another. This scene is a lot for us western climbers to take in so I can't imagine what our Sherpa partners are really feeling and thinking as we all witness the worst disaster in Everest history happening in front of our eyes.

We've been getting a few questions and hearing a few comments that I'd like to try to address:

- This accident was just that – an accident; an act of nature where we humans happen to be in the way. It was not caused by "overcrowding". Matter of fact, there were only about forty of us in the entire icefall and we were spread out. There was no one waiting for others in order to move up and no congestion anywhere in the icefall. It appeared to be perfect climbing conditions right up until the moment the thunder struck.
- The avalanche took place just below camp 1 at about 19,000 ft and the time was approximately 6.45 a.m.
- The Sherpas that were lost were carrying loads to support the upper camps. The fixed lines and ladders through the icefall were already in place. There were very few western climbers in the area and all of us had our climbing Sherpas by our sides and they all survived.
- The trash scene on Mt Everest is not what it used to be. Through the great efforts of many organizations and individuals this mountain has been cleaned up and looks wonderful. All too often we hear stories about the abuse of nature but we rarely hear when people have gone to great lengths to reverse the damage. Everest is one of those stories. Excessive trash did not cause this to happen. There is absolutely no garbage that I saw anywhere in the icefall. Actually we should all be proud of how good this place really looks. This was a random act of nature.

This is a tough time for everyone here on the mountain but accidents, and even death, are part of the deal. If climbing Everest were easy and risk-free, I suspect we'd all take a hike to the top of the world. The price that has been paid over the last twenty-four hours is a large price indeed. I guess the climbing Sherpas as well as all of us western climbers need a few moments or days to re-evaluate what's worth what in this life.

Early this morning I read a comment written about me where the author said, "I hope he finds what he's looking for up there." I appreciated that notion because it got me to thinking about what am I looking for, and I think I have found it whether I see the summit of Everest or not. I'm looking for an adventurous life. I want to see the whole world and all of its people. I want to lay in my deathbed and know that I did and saw all that I wanted to in the time I spent spinning through space on this ball of mud. I want to know that I lived fully! So far in this life the things that I regret the most are the things I didn't do; the things I didn't have time for; the situations that scared me too much. I want to push myself to do and see until I can't anymore. I want to inspire my two boys to aim high, to take from this world and give to mankind more than they can imagine now. I hope I have a lot of life left to live and I hope I keep finding what I'm looking for. I'm glad my friend brought this topic up because I needed to remember today just why I'm here.

I'm so flattered that so many of you are following this adventure. It's awesome that I get to follow my dreams and I remember every day that all of this would be hollow and meaningless without all of you being part of my life.

Please send positive thoughts or prayers to the families of our fallen Sherpa brothers.

Peace – Jon

Monday, 21 April 2014

Time to sit patiently and see what life brings us

Just a note to summarize the last few days. Our Sherpa friends have decided to use this tragedy to further their cause with the Nepal government. All of the climbing Sherpas (as opposed to the Sherpas that help us establish and maintain base camp) have left the mountain and have stated that they will not return until their requests are met by the Nepalese government. What they're asking for is certainly deserved and we support their cause 100 per cent. They simply want the families of the deceased to be taken care of as well as assurances that they themselves and their families will be taken care of should they be hurt or killed while climbing Everest. There are other requests on their list (fifteen in all) but this is the general idea.

As I mentioned we feel that most of what they're asking for is valid and overdue. From what we understand 10 per cent of Nepal's GDP is based on Everest revenue. It may be true that we climbers have substantially increased the quality of life here in the Khumbu Valley with all the money that's spent here climbing this mountain and trekking about but we hope that the government remembers that the climbing Sherpas are the ones putting their lives on the line, right alongside us, on a daily basis. We cannot climb this mountain without them by our sides just as they were not able to climb it without our logistics and resources; we make a perfect and inseparable team. From the very beginning (1953) until today, Everest is climbed not by individuals but by partnerships.

There have been some horribly misinformed comments made lately about the relationship between the Sherpa people and western climbers. As I mentioned, both parties consider the other as equal partners in this quest. We take care of each other twenty-four hours a day. When the avalanche hit, it was actually western climbers (many of whom were actually from our party) who spent the day, on the scene, treating the wounded and extracting the dead. We did not run from the scene. As a matter of fact, our western guides from camp one and from the "football" field rushed towards the debris into the danger and were some of the first on the scene. We have several MDs as clients on our climbing team and some of these docs spent their entire day volunteering their time down at BC medical treating the wounded and pronouncing the unfortunate dead. I write all of this to clear the air of the misinformed nonsense about our relationship with our Sherpa partners. We and the Sherpa people are a team of equals and there were many tears spilled and stomachs turned as we brought our friends down one by one.

We don't know how long it'll take this government to respond to the Sherpas' requests and we have limited time to move up this mountain. Several teams have already thrown in the towel and are headed downhill out of BC now. As for Marcus and me, we've decided to give it our all. We came here to climb E and we'll wait here patiently until our expedition leader tells us we can go up or we must go down. I think we're ready to climb this one. I think the weather is looking better by the day. The mountain conditions are certainly acceptable and we have the absolute best team (IMG) behind us.

Avalanches happen in the mountains. As we lay in our tents we hear them crash down around us several times every day. Unfortunately, this is part of the risk; part of the adventure that we all signed up for. If the government and the Sherpas come to an agreement soon, Marcus and I will continue trudging uphill until we can go no further. If they decide to not give us that opportunity this year, we'll go home early, hug and kiss our loved ones and know that we've been lucky to have had the opportunity to spend time in these mountains and share many wonderful times in the Khumbu Valley with our mountain-loving Sherpa brothers.

Jon

Friday, 25 April 2014

A final thought or two as we prepare to come home

Marcus and I are headed home. This trip may not have seen us on top of Everest but it has provided more life experience than I had ever expected or bargained for. What a trip!

After getting back to Kathmandu and seeing all the press, I can't help but to step back from it and think "I just wanted to come climb a mountain." But as we all now know, Marcus's and my climb has instead become a pawn in a much bigger story.

The loss of sixteen Sherpas' lives, watching their bodies be brought down one by one and the near miss for Marcus and myself, has together somehow changed mountaineering's position on my list of life's priorities.

I've enjoyed a great decade of climbing the world's highest peaks and I've certainly enjoyed sharing these times with all of you back home. However, I think it's time for this chapter of my life to come to an end. It's nice that I have this option, the choice to decide to end this chapter and move on to the next life experience; to spend the next six years participating in my boy's life on a day-to-day basis before he leaves for college; for sixteen men on Everest they'll never get that choice.

We've all heard about these life-illuminating events and we've all surely experienced something that has set us back on our heels and made us re-evaluate what means what; this expedition has done just that for me. I feel so lucky to be headed home; to get to be there for my boy as he grows; another shot at living a full life (I may have used up all of my "get out of jail free" cards at this point:-) and a chance to appreciate all my friends and family once again.

I'd also like to say thank you to all of you who have taken the time to send thoughtful and appreciated notes offering support for the disappointment that Marcus and I must feel. We have read each and every one of them and they've meant more to us than you know. It's true that missing the summit of Everest is a great disappointment but what we have witnessed and been a part of has impacted us much more than the summit ever could.

Life is a great and unpredictable journey. We each make of it whatever we choose. I think that if we want to focus on the worst, on the negative, surely that's exactly what we'll find and what life will deliver. If we decide to do the best we can, to try to see the best in others and to remember that we only have so many days on this planet to practice this . . . We'll each do OK.

Thank you all for participating in this adventure with Marcus and me. With each passing year and adventure, it seems to become clearer and clearer to me how simple life really is. As someone once said, we just need to watch our words around others and our thoughts when we're alone . . . Life is simply a reflection of the thoughts we choose to think . . .

Today I choose to think about all the wonderful friends and family that share my life. I'm a lucky guy . . .

Enjoy your journey! JR

Envoi

A Prayer for Everest

Wilfred Noyce

Written before the Mountain, 1953

That I may endure,
And love of friends confirm me;
That I lend my ear
Kindest to those who vex me;
That I may be strong,
My will guide the faint footsteps;
That heart and lung
May learn, rhythm is conquest;
That in the storm
My hand may stretch to help,
Not cringe in the glove to warm;
That courage of mine
Bring to friends courage too,
As I am brought by them;
That in the lottery
(My last, my worthiest prayer)
No envy bleed,
When, as I know my heart,
Others succeed.
Here be content, the thought:
I have done my part.

From *South Col*, Wilfred Noyce, 1954

Appendix I:

Climbing Everest – Facts and Statistics

The First Ascent:
29 May 1953, by Sir Edmund Hillary, NZ, and Tenzing Norgay, Nepal, via South Col

The First Ascent Without Oxygen:
8 May 1978, Reinhold Messner, Italy, and Peter Habeler, Austria, via South-East Ridge

The First Solo Ascent:
29 August 1980, Reinhold Messner, Italy, via North Col

The First Ascent by a Woman:
16 May 1975, Junko Tabei, Japan, via South Col

The First Winter Ascent:
17 February 1980, Leszek Cichy and Krzysztof Wielicki, Poland, via South Col

The First Ascent of the North Ridge:
25 May 1960, Wang Fu-zhou and Chu Yin-hua, China

The First Ascent of the West Ridge:
22 May 1963, Willi Unsoeld and Tom Hornbein, USA

The First Ascent of the South-West Face:
24 September 1975, Dougal Haston and Doug Scott, UK

The First Ascent of the East Face:
8 September 1983, Lou Reichardt, Carlos Buhler and Kim Momb, USA

The Fastest Ascent:
21 May 2004, Pem Darjee, Nepal, 8 hours and 10 minutes (from Everest South Base Camp, with supplemental oxygen)

The Oldest Summiteer:
23 May 2013, Yuichiro Miura, Japan, 80 years and 224 days

The Youngest Summiteer:
22 May 2013, Jordan Romero, United States, 13 years, 10 months and 10 days

Most Ascents:
11 May 2011, Apa (Sherpa), Nepal, 21 ascents

Fastest Descent:
26 September 1988, Jean-Marc Boivin, France, in 11 minutes, paragliding

First Person to climb all four sides of Everest:
28 May 1999, Kusang Dorje (Sherpa), India.

Deaths on Everest:
266 (to 2015)

The worst year for deaths was 2014, with 17 fatalities. More than 4 percent of climbers have died scaling Everest.

Appendix II

Maurice Wilson – The Lone Climber
of Everest by A.J. Russell

Wilson was the first man ever to attempt Everest solo. He did so in 1934, having flown to India from Britain – by himself – the year before.

Captain Maurice Wilson was a young man from Bradford, son of a manufacturer, and for his courageous services in the Great War he was awarded the Military Cross. But he thirsted for more stirring adventures. To those twin worlds which are accessible only to the bravest of men – flight and mountaineering – he was an unknown newcomer, perhaps an intruder. But he had a firm jaw, a lithe and powerful body and such courage as only the very few can know. He had no fear of facing alone what the majority of mankind would turn from in terror when in the company of brave companions.

Of self-confidence he had a boundless store. He studied books on Everest. He was impressed by the achievements of the three great expeditions that had attempted unsuccessfully to storm that unconquered and unconquerable peak. Himself, an apostle of loneliness and somewhat of a mystic, though of a practical and adventurous order, he was the type of man to be deeply stirred by that story of F. S. Smythe, victor of Kamet, who nearly reached the top of Everest.

Smythe recorded in *Everest 1933* that after his companion Eric Shipton had fallen out from sickness, he had an uncanny experience of a presence from the Beyond accompanying him when climbing alone at 27,000 feet. Smythe said the feeling was so strong that it completely eliminated all sense of loneliness. It seemed even that he was tied to his invisible companion by a rope and if he had slipped "He" would have held him safe. He remembered constantly glancing back over his shoulder and once, after reaching the highest point, he stopped to eat some cake; as he did so he carefully divided it and turned round with one half in his hand. Then he experienced almost a shock to find no one with whom to share it. To Smythe it had seemed that this presence was strong, helpful and friendly; and it was not until returning down to the highest camp that the link connecting him with the Beyond was snapped and, his comrades now only a few yards away, he felt really alone.

Shackleton, too, recorded a similar experience when plodding "farthest south" in the Antarctic.

Maurice Wilson believed in such experiences and had had them himself. He claimed that the Beyond had inspired his lone attempt on Everest. He believed, too, that the supernatural was on the side of the ascetic, the man who hardened himself by frequent fastings to the rigours of life, including those of gale-swept mountain ridges. The *yogi-man*, the man who had conquered all his physical cravings, and not the highly skilled European climber, he contended, was the likeliest conqueror of Everest. Furthermore the victor was less likely to come from one of those highly organized British expeditions of a dozen European climbers supported by a hundred Nepalese porters, encumbered by much baggage, than from a tiny party of one ascetic climber accompanied by two or three natives, travelling as light as possible.

So before he left England he began to practise long and arduous fasts. In time he found that a period of eight or ten days without food was no hardship; rather was it a preparation. That these long fasts did not lessen his courage or undermine his physical strength was shown in a number of ways. He joined the London Aeroplane Club and took a pilot's certificate. His early flying experiences were not without serious incident. Once he descended suddenly and crashed into a tree. A schoolboy walking along the highway was surprised to be hailed by Wilson, an airman in distress, in a topsy-turvy machine. The astonished lad did his best and the airman scrambled free, none the worse for his misadventure.

Soon after this, according to the airman, the real fun began. The best description obtainable of those adventures is given by himself in a letter which he wrote to me from India. He introduced himself thus:

"My dear friend, I know you but you don't know me though you will do so at the end of ten minutes. I am Maurice Wilson, the flying 'nut' (as some people think), who is out to do a solo climb on Mount Everest. And here's the story. If in its details I appear to be blowing my own trumpet don't let it worry you; there's nothing personal about me from start to finish.

"I received the inspiration to climb Everest and proceeded to develop it. This was to get myself thoroughly fit, learn to fly myself, buy a machine and do the job. And I proceeded, studying all known conditions of Everest in the meantime. I returned to England at the end of the year, took my pilot's licence and bought a machine. After only forty hours flying I was ready for the job.

"My original plan was to take off quietly, presumably on a flight to Australia, and without the permission of the Nepalese Government. I intended to do the job from Purnea the base of the Houston flight over Everest. At the persuasion of a friend (and I now know he was right) I got a certain amount of publicity before leaving. Unfortunately along came a letter from the Air Ministry inquiring if recent reports were true, informing me at the same time they did not think it probable that the Nepalese Government would allow the permit; yet not asking if they could be of assistance in securing it.

"I replied, foolishly perhaps, that the information was true, though their attitude would have been more appreciated had they offered assistance. Then came a two-page letter which I ignored and, twenty-four hours before leaving, a two-page wire of warning, which I also ignored.

"The gloves were off; what next?

"I took off on 21 May, 1933. Six weeks before I had been notified that my permit to fly through Persia was awaiting me at Cairo. I rang the officials up on arrival and I registered immediately that there was *nothing doing*! The chief proved really too affable under the circumstances. 'Sorry old man, there's no permit here for you. If there's anything I can possibly do for you just let me know' – and offered me the world! Well, Everest wasn't Cairo, so on I pushed to Baghdad, where I discovered a new route down the southern side of the Persian Gulf, through Bahrain, a British Protectorate, and in use by the Imperial Airways. The only map I could buy of this route showed half the Gulf. For fuel I trusted to luck and to what I could pick up at Bahrain, but, on the instructions of the British Consul, this was refused to me. The consul had the audacity to suggest that I should fly north, one hundred and eighty miles over water and land in Persia, there to inquire about a permit for doing so. The alternative, he later gave me, was to fly to Baghdad.

"I had to bluff.

"The next morning I went along and told him that the flight to Baghdad was the better idea. There was a map in the vestibule and while he was inside writing out my fuel permit I roughed out the distance to Gwadar, *the next stop on my forward route to India,* and took the scale of the map on my coat sleeve.

"Later I worked out that my tankage (with the extra fuel obtained on the new permit) would leave me thirty miles to spare, that was if my gamble on fine weather came off. With that I stuck an additional four-gallon tin of petrol in my front locker, filled up my tanks and took off. To make short of a long story I was nine and a half hours in the air, nine hours out of landing distance and five hours without sight of land. My rev-counter suddenly went bung, the indicator flew back to zero, and I had a momentary hustle for my life-belt, but I landed at Gwadar safely ten minutes before dark, with petrol just on the nod to extinction.

"After a wonderful night under starlit skies I reached Karachi. Here again they tried to stick me up with results as before – I flew on and on. The same at Allahabad, on I went undeterred and arrived at my base, Purnea, to lay up for a day or two before my last hop to the foot of Everest.

"But here officialdom won. At 7 a.m. on the morning after my arrival came the local magistrate and the chief of police with the pleasant information that my plane had been seized by the government and that I would not be allowed to use it until further notice; the further notice was the arrival of the monsoon. Twenty-one days later, when this had truly arrived, my aeroplane was released.

"My next concern was to get this machine under cover. I had received an invitation from a Major Kent to visit his aerodrome some two hundred and fifty miles away; and off I flew on the first possible day. Couldn't get a kick out of the engine after being so long in alternate rain and sunshine. I know nothing about aeroplane engines, but set to work. After five hours with the instruction book I had the thing running and giving better 'revs' than it had ever done since delivery from the makers. Then I took it on to the field. It was hopeless – the machine wouldn't rise. I know nothing about aeroplane rigging, but after some time with the rigging instruction booklet, managed to get away. Unfortunately Kent's aerodrome had no hangar accommodation and I took off to Lucknow. After half an hour's flying I was into the monsoon again with clouds at four hundred feet, and had to look for a landing. With petrol running short, could I come down?

"An old planter had turned his polo ground into an aerodrome and had marked it with the circle and name of the place, ready for the time when flying should take a flip in his part of the country. I was his guest for a week on account of the weather and made a valued friend. As my machine was now of no further use to me for the Everest climb, I made him an offer. I had an intuition that he would buy it. He did.

"I came up to Darjeeling with a view to getting through on foot to Everest. Here the local government official appeared to take great pleasure in telling me that his orders were to block me. In view of these hold-ups doesn't it seem to you somewhat uncanny that I am as optimistic as ever about my job of climbing Everest, *the one I've been given to do?*"

That was the letter which Maurice Wilson sent to me from India. He concluded by asking me to try and get permission from the India Office to allow him to climb Everest alone. That could not be obtained and I advised him against the attempt. At that time only his intimates believed that he would translate his eccentric idea into practice. Everybody solemnly warned him against his project. Friends and acquaintances pointed out to him the impossibility of achieving alone what the best climbers in the world had been unable to accomplish assisted by every device known to mountaineering carried by a large force of porters – oxygen cylinders, ropes, ice-axes, cooking apparatus, haversacks, medical supplies, wireless equipment and quantities of other impedimenta. His reply to all expostulations was that victory would surely come to the man who travelled fast and light. Amundsen had beaten Scott in the race to the South Pole by a lightning dash. He, like Amundsen, was perfectly fit, possessing sufficient endurance to reach the physical limits of the world's altitudes. Already men had climbed 28,000 feet of the 29,000 feet of Mount Everest, and no one should dissuade him from making his lone attempt on that last one thousand feet.

Wilson knew that the people of the Himalayas regard Everest as holy ground just as a generation ago the Swiss so regarded their unclimbed mountains. The Swiss then assumed, as the Tibetans and Nepalese do nowadays, that the avalanches and the disasters to mountaineering parties, as well as poor harvests, were caused by unfriendly spirits inhabiting the peaks, who were enraged by man's attempt to desecrate their sacred abode. But Wilson would reason that Mont Blanc, once the monarch of mountains and thought to be inaccessible to man, was nowadays regarded as a comparatively easy climb. And the Matterhorn, not long since known as the unscalable pyramid, was now being climbed daily; indeed a guide would make two ascents up that once inaccessible peak in one day. Wilson expected to be the forerunner of similar conquests of Everest, though it was about twice the height of these Swiss mountains and situated in the most secluded country of the world. So he set forth on his astounding adventure.

When in May, 1933, he left England, the London press was welcoming home the Marquis of Clydesdale, who was the first man to fly over Everest. At that time the Ruttledge Expedition – holding a government permit – was already at the foot of the mountain engaged in its exploratory assaults. Prevented by the Indian officials from slipping in ahead of Ruttledge and scooping the honour of victory like Amundsen did from Scott at the South Pole, Wilson had to wait until 1934 for his lone attempt.

For a brief period only in each year is the mountain open to climbers – from May to July. Before May, the deep snow, the intense cold and the blizzards that rage round the world's mother mountain provide her with natural defences that no human being can penetrate. After June the monsoon arrives, the temperature rises, the snow thaws, the sides of Everest stream with melting ice and all footholds are obliterated as soon as they are made. Dangerous at all times, it becomes a certain death trap. Anyone then attempting to scale the wind-swept roof of the world must inevitably be carried down to disaster by one of its ceaseless cascades of snow and ice. Though in May and June the destroying avalanches are not so frequent, the climbers must still undertake appalling climbing feats round buttresses with terrific drops and up slippery snow slopes ending in dizzy precipices, and always with the threat of being overwhelmed from above by a thunderous fall of snow.

In one of the early attempts on Everest the intrepid Mallory was swept away in an avalanche, and eight of his party were killed. He was saved because he happened to be roped to others further up the slope. Wilson took no ropes with him up the mountain. His equipment was a small cylinder of oxygen, a height recorder, a camera to make photographs by which he proposed to prove that he had actually reached the summit and warm clothing. He had trained himself to live on dates and cereals.

After being released from what was virtual arrest in Purnea, he promised not to attempt a flight to the base of Everest. But he made a significant move to Darjeeling, the usual starting place of an Everest expedition where, without acquainting the authorities, he engaged a few porters. News presently reached London that in the disguise of a porter he had slipped out of Darjeeling *en route* for Everest. He was certainly travelling light. The Ruttledge expedition of the previous year had comprised fourteen British officers, ninety porters and 300 baggage animals. Wilson had three porters only. Travelling from Darjeeling by forced night marches, he crossed the Sikkim Himalayas without being recognized. Safely in Tibet, he now changed back into European clothing for, unless there were sudden direct orders from Lhassa, which was unlikely, there was now no likelihood of his being stopped and turned back. In fact he was travelling so fast that no transport in that desolate region could have overtaken him.

By 18 April he reached the first stage of his assault, the famous Rongbuk monastery, outpost of civilization, beating by ten days the thirty-five days taken by last year's expedition. This was in itself a remarkable feat seeing that part of the route had to be covered at night for fear of detection. He was glad to reach the Rongbuk monastery, which has more than once befriended the foemen of Everest. Occupied by 300 monks, and over sixteen thousand feet up, it is about the highest habitation in the world. Wilson tarried one day only at the monastery. Refreshed and encouraged, he pushed on up the mountain to what was the Base Camp of 1933. From here the summit of Everest appears to be a triangular pyramid, the downward dip of which very much resembles the tiles on a steep roof. There are few handholds; careful and balanced climbing is necessary to avoid a sheer drop of nearly 10,000 feet. These tiles or slabs continue down to a great ridge, which runs north-west at a considerable angle.

Scarcely giving himself time to rest, Wilson continued upwards to Camp One, a delightful elevated spot providing glorious views, one of which, the Pumori Pyramid, rising sharply above a circle of peaks, suggests the upthrusting tooth of some gigantic tiger.

His next stop, Camp Two, took him nearly 2,000 feet higher to a sunny spot protected from severe winds by ice ridges, but with the temperature many degrees below zero. Already well above the levels of the Swiss mountain peaks, he now resumed his ascent through troughs of ice with the winds blowing the snow from the crests of the open glacier about him. Again he came to rest in an enchanted land of ice towers – blue and white pinnacles – surrounded by lofty peaks urging him still higher into the blue of heaven. He was now nearing an altitude of 23,000 feet beyond which, only a few years ago, no man had ever climbed.

Immediately above him there now rose the steep and shining ice wall of the North Col, that tragic glacier which forms a saddle joining the north peak with the shoulders and summit of Everest. Discovered by Mallory more than ten years ago, it provides the only negotiable route to the top. It was on this North Col that the avalanche occurred which swept eight porters to their doom.

When the tired coolies of the 1933 expedition caught sight of the North Col they burst into a song of joy. For the ascent to its base is hard going and some of the grumblers had suggested giving in. But a few stern words from their leader stimulated them to further effort and they reached camp.

Here the view is not quite so thrilling as further down, for the main bulk of Everest is masked by the towering Col and the north peak. But the scene is an inspiring one for, says Ruttledge, after the last slopes have been taken "with heads down and the senses dulled by altitude" there appears the north-east shoulder, six thousand feet of slab and avalanche-swept valley, beyond which, on the right "is a rock-strewn cone, flying a long pennant of cloud and snow far across Nepal. It is the summit. At long last Mount Everest is tangible, no longer the fabric of dreams and visions." Just below the peak lie a heap of stones, which are seen to be really huge boulders, fifteen feet high, dislodged from the summit.

Wilson eagerly surveyed the goal of his ambitions and prepared to resume his climb. His three porters looked apprehensively at the terrible North Col over whose saddle they must approach that mighty peak, and their courage gave way. Mallory, dauntless pioneer of this glacier, had found it necessary to be supported by ropes wound round a rock as he climbed an ice chimney to the top of that obstacle. Those other intrepid mountaineers who had followed him had all been similarly supported. The porters were quite prepared for the ascent . . . with the same kind of support. But without ropes they would proceed no further.

Wilson expostulated! Vainly did he argue that so far all had gone well, and that the omens were propitious for the future. Resolutely they refused. Though they had already broken speed records for climbing more than two-thirds of the terrible mountain, they feared to face certain death on that almost perpendicular North Col. It was still six weeks or more before the monsoon could arrive, but Wilson would not wait for further equipment. He had set out to climb Everest alone, and alone he would go. If his strength held he might reach the top in two or three more days and be back in four or five. He ordered his three porters to wait for a fortnight; if by then he had not reappeared they were free and could return to India.

On 17 May 1934, in a temperature of perhaps fifty degrees below zero, he resumed his ascent, carrying with him three loaves, two tins of porridge, a small tent, a camera and the inevitable Union Jack. Those who know Everest say that he had no chance; he must perish from cold and hunger or crash to death over a precipice. Never before had two men roped together been able to accomplish what he was expecting to achieve alone. Oates in the Antarctic, leaving Scott and stumbling out alone into the blizzard, may have done a nobler action than Wilson's; but for bravery there was no distinction between them.

Wilson's three porters watched him toiling upwards until he was lost from sight in the ice cones above. For days their gaze constantly sought that triangular peak above them. Would this mad sahib suddenly emerge from the valley and appear silhouetted against the blue sky on the ridge above? They waited for a week, by which time, as no sign had appeared, they thought that his chances of life had dwindled to vanishing point. But they knew his courage and his qualities of endurance and were not easily disillusioned. Perhaps he had found some of the stores left behind by the previous expedition and was taking the climb more leisurely than he had first intended.

A fortnight passed and never a sign of the lone climber. They were now at liberty to return. No ordinary human being could hope to have lived alone on that mountain for a fortnight. But this Englishman was no ordinary man. He had talked about the miraculous powers of the *yogi-men*, and he was one of them. Perhaps he was being supernaturally sustained. That mysterious companion who had accompanied Smythe last year might even now be supporting their own leader and guiding him to the summit there in triumph to plant his little coloured flag.

Another week passed, and yet another. It was only after they had waited a full month that, with the monsoon nearly due, they decided to forsake the mountain and their intrepid leader.

They gathered up their scanty equipment and returned to Darjeeling. Here they confessed to the authorities that they had participated in an unauthorized attempt on Everest and had last seen Wilson following the tracking of Ruttledge up the mountain. There was now no possibility of his being alive.

Some time later the mystery of Wilson's disappearance was solved by Eric Shipton, leader of an Everest advance party, who had been with Smythe in 1933. Wilson's body was lying unprotected in the snow. He had not died of hunger, for he had contrived to discover the provisions left by Ruttledge. But his little tent had been blown away and was found at some distance from the body; and this would suggest that, utterly exhausted, he may have been unable to go further and had frozen to death. Eric Shipton buried the body in a crevasse near the spot where it was found. Wilson's diary, found with him, was brought back to Darjeeling.

Appendix III

Diary of the 1953 British Everest Expedition, compiled by Wilfred Noyce

1952

1 Sept	Wylie started work as Organizing Secretary.
8 Oct	Hunt, Leader of Expedition, arrived in London.
30 Oct	First Equipment Co-ordination Meeting.
5 Nov	Selection of Party completed.
17 Nov	First Alpine Test Co-ordination Meeting.
	First Conference of whole Party.
	Measuring of Party for clothing, etc.
25 Nov	Second Alpine Test Co-ordination Meeting.
28 Nov	Second Equipment Co-ordination Meeting.
1–10 Dec	Visit to Paris, and
	Alpine Test of Equipment at Jungfraujoch by Hunt, Wylie, Pugh and Gregory.
15 Dec	Third Equipment Co-ordination Meeting.
	Second Party Conference.

1953

1st half January

Packing Plan organized by Evans and working party.

2nd half January

Packing starts at Lusk's, Wapping.

17–19 Jan	Oxygen frame carrying tests, at Helyg, North Wales.
20 Jan	Final Equipment Co-ordination Meeting.
	Trying on of clothing, etc., at Lusk's.
	Third Party Conference.

22 Jan	Decompression Chamber tests at Farnborough.
25–26 Jan	Visit to Zürich by Hunt and Evans.
5 Feb	Final Party Conference.
12 Feb	Main party and baggage sail for India on *S.S. Stratheden*.
20 Feb	Advance party, Evans and Gregory, fly to Kathmandu.
28 Feb	Main party arrives Bombay.
8 March	Whole expedition and baggage assembled at Kathmandu.
10 March	First party and 150 coolies leave Kathmandu.
11 March	Second party and 200 coolies leave Kathmandu.
26 March	First party arrives at Thyangboche.
27 March	Second party arrives at Thyangboche.
29 March–6 April	First Acclimatization period.
9–17 April	Second Acclimatization period.
12 April	Icefall party reaches Base Camp (17,900 feet).
13 April	Icefall party starts on Icefall.
15 April	Hillary, Band and Lowe establish Camp II (19,400 feet).
17 April	Same party reaches ice block below Camp III site.
21 April	First half main body of stores arrives at Base from Thyangboche, including in party Morris of *The Times*.
22 April	Second half main body of stores arrives at Base from Thyangboche, party including Major Roberts with the Assault oxygen.

Camp III established at head of Icefall (20,200 feet).

Base Camp established on Khumbu glacier (17,900 feet). |
24 April	Low Level Lift started to Camp III.
24–25 April	Reconnaissance of Western Cwm as far as Swiss Camp IV (21,200 feet).
26 April–1 May	High Level Lift between Camps III and IV.
1 May	Camp IV established (21,200 feet) by Hunt, Bourdillon and Evans.

2 May	Preliminary Reconnaissance of Lhotse Face by Hunt, Bourdillon and Evans.
2–5 May	Rest period for Ferry teams.
3 May	Reconnaissance party to Camp V (22,000 feet).
4 May	Bourdillon and Evans, with Ward and Wylie in support, up to Camp VI (23,000 feet) on Lhotse Face Reconnaissance.
5 May	Bourdillon and Evans above Camp VI on reconnaissance. Ferry work starts again in Icefall and (on May 8) in Western Cwm, as far as Camp V.
6 May	Lhotse Face Reconnaissance party returns to Base.
10 May	Lowe and 4 Sherpas up to Camp V for Lhotse Face.
11 May	Lowe and Ang Nyima, based on Camp VI, start work on Lhotse Face. Westmacott and 3 Sherpas in support at Camp V.
16 May	Major Roberts arrives Base with oxygen, accompanied by Morris of *The Times*.
17 May	Lowe and Noyce establish Camp VII (24,000 feet). Ward up to VII, stays with Lowe and Da Tensing.
18 May	Last Low Level Lift. Advance Base established at Camp IV.
20 May	Noyce and 8 Sherpas, ascending to Camp VII, meet Lowe, Ward and Da Tensing descending.
21 May	Noyce and Annullu complete route over Geneva Spur to South Col. Wylie and 9 Sherpas reach Camp VII.
22 May	Wylie with 14 Sherpas, Hillary and Tenzing ahead, to South Col. Dump loads. 1 Sherpa does not complete climb.
24 May	First Assault party, consisting of Bourdillon, Evans, Hunt, Da Namgyal and Ang Tensing (alias Balu), reach South Col.
25 May	First Assault party stays South Col. Second Assault party reaches Camp VII.
26 May	*First Assault.* Bourdillon and Evans reach South Summit. Hunt and Da Namgyal carry loads up S.E. ridge and dump at 27,350 feet.

Hillary and Tenzing (Second Assault party), supported by Gregory, Lowe, Pemba, Ang Temba and Ang Nyima, reach South Col (Camp VIII). (Also Dawa Thondup, Topkie, Ang Norbu, Annullu and Da Tensing, carrying extra loads).

Ward and Noyce up to Camp VII in support.

7 Sherpas leave South Col.

27 May   Hunt, Evans, Bourdillon and Ang Temba down to Camp VII.

Second Assault party confined on South Col by very strong wind.

Evans and Ward descend to Advance Base.

28 May   Wylie and 3 Sherpas up to Camp VII in support.

Second Assault. Ridge Camp (Camp IX) established at 27,900 feet by Hillary, Tenzing, Gregory, Lowe and Ang Nyima. The latter 3 return to South Col.

29 May   Hillary and Tenzing from Ridge Camp to Summit, return to South Col.

Noyce and 3 Sherpas set out from Camp VII in support.

Noyce and Pasang Phutar reach Col.

Gregory, Pemba and Ang Nyima descend to Camp IV.

30 May   Hillary, Tenzing, Noyce, Lowe and Pasang Phutar reach Camp IV. Westmacott (who has been maintaining the route through the Icefall) and Morris (*The Times*) have come up and return with the story.

31 May   All except 5 Sahibs and a Sherpa party down to Base.

Last Ferry party to Camp III to bring down loads.

1 June   All except Wylie and Sherpa party (staying at Camp III) down to Base.

2 June   Party assembles at Base.

3 June   Party reaches Lobuje.

4 June   Party reaches Thyangboche.

5 June   Advance party (Hunt, Bourdillon and Gregory) leaves Thyangboche.

7 June	Main party leaves Thyangboche.
13 June	Advance party reaches Kathmandu.
20 June	Main party reaches Kathmandu.

From *The Ascent of Everest*, John Hunt, Hodder & Stoughton, 1953

Appendix IV

"Everest Conquered": The report of the Special Correspondent of *The Times*, 8 June 1953

The "Special Correspondent" was actually James Morris (later Jan Morris), who was attached to the 1953 expedition as official reporter, The Times having acquired the copyright of all messages and pictures from the expedition. Though published on 8 June, the report was filed on 31 May.

Camp IV, Everest, 31 May

The masters of Everest, Hillary and Tensing, returned to this camp (22,000 ft) from the South Col yesterday afternoon in a blaze of sunshine and triumphant emotion, bringing their news with them.

It was a significantly beautiful day among the snows of the upper Western Cwm. All was crisp and sparkling, with the awful block of Nuptse only faintly shining with the curious greasy sheen of the melting surface snow. From the ridge of Lhotse a spiral of snow powder was driven upwards by the wind like a genie from a bottle. From down the Cwm came from time to time a sudden thrilling high-pitched whistle as a boulder screamed down from the heights. Everest itself, its rock ridge graceless against a blue sky, was as hard and enigmatical as ever.

It was a day for great news. Here in the camp on the north side of the Cwm there was already yesterday morning a tension, nerve-racking and yet deliciously exciting. At 9 a.m. on the previous day, 29 May, the two summit climbers had been seen by their support group, Gregory, Lowe and a

Sherpa, already crossing the South Summit at about 28,500 feet, and going strongly up the final ridge.

The weather had been perfect, the gales of the preceding days which had so ravaged Camp VII on the South Col had died down. Hillary and Tensing were known to be two of the most powerful climbers in the world, and were using the well-tested open circuit oxygen equipment. Reports brought down from the South Summit by Bourdillon and Evans, who had reached it on 26 May in the expedition's first assault, seemed to show that the unknown final ridge was not impassable, though undoubtedly difficult.

Because of these several encouraging factors, hopes at Camp IV were dangerously high, and the feeling of taut nerves and suppressed wild convictions was immeasurably strengthened when, just before lunch, five tiny figures were seen making their way across the traverse at the top of the face of Lhotse. They could only be the summit team and their supporters from the South Col. They were moving fast, and in three hours they would be in the Cwm. The camp was now alive with stinging expectation. Here in the camp Colonel Hunt sat on a wooden packing case, physically immobile, his waterproof hat jammed hard over his head, his face white with plastered glacier cream. Four or five of the climbers vacantly fingered newspapers in the big pyramid tent. One man sat outside with binoculars reporting the progress of the descending party.

"They must be getting to Camp VI," the watchers said. "They are hidden behind that serac [irregular-shaped pinnacle of ice on a glacier, formed by the intersection of crevasses] with the vertical crack in it – you know the one." "Two of them are sitting down; now they are up again." "Only another hour to wait. What are the odds?" At last, soon after 1.30, just as the radio was announcing the reported failure of the assault, the party emerged above a rise in the ground 300 yards or so above the camp, their blue windproof jackets sharp and cheerful against the glistening snow. Hillary and Tensing were leading. All at once it was through the camp by the magic wireless of excitement that Everest had been climbed.

There was a sudden rush up the snow slope in the sunshine

to meet the assault party. Hillary, looking extraordinarily fresh, raised his ice axe in greeting. Tensing slipped sideways in the snow and smiled, and in a trice they were surrounded. Hands were wrung ecstatically, photographs taken, there was the whirr of the ciné-camera, and laughter interrupted congratulations.

Hillary and Tensing, by now old climbing colleagues, posed with arms interlocked, Hillary's face aglow but controlled, Tensing's split with a brilliant smile of pleasure. As the group moved down the hill into the camp a band of Sherpas came diffidently forward to pay tribute to the greatest climber of them all. Like a modest monarch, Tensing received their greeting. Some bent their bodies forward, their hands clasped as in prayer. Some shook hands lightly and delicately, the fingers scarcely touching. One veteran, his pigtail flowing, bowed to touch Tensing's hand with his forehead.

"We so far forgot ourselves," wrote an English climber of an earlier generation, "as to shake hands on the summit." This expedition so far forgot itself that everywhere one fancied that sunglasses were steaming embarrassingly: and suddenly, as if spontaneously, each climber, Hillary and Tensing the first of them, turned to Colonel Hunt, reflective in the background, and shook his hand in recognition of the truth that in a team venture of great happiness and success his has been the friendly hand which inexorably as it seems has led the expedition to success.

In the pyramid tent, over an omelette served on an aluminium plate, Hillary told the story of the final climb. The tent was uncomfortably crowded. Newspapers were all over the floor, and in one corner the discredited radio lay scornfully tilted on a cardboard box. The climbers sat around on packing-cases, groundsheets and bedding rolls. From time to time the flushed face of an excited Sherpa would appear through the tent door with a word of delight.

Hillary's account began with the events of 28 May, when he, Tensing and the support party – Gregory, Lowe and a tough young Sherpa, Ang Nima – left South Col to establish Camp VIII on the ridge below the South Summit. Colonel Hunt had already dumped most of the necessary stores at about 27,500 feet during the first "reconnaissance-assault". Now the camp was to be established at a point as high as possible so that the next day Hillary and Tensing, relying in large measure on their limited oxygen, would not have so far to climb. It had been planned that two Sherpas would accompany the party, but one was sick and as a result the amount of oxygen carried had to be reduced.

The party left Camp VII on the South Col, about seven, and set off up the back-breaking steepness of the ridge to find a suitable camp site for climbers carrying 50 lb to 65 lb each and Sherpas 40 lb to 45 lb. It was a difficult climb. For what seemed hours no possible site showed itself, and the ridge was covered with difficult snow. Oxygen began to run short, and Gregory and Ang Nima had to use some from the assault cylinders. Tensing remembered a possible tent site just below Lambert's Point. Successive ridges in the rock proved impracticable, but at last the place was found at an estimated 27,800 feet. Camp VIII was established – incomparably the highest camp ever put up on a mountain – and Gregory and Lowe, their mission brilliantly accomplished, returned to the South Col.

Hillary and Tensing were left alone in their eyrie. They spent the next two hours pitching a tent on the snow-covered rock, but were handicapped by the lack of rock pitons. The tent platform was on two levels, with a step in the middle. Tensing sat in the lower half, Hillary in the top.

As darkness gathered they took a little sleeping oxygen, but throughout the night they sustained themselves with sardines and biscuits – "paradise" is Tensing's word for them. It was a calm night though a cold one – the temperature at one time was minus 27 deg. Centigrade. At four in the morning they thawed their boots over the Primus stove, and half an hour later looked out of the tent. It was a glorious clear morning, calm and peaceful. They could see far down the valley to the monastery of Thyangboche, the expedition's original rear base, on its lofty wooded hill.

They were away from camp by six o'clock on 29 May, and started up through deep, crusty, powdered snow towards the South Summit. There were no signs of tracks left by Bourdillon and Evans and they had to cut steps constantly, taking it in turns to break the trail. They kept going steadily, but Hillary describes this climb to the South Summit as the hardest part of the day. At nine they were on the South Summit, the little knoll of snow-capped rock about half a mile from the summit proper, and were seen by the exhilarated watchers on the South Col. They spent ten minutes there, and took off their oxygen masks without any sudden reaction. Nevertheless their main worry was their shortage of oxygen supplies. To economize, when they moved off again they reduced their flow of oxygen from the normal four litres a minute to three.

They were now on the final ridge of Everest, never reached before. Hillary describes it as "technically good, interesting alpine work". They moved along the west side of the ridge, characterized by difficult cornices, with occasional glimpses of this camp, an infinity below. They crossed safely the one major obstacle on the ridge, a difficult rock step almost vertical. At every moment they expected to see the summit, but time and again minor elevations deceived them. It was at 11.30 a.m., 29 May 1953, that they stepped at last on to the snow-covered final eminence of Everest.

Hillary describes this as "a symmetrical, beautiful snow cone summit" – very different from the harsh rock ridge which is all that can be seen from below. The view was not spectacular. They were too high for good landscape, and all below looked flat and monotonous.

To the north the route to the summit on which pre-war Everest expeditions pinned their hopes looked in its upper reaches prohibitively steep. Tensing spent the fifteen minutes on the summit eating mint cake and taking photographs, for which purpose Hillary removed his oxygen mask without ill effects. Tensing produced a string of miscellaneous flags and held them high, while Hillary photographed them. They included the Union Jack, the Nepal flag and that of the United Nations. Tensing, who is a devout Buddhist, also laid on the ground in offering some sweets, bars of chocolate and packets of biscuits.

At 11.45 they left the summit on the return climb, keeping a careful check on the oxygen gauges. Because of the shortage of oxygen supplies they dare not stay at the ridge camp, and they moved straight down towards the South Col, the going being reasonably good. Above the South Col they met Lowe and Noyce. Noyce was the leader of a rescue or reinforcement party which had come up from Camp IV; it was Noyce's second climb to the South Col. By 4.30 all four were back at Camp VII, and yesterday morning, 30 May, they made their way down the face of Lhotse to the Cwm.

Hillary and Tensing seem in astonishingly good form, with none of the desperate fatigue that has overcome Everest summit parties in the past. Nor have they any other than modest pride in their achievements, and more still in the wonderful success of the expedition as a whole. The heroic quality is undoubtedly in them, as it is in most of this fine team, but yesterday afternoon, after the first flood of emotion, it was agreeably shielded by the aura of not very good omelettes (eaten indigestibly fast), untidy tents, high spirits and home thoughts from abroad.

For within a day or two the expedition will be down at the base camp at Khumbu Glacier on its way home. One obstacle remains before it – the icefall has now changed beyond recognition since the centre of operations moved into the Western Cwm. Three weeks ago it had a certain stark and nasty grandeur; now, under the pressure of the thaw, it resembles nothing so much as a gigantic squashed meringue. It is as if the mountain, thwarted of its isolation, has prepared one last hazard for the climbers, and there is certainly no member of the expedition who will not feel a deep relief when this danger is passed.

Setting foot on the base camp again will be a symbol, undramatic perhaps but vivid, that implacable Everest's sting has been drawn at last. It has been drawn, if one may descend for a moment into the personal, by as good a company of adventurers under as skilful a captain as your Correspondent can ever expect to meet.

Appendix V

The Abominable Snowman

By Ralph Izzard

Said to inhabit Everest and its environs, the hirsute, human-like Abominable Snowman or "Yeti" has been pursued almost as much as the summit of the mountain itself. Some of the evidence of the Yeti's existence (or not) is sifted below by Ralph Izzard, a Daily Mail *journalist, who reported unofficially on the 1953 expedition.*

Snowman literature contains no more entertaining contribution than Appendix B (Anthropology or Zoology with particular reference to the Abominable Snowman) to H. W. Tilman's book, *Mount Everest, 1938.* After setting up the Aunt Sallies of boulder, bear, monkey or man as possible authors of the strange, unexplained footprints that have been seen so frequently across the whole length of the Himalaya, Mr Tilman demolishes each in turn, and concludes by counselling us, until the Snowman exposes himself as either a hoax or something already within our knowledge, to give him the benefit of the doubt. At the time he was writing (1947) Mr Tilman's admirable essay on the Snowman could be regarded as positively the last word on the subject, being an expert summary of all evidence until then available.

In the six years which have now elapsed, a number of other champions have, however, entered the field and Mr Tilman himself has returned to the charge. I submit that no fresh evidence which has been brought to light in any way denies the

Abominable Snowman his identity as a distant animal in his own right – in fact indications seem stronger than ever that we are dealing with "Animal X", an unknown variety, or possibly species, a dangerous beast of marked ferocity, who has little to commend him other than his rather endearing name.

Let us now examine the post-1947 evidence, particularly as it affects Nepal. As preface we can do worse than quote from Mr O. Polunin's contribution in an Appendix ("The Natural History of the Langtang Valley") to Mr Tilman's book, *Nepal Himalaya* (1952). Mr Polunin, a distinguished naturalist, writes:

"From time to time during the last 150 years interesting details of the plants and animals of the high alpine regions of Nepal have come to light when collections made by native collectors have been sent back to Europe. Our knowledge of the adjoining countries of Sikkim and Kumaon have helped us to build up a broad picture of the flora and fauna of Nepal, but probably more than 5,000 square miles of the steepest country in the world lies waiting for detailed investigation by trained naturalists.

"Within this area many hundreds of species of plants, insects and other small animals may remain unknown to the scientific world. In addition our knowledge of the distribution of plants and animals, from east to west, and from west to east, along the Great Himalaya Range, will continue to be full of gaps until Nepal has been fully explored. Nepal lies roughly at the junction of two lines of migration where plants and animals from Kashmir and Afghanistan meet those from Burma and China. No plants, as far as is known, have invaded the high Himalaya from the plains of India, and few have come south from Tibet.

"At the meeting-place of two previously-isolated groups the biologist expects interesting things to happen; hybrids may be formed and new species evolved."

I should add at once that at no place in his illuminating appendix does Mr Polumin have the temerity to mention the Abominable Snowman. He merely sets the stage for us; scarcely penetrated Nepal (at least by Europeans), meeting-place of two lines of migration where, in consequence, strange things may happen.

In his own text (*Nepal Himalaya*) Mr Tilman records two further incidents relating to the Snowman. The first concerns a meeting (in 1949) with herdsmen in the Langtang Himal, about eighty miles west of Everest. "In the course of conversation these herdsmen confirmed the existence, or rather the recent presence, of the Abominable Snowman in the Langtang, pointing out a cave which had been his favourite haunt. Six years previously these beasts (whose existence is surely no longer a matter for conjecture) had been constant visitors, but had apparently migrated elsewhere. The small kind, the size of a child, they called 'chumi', while the big fellow went by the name of 'yilmu'. Since sceptics like to affirm that the tracks made by these creatures are in reality bear tracks, it is worth mentioning that the herdsmen were able to show us some fresh bear tracks. It is noteworthy, too, that although bear tracks were fairly common in the Langtang, we saw no tracks on snow, which confirms the natural supposition that it is a rare occurrence for a bear to go above the snow-line. In the absence of rigid proof to the contrary, it is, therefore, safe to assume that if tracks are seen in snow they are not those of a bear."

In his subsequent journey to the vicinity of Everest (1950) Mr Tilman relates how the Snowman cropped up again – this time at the Sherpa grazing village of Phalong Karpa, at the snout of the Khumbu glacier. "As we sat in the secure circle of the fire, our backs to the stone wall of the hut, the talk turned naturally to the Abominable Snowman. As one might expect, they are found in these parts in numbers, especially around Namche Bazar in the depths of winter when the cold drives them lower. Danu (a Sherpa) affirmed that the previous year (1949) a friend of his named Lakhpa Tensing had had his face so severely mauled by one on the Nangpa La that he died. By running downhill, which is, of course, the only way a man can run at these heights, one can usually get away from these creatures whose long hair, falling over their eyes, hampers them, but the unfortunate Lakhpa had apparently tripped, and lying half stunned by the fall became an easy prey."

Champions of the Snowman – among them I number myself – are, however, indebted to Mr Eric Shipton's *The Mount Everest Reconnaissance, 1951* for the clearest proof yet provided of his existence. Mr Shipton, after reconnoitring the icefall between the Khumbu glacier and the Western Cwm, turned his attention to the country to the west of Everest. It was on a glacier of the Menlung Basin, at about 19,000 feet, that his party came upon and photographed the remarkable series of footprints which have aroused so much comment.

In his book Mr Shipton describes finding the prints and adds: "We did not follow them farther than was convenient, a mile or so, for we were carrying heavy loads at the time, and besides we had reached a particularly interesting stage in the exploration of the basin. I have in the past found many sets of these curious footprints and have tried to follow them, but have always lost them on the moraine or rocks at the side of the glacier. These particular ones seemed very fresh, probably not more than twenty-four hours old . . . Sen Tensing (a Sherpa), who had no doubt whatever that the creatures (for there had been at least two) that had made the tracks were 'Yetis' or wild men, told me that, two years before, he and a number of other Sherpas had seen one of them at a distance of about twenty-five yards at Thyangboche. He described it as half man and half beast, standing about five feet six inches, with a tall, pointed head, its body covered with reddish-brown hair, but with a hairless face. When he reached Kathmandu at the end of November, I had him cross-examined in Nepali (I conversed with him in Hindustani). He left no doubt as to his sincerity. Whatever it was that he had seen, he was convinced that it was neither a bear nor a monkey, with both of which animals he was, of course, very familiar. Of the various theories that have been advanced to account for these tracks, the only one which is any way plausible is that they were made by a langur monkey, and even this is very far from convincing, as I believe those who have suggested it would be the first to admit." (I understand that the proponents of the langur – and it would have to be a giant variety behaving as no monkey normally does – are no longer very happy with their theory.)

Mr Shipton's discovery is also referred to by Mr W. H. Murray in his book *The Story of Everest.* Mr Murray, himself a member of the reconnaissance party, writes: "Some of the prints were particularly clear and must have been left within the last twenty-four hours. Pad-marks and toe-marks could be distinctly seen within the footprints, which were twelve inches long, and where the creature had jumped the smaller crevasses the scrabble marks of its nails could be seen on the far side." Mr Murray, who travelled the same route three days after Mr Shipton, adds that he and his companion, Mr T. Bourdillon, "followed the tracks for the better part of two miles (the animal had chosen the best possible route), until on our second day we, too, had to take to the moraine."

Having made a major contribution to the Abominable Snowman's dossier, Mr Shipton and Mr Murray appear to have been content to let the case for the defence rest. Not so Dr G. N. Dutt, an Indian geologist, who also accompanied Mr Shipton. Dr Dutt has done some research work of his own and has dug up some instances which may have escaped Mr Tilman. Dr Dutt published his findings in *The Times of India* (17 May 1953). After recalling that the first Everest expeditions had also come across "yeti" footprints when approaching the mountain by the northern route, Dr Dutt claims that the earliest published account appears in *Altai Himalaya* (Nicholas Roerich), in which the author describes how a major of the British Army saw a tall man, almost naked, standing and leaning on a high bow.

NOTE – It may be mentioned that Colonel L. A. Waddel in his book, *Among the Himalayas* (published 1898), describes how he came across the animal's tracks on a snowfield in north-east Sikkim in 1889.

Nicholas Roerich was a Russian painter and mystic. He designed the original *mise-en-scène*, for Stravinsky's *Sacre du Printemps*. He left Russia after the Revolution, and following a brief sojourn in America (there is a museum of his paintings in New York) retired to the Himalayas, finally settling, with his family, in the Kulu valley of northern Punjab. *Altai Himalaya* is an account of an extensive journey through Central Asia in the form of 'jottings from the saddle.' Paragraphs are often unrelated. That concerning the Abominable Snowman is sandwiched between a homily on the punctuality of the

English and an anecdote of a "sadhu's" railway journey without a ticket. It runs: "It all began with the unknown traces found by the Everest Expedition (1922 ?). Then in *The Statesman* (presumably of Calcutta), an English major related how, during one of the expeditions into the region of the Himalayas, he encountered a strange mountain inhabitant. At sunrise, amidst the frosty snows, the major walked away from the camp and climbed the neighbouring rocks. Glancing at the nearby rocks, the major, to his astonishment, beheld a tall man almost naked, standing, leaning on a high bow. The mountain inhabitant did not look at the major, his attention being completely attracted by something unseen behind the curve of the slope. And suddenly the man bent, strained himself, and by madly dangerous leaps rushed from the rocks and disappeared. When the major told his people about the meeting they smiled and said; "Sahib has seen a 'snow' man. They are watching the guarded places."

Earnest seekers after truth regarding the Abominable Snowman would, I think, do well to leave Roerich out of their researches. As a mystic he was much given to symbolism and could "see" the outline of men and gods in rock faces and headlands and painted them as such. – R. I.)

Dr Dutt continues: "Another story goes back to the time Sir Charles Bell was Indian Political Officer in Sikkim, a feudatory State north of Darjeeling. Some workmen of the Posts and Telegraph Department were reported missing while they were at work near the Jelap La (Pass). Immediately afterwards the British troops stationed nearby were summoned to search for their bodies and also to account for their mysterious disappearance. A few hours' search resulted in the discovery of a Snowman, who was apparently responsible for the death of the missing persons. It was an easy target for the rifles. The body was alleged to have been twelve feet tall, with shaggy hair and toes pointing backwards."

Dr Dutt then describes how, having the necessary languages at his command, he was able to interrogate Ange Tharkay, the

Sherpa sirdar of the 1951 reconnaissance. According to Dr Dutt, Ange Tharkay, after giving a general description of a Snowman, added a plausible and never-failing method of avoiding death when face to face with the creature. "In such a predicament (said Ange Tharkay) one should not lose courage, but collect pieces of stones, wood – in fact anything handy – and throw them one by one at the Snowman. The creature would then collect them with both hands outstretched as if they were prized valuables. As soon as the hands of the Snowman are thus full, the person must scamper to a place of safety."

Dr Dutt also carried on his investigation at Thyangboche Monastery, where: "A Tibetan monk told me that he had seen a 'Shukpa' (Yeti) at the bank of the Imja Khola at dusk. The creature was drinking water there. The monk took fright and fled to his village." (This appears to be a distinct visitation, not to be confused with the commonly recounted story of the appearance of a Snowman on a field beside the monastery when a festival was in progress attended by some scores of Sherpas and visiting lamas from Rongbuk Monastery. There are innumerable witnesses to this incident, which may be the same as that told by Sen Tensing to Mr Shipton. If this is so, the date of the occurrence would be 1949.)

Dr Dutt's most graphic story relates to a fight between a Sherpa strong man and a Snowman. He writes: "A man of Monjo, a village in the valley of the Dudh Kosi, told me a story relating to his father who was a man of great strength and courage. He was told by the elderly people of the village that there was a meadow of soft grass and junipers about 6,000 feet up on the southern slopes of the 22,340-foot Kangteka peak, and that if the Snowmen were not there it would have been ideal pasture land for the yaks. Once grass grew scarce in the vicinity of the village and consequently the milk supply of the yaks decreased considerably. The spirit of adventure of the strong man prompted him to go in search of pastures new. He collected all the yaks of the village and went up. Having left them to graze, he took the opportunity to search for the Snowmen, who were supposed to haunt the place.

"Two black shadows fell across his path suddenly from one of the overhanging cliffs. Looking up, he saw one of them vanish quickly and the other one advance. In a few minutes he found himself struggling with a monster. After a bloody duel the villager extricated himself from the clutches of the creature with a superhuman effort. When he returned his fellow villagers found him swaying with giddiness and blood oozing from his eyes and nostrils. He fell into a swoon and was revived with a strong dose of 'rakhsi' – Nepalese wine. Incoherently he muttered about his almost fatal encounter with the Snowman.

"Thinking that the Snowman had died, the villagers went to the scene of the struggle early next morning. The crushed grass, the dislodged stones and the ground in general bore testimony to the previous night's struggle; the Snowman was, however, not found. The villagers concluded that the body of the Snowman must have been carried away by one of its companions.'

Dr Dutt concludes with an eerie story of his own. "Almost all the residents of the high-altitude pastoral villages believe in the existence of the 'Shukpa' (Yeti). The men were afraid to remain alone in their potato fields, especially when evening approached. The lowest altitude they were found to descend was around 13,000 feet here, but I found footprints as high up as 20,000 feet. The imprints on snow could definitely be identified as the footprints of an animal walking on two legs but, however indistinct they were, the dwellers of the snows did not appear to be walking with toes reversed.

"At the time I was exploring the Cho Oyu (26,750 feet) region on 12 October, 1951, I camped by the side of a lake at the foot of the Kyojumba glacier. Next morning I went up the slope between two rocky promontories, leaving the main glacier on my right. The col in front was about 1,500 feet high. Since there was no track, all I could do was scramble between rugged boulders, some as large as fifty feet across. It was 10 a.m. The sun had begun to melt the snow on the rocky slopes. Melting snow and dislodged rocks made the track treacherous. Although something told me that my movements were watched, I was so preoccupied with finding a safe route up that I did not pay any attention to the foreboding. Finally I reached the top of the col, enjoying the view. Cho Oyu faced me directly and only Pumori and its smaller satellites prevented me from seeing gigantic Everest.

"I did not stay long here to enjoy the landscape because the wind and glare were telling on my nerves. All the time I was on snow I was following large, queer footsteps which ran in the opposite direction. As I was alone, the discovery of the footprints urged me to return quickly.

"Back to the col, I took a minute's rest, wiped the sweat off my goggles and almost involuntarily looked up. I fancied I saw a creature watching me from the ridge to the left. By the time I put on my glasses it was out of sight. All that I was able to see in that short interval was that it had grizzly brown hair on its head. When I told this to my porters afterwards they severely reprimanded me for going up alone.

"Was it mere hallucination? It is true my eyes had been aching at the time I saw it, but all the time I was up the rocky slopes I had a feeling that someone was watching my movements. Suddenly I realised – and as I did so a shudder went through me – *those footsteps went up towards the west ridge.*"

Many of us, and not only the hypersensitive, have felt the sense of a "presence" at high and desolate altitudes and can sympathise with Dr Dutt. Nine times out of ten this "presence" is felt to be malevolent rather than benevolent, although an outstanding exception is the experience of Frank Smythe during the failure of the final attempt on Everest made by the 1933 expedition. Returning to rejoin Shipton at Camp IV, after his forlorn solo effort to reach the top, Smythe records that he felt an overwhelming sense of being accompanied by a companion whose function it was to watch over his safety. So strong was the feeling that when he sat down on a rock to eat some food and being in the dream state that overcomes exhausted men at high altitude, he divided the food in half and turned to offer a portion to his "friend". It almost startled him to find no one there.

But whether or not Dr Dutt was suffering from hallucinations and was deceived in what he saw, nothing can wash out the footsteps he discovered, and Dr Dutt is the sort of man who can be relied upon to recognise a footprint when he sees one.

If we ruthlessly discard Dr Dutt's brief glimpse, unbelievers certainly have a telling point when they challenge that no completely reliable witness – certainly no European – has actually *seen*, a Snowman in recent times. (The latest recorded viewing by a European that I can find was by Mr A. N. Tombazi, who relates in his book, "*Account of a Photographic Expedition to the Southern Slopes of Kanchenjunga*," that in 1925 he sighted what *may*, have been an Abominable Snowman at a distance of two to three hundred yards while camped under Mount Kabru at a height of 15,000 feet. It may be pointed out that this location is not many miles from the Zemu Gap (Sikkim) where in 1937 Colonel Sir John Hunt discovered one of the first sets of authentic footprints. Our case for the Snowman, therefore, relies chiefly upon the tradition and the tracks.)

Traditions are tricky things to trace down. The tradition of a Snowman is certainly widespread. Mr Ronald Kaulback, when exploring across the Tibeto–Burman frontier, records it as far east as the Upper Salween – where he also came upon the tracks in a region where there were neither bears nor monkeys. In 1948, when I was myself on trek in the Himalayan foothills of northern Assam, the tribesmen there spoke confidently of "naked men of the snows" who dwell in the higher mountains to the north. We have seen that the tradition is particularly strong both in Sikkim and around Namche Bazar in eastern Nepal. It occurs again farther west in Nepal, and taking the Himalayas as a whole is to be found as far west as the Karakorams.

Local names naturally vary according to the language or dialect spoken in any particular district, but it may be noted that whatever the local name, throughout the whole length of the Himalaya – rather more than 1,500 miles – where across vast stretches lateral communication is next to impossible, all names mean roughly the same thing in English. "Shukpa" and "yeti" can both, I think, be safely translated as the "wild (in the sense of untamed) men of the snows". I understand the alternative Tibetan name "Metch Kangmi", which originally gave rise to the rather joyous translation of "Abominable Snowman", has not been rendered quite accurately. "Kangmi" certainly means "Snowman", but "Metch", to a pedant, more closely denotes "unkempt" or "unwashed", to a repulsive degree. We are, I think, indebted to Mr Tilman for the happy Latin classification *Homo niveus odiosus*.

One must make allowances for the observations of frightened and imaginative men when attempting to describe the appearance of an Abominable Snowman. He has more than once been described as up to twelve feet tall – he is probably nearer six. He is invariably described as covered all over in reddish hair except for the face, but the hair of the head is long and falling over the eyes hampers vision. The feet – by accurate measurement – are between twelve and fourteen inches long and broad in proportion (the shoe would certainly fit no known monkey). The more imaginative Sherpas believe that the feet of the Snowmen are turned back to front to enable them to walk uphill more easily. (Rather pleasing flattery this, for to the music-hall mind it emphazises that the best way to elude one would be to run downhill, in which case the Snowman would presumably stand every chance of stubbing his toe and turning a back somersault.) So much for tradition.

Our own case rests chiefly on the track. One must concede that doubtless there is a perfectly logical explanation for numbers of tracks that have been reported from time to time, did one but know all the relative circumstances. But this does not alter the fact that numbers of other tracks have been reported for which no logical explanation is conceivable, and reported by men who not only know what they are talking about, but whose integrity is unquestioned. Surely, as Mr Tilman writes in his essay, "if fingerprints can hang a man as they frequently do, footprints may be allowed to establish the existence of one."

The question we have to answer is who or what made the prints? The possibilities, as outlined before are boulder, bear, monkey or man and, one hastens to add, "animal X", a hitherto unknown species.

Thanks to Mr Shipton's remarkable photographs, we can throw away the boulder, for boulders do not have five toes, although it may be said that a boulder falling from a height and bounding down a glacier can make a very realistic series of tracks. I discovered one such halfway up the Khumbu glacier, to the great perturbation of Sherpa Kirkia, who, snuffling like a bloodhound, immediately set off on the scent and refused to relax until he had found the spot where the offending rock had come to rest. I later learned that the Swiss expedition of the previous year claimed that while negotiating the Khumbu glacier, which was then shrouded in heavy mist, they passed through a herd, flock, school or whatever it is of our friends, but without being able to make any positive identification. (*Everest, 1952*; Andre Roch). Kirkia had accompanied the Swiss and the main cause of his anxiety when with me was the fact that the spot where the pair of us had discovered our false trail coincided almost exactly with the position where the Swiss subsequently came upon genuine tracks of *l'abominable homme des neiges*.

As for the bear, almost all Himalayan travellers can tell a bear's print at a glance, for they are common at lower altitudes. This would be certainly true of such men as Colonel Hunt and Messrs Shipton and Tilman – particularly so of the last two, for at the close of one expedition – which I personally would consider rather too lightly provisioned – they were forced in order to sustain life to become rivals with the local bear population for the district's few available bamboo shoots.

And although Mr Bertram Mills has shown us that bears can be taught to ride tricycles, they do not normally walk on two feet. This fact, I consider, also rules out the monkey if nothing else does. I am open to correction, but to my knowledge the only monkey or ape that walks naturally on two legs is the gibbon, and the gibbon only leaves tropical forest for excursions to such places as the London Zoo.

The theory that the tracks were made by a man is a little more difficult to disprove. It is known that in Tibet, where there is no capital punishment, criminal offenders are exiled from their communities and could possibly have taken to a caveman – or one might say Snowman – existence in the mountains. If this be so it is remarkable that all seem to have size fourteen feet and seem to exist on nothing at all unless it be the odd Sherpa or two, a rather indigestible diet for any man. It is also known that Hindu ascetics can sometimes be met on pilgrimages to the snows. Mr Tilman again in his same essay recounts a charming story of a Captain Henniker, Royal Engineers, who in 1930, on the summit of a 17,000-foot pass in Ladakh, met a man completely naked except for a loincloth. "It was bitterly cold and snowing gently at the time. When he expressed some natural astonishment he met with the reply, given in perfect English, 'Good morning, sir, and a Happy Christmas to you' (it was actually July). The hardy traveller was an M.A. of an English University (Cambridge, one suspects), and was on a pilgrimage for the good of his soul." This delightful little anecdote is included purely for its entertainment value, for although 17,000 feet in Ladakh is inhospitable enough, even in midsummer, it cannot match the utter desolation and apparently complete pointlessness of the places where "yeti" prints are most often found. Mr Tilman himself hastens to spike Captain Henniker's guns with his own forceful confutation of the "homo sapiens" theory. "We mountaineers may be wrong in thinking that a liking for the high snows is peculiar to us, but I should be astonished to find a native, Tibetan or any other, however, guilty, ascetic or careless about washing who shared our taste for such places. There are ascetics to be found living not far below the snout of the Rongbuk glacier, but they remain immured in their caves, tended by their admirers and never in my experience mortify the flesh further by a promenade up the glacier."

We are therefore left with "animal X" – an unknown variety or species.

That it has not yet – or rather recently, for the earlier trails are now too cold to follow – been seen by a European is not entirely surprising. European mountaineers in the Himalaya are still far from frequent, and they go there more often than not with the single-minded purpose of placing their feet on the summit of a particular peak. Sad though it be for the interests of science, nothing will divert them from this main objective. Then, when one remembers the vast network of unexplored forest-clad mountains and valleys the Snowman can roam at will, it is scarcely surprising that he keep out of the path of the very occasional small party which happens to come his way

– quite apart from the fact that, like any number of other animals, he may be a creature of almost entirely nocturnal habits.

Few of us who have gone into this matter of the Snowman's credentials will not agree with Colonel Hunt when he says that sufficient reliable evidence now exists to warrant the organization of an expedition founded on a proper scientific basis and charged with the sole objective of proving or disproving his existence. Until that moment comes our abominable friend will continue to shamble on his mysterious errands, credited by some, discredited by others, but with this to be said about him – there is now vastly more evidence that he does exist than there is to prove that he does not.

From *The Innocent on Everest*, Ralph Izzard, Hodder & Stoughton, 1955

Bibliography

Ahluwalia, Major H.P.S., *Higher Than Everest*, New Delhi, 1973

Ahluwalia, Major H.P.S., *Climbing Everest*, New Delhi, 1976

Ahluwalia, Major H.P.S., *Faces of Everest*, New Delhi, 1978

Ament, Pat, *Climbing Everest: A Meditation on Mountaineering and the Spirit of Adventure*, Camden, ME, USA, 2000

Anker, Conrad, and Roberts, David, *The Lost Explorer*, New York, 2000

Anonymous, *Another Ascent of the World's Highest Peak – Qomolangma*, Beijing, 1975

David Barnes, M., *After Everest*, London, 1977

Blessed, Brian, *The Turquoise Mountain*, London, 1991

Bonington, C.J.S., *The Next Horizon*, London, 1973

Bonington, C.J.S., *Everest South West Face*, London, 1973

Bonington, C.J.S., *Everest, The Hard Way*, London, 1976

Bonington, C.J.S., *The Everest Years*, London, 1986

Boukreev, Anatoli, and DeWalt, G.W., *The Climb*, New York, 1998

Breashears, David, *High Exposure*, New York, 2000

Broughton, G. (ed), *Climbing Everest*, Oxford, 1960

Bruce, Brig-Gen. C.G. et al, *The Assault on Everest 1922*, London, 1922

Bruce, Brig-Gen. C.G., *Himalayan Wanderer*, London, 1934

Bryant, L.V., *New Zealanders and Everest*, Wellington, N.Z., 1953

Burgess, Alan and Palmer, Jim, *Everest Canada: The Unclimbed Ridge*, New York, 1984

Burrard, Col. Sir S.G. and Hayden, H.H., *A Sketch of the*

Geography and Geology of the Himalaya Mountains and Tibet, Calcutta, 1907–8

Carr, Herbert (ed), *The Irvine Diaries: Andrew Irvine and the Enigma of Everest 1924*, Reading, 1979

Clarke, C., *Everest*, London, 1978

Coburn, Broughton, et al, *Everest*, Washington D.C., USA, 1997

Coffey, Maria, *Fragile Edge*, London, 1989

Denman, E., *Alone to Everest*, London, 1954

Dias, J., *The Everest Adventure: The Story of the Second Indian Expedition*, Delhi, 1965

Dickinson, Matt, *The Death Zone*, London, 1997

Dittert, R., et al, *Forerunners to Everest, The Story of the Two Swiss Expeditions of 1952*, London, 1954

Dyhrenfurth, G.O., *To the Third Pole*, London, 1955

Eggler, A., *The Everest-Lhotse Adventure*, London, 1957

Evans, C., *Eye of Everest, A Sketch Book from the Great Everest Expedition*, London, 1955

Fellowes, Air Commodore P.F.M. et al, *First Over Everest, the Houston Mount Everest Expedition*, London, 1933

Finch, G.I., *Climbing Mount Everest*, London, 1930

Finch, G.I., *The Making of a Mountaineer*, London, 1924

Firstbrook, Peter, *Lost on Everest: The Search for Mallory and Irvine*, London, 1999

Fleming, J., and Faux, R., *Soldiers on Everest*, London 1977

Gillman, Peter, *Everest: Eighty Years of Triumph and Tragedy*, London, 2001

Green, Dudley, *Mallory of Everest*, Burnley, 1991

Grylls, Bear, *Facing Up*, London, 2000

Habeler, P. *Everest, Impossible Victory*, London, 1979

Haston, D., *In High Places*, London, 1972

Hillary, Sir E.P., *High Adventure*, London, 1955

Hillary Sir E.P., *Nothing Venture, Nothing Win*, London, 1975

Hornbein, T.F., *Everest, The West Ridge*, San Francisco, 1965

Howard-Bury, Lt Col. C.K. et al., *Mount Everest: The Reconnaissance*, 1921, London, 1922

Hozel, Tom, and Salkeld, Audrey. *The Mystery of Mallory and Irvine*, London, 1996

Hunt, Brig. Sir J., *The Ascent of Everest*, London, 1953

Hunt, Brig Sir J., *Our Everest Adventure*, Leicester, 1954

Indian Mountaineering Federation, *Indian Mount Everest Expedition 1965*, New Delhi, 1965

Izzard, R., *Innocent on Everest*, London, 1955

Japanese Alpine Club, *The 1969–1970 Mount Everest Expedition*, Tokyo, 1972

Kamler, Kenneth, *Doctor on Everest*, New York, 2000

Kohli, M.S., *Nine Atop Everest*, Bombay, 1969

Kotani, A., and Yasuhisa, K., *Japan Everest Skiing Expedition*, Tokyo, 1970

Krakauer, Jon, *Into Thin Air*, New York, 1997

MacIntyre, N., *Attack on Everest*, London, 1936

Malartic, Y., *Tenzing of Everest*, London, 1954

Mantovani, Roberto, *Everest: The History of the Himalayan Giant*, Seattle, 1997

Marshall, H., *Men Against Everest*, London, 1954

Messner, R., *Expedition to the Ultimate*, London, 1979

Messner, R., *The Crystal Horizon: Everest – The First Solo Ascent*. Marlborough, UK, 1989

Messner, R., *Free Spirit*, Munchen, 1989

Miura, Y., *The Man Who Skied Down Everest*, London, 1979

Morin, M., *Everest: From the First Attempt to Final Victory*, London, 1955

Morris, James, *Coronation Everest*, London, 1958

Murray, W.H., *The Story of Everest*, London, 1953

Noel, Captain J.B.L., *Through Tibet to Everest*, London, 1927

Norgay, Jamling Tenzing, *Touching My Father's Soul*, San Francisco, 2001

Norton, Lt Col. E.F. et al, *The Fight for Everest: 1924*, London, 1925

Noyce, C.W.F., *South Col: One Man's Adventures on the Ascent of Everest, 1953*, London, 1954

Noyce, C.W.F. and Taylor, R., *Everest is Climbed*, London, 1953

O'Dowd, Cathy and Woodall, Ian, *Everest Free to Decide*, Sandton, South Africa, 1997

Pye, David, *George Leigh Mallory, a Memoir*, Oxford, 1927

Rebuffat, G., *Mont Blanc to Everest*, London, 1956

Roberts, D., *I'll Climb Mount Everest Alone: The Story of Maurice Wilson*, London, 1957

Robertson, D., *George Mallory*, London, 1969

Ruttledge, H., *Everest: The Unfinished Adventure*, London, 1937

Ruttledge, H. et al, *Everest 1933*, London, 1934

Sayre, W.W., *Four Against Everest*, New York, 1964

Serraillier, I., *Everest Climbed*, Oxford, 1955

Shipton, E.E., *Upon That Mountain*, London, 1943

Shipton, E.E., *The Mount Everest Reconnaissance Expedition, 1951*, London, 1952

Shipton, E.E., *The True Book about Everest*, London, 1955

Singh, Brigadier Gyan, *Lure of Everest*, Bombay, 1961

Smythe, F.S., *Camp Six*, 1937

Snaith, S., *At Grips with Everest*, London, 1937

Somervell, T.H., *After Everest: The Experiences of a Mountaineer and Medical Missionary*, London, 1936

Steele, P., *Doctor on Everest, London*, 1972

Stephens, Rebecca, *On Top Of the World*, London, 1994

Stokes, Brummie, *Soldiers and Sherpas*, London, 1988

Swiss Foundation for Alpine Research, *Everest: The Swiss Everest Expeditions*, London, 1954

Tasker, Joe, *Everest the Cruel Way*, London, 1981

Tilman, H.W., *Mount Everest 1938*, Cambridge, 1948

Ullmann, H.J.R., *Tiger of the Snows*, New York, 1955

Unsworth, Walt, *Everest*, London, 1981

Venables, Stephen, *Everest Kangshung Face*, London, 1989

Webster, Ed, *Snow in the Kingdom: My Storm Years on Everest*, Eldorado Springs, USA, 1998

Weathers, Beck, *Left for Dead*, New York, 2000

Younghusband, Sir F.E., *The Epic of Mount Everest*, London, 1926

Younghusband, Sir F.E., *Everest: The Challenge*, London, 1935

Sources & Acknowledgements

The editor has made every effort to obtain permission for use of copyrighted material from the relevant copyright holders. The editor apologises in advance for any errors or omissions made. Queries regarding the use of material should be addressed to the editor c/o the publishers.

"We Had Found George Mallory" by Conrad Anker/*The Lost Explorer* by Conrad Anker and David Roberts, Simon & Schuster, 1999. Copyright © Conrad Anker and David Roberts. Reprinted by permission of Simon & Schuster (US)

"The Skies Were Already Darkening" by Peter Boardman/ *Mountain Life*, January 1976

"Lost Somewhere High" by Chris Bonington/*The Everest Years*, Hodder & Stoughton, 1986. Copyright © 1986 Chris Bonington

"Hope Lost" by Anatoli Boukreev/*The Climb*, Anatoli Boukreev and G. Weston DeWalt, St. Martin's Press, 1998

"Two Eagles" by Maria Gulley/*Fragile Edge*, Chatto & Windus, 1989

"Everest Unofficial" by Earl Denman/*Alone to Everest*, Collins, 1954

"Nightmare" by Matt Dickinson/*The Death Zone*, Hutchinson, 1997

"First Over Everest"/*First Over Everest*, John Lane, 1933

"We Shall Get to the Top" by George Finch/*The Assault on Mount Everest 1922*, ed. C. Bruce, Arnold, 1923

"Onwards, and Onwards!" by Wang Fu-chou and Chu Yin-hua/"How We Climbed Everest", *Mountain Craft*, 1962

"Breaking the Ice" by Bear Grylls/*Facing Up*, Macmillan, 2000. Reprinted by permission of Macmillan.

"Only the Air That We Breathe" by Peter Habeler/*Impossible Victory*, Arlington, 1979

"The Final Frontier" by Tom Horbein/*Everest: The West Ridge*, Sierra Club, 1965.

"Reconnaissance" by Lt Col. C.K. Howard-Bury/"The 1921 Mount Everest Expedition", *Alpine Journal*, no. 224, 1922 [abridged]

"The Longest Day" by Raymond Lambert/*Forerunners to Everest*, R. Dittert, G. Chevally, R. Lambert, Allen & Unwin, 1954

"Tight Corner" by Jack Longland/BBC radio talk reproduced in *Tight Corners*, George Allen & Unwin, 1940

"Avalanche" by George Leigh Mallory/*The Assault on Mount Everest*, Brigadier-General Hon. C.G. Bruce et al, Edward Arnold, 1923

"It Has Been a Bad Time Altogether" by George Leigh Mallory/*The Fight for Everest: 1924*, Col. E.F. Norton, Longman, 1925

"Solo" by Reinhold Messner/*Free Spirit*, Hodder & Stoughton, 1991. German copyright © 1989 R. Piper Gmbh & Co. KG, Munchen. English translation copyright © 1991 Hodder & Stoughton.

"In Disguise to Tibet" by J.B.L. Noel/*Through Tibet to Everest*, Edward Arnold & Co., 1927

"The Dream Comes True" by Tenzing Norgay/*Man of Everest*, Tenzing Norgay and James Ramsey Ullman, G. Harrap & Co. Ltd., 1958

"The Most Hateful Place in the World" by E.F. Norton/*The Fight for Everest: 1924*, Longman, 1925

"The Face" by Wilfred Noyce/*South Col*, Wm Heinemann Ltd., 1955. Reprinted by permission of John Johnson Limited

"The Last Climb" by Noel Odell/*Alpine Journal*, No. 36, 1924 [abridged]

"The Whole of a Magnificent Planet to Myself" by Cathy O'Dowd/*Everest: Free to Decide*, Cathy O'Dowd and Ian Woodall, Zebra Press, 1997. Copyright © 1997 Struik Publishers

"Don't Leave Me Here to Die" by Cathy O'Dowd/*Just for the Love of It*, Free to Decide, 1999

"The Blackest Day" by Jon Reiter/http://jononeverest. blogspot.co.uk. Reprinted by permission of the author

"The Long March" by Hugh Ruttledge/*Everest 1933*, Hodder & Stoughton, 1934

"Great Effort" by Hugh Ruttledge/*Everest 1933*, Hodder & Stoughton, 1938

"The Death of Harsh Bahuguna" by Murray Sayle/"Sorry, Harsh, you've had it", *Sunday Times*, 2 May 1971. Reprinted by permission of News International Syndication

"The Hard Way" Doug Scott and Dougal Haston/*Everest – The Hard Way*, Chris Bonington, Hodder & Stoughton, 1976. Reproduced by permission of Curtis Brown.

"High Life" by Eric Shipton/*Upon That Mountain*, Hodder & Stoughton, 1943. Reprinted by permission of Baton Wicks (UK) and the Mountaineers (US) from *Shipton: The Six Mountain Travel Books*, 1990

"The Shoulders of Giants" by Gyan Singh/*The Mountain World 1962/3*, ed. Malcolm Barnes, George Allen & Unwin 1964. Copyright © 1964 Schweizerische Stiftung fur Alpine Forschungen, Zurich

"Alone" by Frank Smythe/*Camp Six*, Hodder & Stoughton, 1937. Reprinted by permission of Baton Wicks (UK) from *The Six Alpine/Himalayan Climbing Books*, 2001

"Higher Than The Feet of Man Had Trod Before" by T. Howard Somervell/*After Everest*, T. Howard Somervell, Hodder & Stoughton, 1936. Reproduced by permission of Hodder & Stoughton

"On Top of the World" by Rebecca Stephens/*On Top of the World*, Macmillan, 1994. Reprinted by permission of the author.

"Grim Nights" by Joe Tasker/*Everest: the Cruel Way*, Methuen, 1981

"The Mountain Turned White" by H.W. Tilman/"The Mount Everest Expedition of 1938", *The Geographical Journal*, Vol XCII No. 6, 1938

"Escape" by Stephen Venables/*Everest: Kangshung Face*, Hodder & Stoughton, 1989. Reprinted by permission of the author and Curtis Brown

"Dead Man Walking" by Beck Weathers/*Left for Dead*, Villard Books, 2000. Copyright © 2000 by S. Beck Weathers. Used by permission of Villard Books, a division of Random House Inc.

"Tone, We are at the Top" by Nejc Zaplotnik/*Everest*, Nejc Zaplotnik and Tone Skarja (trans. Stanko Klinar), Mladinska, 1981